Sociology and the Race Problem

James B. McKee

Sociology and the Race Problem

The Failure of a Perspective

UNIVERSTY OF ILLINOIS PRESS
Urbana and Chicago

© 1993 by the Board of Trustees of the University of Illinois
Manufactured in the United States of America
1 2 3 4 5 C P 5 4 3 2 1

This book is printed on acid-free paper.

Library of Congress Cataloging-in-Publication Data

McKee, James B., 1919-
    Sociology and the race problem : the failure of a perspective /
James B. McKee.
        p.   cm.
    Includes index.
    ISBN 0-252-02022-7 (acid-free paper).—ISBN 0-252-06328-7 (pbk.)
    1. Blacks.   2. Afro-Americans.   3. United States—Race relations.
I. Title.
HT1581.M35   1993   92-42293
305.8'00973—dc20   CIP

Contents

Acknowledgments

The debts I owe are undoubtedly many, but some I recognize and can acknowledge. My first debts are without doubt to Alfred McLung Lee, Hans Gerth, and John Useem; each in his own way provided me with a basic lesson in being a sociologist. My effort here to reflect critically on a body of sociological work owes much to my reading of Robert Lynd, C. Wright Mills, and Alvin Gouldner, and to the work in the sociology of sociology that flourished spiritedly but briefly before and after 1970.

In the making of this book, I am indebted to Richard Martin, executive editor at the University of Illinois Press, who expressed strong interest in the manuscript even before it was completed; his occasional promptings encouraged me to bring it to closure. Lewis M. Killian read the manuscript and provided useful suggestions for revision; but most of all his kind words of recommendation to the Press gave me the confidence that what I had written was worthy of publication. Louie Simon copyedited the manuscript with skill and a fine eye for detail.

I am also indebted to my wife, Alice, for her unflagging support of my long effort to complete this book. My debt to her cannot be measured, only acknowledged with love and gratitude.

Introduction

Early in the twentieth century, after decades of unchallenged acceptance, scientific racism finally lost credence among biologists, who then yielded the problem of race to social science. Three disciplines—first, anthropology, then sociology and psychology—contributed, each in its own way, to the development of a social scientific study of race relations. But it was only among sociologists that such study became a full-bodied specialty. By mid-century they had worked out a fairly coherent interpretation of the prevailing racial reality in the United States and presumed to possess an understanding of the possibilities of racial change. Their influence reached well beyond academic journals, textbooks, and college classrooms to affect the thinking of a broader stratum of educated citizens.

A full accounting of this development of the sociology of race relations in the United States can be justified on the ground that it remains a neglected chapter in the history of American social science. But that reason alone hardly circumscribes the purpose of this book. Its intent is to do more: to explore critically the now acknowledged failure of the sociologists of race relations to understand fully their own object of study.

That failure became evident in the early 1960s when, unanticipated by any sociological scholar, the prevailing relations between the races burst their bonds. A militancy of protest, a burst of race-conscious symbolism, a powerful surge of racial struggle, indeed, every imaginable form of demonstrative action by a no longer quiescent black people moved irresistibly from south to north, culminating in a wave of destructive violence in northern cities. National commissions were appointed to tell an uncomprehending white citizenry and a confused civic and political leadership what had happened and for what reasons.

A crisis in the nation's racial practices became an intellectual embarrassment, even a scholarly disaster, for sociologists. Not one of them could say, "I told you so," or "I warned you," for none had. Indeed, not only had they failed to foresee the coming of new forms of racial struggle, they had even denied such a possibility. The sociologists and social psychologists most familiar with the social scientific literature on race relations found therein no reason to expect the emergence of the black-led civil rights movement in the South in the early 1960s and even less reason to anticipate the transition to black militancy and then to widespread racial violence in the urban North. To the more thoughtful among them, it became painfully evident that the sociology of race relations had failed to understand what was going on in the world of racial interests and actions.

The issue at stake was not a technical one of inadequate research methods or of insufficient research funds, as some were to claim; nor was it comparable to the embarrassing error of pollsters wrongly predicting the outcome of an election. Instead, it was the failure of a distinctly American sociological perspective to explain the changing pattern of race relations in the United States. The sociologists of race relations had not simply failed to predict a specific event; rather, they had grievously misread a significant historical development. The race relations that appeared in their writings were incongruent with the race relations to be found in the society around them.

Some three decades later, no full accounting of that failure has yet been undertaken. What sociologists did not do for themselves, furthermore, other scholars did not do either. Historians did not extend to the later social scientific work in race relations the engrossed interest they have long displayed—and still do—in the earlier era of scientific racism. They have undertaken no comparable reading of the later texts, no detailed scrutiny of scholarly performance. It is not to historians, then, that one can look for a critical examination of the sociological scholarship in race relations since the 1920s or for efforts to explain its failure to anticipate the decade of militant struggle by black Americans in the 1960s.

It is the contention of this study that the failure of the sociology of race relations was not due to the limitations of its empirical research, of its inability to develop a theory of race relations, of its overemphasis on prejudice, of its association with liberalism, or of other factors attributed to it by sociological critics. Instead, it was a failure of its basic perspective on race in American life, that is, of the beliefs, values, and assumptions sociologists brought to bear on the persistent and always difficult problem of race. From the elements of that perspective, sociologists constructed a coherent sociology of race relations that, nevertheless, proved in time incapable of recognizing the direction that racial change was taking in American society. That, in turn, warrants a critical examination of the perspective.

The Tasks of the Study

Sociologists have always been reluctant to acknowledge that their work reflects a perspective that differs in style and type of sociology, as between European and American sociology, between greater or lesser emphases on conflict and consensus, between structural and social psychological approaches to social phenomena, and among conservative, liberal, and radical ideological assumptions. But over the last three decades there has been too much scholarly reflection on the underlying premises of scholarly work, including the scientific, for anyone to deny that varying perspectives, growing out of various social contexts, shape and define the very character of scholarly achievement. This book is in that tradition of reflective criticism.

Its starting point is the recognition that the failure to anticipate the racial events of the 1960s meant that sociologists did not understand what was transpiring in the world of racial interests and actions. To ask why is to pose a question only a few sociologists have addressed and none has satisfactorily answered. Though there was no viable theory of race relations to hold accountable, there was a widely shared perspective and a considerable degree of consensus about basic concepts and assumptions. The first task of this study was to reconstruct that sociological perspective, while the second task was to find in its reconstruction the reason for its failure.

These tasks required the reading of a large body of literature, much of it now forgotten. The sociologists of race relations wrote and published papers and books, read and reviewed each other's work, and met in conventions and conferences to engage in face-to-face discussion. For more than four decades over three sociological generations, by their writing, reading, reviewing, and discussion, they became a coherent community of discourse. From that discourse came their perspective on race relations.

But any act of textual interpretation must also recognize that the perspective being interpreted is embedded in a social context, and context can limit, constrain, and even intimidate discourse. What is important in recognizing social context is that the assumptions that sociologists brought to their study of race relations were those peculiar to their own time and place and often shared with others of their social class. But it was also a perspective shared by those of the same race. From its beginning, the American sociological perspective on the race problem was constructed by and reflected the outlook on race of white sociologists, and it remained that way for the several decades of its existence.

Black sociologists, of necessity, had to accommodate to that fact while also struggling to give expression to their own perspective. Even such distinguished sociologists as Charles S. Johnson and E. Franklin Frazier were not exempt from this dilemma. Though they were widely read and cited often and appreciatively by their white sociological colleagues, they nonetheless put forth some assessments of race relations that violated the assumptions of the perspective. When that happened, their deviant views were effectively ignored by those same white colleagues.

To reconstruct the whole of this sociological perspective in its context is not an end in itself but a means to comprehend the failure of the sociologists of race relations to understand fully their own object of study. The critical interpretation thus required is the second task, and it is that which makes of this study more than a historical recounting of a now dissolved perspective.

Race Relations: A Sociological Perspective

The basic argument of this study is that the sociologists of race relations in the United States developed a distinct perspective on race relations, from which came the questions they asked, the concepts they developed, and the body of knowledge they claimed to possess. The concept of a perspective is used here in Karl Mannheim's sense; it "signifies the manner in which one views an object, what one perceives in it, and how one construes it in his thinking." It constitutes an infrastructure of assumptions and values for an interpretation of social events, a cultural outlook that selectively chooses some aspects of a given universe of study and ignores others. Fundamental to any perspective are the underlying assumptions, which may remain unspoken and taken for granted. Alvin Gouldner called them "domain assumptions."[1]

The assumptions that undergirded the sociology of race relations included much that was shared with other sociologists. But it was also a domain of study that was unlike others in sociology in at least three ways: first, race relations were not included in the sweeping reforms of the Progressive Era or even those of the New Deal, leaving them little changed when other aspects of American life had changed immensely; second, in a milieu of strong racial attitudes and emotions, studying race relations often seemed to sociologists to be a thankless task; and third, in a period when the assimilation of the European ethnics into American life became accepted policy, nonwhite populations were viewed as unassimilable.

As a consequence, the sociology of race relations developed at its own pace, with its own vocabulary, and always with a deep concern for the attitudes of a racially intolerant white population. A milieu that for a long time could justifiably be called racist provided the social context from which sociologists developed a perspective on race relations, and it is not surprising that they, too, were not immune to that context.

This perspective was at the same time sociological, theoretical, and interpretive. It was sociological because it transformed the biologically oriented race problem into a study of social relations; theoretical because it intended (though it failed) to be a scientific theory of race relations, but also because it was conceptually coherent in its analysis of race relations; and interpretive because that conceptual coherence provided a discourse for interpreting the structure of race relations in American society, however inadequate that interpretation would eventually prove to be.

Such a perspective, furthermore, was not shaped and refined by data developed from research. Little if any research findings ever challenged what sociologists believed to be true of race relations or led to new propositions. Instead, the perspective changed only when social events forced it to do so, as when, for example, the nation's abandonment of legal segregation shifted the perspective from a noninterventionist stance to an interventionist one.

Before sociology's claim to the study of race relations could be made, the race problem belonged to biology, for therein was to be found the scientific case for the natural inferiority of the former slaves. As measured by nineteenth-century natural evolution, blacks had not advanced biologically; as measured by social evolution, they had not advanced culturally. Then, by the new unit-inheritance biology at the outset of the new century, they were judged to be a biologically inferior race, and the natural incapacities that implied meant also they would be judged to be culturally inferior.

But that seemingly solid scientific case for the inferiority of the black population did not long remain intact. In the second decade a new genetics invalidated any scientific case for racial inferiority, and the anthropologists provided a vigorous challenge to the claims of cultural inferiority. Sociologists accepted one of these arguments but not the other. However reluctantly most of them were to do so, they discarded the idea that black people were biologically inferior, but, despite the arguments of anthropologists, they retained an image of them as culturally inferior. In those two decisions was the beginning of the sociology of race relations.

The first decision—to accept the geneticists' position on race—put sociologists for the first time in a far more advanced position than they found comfortable. While science had rejected the prevailing conception of racial inferiority, American society, including the educated middle class, gave not the slightest indication of budging from its established racial convictions. Belief and practice remained unaltered. In American society blacks were still an unassimilable people, which gave sociologists good reason to suggest than their assimilation would occur in some unspecified future time.

The second decision—that blacks were culturally inferior—can only be understood by returning to the origins of sociology in the nineteenth century, specifically, to the creative typologies of Henry Maine, Emile Durkheim, and Ferdinand Toennies that drew a sharp distinction between what was modern and what was traditional (premodern). That typological distinction permeated the thought of the first generation of American sociologists, who were concerned with the modernizing of a nation still largely rural and agricultural but undergoing transformation to an urban and industrial society. As late as the 1920s, sociologists were still very much involved in making typological comparisons between modern and traditional peoples and societies. Black people were seen as a premodern people, culturally backward by modern standards and still isolated from the socializing currents of modern life.

From this context of evolutionary change, a new perspective on the race problem grew around two dimensions. The first was a belief in a massive trend toward the modernization of American society, which required all persons within it, including the nonwhite races, to master the demands of modern civilization. For the blacks, becoming modern would accomplish assimilation into American society, even though, for the foreseeable future, white rejection of racial assimilation was an insurmountable barrier. The second and perhaps more powerful belief was that the black American was so culturally inferior that, even if there were not white rejection, assimilation was possible only in some distant future.

The Promise of Assimilation

The sociologists who established the sociology of race relations never doubted that American society was undergoing a massive change toward an increasingly modern society, and such change was thought to be most evident in such powerful processes as industrialization and urbanization. This was the basis for one of the fundamental assumptions of the perspective on race relations: that these trends toward an increasingly secular and rational society meant that modern social organization would be increasingly incompatible with the practices of a traditional society. It seemed to them that American society would in time abandon such practices, including those of racial segregation, and would achieve an assimilation of all racial and ethnic peoples into one homogeneously modern society. Thus, given enough time, assimilation was inevitable.

But if sociologists came to believe that assimilation was inevitable, they also assumed that such change would come only gradually, not by a wrenching adjustment to violent struggle. This was an idea that the social evolutionists borrowed from natural evolution ("nature never makes leaps"), and that was retained by the postevolutionary generation. It was a comfortable assumption, for gradual change could be measured as social trendlines into a predictable future, a steady, gradual process of progressive movement. The measure of declining prejudice among white people became one reassuring indication of such a gradual trend, and one basis for asserting that, however slowly, race relations were gradually improving.

While sociologists found it intellectually congenial to borrow the concept of gradual change from evolutionary theory, they rejected the theoretical centrality that the social evolutionists had given to social conflict in human affairs. Influenced strongly by pragmatism, they could find no intellectual utility in the concept of conflict. They shared the aversion of an educated middle class to the destructive consequences of civil unrest, shunned disorder and violence, and feared the dangers to social order when those below them, whether white or black, reverted to violent actions.

These, then, were the several elements of the perspective that began with the assumptions that blacks were at that time a culturally inferior people but that a powerful trend toward modernity would sweep away the incompatible elements of traditional society, including racial segregation and discrimination. This perspective made possible the confident optimism of sociologists in the eventual assimilation of blacks into a hitherto white society.

The Culturally Inferior Black

The elements of the perspective that made sociologists confident of racial assimilation, however, were offset by two other caveats that suggested that the eventual assimilation of blacks would only occur in some distant future. The first of these was that the racial intolerance of the white population constituted an insurmountable barrier to racial change. While the trend toward modernity would in time surmount racial segregation, for the present it was impossible to overcome that white barrier and foolish to try. In the 1920s and 1930s, the sociologists of race relations were cautious academics who were not given to challenging the status quo or to providing a voice for an oppressed minority.

The second caveat was an image of blacks as so culturally inferior as to be incapable of functioning effectively in modern society even if given the opportunity. Within the United States the southern rural black became for sociologists their most obvious example of a premodern people. Even when no longer defined as biologically inferior, black Americans were portrayed by some sociologists as still almost primitive, having barely progressed beyond their African origins. Because they had lived in rural isolation in the South, they were regarded as the nation's most backward people, and that was how they appeared in the sociological literature. A somewhat more benign view, which flourished in the 1920s and was commonly held by anthropologists and by some sociologists of race relations, was that blacks were a folk people. But whether backward or folk, they were clearly thought of as a people not yet modern and barely able, if at all, of moving from an isolated, near-primitive existence into the modern world.

However backward and culturally inferior they were portrayed to be, it also became a basic assumption that blacks had lost their African cultures of origin and as a consequence possessed no other culture than the American. They were, it was often said, Americans in dark skins. While sociologists believed that isolated rural blacks had only a minimal command of American culture, they also believed that they shared the values and aspirations of other Americans. The sociologists of race relations never doubted that blacks wanted nothing more than to be accepted by white Americans, to assimilate, and thus to disappear as a separate people.

There was a logical extension of this image of the American black: a people so culturally inferior would lack the capability to advance their own interests by rational action. Viewed as lacking a trained and experienced leadership, as still ignorant and mostly uneducated, and as incapable of participating in the political process, blacks were portrayed as a people unable on their own to effect changes in race relations and thus dependent on white leadership; race was still the "white man's burden."

These various assumptions and beliefs, taken together as a coherent whole, constituted sociology's perspective on race relations. From its beginnings in the 1920s and for the following three decades it gave direction and purpose to the way sociologists studied the problem of race. This book is an effort to provide a long overdue critical assessment of that sociological perspective. It begins with the circumstances that led to the decline of the once dominant biological theory of race, the consequent emergence of a sociology of race relations in the 1920s, and follows its construction and its changes until the decade of the 1960s, when its failure to be congruent with the world of racial action and practice brought on serious criticism and ended its hegemony of four decades.

The Sociological Response to Failure

By the early 1960s some sociologists were aware that what was going on in American race relations was no longer evident in their writings, that they had not anticipated the widespread revolt of blacks in the South, and that their work could no longer serve as a guide for the future of race relations. Others, however, resisted any criticism, particularly criticism from blacks within the university.[2] On the one hand, a small body of self-criticism emerged, providing a response to sociology's evident failure to understand fully its own object of study. The response of most sociologists, however, was like that of Frank Westie, who in 1964 published a long essay in the *Handbook of Modern Sociology* assessing the state of the sociology of race relations that simply ignored what had occurred since 1960.[3]

The criticism began with a paper by Kurt Back presented at the 1962 meeting of the American Sociological Association and later published in *Phylon*. It was followed by Everett C. Hughes, a distinguished elder of the discipline, and one of the last of the students of Robert Park, on the occasion of his presidential address in 1963. During the rest of the decade, however, only three other efforts were made by sociologists to address the issue: a paper by Robin Williams, Jr.; a second paper by James Fendrich and Lee Sloan; and comment by Pierre L. van den Berghe in barely more than six pages in his *Race and Racism: A Comparative Perspective* (a book that on its own merits drew wide recognition and acclaim).[4]

In the early seventies, however, five sociologists (including van den Berghe a second time) returned to the issue and extended the effort at a self-assessment in the sociology of race relations. Two of these attempts were journal articles: by L. Paul Metzger in 1971 (which offered a penetrating critique of sociology's commitment to assimilation) and by James W. Vander Zanden, then the author of a standard textbook in race relations, in 1973. In 1972, between these two papers, three books were published, though two of them were collections of essays in which it was only the editorial comment that contributed to the ongoing criticism. One of these was van den Berghe's *Intergroup Relations: Sociological Perspectives,* a volume of papers on race and ethnic relations selected from the *American Sociological Review;* the other was Robert Blauner's *Racial Oppression in America.*[5]

The third book was Stanford M. Lyman's *The Black American in Sociological Thought: A Failure of Perspective,* a brief work that offered a review of the development of the sociology of race relations since the turn of the century, criticizing it from the anti-Aristotelian (i.e., anti-evolutionary) perspective that asserted that nothing changes in an orderly, foreordained way and that the outcomes of human action are unknown. A significant feature of Lyman's work was his bold assertion that, because of that Aristotelian viewpoint, and "despite more than a century of study, blacks remain a sociological puzzle." This hard truth was a strong condemnation of the sociological perspective.[6]

Against this stream of critical commentary, one sociologist, Melvin M. Tumin, argued that sociology had provided ample evidence that "unless real change was initiated by white government and white society, Negroes would take the initiative." Not sociologists, then, but government and the public had disbelieved it on the basis of three mistaken assumptions: that slow and grudging concessions would suffice; that whites had the power to "dictate the terms and conditions and tempos" of change; and that "blacks were docile, unorganized, and without leadership or the capacity for militant protest."[7]

Tumin's identification of mistaken assumptions was insightful and correct, but these assumptions were not restricted to members of the white public and to government officials; they were shared equally by sociologists. Furthermore, his effort to document his claim that "it was all there for the knowing" is not persuasive. While Tumin's summary of major research findings in the sociological literature documented the destructive effects of constant discrimination, it did not support expectations of a black revolt, nor did the authors he cited make such claims.

Criticizing the Sociology of Race Relations

An analysis of the criticisms made of the sociology of race relations yields eight points that were shared by at least several of the critics. Some of them were significant criticisms, others were of less relevance. Only three of them identified components of the perspective: an aversion to the concept of conflict; change as gradual; and the incompatibility of modern social organization with racial segregation.

Perhaps the extensive evidence of overt conflict in the 1960s accounts for the fact that one of the more common criticisms was that the sociologists of race relations avoided making racial conflict a significant dimension of the processes by which race relations would change from segregation to assimilation. Several sociologists also pointed out how strongly sociologists believed that changes in race relations would be (and should be) gradual. Everett Hughes made these assumptions a central point of his address by asking, "Why should we have thought, apart from the comfort of it, that the relations of the future could be predicted in terms of moderate trends, rather than by the model of slow burn reaching the heat of massive explosion?"[8]

Two critics—L. Paul Metzger and Robert Blauner—put major emphasis on the belief of sociologists that modern social organization was incompatible with racial segregation. Metzger pointed out that sociologists believed that institutionalized racism was southern and would be removed by the modernization of an underdeveloped area, and that the remains of racism in the urbanized and industrialized North would disappear with the improved educational, economic, and occupational status of both blacks and whites: "Hence, the belief that racism is incompatible with the major features of modern social organization . . . is, in fact, rooted in what is perhaps the major theme of modern sociological theory—the shift, in Cooley's terms, from 'primary' to 'secondary' relations as the basis of social order." Sociologists had supported this position, argued Metzger, with the assumption that blacks desired assimilation into mainstream America and, despite a caste-like position, they would in time, like the immigrants before them, be absorbed.[9]

It is in this context of an assumption carried over from evolutionary theory that Stanford Lyman's critique becomes relevant. Lyman argued that evolutionary thought was in error in presuming a slow, orderly development that resulted in inevitable human outcomes. Thus, he challenged that fundamental assumption of the sociologists of race relations that there was a basic trend from traditional to modern society that assured the eventual elimination of an old racial order.[10]

For Blauner, in turn, "the most important assumption" was that "as industrial societies develop and mature, race and ethnicity become increasingly irrelevant as principles of group formation, collective identity, and political action." While this assumption is "so strikingly at odds with contemporary realities in the modern world," he said, it is nonetheless a heritage of nineteenth-century social theory.[11]

One of the more severe criticisms made was that the American sociology of race relations was hopelessly parochial; it lacked a comparative outlook and possessed no sense of history. Both Vander Zanden and van den Berghe developed this point in some detail, but they differed on one aspect. Vander Zanden blamed Robert Park's "Chicago School" of race relations based on the Old South for sociology's parochialism, but van den Berghe recognized that Park was a comparative scholar with a historical perspective and exempted him from the criticism he made of other sociologists.[12]

The charge that the sociology of race relations was parochial by virtue of not being comparative was both true and false. It was true that sociologists from the 1920s on were not doing the kind of comparative studies, such as comparing the United States, for example, with South Africa, or with European or Latin American nations, that contemporary comparative scholars practiced. However, if one recognizes that the sociology of race relations was first built around a fundamental comparison between modern and premodern, the charge is false. Drawing upon the evolutionary tradition of nineteenth-century sociological theory, the generation that began the sociology of race relations saw themselves as engaging in comparative study. In the 1950s the studies of modernization were comparative in the same fashion, contrasting a similar conception of modern with the traditional form of social life to be found in the Third World.

For two reasons, nonetheless, there is some warrant to the criticism. The comparison of modern and premodern in race relations was based upon an image of rural blacks as an isolated, backward people, but by the 1960s blacks were an urban people, residents of inner cities and racial ghettos. A change of four decades rendered the older basis of comparison irrelevant. Second, after World War II, sociologists showed little interest in the comparative study of race relations. Instead, the possibilities of contributing to practical efforts at racial change proved to be a far more absorbing interest.

Perhaps the criticism most frequently made was that the sociology of race relations was far too preoccupied with the racial prejudice of white Americans. There was a major error, it was argued, in believing that movement toward racial equality depended on reducing prejudice in the white majority, which meant emphasizing the attitudes of individuals over a concern for group power. Blauner, for example, insisted that white attitudes "are peripheral rather than primary determinants of racial arrangements."[13] The major difficulty with this criticism is that it assumes that all sociologists uncritically accepted the large number of studies of prejudice provided by social psychologists. There is no question that prejudice was a central component of the research on race relations, and social psychologists went from the mere measurement of attitudes to an interest in the psychodynamics of the prejudiced person. But it is also the case that the measurement of prejudice became a bone of contention between sociologists and social psychologists when some sociologists insisted that structural factors were more important than attitudes. There is a reason, to be sure, that social scientists provided so much attitudinal research: it played to an American culture that emphasized individual attitudes as the decisive factors in both causing and solving social problems. But many sociologists of race relations knew better.

In the politically charged atmosphere of the 1960s, a number of critics charged that liberalism provided an ideological framework for many of sociology's assertions about the reality of race relations and, even more so, its admonitions for racial change. John Horton had provided a basis for such a claim by his provocative essay on order and conflict theory in sociology in which he used the sociology of race relations to illustrate contrasting ideologies. Horton was not trying to explain sociology's inability to foresee a collective explosion of militant action, but his assessment of a liberal sociology's essentially conservative assumptions within a normative theory of social order made it evident that sociologists could be blind to the potential for overt conflict in a social problem. L. Paul Metzger noted his agreement with Horton when pointing out that sociology's theoretical framework "rests essentially on the image of American society which has been set forth by American liberalism, wherein the minority problem is defined in the narrow sense of providing adequate, if not equal, opportunity for members of minority groups to ascend as individuals into the mainstream culture."[14]

More than any other sociologist of race relations, Pierre van den Berghe strongly emphasized how much a liberal outlook had influenced sociological work. It had, he argued, "been strongly flavored with a great deal of optimism and complacency about the basic 'goodness' of American society with the cautious, slightly left-of-center, reformist, meliorative, gradualist approach of 'liberal' intellectuals." Consistent with this, he insisted, sociologists had followed Myrdal's lead and interpreted race relations "as a moral dilemma in the hearts and minds of men rather than a complex dynamic of group conflict resulting from the differential distribution of power, wealth, prestige, and other social rewards."[15]

The association of sociology with liberalism in the matter of race relations is evident enough, but a caveat is needed. In Horton's and Metzger's sense, such an association meant that sociologists shared the liberal assumptions about the reality of American society and the emphasis on individuals finding the opportunity to be mobile and thus assimilate. In that sense sociology accepted the liberal image of American society. However, though the prewar generation of sociologists had been modestly optimistic about assimilation (at least about long-run progress), they were not liberal reformers. A close relationship between sociology and reforming liberalism, it should be noted (and the critics did not note it), came about only after World War II. Before then sociologists concerned with race relations remained uninvolved with, and often critical of, that very small body of white liberals who were active on matters of race. From the Progressive Era until the 1940s, race relations were at best marginal to the liberal agenda; most progressives were either indifferent to the issue of race or shared the prejudices so dominant in their day. Even the Roosevelt administration did not display a compelling interest in race relations.

A less compelling criticism was that sociologists had never developed a viable theory of race relations. But there was nothing new in such a criticism; sociologists had been lamenting their failure to produce a theory of race relations well before World War II. Van den Berghe, however, added another dimension to the issue when he argued that race has "little claim for autonomous theoretical status" because it is only "an interesting special case in a broad range of similar phenomena." That being so, "it follows that there can be no general theory of race."[16] But that, too, was not new. Such major figures in the sociology of race relations as Louis Wirth and Herbert Blumer had also suggested earlier that race relations might not have claim to autonomous theoretical status.

A final and lesser criticism said that sociologists tended to study the opposition by whites to racial change, thus revealing a bias toward the study of the forces that maintained segregation.[17] It would seem pointless to accuse sociologists of documenting the maintenance of segregation, by whatever measures, or of describing the persistent forms of discrimination. A continuing measure of the degree of inequality suffered by blacks in American society was (and still is) essential to the study of race relations. The point of the criticism, of course, was that efforts to measure the factors that maintained segregation led to a neglect of the forces that were making for change. Before World War II sociologists saw little evidence of factors producing racial change, except for urbanization and industrialism as long-run trends. But after

World War II they documented in full the measurable decline in prejudice, which for them was the major evidence for racial change, and they also analyzed the consequences of court decisions that reduced racial discrimination.

Taken together, these criticisms did not possess the coherence and completeness of an explanation. Only three of the criticisms were directed toward components of the defining perspective, though the critics seemed not to recognize that. The others were marginal issues. Sociologists did not fail in their study of race relations because they overemphasized prejudice, failed to be comparative, became involved with liberal reform, failed to develop an adequate theory, or studied only the forces maintaining segregation. These criticisms are, at best, partial truths, or wrong. Insightful as the sociological critics were, they did not grasp the whole of the sociology of race relations that had been constructed over the four decades from 1920 because they did not recognize that behind that sociology of race relations was a formative perspective that shaped and developed it. In fact, they never treated the sociology of race relations as an intact body of thought with some reasonable coherence in the organization of its ideas. Nor did they look back far enough for the origins of some of its themes or for the continuities and discontinuities of thought over time.

In the small body of criticism that appeared between 1962 and 1973 it would appear at first glance that each author was contributing to an ongoing scholarly debate over the adequacy of the sociology of race relations. But such was not the case. No essay compared or contrasted its argument with others, debated or disputed any points, and only rarely made any reference to another work. Consequently, there was no effort to find common ground, to sort through the various pieces to accumulate the criticisms made, or to locate those most agreed upon. When the output of such criticism seemed to finish in 1973, no sociologist made any effort to pull it together by summarizing the critical points and asking whether they constituted a fully coherent critique of the sociology of race relations.

Though there was no further critical comment for the rest of the decade, concerns about sociology's analysis of race relations were not yet fully laid to rest. In 1980 Thomas Pettigrew edited a collection of sociological articles on race relations as these appeared in American sociological journals from 1895 to 1980. In *The Sociology of Race Relations* Pettigrew undertook the arduous task of rereading all articles on race, the race problem, and race relations published in the *American Journal of Sociology*, the *American Sociological Review, Social Forces,* and *Social Problems* from 1895 to 1978. He selected forty-five articles for publication, beginning with a piece by W. I. Thomas on race prejudice in 1904, to document the development of the American sociology of race relations.[18]

In his introduction to the book, itself a fine essay on sociology's long effort to deal with the issue of race, Pettigrew built his assessment around the conception of sociology caught in the tension between its role as social critic and its position as "supplicant," dependent on society for support and acceptance. While acknowledging that sociology had too often been the supplicant, not the critic, he still rejected Ernest Becker's "dour judgment" that sociology had degenerated into a technique in the service of the ongoing ideology. These forty-five articles, he believed, demonstrated this tension in the study of race relations: "The sociological literature on race relations, therefore, both *reflects* American society and attempts to *reform* it."[19]

The critical work advocating reform, he acknowledged, was always in the minority: "Analyses that reflect the limitations of their time—and thereby legitimate these limitations with the imprimatur of social science—dominate the journals." Yet, Pettigrew felt justified in biasing his selection of articles toward those that were critical for three reasons: first, these articles, he claimed, were more influential in shaping the discipline; second, he wished to demonstrate that "at least a minor chord of protest and reform had in fact characterized the sociology of race relations"; and third, they "expose their time more critically." Morever, the critical papers were "overwhelmingly liberal and reformist, not radical and revolutionary."[20]

Pettigrew did not address the issue of the sociological response to failure, but he did cite Vander Zanden's assertion that the sociological literature described and documented black disadvantages, attacked the biological arguments, and interpreted black disadvantages as a consequence of white prejudice and discrimination. Concentrating on these three themes, he thought, produced in sociological work three analytic biases: an emphasis on static description; a stress on the reactive and pathological in black life; and a focus on the individual level of prejudiced personalities, not the institutional and societal.[21] His second point—that sociologists stressed the reactive and pathological in black life—provided some limited recognition that sociologists had offered only a denigrating image of the black American.

Pettigrew's task was not to account for the failure of the sociologists of race relations to anticipate the black rebellion of the 1960s. Nonetheless, his analysis of the journal literature from 1895 to 1980 provided an insightful assessment of sociology's study of race in American life as it developed over eight decades. But like the sociological critics from Kurt Back to Stanford Lyman, whose criticisms he did not discuss, Pettigrew also did not get the whole of it.

Pettigrew's book did seem, finally, to cap off the sociological efforts to examine critically the sociology of race relations. But during the 1980s three historians, H. Fred Wacker, Stow Persons, and Vernon J. Williams, Jr., each in turn examined the early decades in the development of the study of race relations. None of their studies went past 1945, and two of them were about the Chicago school and Robert Park.

In his *Ethnicity, Pluralism, and Race,* Wacker was concerned with defending the Chicago school, and particularly Robert Park, from criticisms that he thought often came from a shallow and distorted reading of the sociological heritage in race relations. In turn Stow Persons, in his *Ethnic Studies at Chicago: 1905–1945,* examined the significance of the Chicago school for its exemplification of the Anglo-American interest in assimilating ethnic minorities to the dominant culture to its consequent decline as a scholarly perspective no longer relevant in a new period of ethnic politics and governmental policies.[22]

In contrast to these studies of the Chicago school, the historian Vernon J. Williams, Jr.'s recent study, *From a Caste to a Minority,* examined the sociology of race relations from its beginning in the 1890s until 1945 as a steady movement of sociologists advocating the "full assimilation" of blacks "into the American mainstream, a triumph of ideals of black progress and assimilation."[23] However, none of the problems that are the concern of this book, and that the critics of the 1960s and 1970s wrestled with, are given any recognition.

Despite the fact that another book about the sociology of race relations seems to come forth every few years, and it thus seems that the historical and sociological analysis of sociology's effort to account for race relations in American society remains an unfinished project, there has not yet been any study that has accounted for the whole of that intellectual process. This cannot be done until the sociological perspective on race relations is examined in full. This book makes an effort to get the whole of it.

The Scope of the Study

This study properly begins in the 1920s, when Robert Park and others began to develop a sociology of race relations to replace the biologically defined race problem. But first the stage must be set for understanding why the sociology of race relations emerged when it did by giving some attention to the period before the 1920s, when the monolith of racist belief and segregationist practice brought into being after the Civil War began to crumble and the explanation of race shifted from biology to the social sciences. That is the task of chapters 1 and 2.

These two chapters, like the others in the book, are organized thematically and chronologically. But thematic shifts from chapter to chapter do not permit a straight chronology, with each chapter taking off from a point in time where the preceding one left off. Instead, there is considerable chronological overlap from chapter to chapter.

Chapter 1 examines the emergence of the "race problem" after Emancipation, when the thesis of the racial inferiority of the former slaves was expanded upon in a flood of medical and biological literature during the last four decades of the nineteenth century. It began with a delineation of racial traits by bodily measurement and was joined by a racial interpretation of Darwinian evolution. What happened in social thought was matched in social practice. In the legal order, Supreme Court decisions in the 1890s conferred constitutionality on racial segregation. In the arena of politics, the onset of the Progressive movement early in the twentieth century excluded race relations from the nation's wide-ranging agenda of social reform.

Chapter 2 records the struggle involved in the redefining of the race problem from biology to culture. From the early years of this century well into the 1920s, a powerful eugenics movement used biological theory to sustain claims of racial inferiority of nonwhite peoples and even of immigrants from eastern and southern Europe, until a new genetics shattered their claims to scientific validity. Following the lead of the Boasian anthropologists, some sociologists in the 1920s moved toward a new sociology of race relations, but others resisted for at least another decade, some even longer. But even as they discarded the belief in biological inferiority, sociologists continued to characterize black people as culturally inferior, a conception that was to become a mainstay of the sociological perspective.

Chapters 3 through 6 provide a detailed examination of the development of the sociology of race relations from its beginning in the 1920s to its maturity in the 1950s. Chapter 3 covers the decade of the 1920s into the early 1930s, when a new generation of sociologists, led by the innovative Robert Park, constructed a sociology of race relations and developed a vocabulary that shaped and focused the sociological discourse on race relations for decades to come. Chapters 4 and 5 cover the decade of the 1930s into the early 1940s, but with different thematic emphases. Chapter 4 examines the retreat by sociologists in the 1930s from the study of race relations in the urban North to the study of caste-bound blacks as folk and peasant in the Deep South, producing the conceptual debate over the applicability of the concept of caste to American race relations. Chapter 5, in turn, looks at the first efforts to do empirical studies of black youth, family, and community, accompanied by the emergence of a number of noted black sociologists, particularly Charles Johnson and E. Franklin Frazier. Chapter 6 examines the significance for the sociology of race relations of Gunnar Myrdal's classic work, *An American Dilemma,* a work begun in the late thirties and published during World War II.

Chapters 7 and 8 provide an examination of the sociology of race relations from the mid-1940s to 1960. Chapter 7 examines issues that emerged between 1945 and 1950, including the attempt to absorb the sociology of race relations into a more encompassing framework of intergroup relations; the involvement of sociologists in the practice of liberal reform; the consequences for the study of race relations of a sociological interest in the study of the authoritarian personality and the correlates of authoritarianism; and the debate over the relative importance of prejudice and discrimination. Chapter 8, in turn, pursues these and other issues through the decade of the 1950s; these include the advent of a social psychology of race relations; the thesis that blacks were psychologically crippled by racial oppression; the intent to provide empirical studies relevant for social policy; the participation of sociologists in the Supreme Court decision on school desegregation; and an abortive effort to develop an applied sociology of race relations.

Chapter 9 brings this study to a close by restating its claim that the sociologists of race relations failed to foresee the coming of the black rebellion of the 1960s. The chapter examines the efforts of sociologists to study the rapid change in race relations and assess the degree of racial progress accomplished, which led a number of them to replace the optimism that had been basic to the sociological perspective since the time of Gunnar Myrdal with a more pessimistic outlook on the future of race relations. In effect, sociologists could no longer continue to think about race relations with the same comfortable assumptions that the persepctive had long provided, for that perspective was now in dissolution.

Finally, a brief epilogue speaks to the reconstruction of the sociology of race relations. A starting point can be found in the new emphasis on diversity and pluralism, on the new value placed upon the concept of ethnicity, as well as the new economic and political context in which the struggle for racial equality will be worked out. The book concludes on the question of what the appropriate sociological stance toward the complex of issues formed around the ideas of diversity and pluralism, race and ethnicity, can be, now that the old perspective has dissolved. There is much to rethink.

Notes

1. Karl Mannheim, *Ideology and Utopia: An Introduction to the Sociology of Knowledge* (New York: Harcourt, Brace, 1936), 272; Alvin W. Gouldner, *The Coming Crisis of Western Sociology* (New York: Basic Books, 1970), 31–37.

2. Wilson Record has studied the emergence of black studies in the university as a context of criticism of sociology's study of race relations, particularly by blacks. See his "Black Studies and White Sociologists," *American Sociologist* 7 (May 1972): 10–11, and also, "Response of Sociologists to Black Studies," in James E. Blackwell and Morris Janowitz, eds., *Black Sociologists: Historical and Contemporary Perspectives* (Chicago: University of Chicago Press, 1974), 368–401.

3. Frank Westie, "Race and Ethnic Relations," *Handbook of Modern Sociology*, ed. Robert E. L. Faris (Chicago: Rand McNally, 1964), 576–618.

4. Kurt W. Back, "Sociology Encounters the Protest Movement for Desegregation," *Phylon* 24 (1963): 232–39; Everett C. Hughes, "Race Relations and the Sociological Imagination," *American Sociolgical Review* 28 (Dec. 1963): 879–90; Robin Williams, Jr., "Social Change and Social Conflict: Race Relations in the United States, 1944–1964," *Sociological Inquiry* 35 (Winter 1965): 8–25; James M. Fendrich and Lee Sloan, "Trends in Race Relations Research," *Indiana Social Studies Quarterly* 20 (Winter 1966–67): 22–38; Pierre L. van den Berghe, *Race and Racism: A Comparative Perspective* (New York: John Wiley, 1967).

5. L. Paul Metzger, "American Sociology and Black Assimilation: Conflicting Perspectives," *American Journal of Sociology* 76 (Jan. 1971): 627–47; James W. Vander Zanden, "Sociological Studies of American Blacks," *Sociological Quarterly* 14 (Winter 1973): 32–52; Pierre L. van den Berghe, *Intergroup Relations: Sociological Perspectives* (New York: Basic Books, 1972); Robert Blauner, *Racial Oppression in America* (New York: Harper and Row, 1972).

6. Stanford M. Lyman, *The Black American in Sociological Thought: A Failure of Perspective* (New York: G. P. Putnam's Sons, 1972; Capricorn Books, 1973), 171. Note the use of "perspective" in the title of Lyman's work, as well as that of Metzger and van den Berghe.

7. Melvin M. Tumin, "Some Social Consequences of Research on Racial Relations," *American Sociologist* 3 (1968): 117.

8. Hughes, "Race Relations," 889.

9. Metzger, "Sociology and Assimilation," 635, 639.

10. See Lyman, *Black American*, 23–25, and chapter 7.

11. Blauner, *Racial Oppression*, 3.

12. Vander Zanden, "Sociological Studies," 43; van den Berghe, *Race and Racism*, 4–5.

13. Blauner, *Racial Oppression*, 8.

14. John Horton, "Order and Conflict Theories of Social Problems as Competing Ideologies," *American Journal of Sociology* 71 (May 1966): 701–13; Metzger, "Sociology and Assimilation," 628.

15. Van den Berghe, *Race and Racism*, 7.

16. Ibid., 5–6.

17. Back, "Sociology Encounters," 232; Vander Zanden, "Sociological Studies," 40.

18. Thomas F. Pettigrew, ed., *The Sociology of Race Relations: Reflection and Reform* (New York: Free Press, 1980).

19. Ibid., xxi–xxii, xvi.

20. Ibid., xxi–xxii, xxv–xxvi (emphasis in original).

21. Ibid., xxxi–xxxii.

22. R. Fred Wacker, *Ethnicity, Pluralism, and Race: Race Relations Theory in America before Myrdal* (Westport, Conn.: Greenwood Press, 1983); Stow Persons, *Ethnic Studies at Chicago, 1905–1945* (Urbana: University of Ilinois Press, 1987).

23. Vernon J. Williams, Jr., *From a Caste to a Minority: Changing Attitudes of American Sociologists toward Afro-Americans, 1896–1945* (Westport, Conn.: Greenwood Press, 1989), 1.

1

Sociology and Race:
The First Generation

When the first scholars who were to identify themselves as sociologists emerged on the academic scene in the 1880s and 1890s, they
displayed a deep concern, in the first instance, for the development of
a new science of society, but second, and more pragmatically, with the
possibilities for a wide range of social reforms. From its beginning in
1895, the pages of the new *American Journal of Sociology* gave ample
space to both matters. Discussions of social issues that were deemed
reformable appeared in every issue of its first fifteen volumes, many
written by nonacademic social critics and reformers. But one issue was
little discussed and not defined as reformable: the race problem.

Those first sociologists came on the scene rather late in the period
in which white Southerners recaptured power and legitimacy and
brought the black population under new forms of social control. By
the 1890s a resurgent South had not only effectively denied the former
slaves the freedoms guaranteed them by the Fourteenth and Fifteenth
Amendments, but it had won the acquiescence if not the full support
of the North in reasserting white supremacy. There seemed to be a
tacit agreement that the South knew best how to deal with the black
population and that it was better if the North left the race problem
in southern hands.

The northern acceptance of white domination in the South was
reinforced by the development of racial theories, some of them from
Europe, the rest of native origin, that offered a presumably scientific
argument for the inherent inferiority of the nonwhite races. The beginning of sociology in the American university, therefore, came at a
time when the prevailing belief in the innate inferiority of the "lower

races" found the strongest support from the natural science of that day. There were only a few sociologists (perhaps only Lester Ward and W. I. Thomas) who were even skeptical of the prevailing racial theories; most of them readily accepted the dominant ideas about the inequality of the races.

When the Civil War ended, slaves and slavemasters alike were unprepared for the complete rupture of their established relationship. Neither the nation's political and civic leadership, nor its scholars, had given any serious thought to the future of four million emancipated slaves. In 1866, after the adoption of the Thirteenth Amendment to the Constitution, the unsettled issue of the appropriate place in American society, if any, for the newly freed people demanded a solution that was not readily at hand.

Three issues needed to be solved. There was first the matter of the economic use of these formerly enslaved laborers. There was also the political question of justice and racial harmony; if most white Southerners were little concerned with racial justice, they were much concerned with what they called racial harmony. But there was also a paramount concern about social control over a population deemed to be biologically inferior and little educable. These issues first defined what came to be called the "race problem" or "the Negro problem" (the terms were used interchangeably), and with but little change this sense of the race problem was to remain in place until the 1920s.

Southern whites of the post–Emancipation South were the first to define the race problem and work out a southern solution that restored a structure of racial domination. The period from the Civil War to the last decade of the century became a time of immense struggle, not only over the future of black people, but also over the future of the South, where almost all blacks still resided. By the 1870s, the white elite of the defeated Confederacy had taken back political power and regained economic control and political governance over a still needed black labor. The status of black people, therefore, hardly changed; most of them remained agricultural laborers, but controlled now, not by the laws of slavery, but by the instruments of debt, tenancy, and sharecropping.

By the 1890s those same whites, recognizing the unlikelihood of northern opposition, began the task of instituting legalized segregation and of disenfranchising the black population. In barely more than a decade, they constructed the system of legal segregation and racial domination that was to remain intact until after World War II. In 1896 the Supreme Court's decision in *Plessy v. Ferguson* gave constitutional sanction to a new system of racial domination and control.

As the twentieth century began, therefore, the once enslaved black Americans were still not far removed from the conditions that enslavement had maintained. They were still mostly confined to agrarian labor in the South, they were an impoverished and exploited people, and a new system of coercive controls now closely regulated their lives, despite the formal rights granted them in the Constitution. White Southerners, furthermore, were far more hostile to them than at any time since Emancipation.[1]

Race, Science, and Evolution

From the Civil War to the turn of the century, the struggle of white Southerners to restore racial domination was also a time of sustained effort in Europe and the United States to provide scientific evidence for the claim of a qualitative ordering of the human races. The white South's indigenous conception of racial superiority became interwoven with racial theories that claimed scientific status. These purportedly scientific claims went through a number of overlapping phases: first, a naturalistic effort to identify racial traits by measuring various dimensions of the human body; second, an effort to fit ideas of racial superiority and inferiority into Darwin's evolutionary theory; and then, in the last decade of the century, a theory of inheritance.

In the first phase, an enormous amount of work went into the naturalists' efforts to relate measurable dimensions of the human body—head, face, skull, brain capacity, and genitals, among others— to qualitative differences in some attributes of the human races.[2] This included intelligence, but also other behavioral and psychological dimensions. While the scientific effort was concerned with demonstrating a ranked order of all races, American scientists and physicians placed particular emphasis on the case of the newly freed black.

The onset of Darwin's evolutionary theory did not upset these efforts. Instead, a delineation of racial traits by bodily measurements was joined to the theory of evolution to support the widely held claim that the nonwhite races had proven to be incapable of evolving as had the white race and remained fixed at an earlier stage of development. As the historian John Haller noted, "In time the hypothesis of evolution and the factors of variation and survival of the fittest gave added scientific sophistication to the heritage of the naturalist's racial characterizations."[3]

Many of these characterizations contributed to an imagery of blacks as regressing to an original state of primitive savagery, once freed from the civilizing control that slavery had provided. Other scientists were to claim that blacks could not survive on their own in competition with a superior race. Their physical and mental deterioration and ultimately their gradual extinction were thought to be foreordained by their presumed inability even to learn adequately the superior culture and so to function effectively within its mental and moral standards. Here was one possible solution to the race problem: the gradual extinction of a race unfit for civilization.[4]

The idea that blacks were regressing to a level of primitive savagery became in time a component of a crude and fearful image of the black male held by many Southerners during the period of heightened racial hostility against blacks and served to justify such harsh actions as lynching. W. I. Thomas, one of the few eminent sociologists of the day to dispute the prevailing theories of racial inferiority, placed responsibility for that fearful imagery on the noted social evolutionist, Herbert Spencer: "There is, however, a prevalent view, for the popularization of which Herbert Spencer is largely responsible, that primitive man has feeble powers of inhibition."[5]

It is probable that most scientists did not envision the extinction of black people as the working out of the evolutionary process. But almost without exception they agreed that the scientific evidence demonstrated the superiority of the white population to the black and, in fact, to all the nonwhite races.

Between the Civil War and the beginning of the new century, educated people in the United States became enthralled with Darwin's theory of evolution. The United States, observed the historian Richard Hofstadter, "during the last three decades of the nineteenth century and at the beginning of the twentieth century was *the* Darwinian country."[6] The implication of Darwin's ideas for social life produced the concept of social evolution as a parallel to biological evolution. Social evolution soon became a dominant mode of social theorizing, best exemplified in the work of Herbert Spencer, and was to last into the second decade of the twentieth century. The idea of necessary adaptation from primitive stages of social life through natural selection and a social equivalent of the "struggle for existence" and the "survival of the fittest" (the latter term was Spencer's) provided Spencer with a basis for constructing an evolutionary theory of society and for making an analogy between society and the biological organism.

Race, however, was at best a minor issue for Spencer. Still, as the historian Thomas F. Gossett noted, Spencer's theory had racial implications, and at times Spencer made observations about race. While he hailed the mixture of varieties of the Aryan race in the United States as producing "a more powerful type of man" and a "civilization grander than any the world has known," he also argued that marriages between individuals of different races should be forbidden. For Spencer, biological evolution had produced dominant and primitive races with a difference in mental development: "The minds of primitive races had all the limitations of the minds of children, except that their childhood of intellect was permanent." But he was also a Lamarckian who believed in the inheritance of acquired characteristics; innate racial character, therefore, was malleable, a point on which he agreed with Lester Ward, though Ward made more of the possibilities for racial equality that could ensue from inheriting acquired characteristics.[7]

Race was also only a minor issue for William Graham Sumner, the most influential of the American Spencerians. While he insisted on the existence of racial inferiority and opposed suffrage for black people, in his most noted work, *Folkways,* he also commented on the confusion over nature and culture: "Modern scholars have made the mistake of attributing to *race* much which belongs to the ethos, with a resulting controversy over the relative importance of nature and nurture."[8]

But Sumner's more lasting influence on race relations was his insistence in *Folkways* that humanitarians and reformers could not effectively interfere with the traditional and customary ways of social life, including matters of race. Change would come in time but only as a natural evolution of new ways of life, not by deliberate intervention. In the early decades of the century, a southern leadership was to find much comfort in these words and quote them often in resisting efforts at political and legal change.

If Spencer and Sumner did not make a major issue of race, others did. They used the evolutionary framework to develop a scientific legitimation of a theory of racial superiority. As Gossett observed, "Races were thought to represent different stages of the evolutionary scale with the white race—or sometimes a subdivision of the white race—at the top." There seemed to be no doubt that the subdivision of the white race at the top was that of the Anglo-Saxons. "The Darwinian mood," according to Hofstadter, "sustained the belief in Anglo-Saxon superiority which obsessed many American thinkers in the latter half of the nineteenth century." The central idea was that the democratic institutions of England, from which those in the United States were derived, had originated among early German tribes. Only a distinctive race of people, it was claimed, possessed the inherent capacity to develop the world's superior form of political institutions and culture.[9]

A logical extension of such thinking could justify the economic and political expansion of the superior peoples over the face of the earth. For some, this meant imperialism and military conquest, ideas that found concrete expression in defense of the Spanish-American War and the taking from Spain of its Philippine and Puerto Rican colonies. This growth of imperialistic attitudes in the 1890s strengthened the Anglo-Saxon sense of superiority over the "lesser" races of the world and encouraged the use of racial ideology as moral legitimation for imperialistic expansion.[10]

In the 1890s biological science took a step forward with the development of an experimental biology of unit-inheritance. After the rediscovery of Mendel's laws in 1900, an explosion of experimental research discovered much about the mechanisms of genetic inheritance and variation and produced an enormous confidence among biologists in its potentialities. They gave strong emphasis to inheritance over environment, in part because their very training assumed physical heredity to be the material link between generations, but also because as middle-class Americans of northwestern European ancestry, they shared a cultural belief in their own superior heredity. A number of them entered vigorously into the debates of the day, offering a new scientific basis for theories of racial inequality. These theories soon became the scientific support for the emerging eugenics movement, which for three decades was to use the new biology to argue for sterilization and a restriction on immigration of those they deemed to be biologically unfit.

For most white Americans, both common sense and scientific evidence seemed to be so obvious that one had to accept the prevailing racial theories whether one's political leanings were conservative or liberal. As Haller observed, "For many educated Americans who shunned the stigma of racial prejudice, science became an instrument which 'verified' the presumptive inferiority of the Negro and rationalized the politics of disfranchisement and segregation into a social-scientific terminology that satisfied the troubled conscience of the middle class."[11] This last dimension is important, for claiming the validation of science gave to the new racial ideology a persuasive influence it would not otherwise have had among educated classes.

As a consequence, racial supremacy became an established fact about which few white Americans displayed any regrets or doubts. Both popular and educated beliefs provided an unqualified confidence in the biological and cultural superiority of white people over all others not white. There were few, indeed, who could stand opposed to the intimidating authority of science and to the solidity of popular belief.

The scientist and the nonscientist, the educated and the uneducated alike, were together in their confident, unshakable presumptions about race. If some whites, mostly Southerners, saw in blacks a regression to primitive savagery, and others saw a race so incapable of coping with civilized life as to gradually become extinct, and still others rejected both ideas, only the rare white person failed to agree that race was a problem because of indisputable differences of inherent quality between the races.

It should not be thought that the belief in racial superiority succeeded so well only because it was seemingly validated by science. What scientists did, it must be recognized, was provide support for what they and others already believed. The North was not a bastion of tolerance persuaded otherwise by science. But, from the 1890s on, the North was so focused on its own problems, particularly those of the new corporate economy and the new massive wave of immigrants from Europe, that it had little concern for the blacks in the South. In addition, Southerners made a missionary effort to convince Northerners that they in the South knew best how to handle the race problem and that their portrait of the black was believable. In due time, the North came to accept much of the South's conception of the black American.[12]

Sociology and the Race Problem

When sociology first emerged as an academic discipline in the 1890s, that first generation of sociologists did not rush to examine the race problem or write extensively about it. Though they were deeply committed to the study of social issues, and their basic stance was one of social reform, for them, as for the many social reformists both inside and outside the university, race was not a reformable issue. They wrote no books on the race problem and only a scattering of articles; a few brief comments on race appeared in some books, such as those by Franklin H. Giddings, E. A. Ross, and Lester F. Ward.

Giddings, for example, in his 1896 book, *The Principles of Sociology*, provided a brief excursus of barely more than a page (in a book of over four hundred pages) on the status of the "lower races" typical of the evolutionary thought of his day. That the "lower races" had been in existence longer than the European races and had accomplished less, he argued, warranted "saying that they have not the same inherent abilities." But it was also the case that among these races were unequal abilities for social evolution. The North American Indian, Giddings thought, though "intellectually superior to the negro," was less able to adapt to new conditions: "The negro is plastic. He yields easily to environing influences. Deprived of the support of stronger races, he still relapses into savagery, but kept in contact with whites, he readily takes the external impress of civilization, and there is reason to hope that he will yet acquire a measure of its spirit."[13]

Lester Ward, in turn, was one of the very few voices to argue against the proclaimed inferiority of the nonwhite races. In 1906 he challenged the scientific claims of proof of such inferiority: "It is not therefore proved that intellectual equality, which can be safely predicted of all classes in the white race, in the yellow race, or in the black race, each taken by itself, cannot also be predicted of all races taken together, and it is still more clear that there is no race and no class of human beings who are incapable of assimilating the social achievement of mankind and profitably employing the social heritage."[14]

The contrast of these opposing views, however, did not lead to any extensive debate. Little concerning the race problem, for example, was to be found in the first five volumes (1895–1900) of the new sociological journal, *The American Journal of Sociology*. It contained only one article on race and one book review, but both were about the races of Europe, not the American race problem. In the ten volumes that followed, from 1900 to 1910, the *Journal* published only eleven papers on the race problem—barely more than one article per annual volume— and six book reviews, some of them no more than a paragraph in length.

The articles varied widely in quality. Some were authored by sociologists or by other academics, while some were by writers with no academic affiliation. As a consequence, some were scholarly in style, others were not. They ranged from a defense of slavery and the slave-masters to a bold assertion of racial equality. Under Albion Small's editorship, the *Journal* took on an eclectic approach to the race problem and did not hold to any particular position, though it did not provide an outlet for those bent on denouncing blacks as savage primitives.

Throughout the first decade of the century, race still fell within evolutionary theory and the vocabulary of race reflected that; *Journal* articles spoke of civilization and savagery, of advanced and backward races. "Civilization" defined the highest stage within social evolution; the lesser stages of development were "barbarian" and "savage," and people of African origin were declared to have come from a savage culture.

The most critical view of the black population in the pages of the *Journal* came from those, such as Paul Reinsch, who said that "in the past the negro race has shown no tendency toward higher development, except under the tutelage of other races" and that "in Martinique, Hayti, and the southern states of the union, the vices of the negro populations assume more repulsive aspects than they bear in the African home." In a book review, Charles Ellwood labeled "the average negro a savage child of nature" and in another, Frank Blackmar said of the black that "owing to his ignorance, superstition, indolence, childish nature, and racial characteristics, he is his own worst enemy."[15]

But there were others who, while acknowledging that blacks were inferior, yet believed that they had made progress and would continue to do so. One such was Charlotte Perkins Gilman, who argued that "in a certain number of cases the negro has developed an ability to enter upon our plane of business life" and that this "proves the ultimate capacity of the race to do so." In such progress she saw "the proof that social evolution works more rapidly than the previous processes of natural selection." Despite her bold claims, she was politic enough to make the point that how to promote a "backward race" is "not a question of 'equality' in any sense."[16]

In the first decade of the new century, however, only one other sociologist besides Lester Ward was bold enough to challenge the comfortable conviction of white superiority. W. I. Thomas seemed even more forthright than Ward when he spoke of "our delusion" that whites are a "different order of mind" from the "black and yellow races." Making due allowance, he said, for "our instinctive tendency as a white group to disparage outsiders, and, on the other hand, for our tendency to confuse progress in culture and general intelligence with biological modification of the brain, we shall have to reduce very much our usual estimate of the difference in mental capacity between ourselves and the lower races, if we do not eliminate it altogether; and we shall perhaps have to abandon altogether the view that there has been an increase in the mental capacity of the white race since prehistoric times."[17]

At a time when the evidence from cranial measurements still exercised an influence in the discussions of racial differences, Thomas summarized his argument as follows: "In respect, then, to brain structure and the more important faculties, we find that no race is radically unlike the others." And in anticipation of the debate of nature versus nurture that was just developing, Thomas came down on the side of environment: "it may well be that failure to progress equally is not due to essential unlikeness of mind, but to conditions outside the mind."[18]

Yet, however bold and advanced this argument was, Thomas was not fully abandoning the place of heredity in the problem of race. For one thing, he was soon to offer a concept of race prejudice as innate. Perhaps more significantly, as early as 1906 he argued that races were distinguished by temperament, which he thought to be important in the development of their cultures. Though Thomas was not to hold to this hereditarian conception of racial temperament for very long, others did, and the concept was to remain a component of the sociological analysis of race until at least the early 1930s.

Hovering around the margin of the discipline in this first decade was W. E. B. Du Bois, committed to empirical research as a source of knowledge to replace ignorance about race, and firmly believing that such knowledge was the basis for movement toward racial equality. As both black sociologist and activist, Du Bois had come on the scene in 1899 with the publication of his study of blacks in Philadelphia and had followed that in 1903 with the publication of his classic work, *The Souls of Black Folk*. From 1897 to 1910 Du Bois produced a vast amount of research at Atlanta University while always frustrated by a lack of adequate financing. Yet he received little recognition from white sociologists; he appeared three times in the *Annals of the American Academy of Social and Political Science*, and at the request of Max Weber published a paper in 1906 in the journal Weber edited, before his brief comment on another's paper appeared in the *American Journal of Sociology* in 1908.[19]

Franz Boas: The Anthropological Influence

In advancing their cases against the standard arguments for racial inequality, Ward and Thomas had been greatly influenced by the renowned anthropologist Franz Boas, who had begun in the 1890s to subject the conventional arguments about racial differentials to a severe critique. Scattered among his numerous publications on fieldwork among American Indians were a few papers on the matter of race, the first of which was published in 1894. During 1910 and 1911 Boas gave a series of lectures before the Lowell Institute in Boston and then at the University of Mexico, in which he incorporated much of the material from his previous papers, some of it verbatim. He published the lectures in 1911 as *The Mind of Primitive Man*.[20] At a time when social science had little to say against the racial doctrines of the day, Boas provided a powerful challenge to such thought.

Boas began by pointing out that "civilized man" assumed that the achievements of the European nations and their descendants were far superior to all others, which meant their aptitude for such achievement

was higher, which, in turn, presumably depended upon "the perfection
of the mechanisms of body and mind" of the white race. In effect, a
superior race produced a superior culture. It was this set of assumptions, which wove together both biological and social evolution, that
Boas subjected to a thorough critique.[21] A quick examination of the
history of human development over the ages convinced him that differences in cultural development were the consequence of favorable
circumstances, not racial qualities: "In short, historical events appear
to be much more potent in leading races to civilization than their
faculty, and it follows that achievements of races do not warrant us
in assuming that one race is more highly gifted than the others." In
summarizing the issue later in the book, he incorporated his critical
analysis of evolutionary stages of culture: "Thus all attempts to correlate racial types and cultural stages failed us, and we concluded that
cultural stage is essentially a phenomenon dependent upon historical
causes, regardless of race."[22]

Boas, however, was not ready to abandon the evidence offered by
European physical anthropology, in which he himself was well trained,
which pointed to physically measurable differences among the human
races, especially that of brain size. There is, he argued, "clear evidence
of differences in mental structure between the races, so we must anticipate that differences in mental characteristics will be found." He
thought it probable, therefore, "that some slight difference of this
character will be found between the white and the negro, but they
have not yet been proved."[23]

More important to Boas was the fact that the quantitative measurements of mental faculty revealed a high degree of overlap, which
meant that "the average faculty of the white race is found to the same
degree in a large proportion of individuals of all other races, and
although it is probable that some of these same races may not produce
as large a proportion of great men as our own race, there is no reason
to suppose that they are unable to reach the level of civilization represented by the bulk of our own people." Later in the book he applied
that principle to the American black by saying that "there is every
reason to believe that the negro, when given facility and opportunity,
will be perfectly able to fulfill the duties of citizenship as well as his
white neighbor." But racial difference would still have an effect: "It
may be that he will not produce as many great men as the white race,
and his average achievement will not quite reach the level of the average
achievement of the white race; but there will be countless numbers
who will be able to outrun their white competitors."[24]

Throughout the first decade of the new century, Boas seized every opportunity to advance his argument in both popular and scientific publications. By 1910 his claim that the American black was fully capable of learning the culture and participating as a citizen in the society was well enough known to be quoted with some confidence, as Ulysses G. Weatherly did in an article in the *American Journal of Sociology*. He cited Boas for confirmation of the idea that "we have as yet no unquestionable evidence that it will be impossible for certain races to attain a higher civilization," and also for the even stronger argument that "there is no reason to doubt their [blacks'] capacity to reach the present level of civilization of the whites."[25]

At a time in American history when assumptions of racial inferiority were among the strongest convictions of most white Americans, Boas brought the rational voice of science to dispute those convictions. But he also brought a liberal reasoning. On the last page of *The Mind of Primitive Man,* he said: "I hope the discussions contained in these pages have shown that the data of anthropology teaches us a greater tolerance of forms of civilization different from our own, and that we should learn to look upon foreign races with greater sympathy, and with the conviction, that, as all races have contributed in the past to cultural progress in one way or another, so they will be capable of advancing the interests of mankind, if we are only willing to give them a fair opportunity."[26]

Nonetheless, very few sociologists were directly influenced by Boas during the first decade of the century. Later, his position would become the one recognized as scientific, but by then others, such as a new generation of geneticists, would have had an even stronger voice in discrediting the once scientific case for racial inferiority, including the evidence from physical measurement that Boas had clung to for so long.

The Ground Between

It should not be thought that some very few enlightened scholars agreed with Ward, Thomas, and Boas, while the majority accepted fully and uncritically the arguments about an innate racial inferiority. There was, in fact, a ground between, created in part because of the Lamarckian theory shared by so many evolutionists. Charles Ellwood, for example, would on the face of it seem to be one who believed strongly in the inferiority of the black race, as his several book reviews for the *Journal* made clear. In a book review on "the color line," Ellwood agreed that science supported the author in asserting the inferiority of the black, and that the color line should be retained. But he disagreed that the black was doomed to extinction and also disputed a proposition on the degeneracy of types produced by racial mixture. His belief in black progress was made evident in his assertion that there were "three influences" that modified racial inferiority: an infusion of white blood; natural selection ("the stupid, unintelligent, and vicious being eliminated in competition with whites"); and education.[27]

A case different than Ellwood's but still within that middle ground was that of Charles Horton Cooley, one of the more notable sociologists of the first generation. On moral grounds he opposed unequal treatment of the races, but he seemed to accept racial inequality as a reality. "It is true, no doubt," he said, "that there are differences of race capacity so great that a large part of mankind are possibly incapable of any high kind of social organization." It was also true, he thought, that "two races of different temperaments and capacity ... tend strongly to become castes."[28]

While Cooley could understand the existence of caste sociologically, it was still a moral burden to him. The caste nature of the racial division in the South, Cooley thought, was evident in "the feeling, universal among the whites, that the Negro must be held apart and subordinate not merely as an individual, but as a race, a social whole." Not even those equal or superior to the white majority could be treated "apart from the mass of their race." While Cooley could accept as "probably sound" the argument of "thoughtful whites" that the "integrity of the white race and white civilization requires Negro subordination," he could not morally accept the human consequences: "At the same time it is only too apparent that our application of this doctrine is deeply colored with that caste arrogance which does not recognize in the Negro a spiritual brotherhood underlying all racial differences and possible 'inferiority.' "[29] Cooley was representative of many educated Americans in the first decade of the century whose moral sense was affronted by the harsh inequities of caste, yet who could find no intellectual grounds for denying there was a basis for its existence.

In that first decade of the century, even the most optimistic of those who believed in black progress were well aware of the passionate hostility of southern whites toward blacks and of how much that hostility had crept North. This led to two consequences. One was the belief that white prejudice had become an unalterable barrier to any form of black progress, or to any positive assessment of blacks as human beings. The other was the belief that racial conflict had become inevitable, given the antagonism of most whites to blacks and the increasing resistance of blacks to accepting the fate whites had dealt them. The concern for white prejudice was to become a cornerstone of the sociological analysis of the race problem through mid-century, but the concern for racial conflict would not persevere in sociology beyond the first generation.

The concept of race prejudice entered the sociological vocabulary through W. I. Thomas's influential 1904 paper. In Lamarckian fashion Thomas defined prejudice as an instinct "originating in the tribal stage of society, when solidarity of feeling and action was essential to the preservation of the group." It was "intense and immediate," called out in response "primarily by the physical aspects of an unfamiliar people," and only secondarily by "their activities and habits." It cannot be reasoned with, Thomas said, nor easily legislated against.[30]

The manner in which Thomas defined race prejudice was in keeping with a dominant tendency of the day to attribute to an inherent human nature some seemingly common aspects of human behavior. But the idea of an innate prejudice, an instinctive response to people who were different, was not to last. The scientific belief in instincts was to persist for less than two decades after Thomas's 1904 paper, but the concept of race prejudice would survive the discarding of instinct theory. It would in time be transformed into a cultural rather than a biological term, and later on it became the concept by which social psychology was to make its contribution to the study of race relations.

Racial Conflict

The concern for racial conflict was a common theme for those sociologists who were social evolutionists, and in the first decade of the century, most still were. More basically, conflict was defined as a fundamental element of evolutionary development. Lester Ward, for example, defended the long record of human struggle that was inherent in the concept of evolution from the charges of its newly emerging critics by saying that "the course of human development has been characterized and determined by the struggle of races, peoples, and nations, and whatever progress has been attained has grown out of this struggle, which is a perfectly normal and healthy condition, and, properly understood, does not possess the evil and immoral attributes that have been ascribed to it." He credited Ludwig Gumplowicz and Gustav Ratzenhofer on understanding the significance of race struggle in the evolution of human civilization.[31]

The sociological interest in conflict was not, however, confined to those committed to the evolutionary paradigm. Albion Small, who was both chairman of the Department of Sociology at the University of Chicago and editor of the *American Journal of Sociology*, translated a long essay by Georg Simmel on the sociology of conflict and published it in three issues of the *Journal* in 1903–4.[32]

The centrality of conflict in social scientific thought was evident when the Harvard economist, Thomas N. Carver, presented a paper before the American Sociological Society in 1907, later published in the *American Journal of Sociology,* in which he offered the evolutionary thesis that the basis of conflict was in economic struggle over scarce goods. In the conflicts among interest groups growing out of scarcity, he said, "the institutions of property, of the family, and the state all have their common origin."[33]

The purpose of Carver's paper was not to argue for the significance of conflict in human affairs; he assumed that his sociological audience agreed with him on that. Instead, he wanted to make the case that, given the economic basis for social conflict, the newly organized discipline of sociology was secondary to economics. That Carver was correct in his assumption was evident in the comments of eight discussants, including such prominent sociologists as E. A. Ross, Edward C. Hayes, Franklin H. Giddings, and Lester F. Ward. None of them disputed the significance of conflict in human affairs. Rather, they engaged him only on his claim to the primary status of economic struggle, thus, challenging his claim to the primacy of economics in the social sciences.[34]

That same acceptance of the centrality of conflict was manifest when Alfred Holt Stone, a Southerner and nonacademic who had written and lectured extensively on race, and was about to publish a book of his essays, also presented a paper at the 1907 meeting of the American Sociological Society, entitled "Is Race Friction between Blacks and Whites in the United States Growing and Inevitable?" The paper was also published in the *Journal* the following March; comments on the paper given at the time by eight other scholars were published in the May issue.[35] For Stone, racial conflicts were "the most pronounced concrete expressions . . . the visible phenomena of the abstract quality of racial antipathy," which he defined as "an instinctive feeling of dislike, distaste or repugnance, for which no good reason can be given." Racial antipathy, Stone argued, was "practically universal" among white people, and stronger among Anglo-Saxons: "One of the best indices of the possibilities of increasing racial friction is the negro's own recognition of the universality of the white man's antipathy to him."[36]

Racial antipathy did not necessarily lead to racial friction. When the black accepted the status assigned him by the white race, as had occurred under slavery, according to Stone, there was no racial friction.

Thus, it depended on circumstances. One such circumstance was an increase in population of the "controlled race." Another was when conditions laid down by the stronger race were not accepted by the weaker race. This was what had now happened: "*Post-bellum* racial difficulties are largely the manifestation of friction growing out of the novel claim to equality made by the negro after emancipation."[37]

Without that "novel claim" to equality, the usually adaptable and contented black people, according to Stone, would have accepted the status assigned to them. The claim to equality, he thought, was exacerbated by the presence of another group whom he identified only indirectly. Stone pointed to a "large and steadily increasing group of men, more or less related to the negro by blood and wholly identified with him by American social usage, who refuse to accept quietly the white man's antipathy toward the race."[38] In such indirect language, Stone identified a race-conscious group of racially mixed people who, "by American usage," could not cross the color line. His comment exemplified the growing sociological interest in the American mulatto and the effort to determine that group's place in the race problem.

The group of eight scholars who offered comments on Stone's paper had no significant disagreement with his main point that racial friction was growing. Nor was there, typical of a generation raised on the theory of social evolution, any lamenting of that fact; conflict was a basic dimension of social change and development. One discussant, W. F. Wilcox, saw the two races "unconsciously but painfully drifting toward a substitute for the slave system ... which bids to provide a more stable social equilibrium." That substitute was to be a caste system in the South and one "not so fully" a caste in the North. Another discussant, the Southerner John Spencer Bennett, saw a worsening of racial attitudes in the South and compared this unfavorably with the period before Emancipation.[39]

But the weight of the comments from the other discussants was focused on the North and on the change in the attitudes of blacks on the race problem. The migration of blacks northward, they agreed, would bring the race problem to the North. "We are beginning to be conscious," said Ulysses G. Weatherly, "that there is also a negro problem in the North as well." While in the South, he noted, the black "is as yet largely agricultural," in the North he is "mainly a recent immigrant, and he lives almost wholly in the cities and towns." The result would be a growth of white prejudice. As Weatherly saw it, in the North there was "less personal liking for and patience with the negro than in the South." The result was to be more racial friction. But the black coming north, Weatherly noted, now possessed "a distinct race consciousness." Most others agreed, and Edwin E. Earp claimed that blacks once wanted to be white, but now, because of their race consciousness, they did not.[40]

The one recognized black scholar among the discussants, W. E. B. Du Bois, agreed in the main with Stone's prediction of rising race consciousness and race conflict. Southerners, he said, "could not depend on the acquiescence of the mass of blacks," and would be disappointed if they thought that blacks were "not to aspire and demand equal rights and fair treatment." There would be more race friction in the South, Du Bois predicted, if Southerners thought that "most human beings are to be kept in absolute and unchangeable serfdom to the Teutonic world." Yet, in 1908, the young black scholar was still optimistic and found hope in "patient" blacks and "honest reasonable people."[41]

For the first generation of American sociologists, then, the possibility of racial conflict was accepted with equanimity. For them, conflict was the natural outcome of the antagonism of white people toward those they deemed to be racially inferior, who, in turn, were no longer willing to accept the continuance of an inferior status that had been legally removed a half century earlier. Most sociologists were social evolutionists, and they expected social conflict to accompany social change.

There is an immense paradox in this nation's acceptance of southern control of the race problem, in the South's ability to impose a new legal order of segregation, despite the guarantees of the Constitution, and in science's production of racial ideologies that were so denigrating of the human qualities of black people. All of this resulted in a reinstituting of an order of racial domination and exploitation, a looking to the past for models of relations between peoples.

Yet, at that very time, the nation was beginning a period of social change and reform, the shaping of a new social order and a modernizing of American society. But even as the sweeping reforms of the Progressive Era proceeded on a broad front, the race problem was excluded from consideration.[42] Those reforms, nonetheless, were in the long run to have an effect upon the way in which the nation was to act in its efforts to alter the relations between the races.

Social Change and Social Reform

The last quarter of the nineteenth century was a period of economic growth, industrial expansion, and the emergence of a new corporate capitalism. Millions of ordinary Americans, however, did not agree on the desirability of the social changes underway. Their dissent was marked by the turbulence of political conflict and class struggle and by financial panic and economic depression. Workers struggled against the new corporations in strikes that were often violent, while farmers expressed their discontent through the reform efforts of the Populist movement, the Grange, and the Farmers' Alliance.

Even as the Populist movement collapsed in the late 1890s, a new movement was emerging from within an expanding urban middle class with a wide-ranging effort to develop a political response adequate to the many social problems it recognized. The Progressive movement's most articulate voices were to be found among a diverse range of social reformers: a Protestant clergy, the new profession of social work, journalists and writers (the "muckrakers"), and academics, including sociologists, among others. While the Progressive movement was a new development, middle-class social reform was not. In 1865 a group of mostly New England social reformers organized the American Social Science Association, and for the next forty years it was concerned with crime and poverty, public welfare, political corruption, public sanitation, mental illness, public health, and child welfare—but not race. The black American appeared only infrequently in the pages of its journal. The historian Merle Curti has argued that the neglect "probably reflected the tacit decision of the northern middle classes to leave the black man in southern hands."[43]

But, however much these middle-class reformers avoided the race issue, they did argue strongly for an environmental perspective and provided intellectual support for the later position that was to argue for nurture over nature, for reform and planned intervention over heredity and laissez-faire. More important, their efforts gave birth to major reform organizations as well as to the new social science associations in history, political science, economics, and sociology, all of which appeared around the turn of the century. Like the social reformers, the first generation of sociologists, even those who espoused evolutionary theory, sustained an interventionist perspective. According to Gisela and Roscoe Hinkle, "American sociologists accepted Spencer's individualism but—aside from a few exceptions, notably Sumner—rejected his antivolitional biological determinism and laissez-faire doctrine." American sociologists, they noted, "generally followed Comte's view of progress as susceptible of acceleration by purposive, rational intervention in society."[44]

In this one respect, at least, sociologists were neither unique nor distinctive in their time; rather, they represented in scholarly values and work a deep sense of the possibilities of purposive, rational intervention shared so widely within the American middle class. The

social changes going on in American society at the turn of the century
only increased their belief that some prudent interventionist policy was
the proper task of government. The pages of the *American Journal of
Sociology* were filled with the articles of social reformers who advocated some form of social intervention. Such a worldview made it
relatively easy for sociologists to participate in the theoretical and
ideological transition that was to mark this period in American history.

The Search for Order

If the new corporate leaders of the nation had continued to find
a viable defense of an unregulated capitalism in Spencer's social-Darwinian arguments or in the more customary claims for a laissez-faire
economy, they would have remained in opposition to the social reformers. But even as the new century began, these arguments for an
unregulated economy had lost much of their credibility with the nation's corporate leadership. Two serious issues were most evident to
them. One was the fear of class struggle, evident in the persistence and
obduracy of labor's often intense and violent struggles. The other was
a growing awareness that laissez-faire capitalism had become the victim
of its own unrestrained and unregulated growth. Some restraint now
seemed necessary to avoid chaos in the marketplace.

No analysis of recognized problems, nor a consequent conception
of needed reform, was possible within either the social-Darwinian theory offered by Spencer and so effectively argued by Sumner, or the
more conventional argument for an unregulated economy. A program
of reform had to be developed, as well as a new mode of social thought
to give it legitimacy. In seeking both program and ideas, corporate
leaders found ways to make common cause, not only with their established opponents, but also and more significantly with an emerging
new generation of middle-class reformers that would in time be known
as the Progressive movement.[45]

However different the perspectives of corporate leaders, the older
generation of social reformers, and the new urban progressives were,
they all proclaimed, though not always in unity, a need for broad social
reform and a new ordering of American life. The rapid social change
from an agrarian to an industrial society had unsettled old ways of
ordering social life and produced what the historian Robert Wiebe
called "a search for order."[46] There was a compelling if inchoate sense
of a nation in the making, impelled by the unleashed forces of industrial
and capitalist development. In that fact was the basis for a wide-ranging
program of social reform and a transformation of social theory.

The search for order arose from a widely shared recognition that the basic outlines of a new order were already present in two interrelated developments. First, as the United States became an industrial and urban society there emerged a new ordering of occupations and classes and a new ethnic diversity as a consequence of the great wave of immigrants from eastern and southern Europe. Second, it was also becoming a more integrated nation, organized politically and economically out of the disparate communities and regions that had given a distinctive but varied cultural stamp to American life. A decentralized and communal ordering of social life was giving way to a more nationally centralized one, and to national instead of regional politics.

The first development was not independent of the other, for the transformation from an agrarian to an industrial order could not occur without a reshaping of the institutional structure. Some reshaping took place as a consequence of the industrializing process and the accompanying emergence of a corporate dominated economy. But some other aspects of the reshaping were the result of deliberate efforts to rationalize and systematize the new order-to-be and to create new institutions, new public policies, and new social practices. The result was a far-reaching transformation of American society, which can best be understood largely in terms of four basic patterns of social change: urbanization; the rise of a new urban middle class; a politics of deliberate, rational reform; and the rapid growth of bureaucracy and administration.

Urbanization

Perhaps no more dramatic and readily apparent change was the rapid growth of cities, an urbanization of the population that was the apparent unavoidable concomitant of industrialization. From farms, villages, and small towns, millions of rural Americans moved in an immense human flow into expanding cities, there to be joined by millions of European immigrants clustered in hastily built urban colonies. This rapidity of urban settlement gave to many cities the appearance of a collection of unrelated communities grouped around a central business district and occupying a common political territory.

The early sociological effort to define the new urbanization was often ambivalent and contradictory. On the darker side, the city was readily defined as the repository of the many social problems of the new industrial order. The fragmentation of community, an instability of family life, ethnic strife, pervasive poverty, rootless individuals, crime and delinquency, disease and feeblemindedness—these and other social problems seemed to the early social reformers to exemplify the social pathology of the new industrial city. Sociologists persistently lamented the decline of small towns and rural neighborhoods and the loss of social control evident when people no longer lived together in small-scale, stable surroundings.[47]

But there was also a new, firsthand exploration of the city by an enterprising and imaginative first generation of urban sociologists at the University of Chicago. From their work the city came alive as a multifaceted, many-hued, complicated social ambience, full of conflict and contradiction, but alive with change and opportunity. It symbolized the chance for a better life, personal freedom and worldly riches, new opportunities and a freer way of living. But it was also rootless, exploitative, impersonal and uncaring, indifferent to the luck of the draw for those who gambled on the new life-chances possible in its streets and shops.

The settling of European immigrants in these rapidly growing cities soon brought about pioneering efforts at a new urban social practice, namely, social work and settlement houses, perhaps best exemplified by Jane Addams and Hull-House in Chicago. Even in this development, however, most sociologists, now city-dwelling but not yet culturally urban, viewed the city with its immigrants and poor people from a perspective shaped by their rural and small-town origins.[48] Yet, however limited this perspective, a first generation of American sociologists did undertake a close observation of the seamier, exploitative side of urban life. They also entered into alliances with the developing professions of social work and with the many social reformers who promoted legislation to curb child labor, provide services for the urban needy, and undertake the assimilation and settlement of the newer immigrants from eastern and southern Europe.

These early sociological concerns for the city, however, saw no race problem, for blacks still lived mostly in the rural South. In the decade before 1900, there was as yet very little movement by blacks from rural to urban places, and what movement did take place occurred mostly within the South. After 1900, however, black people began to move to northern cities in increasing numbers, and the formation of the black urban ghettos was underway. But the new breed of urban sociologists seemed to be so obsessed with the promises and pathologies of the northern city, and particularly with the presence of immigrants from eastern and southern Europe, that they did not look southward and anticipate a soon-to-come relationship between city and race.

The New Middle Class

Sociologists, social workers, and social reformers—the lines of demarcation were not yet clearly drawn—were but one part of a new class development, defined not by ownership of property but by education and vocation. Cities proved congenial to the development of the professions; first, established ones, like medicine and law, which in each case grew in numbers and in effective professional organization. But the greatest growth, because of the greatest need, was in teaching. The demands for increasing numbers of literate and skilled people led to increasing demands for more education for ever more people. The number of teachers grew rapidly as compulsory education spread—from six states in 1871 to all forty-eight in 1916—and so in turn did higher education. Teachers could not teach until they had been trained, and higher levels of education for others required better trained teachers. By 1911, forty-two states (out of then forty-six) required professional training for teachers and school administrators.[49]

Social workers, too, increased in numbers in response to a growing concern about urban problems, and they soon developed a conscious sense of their own identity. That sense of identity led them to form the National Federation of Settlements in 1911; a few years later they gained control of the National Conference of Charities and Corrections and renamed it the National Conference of Social Work.[50]

Training for the new professions of teaching and social work provided a crucial new role for the universities, which soon began to cultivate this combination of education and specialized occupation that *profession* signified.[51] The University of Chicago and Harvard University, for example, took the lead in developing new programs of training in social work. The establishment and legitimation of a new profession became a process firmly attached to universities, for it was the credentials provided by a graduate or professional degree that legitimated a profession.

But if these new professionals, as well as journalists, architects, and others, were prominent in the emergence of a new, urban-based middle class, so was a new generation in business and corporate management. Here, too, parallel with professional associations, business people formed chambers of commerce and trade and industrial associations, a process that was extended to include business unionism and marketing cooperatives in agriculture.[52] Also, the reform of government, both local and federal, brought into being civil service, regulatory commissions, and public agencies for welfare programs and the protection of children. New positions and responsibilities created new skills and expertise.

All of this facilitated the growth of an urban middle class in which education, skill, and knowledge became the basis for professional vocations and technical expertise and an enlarged social influence. If that influence did not exceed that of property and money, its place in making social change and defining the future of American society had now been established. It was to become the source of much of the leadership and direction of the politics of Progressive reform provided by eastern and midwestern urban professionals.

The Politics of Reform

The search for a new order was accomplished largely through an impressive array of social reforms. The accomplishments of these reforms ran across a wide spectrum of interests and changes: workman's compensation; an extension of utililty regulation to limit the privileges and duration of franchises; tax assessment and modernization; a shorter ballot; increased appointive positions in government, reserving some positions for experts covered under civil service; central, audited purchasing; the formation of research bureaus; public health and improvements in housing and factory conditions; and, far from least, a major focus on children, the precious resource of future generations. There was also the formation of the Food and Drug Administration and the Interstate Commerce Commission. All of these reforms, furthermore, found support in an atmosphere of moral exposure produced by that vanguard of the investigative reporter, the "muckraker."[53]

Yet, this was not radical reform, for it sought no fundamental reorganization of society. Instead, it was a reform movement rooted in the transition from an agrarian, communal-based society to an industrial, national, and urban one. The regulative intent of the new legislation was not to hobble the development and growth of corporations, even though hostility to this development was one factor in the pattern of support built up for some reforming legislation. It was a politics of reform intended to modernize the United States and make it an industrial society, to consolidate and centralize, to control and regulate in order to guide and direct. It was also a pattern of reform rooted largely in the professionalizing, urban middle class. They were intent on extending middle-class values to the immigrant masses and the working class through education, social work, and child-care programs; making government and public life coherent, efficient, and adequate to the responsibilities of a new national society; building a rational administrative process that both reformed and controlled; putting educated expertise into public service; and seeking to integrate the hitherto unintegrated—the immigrants, the poor, the workers, and children—into a society of promised reward and opportunity for all. But that promise of reward and opportunity did not extend to black people.

Bureaucracy and Administration

The spread of reform commissions and regulatory agencies, of numerous professional and industrial associations, of civil service in city, state, and federal government, of social welfare agencies, and of expanding educational systems ensured that bureaucratization accompanied the modernization of American society. Public and private administration grew as public and private associations increased in size and scope. The enlargement of human organization, in effect, brought administrative processes and perspectives into the lives of an ever larger number of people, and the administration of some aspect of their lives was now the professional concern of a growing body of administrators.[54]

Social reform in the Progressive Era, then, led to public and private administration over a larger sphere of American life. This was so because most social reforms provided for administrative solutions, which in turn depended upon the efficacy of administrative performance. Not only was there an increased administrative dimension in American life, but social reform became increasingly viewed as the administrative responsibility of public agencies. Some decades later, when reform in race relations finally came onto the public agenda, it, too, was defined as the administrative responsibility of one or more public agencies.

The reforms worked out in the Progressive Era provided the formative processes of twentieth-century liberalism. From its roots in the Progressive mentality came liberalism's commitment to social progress without revolution, to piecemeal reform carried out through social policies directed by trained experts, that is, to a process of social engineering directed by rationally applied processes. Such a mode of reform, observed the historian James Weinstein, moved well away from the unregulated competition of the "Robber Barons" and "toward the stabilization, rationalization, and continued expansion of the existing political economy."[55] No longer did middle-class reformers or corporate leaders believe that that government is best that governs least. Government action to assure stability of marketing and finance, and so to curb "irresponsible" social action, was now deemed a social necessity, as were governmental policies to bring rational efficiency and social integration to a new social order.

Even though reformers still encountered opposition from propertied interests and from those business leaders who still championed an unrestrained competitive capitalism, the new corporate leadership developed a politics quite different from those opposed to all social reform. Recognizing that ideological hegemony is threatened unless the needs and interests of other social classes are seemingly attended

to, the new leadership effectively compromised with and accommodated to a broad array of social reformers.

Both accommodation to and cooptation of the liberal agenda became the program of reformist capitalism. Its commitment to industrial
efficiency and engineering merged with a middle-class infatuation with
social engineering in education and urban government. The urban liberal's growing disdain for small-town "Babbitry" and main-street politics joined with the corporate push for federal centralization, for the
growth of executive power at the expense of legislative authority. The
movement toward centralization and away from localized power and
to social reform calculated efficiently by experts protected by both the
authority of expertise and the politics of nonpartisan civil service gave
liberal reformers some reasonable stretch of commmon cause with the
corporate reform leaders.

In company with industrialization and a new corporate capitalism,
then, these social changes—urbanization, the emergence of a new urban
middle class, the growth of bureaucracy and administration, and a
Progressive politics of reform—encompassed most of what constituted
the transformation of the United States into a more centralized and
integrated nation, moving away from the segmented localism of the
nineteenth century. Such a milieu of vast social change and extensive
political reform was the experiential ground on which twentieth-century liberalism took shape. It was also the impetus for a new mode of
social theory, one consonant with the new social order and its highly
altered perspective on social life.

The Transformation of Social Theory

While there had always been some criticism of the theory of
social evolution, particularly by anthropologists, the theory's identification with the social order being reformed promoted an increasingly
critical reading. From outside the scholarly community, the new pragmatic reformers and their administrative allies, who perceived the
world as a milieu of social problems to be treated in piecemeal, engineering fashion, found good reason to reject evolutionary theory. Its
concept of slow, unplanned change hardly fitted their notion of deliberate, rational intervention. Instead, John Dewey's optimistic conception of intelligent, pragmatic change was far more appealing to the
educated American.

Among scholars, evolutionary theory was attacked from a number
of directions, but its resistance to the idea of social reform as planned
intervention was as basic a reason for reform-minded sociologists as

it was for reformers. Despite their acceptance of social evolution, most sociologists, like other middle-class Americans, were thoroughly interventionist in their worldview.

But it was the anthropologists, led by Franz Boas, who offered a forthright challenge to the whole concept of social evolution. They developed an ethnological critique of the theory, especially of its effort to lock the long history of human development into a fixed sequence of developmental stages that had begun from a common set of primordial social institutions derived adaptively from an original human nature. As a result, the theory of social evolution steadily lost its credibility with social scientists. Sociologists, however, were slower than anthropologists to abandon evolutionary theory. According to Roscoe Hinkle, the years 1915 to 1918 marked the end of the period in which evolutionary theory was dominant in American sociology.[56] By then a new mode of theorizing was emerging.

The Rise of New Theory

Theory is the milieu of intellectuals and scholars, but the act of theorizing springs from the ongoing processes of change and development, of conflict and crisis, that mark all social life. In the early years of this century, these fundamental processes had brought into being a new middle class of urban liberals—reformers, administrators, and professionals—and the new theorists were very much of that same social class. The emerging theory was a theory for that class and for the social changes they had worked to bring about.

In shaping new modes of social interpretation, one significant intellectual development was a revolt against the formalism that had dominated social thinking in the nineteenth century. Morton White has cogently detailed this process in terms of the thinkers whose work rejected one pattern and set out to create another. Their names have loomed prominently in American intellectual history: John Dewey, Thorstein Veblen, Oliver Wendell Holmes, Charles A. Beard, and James Harvey Robinson. The intellectual edifice they constructed was a compound "of pragmatism, institutionalism, behaviorism, legal realism, economic determinism, and the 'new history.' " These "styles of thinking," White tells us, "are suspicious of approaches that were excessively formal; they all protest their anxiety to come to grips with reality, their attachment to the moving and the vital in social life." Dewey and others were convinced that "logic, abstraction, deduction, mathematics, and mechanics were inadequate to social research and incapable of containing the rich, moving, living currents of social life."[57]

Dewey, Veblen, and Beard set out basic theses that were to dominate the intellectual landscape of the social sciences until the 1930s. Dewey's doctrine of instrumentalism committed thought to social engineering by placing primary confidence in the method of intelligence, rejecting dualisms of all kinds, and arguing that ideas were the plans of action, not mirrors of reality. Veblen subjected classical political economy to scathing attack as unfruitfully abstract and offered instead a concept of institutionalism that sought to find the connections between economic institutions and aspects of culture. Beard's economic interpretation of the Constitution elaborated Madison's view in the tenth Federalist paper that faction, rooted in property, is the basic problem of democratic society. As White summarized, "Dewey attacked utilitarian ethics, psychology, and logic for failing to study the actual workings of the human mind; Veblen attacked the hedonic calculus as well as the failure to study economic institutions in the wider cultural settings; Beard opposed the analytical school for treating the Constitution as if it were axiomatized geometry rather than a human, social document; and Holmes regarded Austin's theory as an inaccurate account of law as it is practiced."[58]

The work of these new theorists resonated with the worldview of a new middle class and cleared away the theoretical structure of an earlier period. In the process, they laid the intellectual foundation of twentieth-century liberalism in the United States. But there were several points of difference between these theorists and the new middle class. The theorists' rejection of mechanics along with logic and abstraction came from a critique of an earlier philosophy. But mechanical models of process, as Wiebe noted, were congenial to the pragmatically administrative mind of the urban reformers, "though they were markedly different from those in vogue before Darwin." The new thinking was in terms "of a complex social technology, of a mechanized and systematized factory."[59] Such a way of thinking seems to have been a forerunner to the models of the social system that were to emerge in mid-century sociology.

Nonetheless, the theorists were in one basic way consonant with the new class that responded so enthusiastically to their writings: "They criticized some of the more glaring evils of capitalism, but their political affiliation was never revolutionary."[60] They were reformist, problem-solving and flexible, while not abandoning the centrality of property, and accepting, often without much thought, the class structure. But more than anything else, they were commmitted to piecemeal reform and to the administrative controls and practices such reforms required.

This mode of thinking, furthermore, developed ideas that suited the fluidity and impersonality of urban life:

> They pictured a society of ceaselessly interacting members and concentrated upon adjustments within it. Although they included rules and principles of human behavior, they necessarily had an indeterminate quality because perpetual interaction was itself indeterminate. No matter how clear the evidence of the present, a society in flux always contained the irreducible element of contingency, and predictability really meant probability. Thus, the rules, resembling orientations rather than law, stressed techniques of constant watchfulness and mechanisms of continuous management.[61]

In the newer mode of social science, a concern for fluid group interaction swept aside philosophical idealism. Teleology and the concern for essence gave way to the effort to observe behavior and interaction. And science became method and procedures of investigation. A mode of theorizing grounded in the worldview of a new middle class did not give intellectual voice to other worldviews. It did not speak for, or even to, the working class, nor did it allow the voices of racial minorities and recent immigrants to be heard. Unlike continental Europe, there was not present in the United States a sufficient social basis (most likely, a well-organized and militant labor movement) for a theory grounded in political and intellectual opposition to capitalism. Labor unions were weak and organization of the working class sporadic. An incipient socialist movement seemed at one time to be possible but for a complex of reasons did not develop.

This lack of a systematic and sustained organization of the historic left narrowed the ideological range within which political and intellectual issues were fought out in the United States. On one side was a "conservative" politics seeking largely to maintain the unrestrained freedom of action for business, to keep the open shop in labor relations, to maintain the established class, ethnic, and religious domination inherited from the past century, and to promote growth and expansion of national power and of a national economy.

Its opposition came, not from a socialist or social democratic movement, as in Europe, but from an emergent new liberalism, which sought to reform capitalism in ways that promised to make it more responsible and also to integrate the hitherto unintegrated into the social and economic opportunities that an expanding capitalism promised to offer. Its opposition to old forms of social privilege was rooted in this idea of the reforms necessary to make the United States a modern society, one in which material reward and individual freedom were to be shared widely enough to give it legitimacy. The social reforms that reordered the pattern of American life, therefore, were worked out in a struggle over alternate conceptions, conservative and liberal, of the United States as a capitalist society. And for a still developing sociology, this reformist struggle formed the social framework within which new social theory took shape.

Race: The Unreformable Problem

Despite the broad sweep of social reform during the Progressive Era, however, the race problem remained well beyond reform's reach. Even the most progressive Americans were not ready to rethink their assumptions about race. For practically all white Americans the preeminence of biological judgments about human qualities was still unchallenged; among the more educated, the specific assumption of Anglo-Saxon superiority remained an unquestioned principle.

Among scholars and scientists, support for a theory of racial superiority was far too powerful to be threatened by the growing attack on the credibility of social evolution. In part that was because the theory of biological evolution was unscathed by the attacks on social evolution. But a more important factor was the development after 1900 of a new biology that began to explore the mechanisms of inheritance and variability. A new generation of biologists decreed inheritance to be more significant than environment, thus adding a new and persuasive argument to white Americans' convictions of their racial superiority.

What also remained intact was the entanglement of social and biological thinking. Most of the first generation of sociologists reasoned within a paradigm of sociobiology, in which instincts and inherent temperaments were presumed to be decisive in shaping human behavior and in allocating individuals to social positions within a necessarily stratified social order. In addition, the widespread acceptance of the Lamarckian notion of the inheritance of acquired characteristics helped further to entangle biology and culture. So powerful was the interweaving of the two that only a few sociologists could yet envision their discipline free from biological determinants.

The racial beliefs of those sociologists who accepted the prevailing biological theories of racial superiority were only strengthened by the growth of the eugenics movement, which emerged after 1900 from a backlash against the flood of immigrants from eastern and southern Europe. Its aggressive campaign to stem the flow of immigrants and to reduce the biological reproduction of those defined as unfit kept the issue of racial differentials in the foreground of public concern. The eugenicists were not concerned with the former slaves but with those European immigrants they deemed racially inferior. Nonetheless, backed by claims of scientific evidence from the new biology, the eugenicists' concerted efforts in ideas and actions heightened the white American's sense of inherited differentials in human qualities and reinforced the prevailing assumptions of superiority and inferiority among the human races.

The milieu of social reform had created an environment in which a sociology committed to rational change had been freed from the powerful restraints of an evolutionary paradigm. But the race problem could not as yet be included among the diverse social problems sociologists examined with an intent to encourage social intervention. Race was still imprisoned within a condemning biology, and a conception of the race problem founded on other than biological assumptions was not yet imaginable. Left behind in the ideological swamps of pseudo-scientific thought, the matter of race was denied any share of the progressive developments that were altering the shape and sound of American society.

Before a genuine sociology of race relations could emerge, three changes had to occur: first, the scientific justification for existing racial beliefs had to end; second, sociology had to be extricated from its Lamarckian interweaving of biology and culture; and third, the eugenics movement had to run its course. Only then could the race problem be defined as a matter of social relations, not of biological qualities, and as susceptible to rational intervention.

Notes

1. For a detailed analysis of this period, see Joel Williamson, *The Crucible of Race: Black-White Relations in the American South since Emancipation* (New York: Oxford University Press, 1984), part 2. See also C. Vann Woodward's classic study, *The Strange Career of Jim Crow* (New York: Oxford University Press, 1955), chapter 2.

2. For a detailed analysis of late-nineteenth-century scientific efforts to demonstrate racial inferiority, see John S. Haller, Jr., *Outcasts from Evolution: Scientific Attitudes of Racial Inferiority, 1859–1900* (Urbana: University of Illinois Press, 1971).

3. Ibid., 94.

4. Ibid., chapters 2 and 7.

5. W. I. Thomas, "The Mind of Woman and the Lower Races," *American Journal of Sociology* 12 (Mar. 1904): 442.

6. Richard Hofstadter, *Social Darwinism in American Thought* (Philadelphia: University of Pennsylvania Press, 1955), 4.

7. Thomas F. Gossett, *Race: The History of an Idea in American Thought* (Dallas: Southern Methodist University Press, 1963), 151, 153–54.

8. William Graham Sumner, *Folkways* (Boston: Ginn and Co., 1906), 74.

9. Gossett, *Race*, 144; Hofstadter, *Social Darwinism*, 172–73.

10. On the relation of racial ideology to imperialism, see Hofstadter, *Social Darwinism*, chapter 9; Gossett, *Race*, chapter 13; George M. Frederickson, *The Black Image in the White Mind: The Debate on Afro-American Character and Destiny, 1817–1914* (New York: Harper and Row, 1971), 305–11.

For the origins of racial imperialism, see Reginald Horsman, *Race and Manifest Destiny: The Origins of American Racial Anglo-Saxonism* (Cambridge: Harvard University Press, 1981).

11. Haller, *Outcasts*, x.

12. The North's acceptance of the southern position on race has often been noted by historians. For a recent discussion, see Williamson, *Crucible of Race*, chapter 10.

13. Franklin Henry Giddings, *The Principles of Sociology* (New York: MacMillan Co., 1896), 328.

14. Lester F. Ward, *Applied Sociology: A Treatise on the Conscious Improvement of Society by Society* (Boston: Ginn and Co., 1906), 110.

15. Paul Reinsch, "The Negro Race and European Civilization," *American Journal of Sociology* 11 (Sept. 1905): 156, 166; Charles Ellwood, review of *The Negro and the Nation: A History of American Slavery and Enfranchisement*, by George Merriam, *American Journal of Sociology* 12 (Sept. 1906): 275; F. W. Blackmar, review of *Studies in the American Race Problem* by Alfred Holt Stone, *American Journal of Sociology* 14 (May 1909): 839.

16. Charlotte Perkins Gilman, "A Suggestion on the Negro Problem," *American Journal of Sociology* 14 (July 1908): 78–80.

17. Thomas, "Mind of Woman," 440–41.

18. Ibid., 447, 449.

19. See W. E. B. Du Bois, *On Sociology and the Black Community*, ed. Dan S. Green and Edwin D. Driver (Chicago: University of Chicago Press, 1978); also Elliott M. Rudwick, *W. E. B. Du Bois: A Study in Minority Group Leadership* (Philadelphia: University of Pennsylvania Press, 1960; republished in paperback as *W. E. B. Du Bois: Propagandist of the Negro Protest* [New York: Atheneum, 1968]).

20. Franz Boas, *The Mind of Primitive Man* (New York: MacMillan, 1911). The paper, "The Mind of Primitive Man," was Boas's presidential address to the American Folk-Lore Society and was published in the *Journal of American Folk-Lore* 14 (Jan.–Mar. 1901): 1–11. His first paper in 1894 was "Human Faculty as Determined by Race," *Proceedings of the American Association for the Advancement of Science* 43 (Aug. 1894): 301–27.

21. Boas, *Primitive Man*, 2.

22. Ibid., 2, 17, 249.

23. Ibid., 115.

24. Ibid., 249.

25. Ulysses G. Weatherly, "Race and Marriage," *American Journal of Sociology* 15 (Jan. 1910): 438.

26. Boas, *Primitive Man*, 278.

27. Charles Ellwood, review of *The Color Line: A Brief in Behalf of the Unborn*, by William Benjamin Smith, *American Journal of Sociology* 11 (Jan. 1906): 571–74.

28. Charles Horton Cooley, *Social Organization* (New York: Charles Scribner's Sons, 1909), 28, 218.

29. Ibid., 218–19.

30. W. I. Thomas, "The Psychology of Race Prejudice," *American Journal of Sociology* 9 (Mar. 1904): 607, 610.

31. Lester F. Ward, "Social and Biological Struggles," *American Journal of Sociology* 8 (Nov. 1907): 293, 298.

32. Georg Simmel, "The Sociology of Conflict," *American Journal of Sociology* 9 (Nov. 1903): 490–525; (Mar. 1904): 672–89; (May 1904): 798–911.

33. T. N. Carver, "The Basis of Social Conflict," *American Journal of Sociology* 13 (Mar. 1908): 634.

34. The discussion by eight sociologists can be found immediately after Carver's article, 638–48.

35. Alfred Holt Stone, "Is Race Friction between Blacks and Whites in the United States Growing and Inevitable?" *American Journal of Sociology* 13 (Mar. 1908): 676–97; "Discussion of the Paper by Alfred H. Stone, 'Is Race Friction between Blacks and Whites in the United States Growing and Inevitable?'" *American Journal of Sociology* 13 (May 1908): 820–40.

36. Stone, "Race Friction," 677, 679, 686.

37. Ibid., 680, 682, 684.

38. Ibid., 694–95.

39. "Discussion of Paper by Stone," 820–22, 825–28.

40. Ibid., 824, 833.

41. Ibid., 834–38.

42. For two recent accounts of Progressivism and race, see David W. Noble, *The Progressive Mind, 1900–1917* (Chicago: Rand-McNally, 1970), chapter 6, and Frederickson, *Black Image*, chapter 10.

43. Merle Curti, *Human Nature in American Thought: A History* (Madison: University of Wisconsin Press, 1980), 230.

44. Roscoe C. Hinkle and Gisela J. Hinkle, *The Development of Modern Sociology* (New York: Random House, 1954), 7.

45. James Weinstein has provided a fine historical study of the place of corporate leadership in the era of Progressive reforms. See his *Corporate Ideal in the Liberal State: 1900–1918* (Boston: Beacon Press, 1968).

46. Robert Wiebe, *The Search for Order: 1870–1920* (New York: Hill and Wang, 1967). The following section draws upon this work for its basic perspective and some of its substance.

47. For a historical analysis of the anti-city bias so long prevalent in American social thought, including sociology, see Morton and Lucia White, *The*

Intellectual versus the City (Cambridge: Harvard University and MIT Press, 1962).

48. C. Wright Mills has skillfully assessed the rural, small-town, Protestant-ministerial, and middle-class antecedents that so many early sociologists brought to the study of the city. See his classic essay, "The Professional Ideology of Social Pathologists," *American Journal of Sociology* 49 (Sept. 1943): 165–80; reprinted in Irving Louis Horowitz, *Power, Politics and People: The Collected Essays of C. Wright Mills* (New York: Oxford University Press, 1963), 525–52.

49. See Wiebe, *Search for Order,* chapter 5.

50. Ibid., 120–21.

51. Burton J. Bledstein has provided a critical analysis of the emergence of professionalism in the United States and its close association with the development of higher education. See his *Culture of Professionalism: The Middle Class and the Development of Higher Education* (New York: W. W. Norton, 1976).

52. Wiebe, *Search for Order,* 123–27.

53. Ibid., chapter 7.

54. Ibid., 145–55.

55. Weinstein, *Corporate Ideal,* x.

56. Roscoe C. Hinkle, *Founding Theory of American Sociology, 1881–1915* (Boston: Routledge and Kegan Paul, 1980), 300.

57. Morton White, *Social Thought in America: The Revolt against Formalism* (New York: Viking Press, 1949), 6, 11.

58. Ibid., 14–15.

59. Wiebe, *Search for Order,* 146.

60. White, *Social Thought,* 46.

61. Wiebe, *Search for Order,* 145.

2

From Biology to Culture: Redefining the Race Problem

The historian John Haller once said that in the United States late in the nineteenth century "the subject of race inferiority was beyond critical reach." American society, he said, "betrayed no sentiment, popular or otherwise, that looked to a remodeling of its social and political habits of race. There was neither concealment nor delicacy among its beliefs."[1]

What Haller said about the late nineteenth century still applied during the first two decades of the twentieth. The Supreme Court's decision in *Plessy v. Ferguson* in 1896 gave a constitutional status to racial segregation, so that a legally segregated nation was a firm reality as the twentieth century opened. The prevailing racial climate was not conducive to any balanced public discussion of the merits of racial thought, let alone the building of a case to challenge existing racial practices.

The Boasian argument that "primitive man" was fully capable of learning civilized culture without necessarily being the full mental equal of the white race was to continue on for another decade after the publication of *The Mind of Primitive Man* in 1911.[2] In that decade, however, there were developments more significant than the continuance of the Boasian argument. There was first the growing power of the eugenics movement, which kept the hereditarian position dominant in public discussion, and second, the development of the IQ tests, which purported to document again, but with a new scientific instrument, the racial inferiority of nonwhite peoples. But there were also contravening developments: the rejection of Lamarckianism and the consequent independence of culture from biology, and a new genetics that discredited the very biological theory that the eugenicists were using to make their case for the superiority of white Anglo-Saxons over all others.

By that second decade, the claims of the eugenicists had set in motion a long and acrimonious debate over the relative importance of biological heredity and cultural environment, of nature and nurture, in shaping the basic qualities and competencies of the human being, as well as the social policies that the acceptance of either position would logically support.

Heredity and Environment: The Continuing Quarrel

From the end of the Civil War to the onset of World War I, some twenty-four million immigrants entered the United States. But from 1880 on, they came increasingly from eastern and southern Europe, were often of peasant origin, sometimes illiterate, and on arrival did not speak English. They were also Catholic, Orthodox, or Jewish, not Protestant. Their search for employment brought them to the newly developing industrial cities, and their search for housing led them to cluster in neighborhoods of their own.

Whatever the economic imperatives for unrestricted immigration, the immigrants' easy access to the United States set off a hostile, nativistic reaction. To the middle-class, Protestant mind, these newer immigrants came to be associated with all the social disabilities identified with urban life. Poverty, crime, disease, and feeblemindedness, viewed as issues of inferior heredity, were not new problems; they had first emerged in the decades after the Civil War. The flood of immigrants from eastern and southern Europe gave new fuel to these issues, however, and heightened a strong demand for policies to control what some defined as a threat to the quality of American civilization. The new eugenics movement was an effort to build a case against the continued acceptance of immigrants deemed to be of inferior stock and to invoke social policies based upon a scientific case for the greater importance of heredity over environment. Its emphasis, however, was less on nonwhite peoples and more on the claimed racial differences among the European peoples.

The sociologist Floyd House once observed that until the onset of the controversy over immigration, the longstanding American interest in race was solely in the relation of white and black people. House noted that, "At about the end of the nineteenth century, a new factor was introduced in the discussion of race relations in the United States, in the shape of an argument for 'Nordic' superiority and supremacy which originated in Europe, but was brought to the attention of the American reading public by a series of books."[3]

Though there was a steady flow of material from Germany on racial differences among the Europeans, the more influential ideas came from England and were largely the work of Francis Galton, a cousin of Charles Darwin. In his *Hereditary Genius* (1869), Galton had pursued themes that were to dominate the research around the eugenics issue: the biological inheritance of intellectual distinction; the relation of innate ability to social class; the inferiority of the nonwhite races; and the superiority of Anglo-Saxons to other branches of the white race. In his pursuit of these issues, Galton made significant contributions to the development of statistical methods and originated mental tests. He coined the popular phrase of the eugenics perspective, "nature and nurture," as well as the label, "eugenics," for the movement to impose biological policies on society. When a fledgling eugenics movement began to organize in the United States, Galton had already provided its name and its basic ideas. For the edification of American sociologists, he published two papers in the *American Journal of Sociology*.[4]

Science, Eugenics, and Ideology

While the eugenics movement began with established thinking about racial inferiority, as well as an assured sense of superiority among Anglo-Saxons, it drew enthusiastic support from a new development in biology in the 1890s, an experimental biology made possible by the rise of the new graduate, research-oriented universities. After the rediscovery of Mendel's laws in 1900, an explosion of experimental research discovered much about the mechanisms of genetic inheritance and variation and produced an enormous confidence among biologists in its potentialities.[5]

The new biologists gave strong emphasis to inheritance over environment, in part because their very training assumed physical heredity to be the material link between generations, but also because as middle-class Americans of northwestern European ancestry they shared a cultural belief in its greater importance. They also shared a deep concern for what they felt to be a number of worrisome problems of "pauperism," crime, and the "defectives," which they took to be evidence of the decline of American stock. Consequently, many of them became actively involved in the eugenics movement.

For the eugenicists, the new biology provided a stimulus to action and an immeasurable degree of support in advancing its cause. As Hamilton Cravens noted, "In the next thirty years the American eugenics movement would disseminate hereditarian ideas in the mass media and the educational system, fan the fires of the nature-nurture controversy, and even leave its imprint on federal and state laws."[6] By advocating social policies that claimed to preserve the nation's superior racial stock and remove the biologically unfit, the eugenics movement linked up with the belief in social reform and social intervention so characteristic of the Progressive Era.

The eugenicists pressed for adoption into law two basic reforms: sterilization of the unfit—the eugenics policy that garnered the greatest support from the biologists—and restrictions on immigration. An early measure of success for the movement was getting the state of Indiana to adopt a sterilization law in 1907; by 1915 twelve other states had passed similar acts and by 1931 thirty states had done so.[7] The slums and immigrant ghettos in America's growing cities and the widening middle-class concern about disease, mental disorder, and feeblemindedness provided the eugenicists with an opportunity to advance an essentially biological explanation for these conditions and to advocate sterilization as a biological solution.

What was distinctive about the eugenics movement was the common social origin of the majority of its members: they were professionals and businessmen, and mostly native-born, white, and Anglo-Saxon Protestant. The values and prejudices of such a social class were the source of its anxieties about American society, and these gave impetus to its interest in eugenics. At the same time, there were always a few people associated with eugenics who were not of the same class or social origin or who did not share all its values and prejudices: Margaret Sanger, for instance, who joined to enhance the cause of birth control, and the sociologist E. A. Ross, noted for his involvement in progressive causes, but who supported both immigration restriction and sterilization.[8]

Despite these and other instances, however, the eugenics movement remained within the control of the business and professional leaders who gave it a direction and a program. They drew strong and often quite vocal support from many biologists, such as Charles B. Davenport, perhaps the strongest advocate of eugenics among the leading biologists of his day, and they had the tacit support of still others, such as Paul Popenoe, author of a widely read textbook. According to Kenneth Ludmerer, "Every member of the first editorial board of *Genetics* (1916)—a group which included such respected geneticists as T. H. Morgan, William E. Castle, Edward M. East, Herbert S. Jennings, and Raymond Pearl—participated in or gave support to the eugenics movement at some point during the movement's early history."[9]

Some eugenicists wrote for a middle-class, nonscientific audience, providing popular tracts that sounded a note of alarm about the threat to the superior stock of the nation. The very presence of the immigrants, they argued, threatened the quality of American life and the national capacity for future achievement. That was the message of Madison Grant, a wealthy lawyer and longtime officer of both the American Eugenics Society and the Immigration Restriction League, in his influential and widely read book, *The Passing of the Great Race*. Published in 1916, Grant's book had a preface written by Henry Fairchild Osborne, a distinguished paleontologist and the president of the American Museum of Natural History, putting the continued support of science behind the hereditarian position. Others wrote on the same theme; prominent among them was a Boston lawyer, Lothrop Stoddard, whose *Rising Tide of Color against White World-Supremacy* (1920) was one of the most widely read.[10]

In their writings and speeches, the eugenicists successfully employed the support of science to validate their claims about the inferiority of the newer immigrants and the consequent need to restrict immigration. From the turn of the century, for almost three decades the issue of race could not be extricated from the eugenicists' preoccupation with putting in place policies to offset the proclaimed genetic inferiority of the newer immigrants and the urban lower class in general.

The Case against Heredity

Despite the fact that most biologists supported eugenics, a few social scientists still dared to contest its theories and policies. If, at the outset of the century, the case for heredity largely prevailed over the environmental perspective, the latter always had its own adherents, who contested vigorously the claims of the hereditarians to the mantle of science. Lester Ward and Charles Horton Cooley were the first sociologists to challenge the hereditarians of that period.

In 1897 a young Charles Horton Cooley, taking up one of the hereditarians favorite issues, the study of men of genius, challenged Francis Galton's well-known argument that genius is hereditary by insisting that all of Galton's cases had required literacy and access to books. But he went further and offered a comparison between West End Jews in London and poor East End Jews employed in sweatshops. There were measurable physical differences between them, he pointed out, with the East End Jews averaging three inches less in stature as well as in other measurements. There was also an intellectual deterioration, he noted, even though it could not be measured.[11]

Lester Ward, in turn, devoted the larger part of his *Applied Sociology* (1906) to an intellectual attack upon the hereditarian arguments of the eugenicists. He, too, challenged Francis Galton on the matter of inherited genius by showing, much as Cooley did, that opportunity and education were present in all the cases Galton analyzed. Ward consistently argued that the superiority of race and class was as much a matter of social as of biological heredity (he was still a Lamarckian) and equal opportunity for all classes and races would eventually remove differences in achievement. This was the basis for his noted statement that "no race and no class of human beings" were "incapable of assimilating the social achievement of mankind and of profitably employing the social heritage."[12]

Two decades after the publication of his first paper, Cooley restated his objection to the eugenicists' conception of society. Most of them, he pointed out, were biologists and physicians who did not see society as a psychological organism with a life process of its own: "They have thought of human heredity as a tendency to definite modes of conduct, and of environment as something that may aid or hinder, not remembering what they might have learned even from Darwin, that heredity takes on a distinctively human character only by renouncing, as it were, the function of predetermined adaptation and becoming plastic to the environment."[13]

The plasticity of heredity to the environment and the changes in physical attributes as a consequence of changed environment were lessons that sociologists were to learn mostly from the work of Franz Boas. From the perspective of physical anthropology's concern with measuring head form, Boas was interested in the process of growth and the influence of environment, which brought about the conditions that modified inherited form. From the early 1890s on, he undertook a series of studies of measurements of school children, culminating in his influential study of the children of immigrants. He carried out this study between 1908 and 1910 for the U.S. Immigration Commission, which had been formed to undertake a broad investigation with the intent of developing a case for the restriction of immigration.[14]

At the outset of his report to the commission, Boas summarized his results in bold language. There had been, he asserted, "decided changes in the rate of development" of immigrant children, but also a "far-reaching change in the type" of each immigrant group. These changes "could only be explained as due directly to the influence of environment." His own results were so definite, he felt, that "While heretofore we had the right to assume that human types were stable, all the evidence is now in favor of a great plasticity of human types, and permanence of types in new surroundings appears rather as the exception than the rule."[15]

Despite the boldness of Boas's introductory remarks, however, the body of his report was more cautiously phrased, including his insistence that there was a strictly limited plasticity of immigrants in new environments. He disavowed the idea that all European types would become the same in the United States, even though a number of journalists had used his observation that head form showed a tendency to move toward an intermediate form to support the idea that a melting pot of immigrant assimilation was producing a new American race.[16]

Boas's studies on changes in the bodily forms of immigrants had a basic implication for public policy out of step with the bulk of the commission's reports, particularly his contention that immigration from southern Europe was not to be feared. More than that, he called into question what had been so fundamental to physical anthropology, the study of head form. His critique of racial formalism, noted the anthropologist George W. Stocking, "undercut many of the traditional hierarchical assumptions of racial thinking in its broader and more popular forms."[17]

Boas's considerable influence on sociology, however, extended beyond the issue of race. Much of his professional career was a prolonged (and successful) effort to advance the independence of culture from biology and to establish cultural anthropology as an academic social science. He trained a number of notable cultural anthropologists, such as Alfred Kroeber, Robert H. Lowie, Edward Sapir, and Alexander Goldenweiser. Their efforts to advance the autonomy of culture and the independence from biology of social and cultural analysis contributed significantly to the development of sociology. But the prevailing issues then included not only biology's claim about the fixed inheritance of human attributes; there was also the matter of the still existent influence of Lamarckianism on social theory.

Biology and Culture: The Lamarckian Issue

At the beginning of the century, sociological thinking was still entangled with Lamarckianism, the now largely forgotten doctrine of the inheritance of acquired characteristics. A very old idea still widespread until Darwin's time and associated with evolutionary ideas (Spencer was a Lamarckian, as was Lester Ward), it was used to explain the origin of racial differences. Racial traits, it was thought, developed in an adaptive process and were then transmitted by inheritance. The formation of races, then, was in part a social process. One consequence of this was to give support to the idea of national and cultural groups as historical races. W. I. Thomas, for example, claimed that "the formation of artificial or historic races ... among a heterogeneous population brought by hap and chance into the same geographical zone, is taking place before our eyes at the present moment, and is a matter of history; and we are safe in assuming that in this process the formation of true races is repeating itself."[18]

Lamarckianism also included a conception of habits becoming organized as instincts. Thus, the sociologist Charles Ellwood, by referring to both instincts and habits as "innate tendencies," could then argue that "the negro child, even if reared in a white family under the most favorable conditions, fails to take on the mental and moral characteristics of the Caucasian race. ... His natural instincts, it is true, may be modified by training ... but the race habits of a thousand generations or more is not lightly set aside by the voluntary or enforced imitation of visible models." But the sociologist Robert Park could also argue that freedom from slavery was breaking down "the instincts and habits of servitude" and slowly building up "the instincts of freedom."[19]

The possibility of arguing opposing views of the racial issue suggests some of the complexity of Lamarckianism. On the one side, as Stocking noted, it explained "certain biological (or sociobiological) givens which underlay the social behavior of contemporary man: the racial differences which limited or qualified the generalizations of sociology as to the behavior of man in society."[20] It also explained the evolution of humankind's mental development and, for many, the racial diversity to be found in mental faculties. But the doctrine also suggested that new adaptations could alter old instincts. Although the process could not be rapid, the once inferior races could become equal in habits and instincts.

This was Lester Ward's belief. Lamarckianism permitted him to remain an egalitarian, even though he believed the races were at that time unequal. He vigorously defended Lamarckianism against criticism, because he feared that to give up Lamarckianism would be to surrender to the unqualified biological determinism of the day. Thus, Lamarckianism made a place for the social environment, but, as Stocking pointed out, "it also helped to forestall, by an obfuscation of fundamental assumptions, the assertion of the full independence of the social from the biological sciences."[21]

Even though many sociologists were slow to give up Lamarckianism, it was under attack as early as the 1880s, and by the 1890s that attack had become sustained and widespread. The rediscovery of Mendel's laws and their application to a wider range of hereditary phenomena, as well as the common assertion among biologists that Lamarckians had failed to prove their case experimentally, led to a rapid decline in the acceptance of the doctrine after 1900. Social scientists had no choice but to follow suit. W. I. Thomas, for example, who at the outset of the century spoke of "lower human races" and offered an implicitly Lamarckian conception of "race temperament" to explain the cultural characteristics of different races, by 1912 had abandoned any notion of racial differences. "I have assumed," he said, "that individual variation is more important than racial differences," and he quoted from Franz Boas's *Mind of Primitive Man* in support of his position.[22]

The decline of the Lamarckian doctrine among social scientists was a crucial development, since the study of cultural phenomena could not claim independent status until the separation of biology and culture was complete. Stocking pointed out that Lamarckianism had not been "a central theoretical concept of the social sciences"; rather, "it had provided the last important link between social and biological theory." As long as it remained a viable theory, the independent status of society and culture was probably beyond social science's conceptual attainment.[23]

The Independence of Culture

The abandonment of Lamarckianism by sociologists and anthropologists provided the intellectual condition for asserting the existence of phenomena not biological and explainable in their own terms. Students of Boas had been arguing the independence of culture for almost a decade when both Alfred Kroeber and Robert Lowie in 1917 made a clean break with biology. Kroeber did so with the publication of his classic essay, "The Superorganic," Lowie, with a series of lectures at the American Museum of Natural History in New York (where he was associate curator), which were published that same year as *Culture and Ethnology*. Kroeber rejected the organic analogy and insisted with numerous examples on the distinction between the *cultural* and the *organic;* in similar fashion, Lowie sought to make the case that culture was not biologically determined; neither was it determined by the physical environment or by psychological factors.[24]

In such Boasian-inspired work, not only was culture detached from biology, but social theory was freed from the biological web within which it had been entangled. Floyd House summarized the work of Boas and his students as one of bringing physical and cultural anthropology and the theory of race "into a definite relationship with each other, with the result that there emerges the hypothesis that the facts of culture constitute a distinct realm and are, so to speak, self-determining. They must be studied on their own account, and their origins must be determined historically; no theory of race, heredity, or 'evolution' will account for them."[25]

In 1918 the publication of the first two volumes of *The Polish Peasant in Europe and America* by W. I. Thomas and Florian Znaniecki further advanced the case for the independence of culture. Thomas and Znaniecki explored the Polish peasant's experiences in both Poland and the United States only in sociological and social psychological terms and rejected any notion of biological determinism. They refused to label as racial the behavior of Polish peasants at a time when European ethnicity was still being defined in racial categories.[26]

The movement to separate biology and culture was an encouraging development for those sociologists seeking to escape biology's constraining hold on sociological thought. At the same time, other developments in sociology were having similar effects. The movement of anthropologists and sociologists to reject Spencer's theory of social evolution encouraged new modes of theory in terms of social processes and social interaction. Here Simmel's work had a strong influence on American sociologists, particularly those at the University of Chicago. Even Sumner's concepts of folkways and mores contributed to this development, as did E. A. Ross's work on social control. The newer social psychology that emerged from Cooley's work, as well as that of James Mark Baldwin's, also contributed to this development. This social psychology stressed the social conditioning of the person and the indivisibility of the person and society. When Baldwin in 1911 said that the individual is "a product of his social life and society is an organization of such individuals," a basic grounding for a twentieth-century sociology, free from any Lamarckian connection with biology and from its once dominant evolutionary assumptions, had been established.[27]

More than that, however, found sociological expression in this new literature. There was now a reassertion, not only of American optimism, but of American belief in the rational, self-reliant individual. The eugenicists had advanced a conception of a fixed and unequal human nature, the implication of which challenged some of the most deeply rooted American beliefs in individualism, opportunity, and the progressive development of society. Yet this did not, as the historian Merle Curti noted, "silence the environmentalists. American faith in democracy had always leaned heavily on the assumed importance of equal environmental opportunities."[28]

A liberal social science countered the hereditarians with a conception of society's problems as due, not to human nature, but to purposeful yet alterable policies and institutions. From that conceptual stance came an interest in both education and the socialization of the individual. The strong emphasis that American sociologists have long put upon the concept of socialization originated in this conflict over the significance of biology versus culture for human development. It also provided the social context from which emerged that distinctively American social scientific perspective that came to be known as symbolic interaction.[29]

The conflict, furthermore, was far more than an academic debate. It was a struggle over social policy about the mostly immigrant working class and the poor, and, consequently, about the future shape of American society. The eugenicists spoke for the self-defined interests of those middle and upper strata concerned about sustaining their ethnic and class dominance in society. Below them they saw inferior masses who were in every way a threat to civilization, a menace to be controlled by strong social policies. These policies were basically three: to sterilize all those judged as mentally and morally unfit; to institute strong restrictions on immigration; and to deport those immigrants deemed "defective."

Their critics, in contrast, spoke from a different perspective. Their policy sought to control the immigrant masses and the working class by socialization and education, in short, to assimilate them into American society. The implications of such a policy ran counter to claims of hereditary inequality and suggested that the opportunity to learn and compete was warranted for the children of immigrants from eastern and southern Europe. Horatio Alger, it would seem, could just as easily be Jewish, Italian, or Polish as Anglo-American.

But there were also limits to this new theorizing about the human capacity to assimilate a culture. Nonwhite peoples, but particularly the blacks, were still defined as unassimilable by the large majority of white Americans. For them, the very idea of assimilation meant intermarriage and amalgamation. Many Americans were so intensely opposed to assimilation so defined that the very term could not easily be offered in public discussion when speaking of the race problem. Consequently, social scientists who spoke in behalf of the assimilation of southern and eastern Europeans were mostly silent on the matter of blacks. When they did speak of assimilation in a racial context, they were careful to distinguish it from amalgamation.[30]

The New Genetics and the Triumph of Eugenics

But even as the eugenicists and their critics carried on their debate, new developments in the study of genetics invalidated the very bio-

logical theory on which the case for eugenics rested. Between 1908
and 1913 geneticists in both Europe and the United States agreed that
human development is determined by the interaction of heredity and
environment, not by heredity alone. But, more fundamentally, they
replaced the unit-inheritance principle with a "multiple-gene" theory
for "metrical" characters (e.g., height or intelligence, measured on a
continuous scale). According to Kenneth Ludmerer, "As more and
more 'metrical' characteristics were discovered, particularly in man, the
theory also made possible the realization that Mendel's laws describe
the pattern of inheritance of relatively few traits, thereby invalidating
one of the major genetic asumptions underlying nearly all eugenic
proposals of the period." The consequence for the eugenicists was
clear: "Certain genetic findings, therefore, indicated that earlier views
of inheritance needed to be modified, that eugenic assumptions about
heredity were invalid."[31]

In the face of this new development, most sociologists proved to
be reluctant to abandon their biological beliefs. While they were so
committed to being scientific that they could not deny what science
taught, they were still resistant to the new message from the geneticists.
As a consequence, they looked for other ways to restore a scientific
basis for racial inequality. The assumptions that since Emancipation
had framed the race problem no longer remained intact, but only a
few sociologists were among those eagerly seeking a new framework
in which to study the problem.

For those few there was little if any public to reach out to in support
of new ways of thinking about the race problem. While the arguments
between the hereditarians and environmentalists still raged on in academic and scientific circles, within the larger public the hereditarians
had a one-sided dominance, and the concept of racial superiority was
as firmly in place as it had been in the 1890s. A continuing mindset in
public attitudes did not provide an encouraging milieu for criticizing
American society's understanding of race, let alone advocating social
change.[32]

Even more discouraging for the possibility of any intellectual or
social innovation was the emergence after World War I of a strong
nativistic reaction against many of the social changes then current in
American life, including the growing numbers of immigrants from eastern and southern Europe and the rapid increase in the number of blacks
moving from the rural South to the urban North. The efforts of many
Americans to reassert their values and way of life in the face of impending change were evident in a number of ways: a revived Ku Klux
Klan extending its influence into northern states; a political effort in

behalf of immigration legislation with quotas favoring northern Europeans over those from southern and eastern Europe; outbreaks of anti-Semitic expression; an identification of "radical" with "alien" in a resurgent patriotism; and efforts to ban the teaching of human evolution. Violence, too, was a significant dimension of such a response. The Klan was often violent, always intimidating, and constituted a vigilante force. Violence against blacks in the form of lynchings and riots had persisted from the beginning of the century, but the year 1919 was marked by a sharp increase in violent race riots, large and small, around the nation. The largest and most destructive riot occurred in Chicago; it raged for four days before a state militia brought it under control.[33]

A social milieu so unreceptive, if not overtly hostile, to even the most moderate advocates of racial justice was also a tempering and restraining influence on the possibilities of an analysis of race not founded on hereditarian assumptions. In such a social atmosphere, the eugenicists could easily muster the political influence that would enable them to achieve one of their primary goals: the restriction of immigration by southern and eastern Europeans to the United States.

Despite the findings of the new genetics, before 1920 the eugenicists remained confident of their principles and pressed hard for the attainment of legislation restricting immigration from eastern and southern Europe. The massive set of volumes produced by the U.S. Commission on Immigration in 1911, for example, to which Franz Boas had contributed a dissenting paper, was intended to document the need for such legislation. The onset of World War I in 1914 had interrupted emigration from Europe until the end of the decade and temporarily took from the issue a sense of urgency. But with the renewal of immigration after the war, the political struggle for restrictive legislation began again. In the early 1920s a unique combination of political and attitudinal factors in the United States—a sustained climate of religious, racial, and nationalistic antagonisms—were conducive to such an effort.

That intolerant climate, however, cannot be attributed wholly to programs of organized bigotry, such as those of the rejuvenated Ku Klux Klan, or the Klan's ability to exploit the racial and religious prejudices of masses of ordinary citizens. There was also widespread support from the nation's educated classes. A considerable segment of the nation's political and civic leadership were strong advocates of immigration restriction and supporters of the eugenics movement; indeed, they created, sustained, and directed the movement. They were not only educated in the presumably scientific evidence from biology that the movement used to validate the restriction on immigration, they gave public voice for its image of a racially stratified society. Their own intolerant attitude was a major factor in both the climate of opinion and in the political efficacy generated from it.

If the news of the genetic discoveries that invalidated the eugenicists' claims had filtered through the scholarly community—and they had; sociologists were quite familiar with them—it was as yet little known in wider public circles. In part this was because the geneticists had not come forth with strong public criticisms of the eugenics movement; some still felt it was a worthy cause and continued to participate, while some had not yet wholly accepted the new findings. Yet many geneticists were dismayed by the claims about genetics that the eugenicists used in arguing for immigration restriction. For example, Herbert Jennings, a leading geneticist, "on many occasions . . . publicly spoke out against the excesses of the eugenics movement in order to expose the false biology at its base."[34] But during the early twenties, there were too few such objections from the normally nonpolitical biologists to make a difference; despite such limited efforts, therefore, the restrictions on immigration became law.

Congress first enacted legislation in 1921 that limited the number of immigrants from any European country to a national quota equal to 3 percent of the immigrants from that country already in the United States in 1910, as reported in the census. But for the eugenicists that was not sufficiently restrictive, and in 1924 their renewed efforts produced the passage of a far more restrictive law. The national quotas were reduced to 2 percent and the crucial census year was moved back to 1890. Such a policy clearly favored old immigrant stock from northern and western Europe, mostly Protestant, over the newer immigrants from eastern and southern Europe, mostly Catholic, Orthodox, and Jewish. In addition, the Japanese were added to the existing ban on Chinese immigration.

The new legislation was a major political victory for the eugenicists; it was the high point of their political influence, and was the one policy they were able to achieve at the national level. While they had previously been able to bring about the adoption of legislation on sterilization, this was at the state level, and they were never able to accomplish this in all states. But they were able to get judicial sanction for sterilization; in 1927 the Supreme Court, in a decision read by Justice Oliver Wendell Homes, Jr., upheld Virginia's law providing for the sterilization of the mentally unfit.

IQ and Race

Even as the geneticists were developing a new theory that would in time undermine the eugenics movement, American psychologists were designing the IQ test, an instrument that was soon to become a ubiquitous feature of American education. In doing so, they were creating yet another major struggle between hereditarians and environmentalists.

Designing an IQ test was not a new interest for psychologists, for they had long wanted to measure mental ability. Since Francis Galton's early efforts, biologists and psychologists alike had attempted to measure one or more aspects of mental ability or response, usually intending to demonstrate racial or class differences. But none of these efforts were satisfactory until Alfred Binet in France, along with Theodore Simon, developed an intelligence test for schoolchildren. Binet and Simon wanted to detect degrees of feeblemindedness in children, not to demonstrate intellectual superiority. They acknowledged, furthermore, that environmental and educational opportunity would necessarily affect the test results. The tests, they warned, would only measure approximate intelligence in children from very similar environments.

As Binet and Simon's pioneering work found its way to the United States, American psychologists eagerly seized upon the French import, and by 1916 the psychologist Lewis Terman and his associates had developed the Stanford-Binet intelligence test. But in their eagerness to measure race and class differences in intelligence, they grounded the instrument in a hereditarian theory of intelligence, and Binet and Simon's warning was easily ignored.[35]

In 1917, when the United States entered World War I, a committee of psychologists, including Terman, and chaired by Robert M. Yerkes, at the request of the United States Army developed two tests for conscripted soldiers (one was for illiterates and immigrants unfamiliar with English). The subsequent testing of 1,700,000 soldiers provided a large body of data to assess the distribution of intelligence in the American population. Based on the claim that the tests measured innate intellectual ability, psychologists were quick to assert that here was irrefutable evidence of racial differences in intelligence, but also of the relatively low intelligence of the average adult in American society. Yerkes asserted that the tests demonstrated "the intellectual inferiority of the negro," and that "the negro soldier is of relatively low grade intelligence." He drew from that the claim that education would not be sufficient to put the races on an equal basis.[36]

Throughout the 1920s confident psychologists pronounced intelligence tests to be objective evidence of mental abilities, and doubters were castigated as intellectually backward, like people who did not believe in vaccination. When, for example, the distinguished public philosopher Walter Lippman dared to question some of the conclusions drawn by psychologists from the Army tests, the psychologist William McDougall suggested that to deny that mental ability was not largely a matter of inheritance was to deny the theory of organic evolution. In the pages of the *New Republic,* both he and Lewis Terman relegated Lippman to the company of William Jennings Bryan, the renowned spokesman for the fundamentalist religious opposition to the theory of evolution.[37] The Lippman incident not only demonstrated the supreme confidence of the psychologists in the scientific validity of their new IQ test, but also the intimidating way in which the name of science could be invoked.

Those sociologists who had only reluctantly accepted the new genetics did not, however, hesitate to accept the new IQ test. They responded favorably to the arguments for the scientific validity of IQ measurement offered by the psychologists. Here, at least, was one way they could still claim that science validated the claim of racial inferiority. But some of them, such as those who wrote on social problems, did more. Reaching back into evolutionary theory, they resurrected the old argument for natural selection and inserted it back into the explanation of the race problem.

The Race Problem in the 1920s

What in the 1920s was interchangeably called "the race problem" or "the Negro problem" seemed at first glance little changed in the United States since the 1890s, when sociology first became involved in the nation's concern about race. The racial attitudes of white people held firm, and social practice sustained an unchallenged pattern of segregation and discrimination. The "color line" remained unaltered, though its exact boundaries were imprecise in northern cities where blacks had not previously lived in anything but the fewest numbers. Still, by a wide consensus, it was agreed that blacks—along with Chinese, Japanese, and American Indians—were an unassimilable people.

Nonetheless, there were changes in the way the race problem was defined. By the 1920s little was heard any longer about the capacity of black people to survive without the firm controls exercised by the slavemasters. In 1920 the Census Bureau recorded 10.4 million blacks, more than double the number recorded at the time of Emancipation; clearly, they were not becoming extinct. Much less was also heard about a reversion to barbarism, and the rage of southern violence against blacks premised on such an image was in decline. Lastly, with large numbers of blacks now moving north, it could no longer be claimed that the race problem was a southern problem and best left in the control of white Southerners.

The race problem had persisted as a prolonged public issue because there was never a consensus as to the nature of the problem or its solution. While there was no doubt that almost all white people agreed on the inherent inferiority of the black population, they did not agree as to what that implied about the capacity of blacks to participate in the social order or what long-range future for race relations should be pursued. Furthermore, by the 1920s social scientists were painfully aware that scientific claims of racial inferiority had been refuted by a new genetics and, however reluctantly, they had to acknowledge a new scientific position on race.

Between 1920 and 1933 five well-known social-problems textbooks provided one or more chapters on the race problem. These were Gillin, Dittmer, and Colbert's *Social Problems,* Grove Dow's *Society and Its Problems,* Elbridge and Clark's *Major Problems of Democracy: A Study of Social Conditions in the United States,* Gillette and Reinhardt's *Current Social Problems,* and Ellwood's *Sociology and Modern Social Problems.* There also appeared in that period two other works of some significance: Jerome Dowd's *The Negro in American Life* and John Commons's *Races and Immigrants.* Jerome Dowd was a Southerner and an economist by academic status, but his work on race was well-known to American sociologists. He had earlier written a two-volume work on the American blacks, had appeared as discussant and book reviewer in the *American Journal of Sociology,* and had read a paper on segregation before the American Sociological Society. John Commons was the renowned Progressive and institutional economist at the University of Wisconsin.[38]

An examination of these books reveals how many (perhaps most) sociologists still regarded the race problem in the 1920s. Much of what they had to say descriptively of black life had already been said in 1910 by a young southern sociologist, Howard W. Odum, in his influential and often-quoted study of black life in southern towns.[39]

Howard Odum: The Social Conditions of Black Life

What made Odum's study so influential was his detailed and unremittingly negative view of the social and moral factors he attributed to the social life of the black community. His 297-page examination of southern small-town life in the early years of the century provided a litany of deficiencies and defects in the social and moral conditions of black life, and these were to influence the literature on the race problem for a quarter century after their publication in 1910. In the 1920s these deficiencies and defects were still evident in the social-problems literature.

Odum seemed to be constantly appalled by what he observed, especially in regard to children:

> Perhaps nowhere in Negro life does the problem of immorality appear more stupendous than among the children. Innocently they reflect all that is not innocent; guiltless, they show the superlative to filth and indecency. The amount of knowledge of evil and evil practices possessed by small children is unthinkable. Their practices are no less appalling. The unconscious depth of depravity to which the children have already come is appalling. . . . Nor is it surprising that the children become so early in life masters of the unclean and immoral. They hear unclean words and witness obscene deeds on every hand. They but reflect on a small scale what their elders embody in their daily life.[40]

Odum seemed not to find anything morally redeeming in the lives of black people or anything promising for their future. Neither the schools, the churches, nor the many civic organizations appeared to be positive forces for social and moral improvement: "One of the crying weaknesses in the negro school is the lack of moral strength on the part of the women teachers. It is but natural that children accustomed to gross immoralities at home and sometimes seeing indications of the same tendency on the part of teachers, should be greatly affected by it at school. Thus with mental stupidity and moral insensibility back of them, the children are affected already in practice and thought, in deeds and speech."[41]

Odum was no less severe in judging the pastors of black churches, criticizing them as "perhaps responsible for much of the present conditions." They seemed not to recognize the needs of their people, seldom to care "for high principles in life," and to possess an ignorance he found "appalling": "Open and hidden deception, the drinking of spiritous liquors, illicit relations with members of his congregation—such a state of affairs is not unusual." Furthermore, Odum claimed, black pastors are often not truthful and they unduly stressed the material needs of their church. But if the black churches failed at moral instruction, so did the Sunday schools operated for blacks by white churches: except for some individual cases, "years of patient work show no visible results in the schools. . . . No change in the religious conditions or improvement in the moral status can be traced to this source."[42]

No less wanting, as Odum saw it, was the housing blacks inhabited. Though some few blacks occupied decent housing, "the average negro house presents an exterior with the appearance of neglect," but the "inmates are, however, apparently satisfied." Odum described the interior of the houses as crowded and dirty, while the "personal habits" of blacks "are filthy.... Filth and uncleanliness is everywhere predominant." Under such conditions, disease was prevalent.[43]

Odum thought such social conditions to be "the soil from which the vices commonly practiced among the negroes arise." For example, "crime and vice among the negroes in Southern communities have assumed alarming proportions." While Odum acknowledged that "the conditions under which the negroes live are not conducive to good conduct, to the growth of strong character, or to the development of a healthy social organism," he nonetheless insisted that much crime and vice was due to the "chief traits of character and disposition" of black themselves. A comparison of enslaved and present-day blacks, argued Odum, revealed, first, a loss of humor, politeness and courtesy, respect and reverence toward the aged, kindness and attention to the sick and the care of children, and trustworthiness. In turn, however, "certain negative tendencies" of slaves had become magnified: laziness had developed into shiftlessness and vagrancy; carelessness in performing tasks into the inefficient laborer; improvidence into lack of managing ability and financial aptitude; skill in inventing tricks to deceive the master into tendencies to conceal both stolen goods and criminals. Therefore, summed up Odum, "The tendencies of the present-day Negroes ... still reflect forcibly the prevalent traits of the Negro in Africa."

Such traits, under the prevailing social conditions, produced a rate of crime much higher than that of white people: "Nurtured with some hatred toward the whites, taught no morals, with a fanatical religion, itself leading to erratic actions, with little regard for common decency, and bred in filth and adultery, the negro is considered peculiarly liable to crime. The reformed negro criminal is rarely seen, and it is well known that the negro offender is not cured by the ordinary punishments."[44] Odum often asserted such claims about black people on the basis of common knowledge: "it is well known that . . ." In this way he inserted into his sociological analysis the common judgments of middle-class southern whites on the conditions of black life.

A decade or more later, during the 1920s, Odum's bleak picture of black life was fairly well replicated in the social-problems literature. Gillin, Dittmer, and Colbert, for example, argued that blacks had undergone three centuries of "moral stunting" under slavery; therefore, "it is not to be wondered at that there still exists a considerable amount of moral looseness, juvenile neglect, family desertion, neglect of the aged, and brutality." Dow, in contrast, said that, while "immorality flourishes" among blacks because of conditions under slavery, it is also "because of their past history in Africa, where the climate tended to the preservation of those with a high birth-rate and thus caused the negro to inherit stronger passions than the white man. These, joined with his weaker will power and greater temptation under present conditions, naturally produces higher rates of irregularity and vice."[45]

Along with Dow, Gillette and Reinhardt also stressed the prevalence of crime, disease, poverty, and poor education and illiteracy among blacks, while Ellwood stressed criminality and pauperism.[46] For the social-problems sociologists, the deficiencies of black people, culturally and biologically, or both, defined a significant dimension of "the Negro problem." The language was less morally charged than was Odum's, but the message was the same.

Heredity, Environment, and Natural Selection

The social-problems sociologists in the 1920s differed from Odum on one matter: for them, the prolonged debate over heredity and environment was a bothersome issue. Not one of them took an unequivocal stand for the environment, yet most of them acknowledged that science now denied validity to any claim of innate racial superiority. Gillin, Dittmer, and Colbert, for example, observed that "anthropologists and students of ethnology are agreed that race differences cannot be interpreted as implying that some races are superior to others." Jerome Dowd made a similar statement, agreeing that "we have reason to believe that all races of men have the same mental faculties" and "differ in no important degree" in their ability to learn. Eldridge and Clark, in turn, admitted that the "consensus of scientific opinion" was that no race "was demonstrably superior or inferior to any other race," while yet insisting that "it is not unlikely that there are some hereditary intellectual differences between races and nationalities." Charles Ellwood also argued that "it is the weight of opinion that racial heredity is a very real factor" and "cannot be left altogether out of account in studying social problems." In contrast to these, Grove Dow seemed to give little credence to innate racial differences. Though he held on to the possibility that some characteristics attributed to black people might be innate, he insisted that "natural selection and environment are much stronger."[47] It was the concept of natural selection that provided the key to a new defense of the claim to the racial inferiority of black people.

If Grove Dow more readily dropped the concept of racial heredity than other social-problems sociologists did, neither he nor they were ready to accept unreservedly the new scientific dictum on race. Instead, they returned to the theory of biological evolution to find in the concept of natural selection an instrument by which they could reclaim the superiority of the white race. Grove Dow claimed that natural selection had produced a mentally and culturally inferior people; it had made the black docile, easygoing, lazy, and indifferent to the future. Since a living came easily from nature and "the negro was not compelled to use his ingenuity or tax his intellect . . . his mental capacities did not develop." Because nature "did not select the shrewd and cunning as in the cooler climates . . . we find the negro possessing a strong physique but an inferior intellect." A similar argument was made by John Commons, who insisted that "nature conspires to produce a race indolent, improvident, and contented." Perhaps his most revealing comment was that "Other races of immigrants, by contact with our institutions, have been civilized—the negro has only been domesticated."[48]

Gillin, Dittmer, and Colbert, in turn, argued that "Each race seems to be superior for the environment for and within which it was selected." Jerome Dowd claimed that, due to natural selection, the races cannot equally adapt to the same environmental conditions, "nor to attain the same accomplishments." Charles Ellwood argued that, because "the negro race is that part of mankind which has developed in the tropics," the negro is "lazy and shiftless," for those are the qualities of the person favored for survival in the tropics. In similar fashion, "nature fixed in the negro strong sexual propensities in order to secure" a high birth rate to offset a high death rate. Blacks are superior to whites in the capacity to survive in the tropics, he argued, but whites are superior to blacks in adapting to a complex civilization under different climatic conditions.[49]

For most of the social-problems sociologists, then, the concept of natural selection provided a way to hold to a conception of racial inferiority without seeming to abandon a scientific position. Without any significant evidence, they put natural selection in an imagined context of an Africa of endlessly bountiful jungles that would produce people indolent and mentally undeveloped. Though the assertions of the new genetics were not to be denied, the evolutionary notion of natural selection would restore the case for white supremacy.

Origin of the Problem

For sociologists, every social problem had an origin, social or natural. For those who still held to hereditarian views, it was sufficient to identify natural heredity as the source of the race problem. But for those who gave some credence to the scientific position disputing the hereditarian claims—and most did—then other factors had to be identified. The two most common were population movement and racial differences, the latter of which became an argument for cultural inferiority.

For some sociologists the race problem could be located within the more encompassing population problem. The steady flow of immigrants to the United States, as well as the population shift from country to city, had made the issue of population composition, quality, growth, and movement a major concern for sociologists, and the study of population had become a strong specialty within the discipline. Since the movement of population brought on social change and conflict and disrupted established ways of life, the movement of racially different populations made race a social problem.

This was the position taken by Gillin, Dittmer, and Colbert. As they saw it, "Race antipathies and national tolerances bear a direct ratio to the intensity of inter-population competition." The migration of one race into the midst of another *"recognized* as different in *cultural background* and *physical characteristics"* complicates human relations and, when the number of migrants increases, produces racial prejudice, which persists as long as the differences are recognized by either race. The native population feels its prestige threatened, defines the migrants as inferior, and draws a color line; "then it is that trouble begins."[50]

Though with a less developed rationale, Eldridge and Clark also defined the race problem as a population problem; so did John Commons. Eldridge and Clark used that approach to support the recent passage of legislation restricting immigration: "We seemed justified on excluding immigration from any except Caucasian countries, for a large population from other countries would create here additional race problems similar to the so-called Negro problem, something that should clearly be prevented." Grove Dow, in turn, thought racial hatred "almost innate," so that racial contact due to population movement brought on "friction and generally war." This resulted in the subordination of one race to another, and always black to white. Subordination, however, did not seem to bring racial harmony; instead, a continuing racial friction remained between the races.[51]

But it was also possible to take racial migration for granted and locate the origin of the race problem in differences among races. That was Jerome Dowd's position. He argued that whether races were inherently equal or unequal mattered little, since the race problem would be the same "even if all races were, in fact, equal," which, he acknowledged, he did not believe. The "essential fact" was that all races differ physically, psychologically, and in tradition and culture, "and these differences give rise to the race problem."[52]

For some, however, racial differences translated into cultural differences, which, in turn, meant cultural inferiority. Gillin, Dittmer, and Colbert, for example, had first defined race as a population problem but followed that with an assessment of the differences between the races due to culture. If inherent superiority or inferiority had no basis in fact, they argued, "then we must examine the cultural backgrounds in order to find the real basis for the problems of race relations in the United States." Historically, they pointed out, there developed "two very different types of culture—one for the white man and one for the negro." These were two incompatible cultures: "the slave culture for the negro; and the free culture for the white." The slave culture supplanted any culture brought from Africa, and, "allowing for differences in temperament, it is quite possible to find in the slave culture ample explanation for most of the 'negro characteristics' which hamper his progress, and which are often ascribed to his original inferior nature."[53]

Even Charles Ellwood, who still believed in inherent inferiority, and Grove Dow recognized the importance of slavery in developing a distinctive culture among blacks. Slavery, Ellwood asserted, was both "beneficent" and "malificent" for the blacks. It secured "a better type of negro physically . . . and a more docile type mentally; but the chief beneficent influence of slavery on the negro was that it taught him to work, at least to some extent." However, "slavery did not fit the individual or race for a life of freedom and did not raise moral standards much above those of Africa." Grove Dow agreed that the black learned to work under slavery, but "under compulsion, under conditions that made him hate manual labor." But he also saw other negative consequences from slavery: an undeveloped family life, for one, thus, "little family morality . . . and little skill in the training of children"; and a lack of self-control and the ability to plan or to make provision for the future.[54]

To add, therefore, to the argument they made about the consequences of natural selection in Africa, sociologists attached the argument that harmful cultural attributes derived from slavery ensured that blacks would be culturally inferior even if no one could any longer make a scientific case for their mental inferiority.

The Social and Psychological Characteristics of Blacks

Southern whites had long maintained an ambivalent, even contradictory image of the black person. From one perspective, it was in the nature of blacks to be cheerful, good-natured, and happy; from another, blacks were a shiftless and immoral people. In 1910 Odum had denied the image of blacks as cheerful and good-natured; while that was true of blacks in the past, now, he claimed, the adults were often sullen and rude. They were a people possessed of "primitive emotions" that were volatile and unstable; both anger and excitement were easily aroused and often uncontrollable. These "primitive emotions predominate to a marked degree among the negroes. . . . His whole being is volatile, without continuous or stable form, easily disturbed, as easily quieted. . . . A strong physical organism with powerful sensuous capacity thus gives the Negro a rich emotional nature, which together with habituation and facility, with little inhibition save that of conflicting emotions, renders him preeminently subject to the feeling states."[55]

Odum's imagery of black people was still evident in the writings of some sociologists in the 1920s. By incorporating much of white southern lore about black people into his own analysis, Jerome Dowd, for example, offered a detailed delineation of what most white people in the 1920s believed to be the psychological character of blacks. He characterized them as having the minds of children, being cheerful, impulsive, vain and fond of showing off, emotional, restless, and given to fits of anger that were soon forgotten. They were, he proclaimed, the most pronounced of extroverts among the races: impulsive, talkative, and interested only in the present. And they were a gregarious people who loved crowds. But, according to Dowd, black people also lacked rational correlation, their imaginations reproduced concrete images, not abstract ideas, while their minds possessed feeble inhibiting powers; and they were very imitative. They were a people given to loafing and vagabondage; and they were sexually incontinent.[56]

Much of what Dowd said about black people was also said by the others. Gillin, Dittmer, and Colbert, for example, thought that the slave had been busy, happy, and loyal, and that the "shiftlessness, lack of foresight, easy-going nature and indifference" of blacks were traits developed under slavery. But both Charles Ellwood and Grove Dow thought that these same traits were the outcome of natural selection in a tropical environment, while Commons thought blacks to be indolent and improvident by nature. Dow also attributed a larger range of traits presumably characteristic of the black to natural selection: "a greater power of memory, stronger sexual passions, submissiveness rather than pugnacity, a larger sense of sociability, and a greater ability to read character and interpret one's thoughts; that he is emotional in religion; that he has a smaller capacity for group organization and for government; that he is more influenced by imitation, emotion, and emulation than by rational thinking and purposeful direction."[57]

The image of the black person that emerges from these texts is a confused mixture of the innate and the cultural without benefit of distinction. But however the innate and the cultural were indiscriminately combined, the resulting image of the black remained that of an inferior people. What was only dimly evident here, but would soon be more evident in the work of other sociologists less inclined to hold fast to notions of innate inferiority, was the beginnings of a new tendency: to abandon the idea of inherent inferiority and replace it with the idea of cultural inferiority. Even as black people were about to be freed from the bondage of biological inferiority, they were soon to be confined by that of cultural inferiority.

Solving the Race Problem

For sociologists in the early decades of the century, the race problem was unique in that it offered no rational basis for social intervention and seemed to defy solution. Jerome Dowd, for example, contended that "there seems to be no solution from the standpoint of social science" and that "the Negro problem ... is one of a type for which human experience has thus far found no solution." Grove Dow also called it "insoluble." Gillin, Dittmer, and Colbert, in turn, thought that neither "full social cooperation" nor "full social coordination" was possible in the United States when ten percent of the population was racially different.[58]

Yet, despite the proclaimed difficulty of finding any solution, the sociologists concerned with the race problem still argued that the problem could not be left where it was. Whatever solutions the social-problems texts had to offer had already been presented in fuller detail by Odum in 1910. Though he viewed the conditions of life among blacks as utterly deplorable and morally unredeeming, Odum nevertheless believed there was hope for progress. That hope lay in the "developing of the Negro's ability" and his "advantageous adjustment to the civilization in which he was to achieve his place." But that "place" would always be segregated and socially unequal and that "adjustment" required moral as well as practical instruction. Any amelioration of the social conditions of black life, furthermore, "must come through continuous growth," not by leaps and bounds; there must be a "persistent, continuous process" of training "which will give a permanent character-basis upon which to build." To accomplish that, whites had to assume responsibility for racial progress and for training black people; the black, Odum insisted, "should be intelligently assisted to make his way." He believed that what he advocated was all that was reasonable and possible, but if even that was to be accomplished, there must be legal justice and fair play for black people.[59]

As a prelude to the presentation of his own solution, Odum, in a tone of mild ridicule, noted how many solutions, none of them worthy of being taken seriously, had been offered in the vast literature on the race problem. He never discussed what those solutions were, but the text by Gillin, Dittmer, and Colbert specified eight solutions to be found in the discussions of the race problem: political action to secure unrestricted civil rights; race amalgamation; returning blacks to Africa; a separate and independent state or reservation for blacks; a return to the caste system guaranteeing white supremacy; permanent racial segregation; scattering blacks so widely across the nation as to render them politically and socially negligible; and education and interracial cooperation. The authors offered reasons why each of these could not be accepted as a permanent solution; there was "no panacea for the problem of race relations." But they did see in education and interracial cooperation a path to racial progress, though education had to remain segregated, and they cited examples of southern communities making small changes that promoted economic progress for blacks as well as enhancing racial harmony.[60]

Grove Dow also tried to sort out both short-term and long-term solutions to the race problem, but he, too, thought it was "too complicated and involved to admit of solution at this time." He regarded "absorption," "equality," and "colonization" as "impossible solutions" and accepted the southern caste system as "probably the only attitude that we can take toward the negro where he exists in any greater numbers, but it is by no means a solution; it is the very condition we are attempting to solve." Dow then offered a "compound solution" of industrial education "to make the negro more efficient and economically productive" as a first step, and a second step of "gradual segregation," by which he meant a relocation of blacks in separate towns, cities, and even states, where "the negro will be industrially self-sufficient, professionally independent, and will be able to work out his own solution." This would not, however, soon bring the black to equality with whites: "It will take many years, possibly hundreds, to catch up completely with the whites."[61]

Other sociologists took similar positions; only education and training in a context of interracial harmony and cooperation seemed to them to provide a basis for gradual improvement in the status of black people. Jerome Dowd called for a development with "proper discipline" so that the blacks' "traits will show the characteristics of the adult." But, he insisted, there will not be "any marked change for generations." Nonetheless, he wanted blacks trained for trades and segregated professions and morally trained to strengthen "desirable traits" and to eliminate undesirable ones. Gillette and Reinhardt also called for cooperative efforts in education as well as in health, because the low status of the Negro injured society. Charles Ellwood, who still retained a strong conception of inherent inferiority, argued for efforts to make blacks a "harmonious and helpful" element by "Americanizing" them, else they revert to barbarism. Most of all, he felt, blacks must be made useful, which required education and training, as well as cooperation by members of both races.[62]

The advocacy of education and interracial cooperation within the structure of segregation would not qualify as a solution to the race problem if racial segregation were defined as an element of the problem. But in the 1920s it was not, except by a small number of white liberals and by the northern black leadership. Instead the race problem was defined by the "defects" of black people and by the conviction of white people that blacks were completely unacceptable as racial equals. Education and interracial cooperation were within those seemingly unchangeable parameters. To its advocates, it qualified as a solution, since it made some demands, however modest, upon white people to make and accept some changes: blacks would be trained to their potential and whites would assume a greater responsibility to cooperate with blacks in achieving that potential.

The rewards for accomplishing this were to be two: first, a black population less discontented because better treated, thus enhancing racial harmony; second, a better trained black population becoming more useful to the economy. To the social-problems sociologists, no more could be done. But what still applied in the 1920s clearly went no further than what Odum had advocated in 1910 or even what Booker T. Washington had called for in the 1890s. Indeed, this was still Washington's program, and some sociologists acknowledged as much.

In the 1920s American sociologists were cautious in their assessment of possible changes in race relations. They sided with neither the very small band of white liberals who advocated civil rights for blacks nor with those whites who assumed black people to be so inherently inferior as to be incapable of further development. Nonetheless, they were much further from the white liberals than from the others. None of them saw any changes possible in the reality of segregation, nor did they advocate it. They also agreed with Odum in his insistence that blacks must accept their place as a separate race, not only because of the fact of different abilities and potentialities, but also because whites were unyielding in not accepting blacks as equals.[63]

After the disfranchisement of blacks in the southern states, it was evident that the civil rights guaranteed in the Fourteenth and Fifteenth Amendments had not become a reality for blacks and would not become so in the foreseeable future. The social-problems sociologists offered no objection to disfranchisement, and one of them, Grove Dow, praised the action. By adopting the Fifteenth Amendment, he said, "the American people committed probably the worst political blunder in the history of the country." The subsequent disfranchisement had been beneficial, he thought, even though it had denied the ballot to a few qualified blacks. For those few blacks qualified by literacy, property ownership, or payment of taxes, he advocated that they be given the vote. It would be a gradual process, he claimed, insufficient in numbers to control politics.[64]

Jerome Dowd and John Commons, however, did take note of the disfranchisement of blacks. Dowd felt it "to be a settled fact . . . that neither the Negro, nor any other colored race, will ever be able to exercise civil rights in the United States to the extent of controlling part of our government." Commons, in turn, took it for granted "that the negro will not again in the near future enjoy the privilege of the free ballot." Other sociologists simply accepted the reality of disfranchisement by making no reference to the issue of civil rights for blacks.[65]

Racial Mixing

In the 1920s mulattoes and other racially mixed people were believed to be a minority of the black population, though as far as whites were concerned they were still to be treated as blacks. There were two issues about the racially mixed: What proportion were they of the black population? Were they a positive or negative factor in the society?

How many blacks were of mixed blood had long been difficult to assess. Charles Ellwood claimed that it "is quite generally accepted by those who have carefully investigated the matter" that "one third of the negroes in the United States have more or less white blood." The census of 1920, however, counted only 11.9 percent as being of mixed blood. But in 1928 the anthropologist Melville J. Herskovits challenged these figures and claimed, on the basis of four years of research, that almost 80 percent of black people were mixed with white or Indian blood or both. Only slightly over 20 percent were still unmixed with the blood of other races.[66]

That they were unique because of their mixed blood, that they usually occupied superior positions in the black community, and that they constituted almost all of the eminent persons defined as black—these were the elements of the image of the light-skinned, racially mixed people in the United States. That is what Edward Byron Reuter sought to demonstrate in 1918 in his influential and often quoted study of the mulatto. John Commons agreed, asserting that mulattoes "differ but little if at all from the white race in the capacity for advancement" because "in their veins runs the blood of white aristocracy." But that did not mean that mulattoes could cross the color line; instead, "A new era for blacks is beginning when the mulatto sees his future as theirs."[67]

Other sociologists, however, thought that racial mixing could only have negative consequences. Gillin, Dittmer, and Colbert made clear their disagreement with those who believed racial mixing to be beneficial. They acknowledged that the hybrid stock may not be inferior, but insisted that too much interbreeding leads to deterioration of the human stock: "*Random mating* of various breeds of dogs produces the mongrel, and this same principle is as true for divergent human races as it is for dogs." This was the view of three sociologists who in the late twenties were still ardent eugenicists and were awaiting more knowledge about heredity to expand the practice of sterilization to rid society of the unfit.[68]

In like fashion, Grove Dow saw only negative consequences in race mixing; he viewed with alarm the reported increase in mulattoes each decade since 1890. But it is the white male, "too often the degenerate blood of some of the best families in America," who causes the problem: "it is the reckless and immoral element of the white population that mingles with the negro, for the mulatto is in nearly all cases illegitimate." But that same illegitimate mulatto was also "too high-spirited" to accept "the social conditions of his negro ancestor." Yet, Dow insisted, the mulatto cannot be accepted by white people, "because intermarriage is impossible without our becoming a mulatto race. So he must be classed as a negro."[69]

Some, however, like Charles Ellwood, saw both positive and negative consequences from racial mixing. Ellwood contrasted the favorable aspects with the unfavorable by saying that "on the one hand it has resulted in creating a class of so-called negroes in whom white blood and the ambitions and energy of the white race predominate, and on the other hand it has also resulted in creating a degenerate mixed stock who furnish the majority of criminals and vicious persons belonging to the so-called negro race." This negative consequence, however, "comes from social rather than from physiological causes" when the illegitimate offspring "of the union of white fathers and negro mothers are frequently the product of conditions of vice."[70]

But not all sociologists attributed great importance to race mixing. It gradually faded away as an issue, and references to mulattoes appeared less frequently in the literature of the next decade. A major reason for this was acceptance of Herskovits's thesis that the majority of blacks were of mixed blood. The idea held by some that a racially mixed segment of the black population would provide leadership and demonstrate superior performance for the benefit of the mass of pure-blooded people of African descent no longer seemed relevant.

A reading of the social-problems textbooks of the 1920s reveals that many sociologists of that time still thought about the race problem as it had been defined since the outset of the century, except for the new scientific position on racial heredity. This they accepted only grudgingly, and some not at all, and those who did substituted a conception of inferiority by natural selection. The race problem remained largely where it had been when slavery was abolished: how to control and find a useful place for a once-enslaved African people. A complex, even contradictory image of black people in terms of limited capacities, a dubious quality of temperament, and moral deficiencies seemed to justify for many sociologists the denial of even a modicum of social equality for the former slaves.

Sociologists in the 1920s still examined race within the conventional parameters of the race problem. Most of them were reluctant to accept unequivocally the notion that genetic evidence did not prove the black innately inferior, and all of them were fully confident that blacks were culturally inferior. Still, throughout the decade, there was a slow movement from biology to culture in the explanation of race.

From Biology to Culture—Slowly

The break with hereditarian theory, so long a basic part of American social science, did not come easily for many American sociologists. In her 1929 analysis of the place of culture in American sociology, Dorothy Gary pointed out that "a great majority" had moved to "an extended qualification" of earlier biological assumptions, while "a significant number have made an outright repudiation of the significance of biological factors."[71] A movement to even a qualified position was made easier for sociologists by the rapid decline of the eugenics movement and the success of those who subjected the methodology of intelligence testing to a severe critique.

The Decline of Eugenics and the Critique of IQ Testing

If the success of the eugenics movement was in the passage of the 1924 immigration legislation, that very success was in part its undoing; no longer could eugenicists warn of the dangers of unrestricted immigration. But the strongest blow to the eugenicist's cause was the frontal attack on its claims to scientific status by a far more vocal number of biologists. Though they had not spoken out loudly enough or often enough to prevent the passage of the immigration legislation, they made their voices heard in the late twenties. The newer work in genetics, they pointed out, simply invalidated the version of biology on which eugenics had been based; its hereditarian arguments had become scientifically untenable. As Cravens observed: "Those who did not hear of the new ideas, or saw no relationship between them and eugenics, could nevertheless follow a drama in their daily newspapers and in popular magazines: the withdrawal of geneticists' support for eugenics and scientific racism."[72]

Since the eugenicists had always claimed the sanction of science for their cause, the withdrawal of that sanction was to be a fatal blow. There was no other source of intellectual support that could provide the legitimation science did. The eugenics movement that had become such a powerful force in American life and that had so effectively shaped public policy was to fade away rapidly during the 1930s.

To be sure, the struggle against the hereditarian theory behind eugenics did not win out fully even in biology during the 1920s; there were reputable biologists still arguing the hereditarian thesis for at least another decade. Their reluctance to accept fully the new genetics gave aid and comfort to all others who wanted still to believe that science sanctioned the belief in racial inferiority.[73]

The period in which psychologists could be as imperious to their critics as Lewis Terman was to Walter Lippman did not last long. If many sociologists seemed to be either impressed or intimidated by the claims drawn from intelligence testing, cultural anthropologists were not. Throughout the 1920s their criticisms led to a spirited exchange of claims and counterclaims and to an increasingly telling critique of intelligence testing from both within and without the field of psychology. Before the decade was over, many psychologists began to reconsider, modify, and even reverse their position.

The criticism from within psychology focused largely on the assumptions and methodology of testing. For psychologists, according to Stocking, a commitment to intelligence testing was not simply an expression of racial ideology; "It was rather a matter of professional commitment to what was in effect a system of instrumentation which seemed to place psychology on a much firmer scientific footing and which happened also to quantify assumptions about race which they shared with most other members of their national culture."[74] Once that instrumentation was shown to be culturally biased, intelligence testing lost its scientific credibility for many psychologists.

That critique of assumptions and methodology, however, was also stimulated by interdisciplinary work between psychologists and other social scientists, such as the collaboration of the anthropologist A. L. Kroeber with Lewis Terman in planning for the development of a "culture-free" intelligence test. Psychologists were also involved with other social scientists in such agencies as the National Research Council and the Social Science Research Council. Some of this interdisciplinary work involved psychologists with social scientists who were critics of the assumptions of intelligence testing. According to Stocking, "Over a period of time, several psychologists publically changed their minds on the issue, and by the late 1930s the whole profession had clearly moved a long way toward the acceptance of the cultural critique."[75] The IQ test was to remain a widely used instrument for measuring schoolchildren, and controversy about its validity was also to remain a live issue. But for the majority of sociologists, it soon became a cultural, not a biological instrument of measurement.

With the recognition that the IQ test did not measure an innate intelligence, accompanied by the decline of the eugenics movement, few sociologists were any longer still holding to a hereditarian position; instead, they were at least accepting the "extended qualifications" that Dorothy Gary spoke of. Some of the qualifications offered, however, were less extended than others. A notable example of this was the Russian emigré sociologist, Pitirim Sorokin, who offered a qualified but nonetheless strong support for the hereditarian position. Another was the sociologist Frank Hankins, who tried to find a ground between the racial egalitarians, whom he firmly rejected, and the mainstream of contemporary biological determinists by rejecting some of the latter's least defensible arguments. These were the last two sociologists of any repute to try to salvage some dimensions of the hereditarian position.

Sorokin: The Emigré View

In a highly influential textbook on sociological theory, Sorokin subjected theories of "race, heredity, and selection" to an exhaustive review of the known literature, much of it European, in a chapter that ran to ninety pages. In a long section on the "valid principles" of the hereditarian school, Sorokin insisted that biometric measurements provided supporting evidence for the hereditarian argument. There are, said Sorokin, "innate" differences among races, classes, and individuals, and these differences are both psychic and mental: "This perfect agreement of all these tests: the historico-cultural, the mental; the absence of geniuses, especially of the highest rank; and the 'superiority' of the mulattoes, seems to indicate strongly (especially together with the further data concerning other races) that the cause of such a difference in the negro is due not only, and possibly not so much to environment, as tò heredity."[76]

Sorokin qualified his argument in two ways. The first was his refusal to use the terminology of "superior" and "inferior" "in view of the subjectivity of these terms." His second was to accept both environmental and hereditary factors as necessary components of human behavior. However, Sorokin did not offer any assessment of their relative importance; several attempts to do so quantitatively, he said, are "subjective and therefore inconclusive."[77]

Sorokin further qualified the hereditarian case by noting that the differences found in biometric measurements and IQ scores "amount to nothing but statistical averages, which does not prevent the existence of a great deal of overlapping." Such overlapping, however, does not "disprove the indicated fact" of class differences in intelligence. He also took pains to point out that European nationalities were not "racial groups in the zoological sense of the word," an error so long prevalent in the American discourse on eugenics and immigration. Each nationality, he asserted, contained varieties of the white race's three branches (the Nordic, the Alpine, and the Mediterranean) and all "in their cultural history have shown brilliancy."[78] By insisting on the cultural achievements of all three varieties of the white race, Sorokin put a considerable distance between himself and those eugenicists who had argued for restricted immigration from eastern and southern Europe, including Sorokin's own Russia.

Sorokin's book remained an influential and widely used text in sociology for another two decades after its publication in 1928. Accordingly, his strong if qualified case for the hereditarian argument, his insistence on the basic validation of facts gathered by biometric techniques and IQ tests, as well as his assertion that heredity largely accounts for the lower IQ scores of blacks, was one of the last influential statements in sociology in behalf of even a qualified support for the hereditarian position.

Hankins: An American View

In his 1926 book, *The Racial Basis of Civilization: A Critique of the Nordic Doctrine*, Frank Hankins, who had long believed in racial inferiority and the cause of eugenics, made an effort to reestablish the ground lost by the geneticists' critique of eugenics. He began by repudiating the idea that "the Anglo-Saxons are the purest of the Nordics and that the salvation of the world depended on the maintenance of Nordic domination." More than two-thirds of his book was taken up with an extended argument about the significance of the racial divisions of Europe, in which he severely criticized the work of Count Arthur de Gobineau, as well as the Americans, Madison Grant and Lothrop Stoddard, among others, thus separating his work from that of discredited racial theorists.[79]

In later chapters, Hankins offered a concept of race as an ideal type of a series of physical traits in a state of flux. Differences between types were relative rather than absolute and overlapped considerably in traits. There were no pure types, nor was there any value in such purity. Instead, he praised racial mixing, even between blacks and whites, insisting that the inbreeding of races has produced "all the important races of man" (342).

Despite these criticisms of a racial theory he once shared, Hankins was in no way a racial egalitarian. He still firmly believed in both physical and mental differences among races. Races are superior to one another in terms of specific traits, he argued, and a race superior in one trait might be inferior in another. He then moved to rescue the concept of racial inequality by adding that it was "quite evident that the superiority of one race over another may apply to those traits which are the most important for the development of an advanced culture" (294).

Hankins acknowledged that the different races overlapped in measurable traits, but some races had a higher proportion of their members capable of higher cultural activities because "(1) they contribute most to the advancement of the arts and sciences, and (2) they are relatively scarce." This thesis rested on Hankins's concept of the superior individual, a small proportion of any group, who are natural leaders; they are inventors, originators, and the creative geniuses who achieve in science, philosophy, and the arts, and on whom the mediocre mass is always dependent. Some races produce many more superior individuals, claimed Hankins, because even a small difference in the average between groups will result "in very great differences in the number of talented persons produced" (301, 305–6). This concept of the superior individual Hankins had taken from Galton, and it was a fundamental attribute of his theory of human civilization.

On the basis of this thesis, Hankins sought to demonstrate the superiority of "white to negro" (Hankins, like Sorokin, never capitalized "Negro"). Black people, he claimed, were inferior to whites in brain structure and, therefore, in intelligence. That mental tests have shown blacks "most deficient" was only to be expected "in the light of neurological differences of white and negro brains." But if blacks were inferior, so were others: "the Spanish, Mexicans, Portuguese, Italians, Poles, Greeks, and various slavic nationals have been less well-endowed than the average native American" (321, 325).

On the matter of heredity and environment, Hankins accepted the emerging position that it was not an either-or proposition; "environment is clearly more important for some things and heredity for others." But that does not make them equally important: "If we are to explain why it is that individuals from substantially the same cultural environments achieve quite different levels in the society to which they belong, we shall in most cases be correct in attributing the major weight to their organic differences." Hankins was here holding firmly to a long-established perspective, namely, that superior individuals rise to higher social levels in "a rough justice in the achievement as a whole." His view was clear: "It appears to us that since the first work of Francis Galton the steady accumulation of evidence favors the view that social stratification in a democratic society is explained more fully by the variation in inherent qualities than by any other factors" (368–69).

If early in the book Hankins had attacked some of the crude racial formulations of his day, if he had dismissed as unscientific the Anglo-Saxon fear of racial mixing, if he now granted there were no pure races and a considerable overlap in measurable traits among existing races, he still argued for the importance of race. For Hankins, "the actual course of history is fundamentally determined by the conjunction of racial, cultural, and geographic factors." To deny that race was a basic factor in building civilization was simply wrong; the theory of cultural evolution "errs as much in one direction as Gobineau and Grant do in the other" (367–68).

Just as Hankins remained committed to a concept of racial inequality, so he also remained convinced of the importance of eugenics as practice and policy. While he disputed some of the eugenicists' arguments, he shared in their fear that "the relative super-fertility of inferior stocks in our population is a threatening herald of population deterioration." The issue was not one of "preserving Anglo-Saxon stock," for much of it "is utterly worthless and should be sterilized at the earliest possible date." Nor was it a matter of drawing racial lines. Instead, it was essential to multiply the more able, regardles of race, and to lower the birth rate of the less able: "For the less intelligent there should be devised and universalized some effective means of birth control." This might include "a gradual extension of the present policies of segregation and sterilization" (346–47, 375).

Rescuing Racial Theory

In a period when cultural theories were gradually replacing biological ones in sociology, Sorokin and Hankins tried to rescue biological determinism and racial superiority from the compelling critiques of the geneticists. They wrote with different emphases that reflected their different origins and interests: Sorokin, the emigré scholar who cited extensively from European sources; Hankins, the native sociologist attuned to the American milieu of scholarly argument about and political struggle over the issue of race. Yet, the influential force of their arguments in the late 1920s can best be seen in their areas of agreement.

Both Sorokin and Hankins were intent on grounding their arguments on scientific evidence and showing respect for that evidence, whatever conclusions it produced. Their claims to be heard, then, were as scientists, not as polemicists for or against claims of racial superiority. There was good reason for such a position. Sociologists had abandoned social reform for science, and they were anxious to claim that sociology was (or was becoming) a science; therefore, they could not with impunity admit to disbelieving any proposition that had been scientifically validated. In order to remain scientifically credible, Sorokin and Hankins defined race in terms of statistically measured overlapping traits and placed strong confidence in biometric techniques and IQ tests as instruments of scientific measurement. Both ridiculed the American conception of Nordic (and thus Anglo-Saxon) superiority; both recognized that national populations were never of one racial origin; and both rejected the older nature-versus-nurture argument by making environment a significant explanatory factor of human behavior, though neither of them was inclined to make environment fully equal to heredity.

Yet they differed in two significant ways. In the first instance, Sorokin stayed closer to the measurement of racial traits and qualities, while Hankins rooted his argument in a theory of civilization that resonated strongly of late nineteenth-century theories of evolutionary struggle. To this he added Galton's notion of the talented few and revealed a strong contempt for the masses of ordinary individuals. Second, Hankins was immersed, as Sorokin was not, in the American situation, sensitive to the nuances of academic argument and to public opinion. He was an embattled partisan using scientific arguments to recapture credibility for the case for racial superiority and a eugenics policy.

Hankins's book did not have the staying power that Sorokin's did, at least within sociology, because issues he argued—the case against Nordic superiority and the case for sterilization—soon faded out with the decline of the eugenics movement. Nor did mid-century sociologists display much interest in theories about the basis of civilization, especially one that made race one of the basic factors. Hankins's book, therefore, was probably the last such effort by an American sociologist. Still, his work had an influence. Like Sorokin, he argued in behalf of those who were reluctant to accept any change in the theory of biological determinism, and he gave them reason to modify but not reject their fundamental position. As a consequence, two decades later remnants of the older racial thinking were still visible in the work of some sociologists.

Like Sorokin and Hankins, many sociologists in the late 1920s, as Dorothy Gary pointed out, straddled the issue; while allowing for the place of culture, they still gave some credence to heredity. Some of them pursued a program of synthesis between heredity and environment by drawing upon the new genetics to deny the familiar nature-versus-nurture opposition and to argue, instead, for what came to be called "organic plasticity," which allowed for varied development of the organism under diverse environmental conditions. In this way the specificity of heredity, as in the older biology, was much diminished, and an indeterminate conception of human nature became feasible. But it also specified limits to plasticity, which could be variously interpreted to allow for a greater or lesser emphasis on heredity. Fence-straddling sociologists, therefore, could avoid an outright commitment to an environmental position.

By virtue of such fence-straddling, sociologists in the 1920s still played a secondary role in the ongoing struggle over a scientific conception of race. An older biology and a new psychology of mental testing dominated the hereditarian thesis, while anthropology staked out the opposing ground. The hereditarians owed the thrust of their argument to biological evolution, for they had long asserted that the races that had evolved as superior produced the world's superior cultures. The cultural anthropologists thoroughly disputed this thesis. Dorothy Gary summarized the cultural position by arguing that "the culturalists have demonstrated, through accumulation of a wealth of historical data on the subject, that race is but a chance carrier of culture." She also stated that the culturalists "have pointed out the ethnocentric character of the white group's judgments and scale of values," as well as "the accomplishments and contributions to world culture of the so-called backward peoples."[80]

This Boasian argument for the independence of culture from biology was further inducement for sociologists to move, however slowly, to a position emphasizing culture over biology. But even as they did move, biology remained a factor for them by virtue of a persisting belief in racial temperament. It was an old idea in social thought, which W. I. Thomas introduced into sociology, and it showed a remarkable persistence well into the 1920s.

Race and Temperament

The idea that each race had a distinct temperament was an idea of ancient vintage, but one that flowered again in the nineteenth century. Temperament, like intelligence, was believed to be innate, and neither environment nor education was likely to effect much change. There was never any clear definition of the concept among those who asserted it to be a racial characteristic, and the list of such characteristics was a long one. Racial temperament was presumed to explain differences in ambition, courage, extroversion, cheerfulness, coolheadedness, passion, honesty, submissiveness, and many others; there was also a scientific temperament and an artistic one.

In all racial thought, a close connection between race and temperament was taken for granted, and the most extravagant comparisons of temperament were made. It would be difficult to find a racial thinker who did not invoke some conception of racial temperament as one aspect of racial superiority. When psychologists developed tests to measure the innate character of the races, according to Gossett, they undertook the measurement of such "racial characters" as integrity, kindliness, courage, unselfishness, reasonableness, refinement, cheerfulness and optimism, motor inhibition, noncompliance, and finality of judgment. Gossett notes, "As one might have predicted, the tests generally showed that Negroes, Indians, Mexicans, and other nonwhite races were ordinarily inferior in their personality traits to the whites."[81]

But one did not have to be a confirmed hereditarian to believe in innate character. Perhaps the most striking instance of this was in the work of Edward Reuter. In his 1927 text, *The American Race Problem,* he said that he was not concerned with race as biology but race as a sociological and social problem, yet he still found reason to make use of the notion of racial temperament. Much variation in human groups, he said, can certainly be accounted for by cultural variation, but not all. Some variation can be accounted for by temperament: "It is possible, and appears probable that as a result of variations, selection, and adaptation to a peculiar environment and natural habitat, the Negro people may possess, as a racial heritage, certain characteristic temperamental qualities." Even as had the social-problems sociologists, Reuter was invoking the theory of natural selection. After enumerating some descriptive terms, Reuter claimed that "they lend support to the presumption of a racial individuality of temperament." But he carefully qualified this claim: "So far as such terms are really descriptive" and so far as they "are not a temporary expression of their recent historical status."[82]

Reuter pressed his conception of racial temperament most fully around the issue of slavery and freedom. Though processes of accommodation and assimilation were basic to his analysis of the adjustment of Africans to their enslavement, their racial temperament, he felt, eased that process and "appear[s] to be as such as to make the initial stages of a slave order relatively easy to establish": "In disposition they are cheerful, kindly, and sociable: in temperament, they are characteristically extrovert, so readily obedient and easily contented. More than most other racial groups they are patiently tolerant under abuse and oppression and little inclined to struggle against difficulties. These facts of racial temperament and disposition make the Negroes more amenable to the discipline of slavery than perhaps any other racial group."[83]

Since Emancipation the former slaves have had but a short time in which to choose their own values, thought Reuter, yet this had already produced "significant changes in the behavior of the group." Though their choice is still narrowly limited, "they show a tendency to select from the complex American culture the artistic rather than the utilitarian values." For this reason, Reuter went on to say, Robert Park had called them "the lady of the races."[84]

Reuter's reference to Robert Park invoked not only the name of the leading sociologist of race relations but also an acknowledged friend of black people and a former close associate of Booker T. Washington. Though Park came to regret his "lady-among-the-races" phrase because of the criticism it was to evoke, particularly from educated blacks, in fact it was an appropriate expression of Park's belief in racial temperament. Writing in 1918, Park made a distinction between racial inferiority and racial temperament: "Admitting, as the anthropologists now seem disposed to do, that the average native intelligence in the races is about the same, we may still expect to find in different races certain special traits and tendencies which rest on biological rather than cultural differences." Beyond all cultural and historical differences, he noted, "it is presumed that Teuton and Latin, the Negro and the Jew . . . have certain racial aptitudes, certain innate and characteristic differences of temperament."[85] Unlike the psychologists, who measured differences among races in relation to the same character traits, Park did not make invidious comparisons; a different temperament was but a different combination of character traits, neither better nor worse than another.

Comparing racial character to the role of the wish in Freud's dream analysis, Park thought of the racial temperament of blacks as clothing itself in external cultural forms taken from white culture, but giving to these forms the "inner meaning, the sentiment, the emphasis, the emotional color" of its own race. Each individual thus receives a "double inheritance," an inherited racial temperament and a social tradition by communication and education: "Between this temperament and this tradition there is, as has generally been recognized, a very intimate relationship."[86]

After a seemingly confident development of his thesis, Park acknowledged that it yet remained to determine to what extent racial characteristics were "actually racial" or due to environmental conditions, and said his thesis was offered "merely as an hypothesis. As such its value consists in its suggestion of a point of view and program for investigation."[87] Park was here acknowledging that racial temperament was not accepted by all sociologists—his colleague W. I. Thomas had abandoned it—though he clearly maintained it as a point of view worth holding.

It is testimony to the power of the inherited tradition of racial thought that even Robert Park, far more sympathetic to the black than any sociologist of his day, and who easily abandoned the idea of inferior intelligence, nonetheless clung stubbornly to the concept of racial temperament (as well as that of acquired characteristics) throughout the 1920s. Park belatedly abandoned Lamarckianism in 1928, while still clinging, in some unclear way, to the concept of racial temperament:

> Changes in race, it is true, do inevitably follow, at some distance, changes in culture. The movements and mingling of peoples which bring rapid, sudden, and often catastrophic changes in customs and habits are followed, in the course of time, as a result of interbreeding, by corresponding modifications in temperament and physique. . . . However, changes in racial characteristics and in cultural traits proceed at very different rates, and it is notorious

that cultural changes are not consolidated and transmitted biologically, or at least to only a very small extent, if at all. Acquired
characteristics are not biologically inherited.[88]

As late as 1931 Park was still clinging to some conception of racial
temperament when he argued that such characteristics of the mulatto
as "restlessness, aggressiveness, and what may be described as the general egocentric behavior of the mulattoes compared to the Negro may,
and probably does, have a temperamental basis."[89]

The concept of a racial temperament was the last vestige of the
argument for the racial determination of human attributes. While it
had remained alive throughout the 1920s, it was to disappear altogether
in the 1930s as sociologists finally moved on to a cultural analysis of
race relations.

By the end of the decade of the 1920s, the racial problem was
undergoing significant redefinition in the social sciences. There were
three redefining factors: the geneticists' invalidation of the biological
theory of racial inferiority; the anthropological effort to separate race
from culture; and, in the face of a compelling critique, the inability of
the psychologists to sustain confidence in the scientific validity of IQ
measurements. Sociologists had been gradually coming to accept these
changes and to move from a biological to a cultural analysis of race.

Given the deeply rooted and long entrenched status of racial beliefs,
however, such movement did not come easily, and remnants of the
old racial theories remained, though often in altered form. Sociologists
like Sorokin and Hankins tried to reconstruct the case for racial inferiority by rejecting some of the more disputable arguments of the
eugenicists and by giving some credence to environmental factors.
Their task was to rescue the hereditarian case by repairing it. Others
turned back to Darwinian theory and took up again the concept of
natural selection in order to rebuild the case for racial inferiority.

Opposed to them were mostly the cultural anthropologists, who
rejected the concept of racial inferiority and argued instead for a cultural analysis that insisted on the equal value of all human cultures
and the ethnocentrism of those who thought otherwise. There was a
growing number of sociologists who accepted the anthropologists' position, except on one point: they firmly rejected the idea that all human
cultures were equal.

Floating uneasily somewhere between these two positions were
those who could not yet bring themselves to abandon fully the idea
that biology still played a role in assessing racial differences. While

Park had rejected racial inferiority before 1920, he still clung to the idea that racial temperaments were at least partly rooted in biology. But there were others who were deeply ambivalent about the whole matter of race. While they did not directly dispute the new genetics, they could not bring themselves to accept it fully, so deeply imbued were they with older racial ideas and feelings. Representative of such sociologists was Edward Reuter, who was to become second only to Robert Park in influence among the first generation of the sociologists of race relations.

While Reuter's *American Race Problem* was a sociological study of American race relations, and he disavowed any interest in race as biology, nonetheless, he still believed in racial inferiority: "It is probable that differences in race mentality exist. . . . There is a very considerable body of apparently unbiased scientific opinion on the side of Negro inferiority. And there are no competent students of racial matters who dogmatically assert an absolute racial mental equality." Then he turned to what science could say: "What has been done is to demonstrate that the customary proofs of racial inequality are scientifically worthless. The Negro may be the intellectual inferior of the white racial stock, but to date no one has marshalled in proof of the position any body of evidence that has scientific validity."[90] Reuter seemed unaware of the contradiction in his argument: there could not be a body of apparently unbiased scientific opinion to support racial inferiority if the customary proofs of racial inequality were scientifically worthless.

Nonetheless, the resistance to abandoning some last hold on biological thought largely gave way during the 1930s, and those few sociologists with an interest in race turned their attention to the construction of a sociology of race relations. In doing so, they finally abandoned the argument for biological inferiority, but they built into the new sociology of race relations a conception of black people as culturally inferior. That conception of cultural inferiority was to remain a basic component of the sociology of race relations until the events of the 1960s made its retention impossible.

Cultural Inferiority

If more and more sociologists were moving from biology to culture in the analysis of the race problem, they were still deaf to the anthropological argument for the equal status of human cultures. The concept of cultural inferiority was not new; it had been a staple of the theory of racial inferiority. A biologically inferior people, it was argued, could not be expected to display cultural skills comparable to their natural superiors. But for those who had abandoned a belief in biological inferiority, a belief in cultural inferiority needed a further rationale.

The necessary rationale was provided by sociologists and anthropologists who explicated the distinction between folk and modern society. Park, for example, saw cultural advance as an outcome of migration and conquest and the extension of trade and commerce, which inevitably brought into contact people racially and culturally divergent. The consequence of unavoidable conflict between a society founded on kinship (folk) and one founded on the marketplace (civilization) was a process of dissolving and disrupting the folk society and eventually assimilating the folk into civilization. In that way Park's judgments bespoke a comfortable acceptance of what he and much of his sociological generation took to be an irreversible evolutionary process, one in which the concept of civilization stood for the undeniable superiority of "modern" to the "simple," the "primitive," and the "folk."[91]

For Park, most blacks were still living in isolated communities in the rural South, a folk culture of peasants still separated from and unassimilated into the larger society. He did not invoke any invidious judgments about them; instead, he provided a description of a people who developed, first, under conditions of slavery and plantation life and continued under conditions of rural isolation. But other sociologists, including Reuter, saw clear evidence of cultural inferiority in this imagery of an isolated rural peasantry.

For Reuter, the contrast of an impoverished, often illiterate rural folk and those of an advanced urban culture made invidious comparisons unavoidable. He perceived a stark contrast between what black people were originally, and still were, and the standards of modern culture. In their origins, they had been "a primitive and superstitious people," whose African religion was "basically, a crude and simple demonology." Now, well after Emancipation, they were still "culturally retarded" and "in many respects, outside the modern culture." Blacks, from Reuter's perspective, had arrived culturally inferior and had remained so because of social isolation and the implacable opposition of the dominant whites to any significant racial change.[92]

A fundamental change was now underway in the manner in which sociologists viewed black people. What had once been defined as a racial hierarchy of genetically derived abilities was now being transformed into an invidious contrast of patterns of cultural development. If black Americans were finally escaping the biological condemnation that had beset them for so long, they were now being relegated to another condemning status, that of the culturally inferior.

Notes

1. John S. Haller, Jr., *Outcasts from Evolution: Scientific Attitudes of Racial Inferiority, 1859–1900* (Urbana: University of Illinois Press, 1971), 210.

2. See, for example, Ellsworth Faris, "The Mental Capacity of Savages," *American Journal of Sociology* 23 (Mar. 1918): 603–19.

3. Floyd Nelson House, *The Development of Sociology* (New York: McGraw-Hill, 1936), 349–50.

4. Francis Galton, "Eugenics: Its Definition, Scope and Aims," *American Journal of Sociology* 10 (July 1904): 1–6, and a discussion by others: 6–25; "Francis Galton on Eugenics: Discussion before the Sociological Society, London," *American Journal of Sociology* 11 (Sept. 1905): 277–96.

5. See Hamilton Cravens, *The Triumph of Evolution: The Heredity-Environment Controversy in American Science, 1900–1941* (Philadelphia: University of Pennsylvlania Press, 1978), chapter 1, "The New Biololgy." Cravens's book provides a thorough review of the heredity-environment issue in the United States in the early decades of the century. For other reviews of the eugenics movement, see Thomas F. Gossett, *Race: The History of an Idea in America* (Dallas: Southern Methodist University Press, 1963), 155–75; Richard Hofstadter, *Social Darwinism in America* (Philadelphia: University of Pennsylvania Press, 1944), 161–67; Donald K. Pickens, *Eugenics and the Progressives* (Nashville: Vanderbilt University Press, 1968); Kenneth M. Ludmerer, *Genetics and American Society: A Historical Appraisal* (Baltimore: Johns Hopkins University Press, 1972); and Daniel J. Kevles, *In the Name of Eugenics: Genetics and the Uses of Human Heredity* (New York: Alfred A. Knopf, 1985), chapters 1–8.

A large body of the literature of the eugenics movement has been collected and reprinted in twenty volumes in five parts; see Nicole Hahn Rafter, ed., *The Sociobiology of Deviance: The Eugenics Movement in the United States* (Millwood, N.Y.: Krau Reprint, 1981).

6. Cravens, *Triumph of Evolution*, 14.

7. For an analysis of how some states dealt with the issue of sterilization, see Pickens, *Eugenics and Progressives*, chapter 6; Ludmerer, *Genetics and Society*, 90–95.

8. It was not uncommon for progressives like Ross to be hereditarians and supporters of eugenics. However, for a study that relates hereditarianism to conservative thought and environmentalism to liberal thought, see Nicholas Pastore, *The Nature-Nurture Controversy* (New York: King's Crown Press, 1949). On Margaret Sanger's involvement with eugenics, see Pickens, *Eugenics and Progressives*, chapter 5, "Margaret Sanger: The Radical and the Restoration of Nature."

9. Ludmerer, *Genetics and Society*, 34.

10. Madison Grant, *The Passing of the Great Race* (New York: Charles Scribner's Sons, 1916); Lothrop Stoddard, *The Rising Tide of Color against White World-Supremacy* (New York: Charles Scribner's Sons, 1920).

11. Charles Horton Cooley, "Genius, Fame, and the Comparison of Races," *Annals of the American Academy of Political and Social Science* 9 (May 1897): 317–58.

12. Lester F. Ward, *Applied Sociology: A Treatise on the Conscious Improvement of Society by Society* (Boston: Ginn and Co., 1906), 110.

13. Charles Horton Cooley, *Social Process* (New York: Charles Scribner's Sons, 1918), 206.

14. *Changes in Bodily Form of Descendants of Immigrants: Partial Report on the Results of an Anthropological Investigation for the United States Immigration Commission*, Senate Document no. 208, 61st Congress: 2d session (Washington, D.C., 1910).

15. Ibid., 2, 5.

16. Ibid., 64–76.

17. George W. Stocking, Jr., *Race, Culture and Evolution: Essays in the History of Anthropology* (New York: Free Press, 1968), 189.

18. W. I. Thomas, "The Scope of Folk Psychology," *American Journal of Sociology* 1 (Jan. 1896): 439.

19. Charles Ellwood, "The Theory of Imitation in Social Psychology," *American Journal of Sociology* 6 (May 1901): 735; Robert E. Park, "Racial Assimilation in Secondary Groups," in his *Race and Culture,* ed. Everett C. Hughes et al. (New York: Free Press, 1950), 214.

20. Stocking, *Race, Culture,* 242.

21. Ibid., 243.

22. W. I. Thomas, "Race Psychology: Standpoint and Questionnaire, with Particular Reference to the Immigrant and the Negro," *American Journal of Sociology* 17 (May 1912): 726.

23. Stocking, *Race, Culture,* 267.

24. Alfred Kroeber, "The Super-Organic," *American Anthropologist* 19 (Apr.–June 1917): 162–213; Robert H. Lowie, *Culture and Ethnology* (New York: Horace Liveright, 1917).

25. House, *Development of Sociology,* 269.

26. W. I. Thomas and Florian Znaniecki, *The Polish Peasant in Europe and America,* 5 vols. (Boston: Richard Badger, 1918).

27. James Mark Baldwin, *The Individual and Society* (Boston: Richard Badger, 1911), 118.

28. Merle Curti, *Human Nature in American Thought: A History* (Madison: University of Wisconsin Press, 1980), 288.

29. On the origins of symbolic interaction, see J. David Lewis and Richard Smith, *American Sociology and Pragmatism: Mead, Chicago Sociology, and Symbolic Interaction* (Chicago: University of Chicago Press, 1980) and Bernard Meltzer, James Petras, and Larry Reynolds, *Symbolic Interactionism: Genesis, Varieties, and Criticism* (London: Routledge and Kegan Paul, 1975).

30. A case in point was an article in which the author sternly chided Southerners for their prejudicial belief in the inferiority of blacks and argued for their assimilation, but he took pains to point out that assimilation as he was using it did not mean amalgamation. See George Eliott Howard, "The

Social Cost of Southern Race Prejudice," *American Journal of Sociology* 22 (Mar. 1918): 577–93.

31. Ludmerer, *Genetics and Society,* 77, 79.

32. For a description of racial thought in this period, see I. A. Newby, *Jim Crow's Defense: Anti-Negro Thought in America, 1900–1930* (Baton Rouge: Louisiana State University Press, 1965).

33. For an analysis of nativist reaction, see John Higham, *Stranger in the Land: Patterns of American Nativism* (New Brunswick, N.J.: Rutgers University Press, 1955); for a description of white-instigated riots against blacks, see John Hope Franklin, *From Slavery to Freedom: A History of Negro Americans,* 3d ed. (New York: Alfred A. Knopf, 1967), 440–44, 474–75, 480–84.

34. Ludmerer, *Genetics and Society,* 123.

35. On the early use of IQ tests in measuring racial differences, see Stephen Jay Gould, *The Mismeasurement of Man* (New York: W. W. Norton, 1981), chapter 5; Gossett, *Race,* 363–69; and Craven, *Triumph of Evolution,* chapter 7.

36. Gossett, *Race,* 368–69.

37. Ibid., 377.

38. See: John Lewis Gillin, Clarence G. Dittmer, Roy J. Colbert, *Social Problems* (New York: Century, 1928); Grove Samuel Dow, *Society and Its Problems: An Introduction to Sociology* (New York: Thomas Y. Crowell, 1920); Charles A. Ellwood, *Sociology and Modern Social Problems* (New York: American Book, 1924); Seba Eldridge and Carroll D. Clark, *Major Problems of Democracy: A Study of Social Conditions in the United States* (New York: Century, 1928); John M. Gillette and James M. Reinhardt, *Current Social Problems* (New York: American Book, 1933); Jerome Dowd, *The Negro in American Life* (New York: Century, 1926); John R. Commons, *Races and Immigrants in American Life* (New York: MacMillan, 1920).

39. Howard W. Odum, *Social and Mental Traits of the Negro: Research into the Conditions of the Negro Race in Southern Towns: A Study of Race Traits, Tendencies and Prospects,* Studies in History, Economics and Public Law, vol. 37, no. 3 (New York: Columbia University, 1910). This was Odum's doctoral dissertation.

40. Ibid., 165.

41. Ibid., 40–41.

42. Ibid., 86–88, 94.

43. Ibid., 152, 159–60.

44. Ibid., 183–86, 266, 188.

45. Gillette, Dittmer, Colbert, *Social Problems,* 214; Dow, *Sociology,* 177–81.

46. Gillette and Reinhardt, *Current Problems,* 444–71; Ellwood, *Sociology,* 158–59.

47. Gillin, Dittmer, Colbert, *Social Problems,* 208; Dowd, *The Negro,* 394; Eldridge and Clark, *Major Problems,* 65; Ellwood, *Sociology,* 196; Dow, *Society,* 167.

48. Dow, *Society,* 163; Commons, *Races,* 39, 41.

49. Gillin, Dittmer, Colbert, *Social Problems*, 170; Ellwood, *Sociology*, 246–49.

50. Gillin, Dittmer, Colbert, *Social Problems*, 74, 206 (emphasis in original).

51. Eldridge and Clark, *Major Problems*, 66; Dow, *Society*, 157–58.

52. Dowd, *The Negro*, 396.

53. Gillin, Dittmer, Colbert, *Social Problems*, 210–12.

54. Ellwood, *Sociology*, 250; Dow, *Society*, 164–65.

55. Odum, *Social and Mental Traits*, 184, 239. Odum devoted all of chapter 7 to the emotional nature of black people.

56. Dowd, *The Negro*, 401–8.

57. Gillin, Dittmer, Colbert, *Social Problems*, 213; Ellwood, *Sociology*, 249; Dow, *Society*, 163, 166–67; Commons, *Races*, 39.

58. Dowd, *The Negro*, 360, 525; Dow, *Society*, 181; Gillin, Dittmer, Colbert, *Social Problems*, 171.

59. Odum, *Social and Mental Traits*, 276, 286, 288, 293.

60. Ibid., 262–64; Gillin, Dittmer, Colbert, *Social Problems*, chapter 15.

61. Dow, *Society*, 182–88.

62. Dowd, *The Negro*, 577–79; Gillette and Reinhardt, *Current Problems*, 497–99; Ellwood, *Sociology*, 266–68.

63. Odum, *Social and Mental Traits*, 286–88.

64. Dow, *Society*, 175–77.

65. Dowd, *The Negro*, 586; Commons, *Races*, 44.

66. Ellwood, *Sociology*, 255; Melville J. Herskovits, *The American Negro: A Study in Racial Crossing* (New York: Alfred A. Knopf, 1928), 10.

67. Edward Byron Reuter, *The Mulatto in the United States* (Boston: Richard Badger, 1918); Commons, *Races*, 209–10.

68. Gillin, Dittmer, Colbert, *Social Problems*, 199–203, 236 (emphasis in original).

69. Dow, *Society*, 181–82.

70. Ellwood, *Sociology*, 255–58.

71. Dorothy Gary, "The Developing Study of Culture," in *Recent Trends in American Sociology*, ed. George Lundberg, Read Bain, and Nels Anderson, (New York: Harper and Brothers, 1929), 187.

72. Cravens, *Triumph of Evolution*, 174. For an informative review of the changes in biology that undercut the scientific legitimacy of eugenics, see Cravens's chapter 5 and Ludmerer's chapter 6.

73. See, for example, Ellsworth Huntington and Leon Whitney, *Builders of America* (New York: William Morrow, 1927); Edward East, *Heredity and Human Affairs* (New York: Charles Scribner's Sons, 1927); and Robert Bennett Bean, *The Races of Man* (New York: The University Society, 1935).

74. Stocking, *Race, Culture*, 301.

75. Ibid., 301–2.

76. Pitirim Sorokin, *Contemporary Sociological Theories* (New York: Harper and Brothers, 1928), 279, 297–98.

77. Ibid., 302, 304.

78. Ibid., 280, 288, 301.

79. Frank H. Hankins, *The Racial Basis of Civilization: A Critique of the Nordic Doctrine* (New York: Alfred A. Knopf, 1926), vii. Further references to this work will appear in the text.

80. Gary, "Developing Study of Culture," 192–93.

81. Gossett, *Race,* 376–77.

82. Edward Byron Reuter, *The American Race Problem: A Study of the Negro* (New York: Thomas Y. Crowell, 1927), 93.

83. Ibid., 104, 7.

84. Ibid., 94–95.

85. Park, "Education in Its Relation to the Conflict and Fusion of Cultures," *Race and Culture,* 264.

86. Ibid., 280, 282.

87. Ibid., 281.

88. Park, "Human Migration and the Marginal Man," *Race and Culture,* 346–47.

89. Park, "Mentality of Racial Hybrids," *Race and Culture,* 387.

90. Reuter, *Race Problem,* 92.

91. Park's ideas are elaborated in the first three chapters of his *Race and Culture.*

92. Reuter, *Race Problem,* 19, 114, 309.

3

From the Race Problem
to Race Relations

Even as they were still shedding the last remnants of the biological interpretation of race, a small body of sociologists were putting the foundations to a new sociological perspective. Until then, race had always been viewed in terms of "the race problem," defined by the white conviction of black innate inferiority and consequent concern about matters of social control and the use of a now legally free labor. While the framework of the race problem was to remain a significant way for sociologists to think about race, there was already underway the development of a new perspective: an interactionist perspective that viewed race as social process—*race relations.*

It was none too soon. However reluctant many sociologists may have been to accept the lessons of the new genetics, the biologists were withdrawing from the race problem and leaving it to the social sciences. Though biology would still have something to say about race as a biological phenomenon, it was discarding the burden of the race problem and would no longer be responsible for sanctioning matters of social policy. At first it was the anthropologists who, by virtue of their pioneering work, inherited from the biologists the authoritative voice on matters of race. Other scholars were more likely to look to them than they were to sociologists for guidance on the newer understanding of racial differences.[1]

But this would not be the case for long. A sociological interpretation of race was in the making, and by the mid-thirties sociology had established itself as the one among the social sciences most persistently committed to a social understanding of race in American life. Though the new study of race relations was to develop within a perspective of social process, its first step was taken within the older framework of social evolution.

Evolution and Race Relations

It is a truism among sociologists that American sociology abandoned the concept of social evolution in the early decades of the century, almost in tandem with the anthropologists, and turned to a nonevolutionary mode of theorizing. But this is only a partial truth. Evolution survived as an unrecognized but nonetheless substantial component of the social thought American sociologists inherited from nineteenth-century European sociology. Evolutionary thinking was most evident in the long effort to characterize modern society—and the United States as a modern society—as the ultimate outcome of a long developmental process. That effort to delineate what was modern led to repeated attempts to contrast it with what was not modern, a scholarly activity with roots running back into the nineteenth century.

While evolutionary thought in the nineteenth century concentrated on the origins of social life and the stages of evolutionary development, many others in that time were less interested in elucidating origins and stages than they were in comparing modern society with its preceding stage of social development in Europe and with nonwestern peoples found elsewhere on the globe. Evolutionary theory provided the conditioning context for a contrasting typology of modern and premodern forms of human association. Henry Maine's delineation of a developmental progression from *status* to *contract* was the first of what was to become a long tradition of typological comparisons, notable among which were Ferdinand Toennies's *gemeinschaft* and *gesellschaft* and Emile Durkheim's *mechanical* and *organic solidarity*. Even Herbert Spencer, after elaborating his three-stage evolutionary scheme, developed a typology of *military* and *industrial* societies.

For American sociologists, who were still concerned with the transition from agrarian to industrial, and also rural to urban, as well as with the integration of peasant immigrants from rural Europe, these typologies struck a sensitive nerve. They spoke to an American sociological concern—the development of the United States as a fully modern society—in a way that at the time had no counterpart in Europe. It was not surprising, then, that in the 1920s a number of sociologists were finding it useful to undertake a typological analysis.

Sociologists were appreciative readers of the anthropologist Robert Redfield's typology, *folk* and *urban*, but there were sociological contemporaries of Redfield who developed typologies of their own: Howard Becker's *sacred* and *secular;* Robert MacIver's *community* and *association;* Howard Odum's *folk culture* and *civilization;* and not least, Robert Park's *culture* and *civilization.* Each of these contributed to American sociology's image of modern society as the endpoint of societal development characterized by a unique combination of attributes not to be found in any past society. And it was the evolutionary perspective that gave to sociologists their confident assessment that "modern" meant a progressive development before which all past societies were in some way inferior. Commerce, money and the market, industrialization and the factory system, urbanization and the city, bureaucracy, rationality, and science were some of the conceptual attributes that served to define the distinctiveness of modern society. (In the 1950s the study of the "modernization" of "traditional" societies in the Third World rested on this same typological comparison.)

Robert Park shared fully in this effort to create contrasting typologies. His typology was the outcome of two related developments: first, the vast movements of people the world over to trade, explore, or conquer; and second, a consequent coming together of culturally diverse peoples within the impersonal milieu of city and market. From such processes came modern society (civilization), the emergence of which undermined local groups and traditional ways (culture). When that happened, folk people were assimilated into secular societies and took on new cultural and national identities. Assimilation, it seemed, was an inevitable and irreversible feature of the evolution of modern societies.[2]

Park differed from other sociologists in the explication of his typology. First, while others were primarily interested in ways of life, Park was more interested in showing how civilization evolved from the processes of movement and migration, trade and territorial expansion, and how a developing civilization absorbed and assimilated a local culture. Second, Park located race relations in this civilizing process; here was how contact between racially different groups ended in the racial domination by one of the other, but also by the eventual assimilation of one people to another.

This location of the issue of race relations in an evolutionary context of typologies of premodern and modern, and of the concept of assimilation as the basic process of transition to modern society, constituted two assumptions that powerfully undergirded the new sociology of race relations in the 1920s. If it removed black people from the context of biological evolution, it nonetheless kept them within the framework of social evolution wherein they were defined as a people at a lower stage of social development. Though not what Park intended, this fitted the idea that blacks were a culturally inferior people.

Park, however, was to do a great deal more to develop a sociology of race relations, particularly by viewing it, not as a fixed status, but as social process, continually changing and developing.

Robert Park: Race as Social Process

Robert Ezra Park, journalist, publicist for the Congo Reform Association, and staff writer and press agent for Booker T. Washington, came to the University of Chicago in 1913 at the age of forty-nine on a part-time basis. It would be ten years before he would receive a full-time appointment. Nonetheless, from the day of his arrival, he was a key figure in the development of the renowned "Chicago School" of sociology. Park's contribution to sociology ranged from a basic theory of society to the study of the city, human ecology, collective behavior, and the immigrants; his work also contributed to the definitive shaping of a new sociology of race relations. He trained a generation of capable scholars and he influenced greatly the work of many more.[3]

Park's most coherent theorizing about social life was worked out in collaboration with Ernest W. Burgess and published in an enormously influential text, *An Introduction to the Science of Sociology*. It was here that he and Burgess set out in general terms the concept of social life as constantly interactional, as social process. Park and Burgess did not invent the concept of social process. Floyd House credits Ludwig Gumplowicz for bringing the concept into sociology, and Albion Small and E. A. Ross for introducing it into their writings as early as 1905.[4]

At the outset, the concept of social process had two meanings: the first, Simmel's idea of forms of interaction in the most general terms; the other, a sequence of social changes, that is, processes of social development. This second meaning of social process was the one used by Small and Cooley, and also by Park and Burgess in their *Introduction to the Science of Sociology*. In that work social process was analyzed in terms of four major types: competition, conflict, accommodation and assimilation.[5] Park's use of these concepts in analyzing race relations became their best known application.

Park had developed a strong interest in, indeed, a fascination with black people in the rural South through his association with Booker T. Washington and time spent at Tuskegee Institute: "I spent seven winters, partly at Tuskegee, partly roaming about the South, getting acquainted with the life, the customs, and the condition of the Negro people." Unlike Howard Odum and Edward Reuter, Park did not find black people morally wanting and did not lament their failure to live by the moral standards of the white middle class. From this experience, Park noted, "I was not, as I found out later, interested in the Negro problem as that problem is ordinarily conceived." Park accepted neither the value put on racial harmony nor the belief that black people were destined forever to be of secondary status in modern society, at best useful as a laboring class. His perspective was quite different: "I was interested in the Negro in the South and in the curious and intricate system which had grown up to define his relations with white folk. I was interested, most of all, in studying the details of the process by which the Negro was making and has made his slow but steady advance. I became convinced, finally, that I was observing the historical process by which civilization, not merely here but elsewhere, has evolved, drawing into the circle of its influence an ever widening circle of races and people."[6]

Park's disinterest in "the Negro problem" was also a disinterest in the social-problems perspective so common to American sociologists in the 1920s. Nor did he show any interest in the very modest ameliorative actions suggested by sociologists for the race problem. If there was conflict in a situation, he saw it as but a phase in establishing a new accommodation; if there was suffering and injustice, these were but the inevitable accompaniments of the advance of civilization. Park revealed his attitude best in his comments on his early experience as secretary of the Congo Reform Association: "I discovered what I might have known in advance—that conditions in the Congo were about what one might expect, what they have since become, though not by any means so bad, in Kenya. They were, in short, what they were certain to be whenever a sophisticated people invades the territories of a more primitive people in order to exploit their lands and, incidentally, to uplift and civilize them. I knew enough about civilization even at that time to know progress, as James once remarked, is a terrible thing. It is so destructive and wasteful."[7]

While Park's disinterest in the Negro problem was consistent with his evolutionary view of race relations, it was also consistent with his noninterventionist perspective, which was sustained by more than one aspect of his thinking: by the view he shared with his colleagues at Chicago of a clinically objective sociology; by his injunction against political involvement; by his disdain for social reform; and by his concept of social conflict as a force for social change.

Along with his Chicago colleagues (and undoubtedly also the majority of sociologists in the 1920s), Park upheld a conception of so-

ciology as becoming an objective science detached from any political
interest that could intrude upon unbiased scholarship. It was the beginning in sociology of an effort to separate the discipline from social
work and its social causes, from various reform movements, from
radical and socialist politics, and even from an interest in social problems. Such separation, sociologists preached, was necessary to provide
the environment and the time to build a science. In describing the
clinical atmosphere in sociology at Chicago, Robert Faris said that
Park "had abundant human sympathies and political preferences, but
he also kept them under control. For example, in the subject of race
relations, Park, a strong friend of the Negro people, successfully cultivated objective inquiry in this area by students of both white and
Negro races."[8]

Park's clinical objectivity also included a strong interest in avoiding
political involvement of any kind. In his review of the Chicago school,
James T. Carey noted that "Park was very forceful in discouraging . . .
any formal links with practical political activity." That philosophy,
however, did not keep Park from a certain amount of civic action. In
1916 he helped found the Chicago chapter of the Urban League and
served as president for its first two years. In 1919, according to his
biographer, Fred Mathews, he "was appointed chairman of a Joint
Emergency Committee set up by the Urban League, the NAACP, the
Negro YMCA, and other groups to look after the interests of Negroes
arrested during the riots."[9]

But Park's most significant participation in civic affairs was his involvement in the workings of the Chicago Commission on Race Relations, formed to study Chicago's destructive race riot of 1919. Charles
Johnson, later to be a noted black sociologist, but then a graduate
student under Park, took direction of the research and the writing of
the report, and Park undertook a strong consultative role in the research process and in the preparation of the final document. Three of
his students were among seven hired to compile the data and write
drafts for the final report, and "the chief researchers in the sub-study
on public opinion were students in his class on 'The Crowd and the
Public.'" Park's perspective was evident in the document's emphasis
on the importance of the press in shaping public opinion; reflecting
his long interest in journalism, he saw the informing role of the urban
press as a more effective reforming process than directed programs of
change.[10]

Park possessed a deep suspicion, perhaps even a contempt of social
reformers. He had felt this way about reformers since at least his early
involvement in the Congo Reform Association, and the feeling was

only further enhanced by his experiences at Tuskegee. Accordingly, it served as another factor in sustaining his noninterventionist perspective. But Park's disdain for social reformers did not imply a fatalistic acceptance of existing race relations. Mathews said that "the mark of scientific neutrality, to Park, was not a total abstinence from moral judgment, or from social action, but rather the willingness to face the facts of social resistance to change." He placed great store on knowledge to enable human beings to alter the circumstances of their existence: "Social science should not cramp men's freedom and destroy their hope; rather it was to be the learned servant of action."[11]

If Park had little use for social reformers, it was because he differed with them on how change was to come about. Park understood and appreciated the place of conflict in bringing about social change, and he viewed racial change as coming about through the struggle of the oppressed group, not by the efforts of a white leadership that wanted to effect change while carefuly avoiding any semblance of social conflict. As Mathews pointed out, "Park assumed that changes were not *granted* but *won;* the dynamic forces must come from the oppressed themselves." Mathews also reports the recollection of Everett Hughes that "not long before he died Park 'shocked a young political scientist by asking why there should be racial peace before there was racial justice.' "[12]

Except, then, for his civic involvement in racial matters in Chicago from 1916 to 1922, Park preferred to focus his work not on the conventional view of the race problem, nor even on the new urban context, but on a study of race relations understood in terms of conceptual constructions of his own: the race relations cycle, on the one hand, and on racial conflict expressed by nationalism and biracial organization, on the other.

The Race Relations Cycle

From the 1920s until the onset of a new generation and a new situation after World War II, Park's conception of a race relations cycle provided an influential model for studying the assimilation of racial minorities into modern society. The cycle was set within the framework of his concept of *civilization,* that irreversible evolutionary development of secular society in which the social contacts of city and market undermined all local culture and ancient ways. The movement of people around the globe produced *contact* between racially different populations on what Park called the "racial frontier." That was the beginning of the cycle. Then followed *competition* and *conflict* over resources. In time conflict ended in *accommodation,* the establishing of a stable though usually unequal social order. One racial group would dominate and control, the other would be subordinated and exploited, even enslaved. But accommodation, in turn, would eventually be followed by *assimilation,* a cultural and physical merging of the two races. For Park this seemed to be an evolutionary law of cultural development: "The race relations cycle . . . is apparently irreversible. Customs regulations, immigration restriction and racial barriers may slacken the tempo of the movement; may perhaps halt it altogether for a time; but cannot change its direction; cannot, at any rate, reverse it."[13]

Despite the inequality found in any accommodative structure, interpersonal intimacy would develop among individuals, and this, Park felt, was "the great moral solvent," the assimilating process that would subvert all separate and unequal structures. Interracial friendships would "cut across and eventually undermine all the barriers of racial segregation and caste." Park purported to have found evidence of this in the period of slavery in the United States, namely, in "the number of free Negroes and emancipated slaves in the South." To Park this proved that it was "the intimate and personal relations which grew up between the Negro slave and his white master that undermined and weakened the system of slavery from within, long before it was attacked from without."[14]

The renown and influence of the race relations cycle during the 1930s and 1940s, however, was due primarily to the use that Park's students made of it, rather than any claims that Park was to make for it. His students seemed to employ the cycle less as a model for research, more as a legitimation for the idea that assimilation was the inevitable endpoint of race relations. Not all sociologists, however, accepted it. Park's emphasis, first on conflict and an often oppressive accommodation, including slavery, and then upon understanding and interpersonal acceptance, seemed contradictory to some sociologists. It was not readily evident that an oppressive accommodation, such as slavery or the postslavery caste system, would lead inevitably, even if slowly and gradually, to assimilation.

After World War II the idea of an irreversible cycle in race relations came under criticism. Some claimed it was an untestable hypothesis, others that it did not fit all cases or allowed too many exceptions, still others that some ethnic situations simply did not end in assimilation. Except for a brief discussion in textbooks, it found less and less acceptance among sociologists. The most influential textbook of the postwar era, George Simpson and Milton Yinger's *Racial and Cultural*

Minorities, first published in 1953, did not even mention the race relations cycle.[15]

Such criticism apparently assumed that Park placed the same importance upon the race relations cycle as his students did. Their widespread discussion had made it seem that this was Park's significant contribution to the sociology of race relations, the one thing on which his reputation would rest. Yet Park only twice wrote about the concept of the race relations cycle. He first presented it in 1926 as a final short section to an article on the Pacific as a racial frontier; it was published in *Survey Graphic,* an influential periodical of the day but not a sociological journal. He did not discuss it again until 1937, when he wrote a brief essay, "The Race Relations Cycle in Hawaii," as an introduction to the book, *Interracial Marriage in Hawaii,* written by one of his students, Romanzo Adams.[16]

Though Park made limited use of the race relations cycle in his writings, it is more important to note that in his essay on Hawaii he offered a conception of the cycle that did not claim that assimilation alone was the outcome of racial change. Instead he argued that with stabilization "race relations will assume one of three configurations": a caste system, as in India; complete assimilation, as in China; or "a permanent racial minority within the limits of a national state, as is the case of the Jews in Europe." Furthermore, "all three are more or less involved in what we may describe as the 'race relations cycle.' This means that race relations . . . can best be interpreted if what they seem to be at any time and place is regarded merely as a phase in a cycle of change which, once initiated, inevitably continues until it terminates in some predestined racial configuration, and one consistent with an established order of which it is a part."[17]

Park's race relations cycle was not his only contribution to the sociology of race relations, but through the efforts of his students, it became better known than his other work. But in that other work Park was intent on placing American race relations in a wider social context than simply that of the American experience with slavery and its aftermath.

Nationalism and Biracial Organization

While Park claimed that an assimilation process had already begun under slavery, he did not assume that it continued after Emancipation. Quite to the contrary, a new situation set in motion new processes based, not on intimate relations, but on an almost complete separation of the races from one another. After slavery the white South soon constructed a caste system based on race and maintained by the "color line," a term common to the racial vocabulary since before the turn of the century. Though as late as the 1930s most sociologists still believed that caste relations prevailed in the South, Park believed that the maintenance of caste was no longer possible: "Although caste still persists and serves in a way to regulate race, many things ... have conspired not merely to undermine the traditional caste system but to render it obsolete."[18]

For Park, furthermore, the isolation of the races from one another, and the often hostile and sometimes violent encounters between the races, required a different conceptualization. He found his answer by comparing the black Americans emerging from slavery with the emergence of nationalities in eastern Europe. Park had thought of this before he went to the University of Chicago, and he presented the idea in his first sociological paper in 1913. The enforced isolation of black people, he thought, was producing an increased consciousness of race and a growth of "race pride." He saw this as an outcome of the struggle "to rise and make for themselves a place in a world occupied by superior and privileged races" and compared it to the process that was producing nationalities in Europe. Like the Slavic groups in eastern Europe, black Americans were becoming "a nation within a nation"— a quote he attributed to his friend, Booker T. Washington: "From what has been said it seems fair to draw one conclusion, namely: under conditions of secondary contact, that is to say, conditions of individual liberty and individual competition, characteristic of modern civilization, depressed racial groups tend to assume the form of nationalities. A nationality, in this narrower sense, may be defined as a racial group which has attained self-consciousness, no matter whether it has at the same time gained political independence or not."[19]

Park regarded this process of forming nationalities as tending to "substitute for horizontal organization of society ... a vertical organization in which all classes of each racial group were united under the title of their respective nationalities." In the emergence of a new biracial accommodation, sustained by race consciousness and pride, he saw a new basis for assimilation. Such a nationalist movement, as Park called it, would enable a race to achieve its "moral independence" and from that "assimilation, in the sense of copying, will still continue." By that Park meant a cultural borrowing and then reworking of cultural materials appropriate to claims of dignity and solidarity. "A race which has attained the character of a nationality," he claimed, "may still retain its loyalty to the state of which it is a part, but only in so far as that state incorporates as an integral part of its organization, the practical interests, the aspirations and ideals of that nationality." A separate nation loyal to a larger state was then a new accommodation from which the processes of assimilation would then develop.[20]

Late in the 1920s, Park returned to his concept of a biracial organization, giving it a schematic form:

The situation *was* this:

All white

All colored

It is *now* this:

White	Colored
Professional occupation	Professional occupation
Business occupation	Business occupation
Labor	Labor

What was significant for Park was that "the races no longer look up and down; they look across. These bi-racial organizations, so far as I know, are a unique product of the racial struggle in this country; they do not exist outside the United States."[21]

If biracial organization seemed to Park to be unique to the United States, that fact did not diminish his insistence on locating the American race issue within a world process of racial conflict and change. In that light, Park saw race and national consciousness as a worldwide phenomenon within a political system developed to control the new world economy. Given that fact, therefore, it seemed inevitable that there would arise "a struggle of the subject people to be free and of people occupying an inferior position to improve their status."[22] Such an improved status was defined in terms of independence and self-determination.

Nationalistic developments, then, were but one aspect of a larger social and communicative process in the world, which assured the eventual assimilation of the world's peoples within the limits of a common culture and a common historical life. From that perspective, the emergence of a nationalistic movement among American blacks could be viewed, as Park viewed it, as both an inevitable political development and a necessary one for a subject people to undertake. To deplore it, as Edward Reuter did, would seem to be useless.

Edward Reuter: Race as a Social Problem

In contrast to Robert Park, Edward Reuter advanced in all his work the idea of race as an American social problem. The very title of his most influential work, *The American Race Problem,* conveyed his conviction that race was best understood as a social problem of fundamental importance. Furthermore, the subtitle, "A Study of the Negro," made it clear that Reuter shared with other sociologists the conviction that "the race problem" and "the Negro problem" were the same.[23]

For Reuter, the American race problem had its roots in the events that followed Emancipation. The white population in the South had crystallized its racial sentiments into a creed that insisted on white economic and political domination and the firm maintenance of a color line to keep the black "in his place." But despite this, the black population made progress, and as it did, it developed a race consciousness that produced "a spirit of resistance" to unequal treatment by whites. The races consequently tended to draw apart, to lose the "sympathetic attitude characteristic of earlier relations" and to become "separate communities." Despite this separation, however, whites and blacks must associate with one another in the same areas and must come into competition. As a practical problem, therefore, the race problem is "a heritage from an earlier social order. It is the problem to maintain some sort of harmonious and mutually satisfactory working relations between the two racial groups in the population" (12–13).

As Reuter saw it, the race problem consisted of two interrelated aspects: the separate existence of the black people, which left them a backward and culturally retarded group, and the resistance of whites to allowing blacks to develop further. Because of the present structure of largely separate social relations between two unequal groups, the nation's social development, that of whites as well as blacks, was retarded. A segment that was 10 percent of the population could not be neglected without harming the entire nation. Furthermore, political democracy was threatened when all persons could not participate. However, participation in democratic affairs required an "intelligent appreciation" of the questions involved, but black people, Reuter felt, lacked any comprehension of a democratic social order. To permit their full participation would be an unbearable strain on the political order; to exclude them, however, was to discard democracy for an "older, arbitrary type of political control without the consent or participation of the governed" (14).

Reuter's unequivocal language left no doubt that blacks were a "culturally backward" people. His portrait of the masses of blacks

offered no redeeming features: "The masses of the Negroes are uneducated and a high percentage entirely illiterate. The sickness and
death rates are high and their health standards are low. Their family
life is on a very low plane. They are economically inefficient. Their
standard of living is inferior. They are prone to a varied assortment of
vices characteristic of a poor and ignorant people" (17).

These matters Reuter explored fully in a series of separate chapters
on health, sex and family life, education, and delinquency and crime.
Even his chapter on religion and church in the lives of blacks contrasted
unfavorably the "emotional" nature of religious service and the failure
of black churches, because of isolation, to keep pace with modern
religion's development as a system "of moral practices and ethical
ideals, instead of a body of supernatural beliefs." He characterized the
black clergy as largely "men of mediocre ability and of limited education," often lacking in high moral standards (331, 326–27).

Reuter devoted most chapters of *The American Race Problem* to
demonstrating that blacks were an impoverished, uneducated, unskilled, and culturally backward people. In doing so, his treatment
differed but little from that of other social-problems sociologists. There
was also little difference in Reuter's ideas about solving the race problem, except on one basic matter: Reuter's belief in an eventual racial
amalgamation. If anything was to be accomplished in finding a solution,
Reuter asserted, social change must come in two ways. First, there had
to be an improving of the cultural level of black people, an "enlight-
ening of the masses" so they could participate in the culture. Second,
there was a need to raise the industrial efficiency of the group "that
they may not be a handicap to the economic evolution." To do so,
their social status had to be raised, their health standards improved,
and their home life purified: "Their moral standards must be brought
into conformity with the prevailing standards of the time" (15).

But none of this could be done unless there was also opportunity
and social justice for black people. They "must be guaranteed economic, educational, political and social rights." He also spoke out for
individual dignity; the black male must be permitted "to be a man and
an American" (14). Though Reuter spoke far more forcefully for justice
and rights for blacks than did the social-problems sociologists, the
difference was still a matter of degree—though in some cases, a considerable degree. A number of them had recognized that even the
modest goals they advocated required some alteration in the most
blatant forms of unfair treatment.

While Reuter could speak to what had to be done, he did not know
how it could be accomplished. The means to achieve the changes he

advocated were not apparent to him. Instead, the problem appeared to be so deeply rooted as to be largely impervious to reform. At the end of his book, Reuter took note of Booker T. Washington's program for the economic and educational advance of the black masses (which most other students of the race problem seemed to support), the National Associaton for the Advancement of Colored People's "aggressive and militant" fight for full constitutional rights, and Marcus Garvey's effort to bring about a return to Africa to create a separate African nation. None of these would do: "The various methods advocated by individuals and organizations as solutions of the race problem may be dismissed with brief comment. There is no solution" (426–27). From Reuter's perspective there was no solution because of the powerful impediment offered by the prejudice of race and caste. Prejudice was "a relatively fixed factor" and there was no reason to assume that it would diminish in the future. Those who advanced programs for racial equality assumed that prejudice could be removed or overridden, but this appeared to be a "vain assumption so long as there are distinguishable physical marks of race and social marks of caste" (431, 434).

The tenacity of the race problem made it "not a thing to be removed by political and administrative measures." In fact, thought Reuter, there was evidence that there could be "increased exclusion of the Negroes and their organization and perpetuation as an inferior caste." In the last paragraph of the book, a few lines after the preceding comment, Reuter turned to the "ultimate" solution: "As a result of intermixture the Negroes as such ultimately will disappear from the population and the race problem will be solved. But in the meanwhile there will be the problem of defining relations in terms tolerable to the members of each racial group" (433–34). That ultimate solution, though assured by the process of racial mixing, seemed to lie in a far distant future, barely imaginable at that time.

Reuter's view that racial amalgamation would eventually end the race problem set him well apart from the social-problems sociologists, who found any such idea unacceptable, if not offensive. Yet he also shared much of their thinking, as in his interest in mixed bloods, in racial traits, and in his evident ambivalence about the rejection of the biological argument for racial inferiority. He was also interested in describing the presumed disabilities of black people. In fact, Reuter's detailed description of blacks in terms of health and mortality, employment and occupation, education, sex and family life, and crime and delinquency provided a model for the specificity of disabilities that would in time become standard among a new generation of sociologists. The disabilities that had provided evidence of the cultural inferiority of blacks were to remain that, while also providing evidence of discrimination against blacks, and these were to define race as a social problem.

But Reuter was also a Chicago sociologist influenced by Park's work in race relations. He bridged Park's interest in the evolution of race relations in modern societies and the more parochial American interest in a particular definition of its own race problem. That bridging was indicative of American sociologists' interest in the matter of race: while they continued to develop a sociology of race relations, they also held on to an older conception of the race problem.

Biracial Organization: A Negative View

While Park saw positive value in the new form of biracial organization in the United States, Reuter saw the matter far more darkly. He agreed that there had been a historic reorganization of the lives of black Americans since slavery, and that emerging from that reorganization was an independent, biracial structure, one which seemed increasingly to separate blacks from whites. He sought to describe that independent existence, particularly in the emergence of a black middle class with a vested interest in such separateness, as well as to explicate what he took to be its negative consequences for blacks and for race relations.

The separate existence of blacks and whites, noted Reuter, emerged after slavery as blind trial-and-error adjustments between two racial groups unprepared for such change. Exclusion and isolation of blacks by whites produced a separate existence where before there had been intimacy and understanding; but once it was underway, blacks found reason to further the process of separation: "The growth of an independent black life reacted in a situation to increase the cleavage between the races; as they gained in experience, so in individual and racial self-confidence, the tendency to a voluntary and complete separation increased. It marked the beginning of a sense of racial unity, a race consciousness, which, however, did not reach an articulate stage before the present century" (159).

Two developments, Reuter thought, increased black commitment to a separate existence. First, a separate existence provided an opportunity for blacks to become merchants and professionals with a clientele assured because of segregation. Second, a segregation first forced on blacks soon became viewed by many educated blacks as an advantage for the race and a source of racial solidarity; and racial solidarity was a benefit in undertaking a continuing struggle against racial injustice. Many blacks, according to Reuter, thought separation also provided the basis for developing a leadership and for lessening friction by reducing interracial conflict. But it also created, some claimed, an opportunity to make a distinctive cultural contribution, while still others felt it preserved the cultural uniqueness of black Americans (404–6).

For Reuter, there were compelling disadvantages to this nationalistic separateness. He offered as one notable example the Back to Africa Movement led by Marcus Garvey, which had blossomed in the 1920s. Garvey, it would seem, had appealed directly to the "black and ignorant masses, ignoring the light-colored masses," and then had attacked them as being "out of sympathy with the masses." As a result, there was bitter opposition from the "mulatto leadership" but an "increased enthusiasm on the part of the black and ignorant classes." Reuter estimated that anywhere from one-third to one-half of American blacks were followers of Garvey's movement. Though he thought the movement "farcical," he viewed it as "a dramatic demonstration of the social unrest of the inarticulate masses" (407–8).

But the consequences of a "Negro nationality" went well beyond the spreading of unrest among "ignorant masses." As Reuter saw the matter, the very future of the race and of race relations in the United States would be adversely affected by separation. What might be helpful in the short run would only be harmful in the long run. In the short run, separation helped to establish a business and professional class to serve blacks, but "ultimately it must react disastrously upon the group and the very classes that at first profit by it." The racial monopoly of a clientele provided by segregation would, claimed Reuter, lower standards: "Inferior service is the price the group pays for the indulgence of a racial sentiment" (410).

But Reuter had an even more important point to make. He saw the development of "peculiar and exclusive" institutions as not merely characteristic of an isolated people, but, far more important, as the act of a culturally backward people. Instead of building a separate existence, the first task of black people was to master the existing culture: "Just as the first need of the child is education, a knowledge of what has been done and a training that will give him a workmanlike control of the tools of culture, so the Negroes need to be assimilated to the existing culture and measure up to the standards of European civilization. To refuse to be assimilated into the existing culture can result in nothing except the retardation of the rate at which the group advances" (411).

So convinced was Reuter that cultural backwardness was basic to all aspects of black life that, unlike Park, he could see very little of redeeming quality even in the literary and artistic efforts of blacks. Though the 1920s was the decade of the Harlem Renaissance, a time of exceptional creativity and achievement among blacks, Reuter could see nothing "of first or even second rank," and said that "the contribution made by Negroes to American literature is slight and contains very little of any permanent value." Their only musical contribution has been the "simple and rhythmical" slave songs "replete with childish imagery and monotonous with much repetition." The slave songs, however, "are no assurance of ability to use an art form." Perhaps the characteristic bent of Reuter's judgments is evident in his comments on jazz and ragtime music. These he associated with "bawdy houses, saloons, and indecent dance halls," which, he claimed, "became popular with the slump of moral and aesthetic standards incident to the European War" and their popularity "is in part due to the general lack of musical taste" (292, 296, 300, 303).[24]

A failure to have mastered the culture and a refusal to accept fully all its elements were not, Reuter claimed, peculiar to blacks; it was also characteristic of various immigrant groups: "Various nationalistic groups retard their advance by a sentimental determination to persist in the use of their own objectively inferior cultural elements—as the Polish refusal to accept a cultural language, or the Irish refusal to accept a protestant religion—because the alternative and superior forms originated with or are in the hands of groups toward which their nationalistic antipathy is directed" (412).

In comparing blacks with immigrant groups, Reuter always insisted that, unlike other nationalistic groups, blacks possessed only an American culture. Of this culture he said, "The institutions developed by the Negroes are more or less faithful copies of corresponding white institutions but, in the nature of the social process, they will be inferior to the originals." Furthermore, he claimed, racial isolation will ensure that inferiority: "Separate institutions are inferior institutions," for with separation the necessary processes of cultural contact and learning are inhibited. "The attention of the race-conscious Negro tends to be upon inferior models" (412–13).

If Reuter interpreted the emergence of an early form of nationalism within the black population as misguided, a development that in the long run would hinder the solving of the race problem, he did not deny its existence nor underplay its importance as a growing reality. Though he disapproved of it, he understood there were reasons for its emergence: "So long as discrimination and exclusion are general, it is folly to oppose the growth of nationality" (420–21).

Reuter, Park, and the Social-Problems Sociologists

Reuter's work in the 1920s can only be assessed by contrasting it with that of Park and with the interpretations offered by the social-problems sociologists, whose analysis of race during the 1920s revealed little change (with one exception) from what it had been over the previous three decades. That one exception was the abandonment of the hereditarian argument for the innate inferiority of blacks. Even then, however, they did not adopt a position of equality among the human races but expressed reservations about the full implications of the new genetics; Reuter was among them. Some went so far as to argue that natural selection in Africa's tropical environment had bred a race incapable of the standard of behavior required of people in a modern civilization. By such an argument they could seemingly remain consistent with science while retaining the basic assumption of the race problem, namely, that blacks were an inferior people incapable of rising to the levels of mind and skill developed by white people.

For the social-problems sociologists, the race problem then remained what it had been since Emancipation: how to make economic use of black labor while also exercising social control sufficient to ensure social harmony. Most of them advocated mild reform, namely, a further development of black labor skills (as Booker T. Washington had in the 1890s) and some improvement in the treatment of black people, that is, a small measure of fair play. Such a suggested reform was an acknowledgment that the skill potential of blacks had been underdeveloped and that social harmony was threatened by the prevalent denial of even a modest measure of fair treatment in the daily interaction between white and black people. But such reform did not contemplate any movement toward equality nor any modification of white domination.

Reuter, in turn, retained the concept of the race problem while also absorbing elements of Park's analysis. His version of the race problem retained the conventional emphasis on the disabilities of black people—poverty, illiteracy, poor family life, and the like—and the notion that these disabilities were not easily subject to change. But unlike other sociologists, who viewed blacks as unassimilable, and perhaps reflecting his long interest in racial mixing, Reuter saw the eventual elimination of blacks as a separate race by racial amalgamation. He had no timetable for what was clearly to be a long drawn-out process, and unlike Park, he did not see in the struggles of a race-conscious people any contribution to that eventual outcome. While he accepted Park's conception of a developing race consciousness and the emergence of a biracial organization, he differed from Park in his strong disapproval of such developments.

But Reuter also argued for opportunity and social justice, as well as personal dignity for the black male, to an extent rare among the sociologists of his day. He did so, however, by locating that argument within the framework of the concern for the modernizing of American society, so common to the sociologists of race relations. He insisted that a nation was held back in economic development if the potential development of 10 percent of its population was retarded by the will of the 90 percent. Whatever may have been Reuter's personal sentiments, his argument was not so much for justice in its own right, as for the granting of opportunity and some social rights for the sake of the further development of the nation.

Reuter did not share Park's deep interest in the worldwide struggle among culturally different peoples for national independence and did not locate the American race problem therein. Instead, he retained the notion of race as one of several American social problems. In narrowing the race problem to a largely noncomparative, uniquely American issue, Reuter's work encouraged the retention of a parochialism about race that was to characterize the sociological study of race relations in the United States for the next forty years.

The Sociology of Race Relations: A Vocabulary

Though Park's indifference to the concept of the race problem did not persuade other sociologists to abandon it, his own work influenced considerably a new mode of analysis. The rudiments of a conceptual vocabulary—assimilation, prejudice, social distance, minority, race and ethnic—appeared, as did the first grudging recognition that race was not only a national issue but was also becoming an urban one. What emerged from this was the outline of something that was less than a theory but more than an aggregate of concepts; a distinct American sociological perspective on race was in the making. Floyd House, a contemporary and close observer of developments in the discipline, recognized this when he noted in 1935 that the study of race had gone from the study of racial heredity and racial traits to the study of cultural traits, but now "even the realistic problems of culture traits and culture differences between racial groups may gain when studied in connection with some inquiry into race relations and their changes."[25]

Assimilation

The idea of assimilating people of divergent origins to a common culture did not originate with sociologists; rather, it emerged from a nineteenth-century debate over the qualities of each new immigrant group to reach American shores; some were defined as assimilable, some as not. For over a century, the English-descended Americans worried about the desirability and possible consequences of accepting newer people into the United States and resisted accepting those they deemed unassimilable. But ideas of the "melting pot" and "Americanization" became powerful currents of American thought even before the eugenics movement went into decline.[26]

Sociologists came to accept the concept of assimilation as their own as they absorbed the issue of immigration as a sociological specialty and contributed to the debate about it. As a consequence, assimilation became a central concept in sociology without prolonged debate and without much concern for any preciseness of definition. The first systematic sociological analysis of the concept appeared in 1901 in a very long essay by Sarah E. Simons, the niece of Lester Ward; the essay was published over five issues of the *American Journal of Sociology* in 1901 and 1902. Simons located assimilation in something less historically particular and parochial than worries about less able immigrants. Instead, she placed it in an evolutionary context of conflict brought on by migration, contact, and conquest, as Park was to do later. Assimilation was a final aspect of this process of conquest and subjugation from which came a new social order. To fit the evolutionary process, Simons defined assimilation as sharing a common language and a community of interests and as a unity of political and social ideals.[27]

In his first sociological paper in 1913, Park pointed out that it was not always clear what assimilation meant: "There is a process that goes on in society by which individuals spontaneously acquire one another's language, characteristic attitudes, habits, and modes of behavior. There is also a process by which individuals and groups of individuals are taken over and incorporated into larger groups. Both processes have been concerned in the formation of modern nationalities." Later in the same essay he defined assimilation as the process by which "we may conceive alien people to be incorporated with, and made a part of, the community or state." In 1921 he and Ernest Burgess defined assimilation as "a process of interpenetration and fusion in which persons and groups acquire the memories, sentiments, and attitudes of other persons or groups, and, by sharing their experiences and history, are incorporated with them in a common cultural life." Finally, in 1930, for the *Encyclopedia of the Social Sciences*, Park defined assimilation as "the name given to the processes by which peoples of diverse racial origins and different cultural heritages, occupying a common territory, achieve a cultural solidarity sufficient at least to sustain a national existence."[28]

The various definitions of assimilation often confused two processes, as Park first noted in his 1913 essay. One process was at the time called "the melting pot," an assimilating process for both immigrants and Anglo-Americans to produce a new culture and a new American. In the other, immigrants adopted the cultural ways they found upon arrival and shed their immigrant culture. In the 1920s this process was called "Americanization"; later, Milton Gordon was to call it "Anglo-conformity," a term he acknowledged borrowing from Stewart and Mildred Cole.[29]

Assimilation, whether seen as "the melting pot" or as "Americanization," did not, however, go uncontested among American intellectuals. From 1914 on, people as diverse as Jane Addams and John Dewey saw persisting value in immigrant cultures, while others—Randolph Bourne and Norman Hapgood, for example—argued forcefully for a culturally pluralistic democracy. But the case for cultural pluralism was most thoroughly argued by the philosopher Horace Kallen, beginning with two esssys in *The Nation* in 1915 and culminating in 1924 in his *Culture and Democracy in the United States.*[30]

While sociologists then and later were to recognize cultural pluralism as a logically possible position, they did not accept it as either desirable or realizable. They were not impressed with Kallen's claim about the value of diverse cultural heritages for enriching a still developing American culture, and they did not accept his arguments for the value of retaining cultural diversity. Diversity, they felt, encouraged separate group identities from which came hostility, stereotypes, and prejudice. For them, cultural pluralism was an anachronism, for they saw only the necessary process of assimilating individual immigrants into the larger society. The dissolving of traditional, particularistic identities was necessary to the forming of modern society.

But they were also confident that reality was on the side of assimilation; separate immigrant groups, from the first generation to the second, they observed, began to crumble before the sheer organizing force of a modern society. Perhaps among the sociologists only Herbert Miller, a student of Park's, saw merit in cultural diversity while still retaining a belief in an eventual assimilation. He thought that the problem was to discover a method of merging together "people of varying backgrounds and intense attitudes" without producing "a uniform standard society" and "with tolerance toward the varying customs and beliefs."[31]

The agreement between sociologists and most Americans on the desirability of assimilation, however, did not carry over to the case of blacks and Asians. For the vast majority of white Americans, racial assimilation was unthinkable, and any assertion of its possibility met with an implacable, even hostile reception. Most sociologists accepted with little evident regret the segregation of a people still deemed vastly inferior and saw no possible change in the foreseeable future. But even those few who did see a need for greater change were intimidated by their assessment of an unassailable wall of prejudice in the present and for some time to come. Consequently, they had little advice on goals and programs, beyond that of education and interracial cooperation within the structure of an unchallenged racial segregation, to offer to a society entering a period of rapid, unsettling change.[32]

Prejudice

If Edward Reuter saw cultural backwardness of the mass of blacks as one aspect of race as a social problem, he also recognized that it was the prejudice of the white majority that made cultural advance so difficult for blacks. In the 1920s American sociologists could not avoid being impressed with the depth and power of the prejudice toward black Americans held by most white people and their seemingly intractable opposition to any conception of black progress, to any notion of greater social opportunity, or to any realization of the civil rights guaranteed in the Fourteenth and Fifteenth Amendments to the Constitution.

When sociologists first began to make use of the concept of prejudice, it was prejudice as a more basic aspect of human nature and a constant element in the relations between cultural and racial groups that concerned them. Very early in the century W. I. Thomas had put forth a conception of race prejudice as essentially biological. He defined it as an instinct of hate, which grew out of experience, was "intense and immediate," incapable of being reasoned with, and "localized in a prejudice felt for the characteristic appearance of others." Such a notion of an innate aversion to others fitted the biological perspective still dominant in 1904. At the same time, Thomas argued that southern antipathy to the black was a matter of "caste-feeling," while it was the Northerner who exhibited true race prejudice, a "skin-prejudice" occurring as a consequence of racial separation in contrast to the intimacy that once prevailed between master and slave. He also added a conception of prejudice as expressing in-group sympathies and out-group antipathies and aversions, a "tendency to exhalt the self and the group at the expense of outsiders."[33]

Robert Park took over this conception of prejudice from Thomas, his longtime friend and colleague, and for some time prejudice as instinctive response underwent little change in Park's work. In 1917 he referred to prejudice "as a spontaneous more or less instinctive defense-reaction," and in the mid-1920s he was still defining it as a "more or less instinctive and spontaneous disposition to maintain social differences." By 1917 Park was well aware that anthropologists disputed the idea that prejudice was innate, and he disputed them: "It has been assumed that the prejudice which blinds the people of one race to the virtues of another, and leads them to exaggerate the other's faults, is in the nature of a misunderstanding which further knowledge will dispel. This is so far from true that it would be more exact to say that our racial misunderstandings are merely the expression of our racial antipathies. Behind these antipathies are deep-seated, vital, and instinctive impulses."[34]

Even as Park was still invoking the concept of instincts, however, others were effectively undermining it as a scientific concept. A younger generation of animal pychologists, notable among whom was John B. Watson, criticized the concept of instinct as a heritage of a philosophical psychology lacking experimental evidence. But sociologists also were active in challenging the scientific validity of the idea of innate instincts controlling human behavior; notable among them were Luther Lee Bernard, Ellsworth A. Faris, and Park's student, Herbert A. Miller. A new generation in both psychology and sociology were receptive to these criticisms and committed to building their disciplines around experimental evidence (as in psychology) or by original social investigation (as in sociology). In a remarkably short period of time, therefore, the concept of instinct lost its once dominant status in both psychology and sociology, and by the mid-1920s it had been rejected by most psychologists and sociologists.[35] Though the concept of instinct had only limited use in the debate about race—its significance was in an instinctive conception of prejudice—its rejection meant that another support for the hereditarian argument was removed.

By 1928, however, Park had moved from instincts to attitudes; prejudice, he said, "is an attitude, a social attitude." What he had once called instinct he now viewed as the first aspect of developing a prejudice: "The fact seems to be that what we ordinarily regard as instinctive, and biologically determined in our behavior and attitudes toward peoples and races other than our own, is merely, in the first instance at least, the spontaneous response ... to what is strange and unfamiliar." The approach of the stranger inspires a sense of insecurity, which, if not dispelled by intimate acquaintance, crystallizes into an attitude. Sentiments arise, and the "racial mark," usually skin color, becomes a symbol of these sentiments. In this situation there occurs "the most irrational, and at the same time the most invincible, elements in racial prejudice."[36] If Park had abandoned instincts, he nonetheless had transferred the contents of the concept of instinctive prejudice into the concept of attitude.

Finally, Park was now analyzing prejudice as a social phenomenon, a phenomenon of change of status: "Prejudice ... is merely the resistance of the social order to change" and so "is merely an elementary expression of conservatism." When there is change, there is conflict, said Park, and conflict arouses animosities. But animosity and prejudice need to be distinguished, for animosities arise in conflict. But when conflict ceases and an accommodation is achieved, animosity subsides: "On the other hand, the racial prejudices, which are the basis of this hostility, may and often do persist."[37]

While Park was for the first time defining prejudice as a social phenomenon, this was not the first time he had assigned it a social function. In 1919, when he still defined race prejudice as an instinct, he put its "practical effect" in economic terms: to "restrict free competition between races." In 1924, when he still saw race prejudice as instinctive, he said that "prejudice ... seems to arise when, not our economic interests, but our social status is menaced." Whatever contradiction or change of mind may be apparent here, Park was consistent in his view that prejudice was "a conservative force, a sort of spontaneous conservation which tends to preserve the social order and the social distances upon which that order rests."[38]

For Reuter, as for Park, prejudice could not easily be changed; it was a highly tenacious and sustaining element in social life, not easily susceptible to alteration. While prejudices were certainly modifiable by changes in cultural conditions and in the structure of race relations, these changes could only occur slowly. Reuter's sense of how difficult it would be to alter prejudice was made evident by his summary statement on prejudice in the concluding chapter of *The American Race Problem*:

> What it is meant to emphasize here is, on the one hand, the futility of the numerous romantic programs that either do not see prejudice as a reality or assume that it will disappear in the presence of sentimentality and, on the other hand, the positive disutility of the militant programs and solutions depending for success upon the overriding of such prejudices or their destruction by direct frontal attack. Prejudice is a reality in the racial situation.

It is not less real and probably not less permanent than the physical marks of race. A practical program must accept it as a primary datum.[39]

During the 1920s, then, the concept of racial prejudice was transformed from a biological instinct to a social attitude. According to Park and Reuter, it was a tenacious and enduring component of group life that could not be easily or quickly eliminated or even altered. Its function was defensive and conservative, protecting the social interests of more advantaged groups against less advantaged ones. For that first generation of sociologists of race relations, the concept of prejudice was primarily a group term, invoking a concept of group consciousness. A later generation of social psychologists, of course, would in time redefine prejudice as an attribute of the individual, consistent with the social psychological tendencies of thought characteristic of American society.

Park recognized that prejudice led individuals from different groups to limit to a greater or lesser extent their interaction with one another. To capture sociologically this process of distancing, Park created the concept of *social distance,* which he called an attempt "to reduce to something like measurable terms the grades and degrees of understanding and intimacy which characterize personal and social relations generally." A sense of distance was not only felt by one person toward another person, "but we have much the same feeling with regard to classes and races." Emory Bogardus then developed a scale to measure quantitatively the sense of distance that individuals felt toward members of various ethnic and racial groups.[40] The idea fitted well the growing interest in quantitative measurement, but it also gave a strong boost to the impetus to develop a social psychological perspective on race, a reflection of the individualizing undercurrent never absent from American sociology.

In a short period of time, the concept of social distance took on a life of its own. What Bogardus had begun with his effort to measure social distance was to become in less than two decades a major preoccupation: to construct a quantitative measurement of prejudice. Such measurement, in fact, became a major and enduring way in which prejudice was accounted for as a significant factor in race relations. The prejudices of dominant groups were defined as measurable attitudinal variables and correlated with other social factors, like age, education, religion, occupation and class, among others. In a short time, this social psychological dimension of race relations was to expand enormously as one type of research, one body of literature, and one perspective on race relations.

The Black and the City

What was inescapable to most sociologists in the 1920s was the unwelcome recognition that American race relations, as process and as problem, were going to be worked out in the urban North, not in the rural South. In cities such as Chicago a new urban form of race relations was emerging. It appeared to be volatile and unstable, with much potential for confrontation and violence, as the Chicago race riot of 1919 demonstrated. This new development, sociologists readily understood, was the consequence of the massive migration of blacks from south to north, and no less significantly, from a rural to an urban setting. In 1910 there were 637,000 blacks in cities of the North and West; by 1930 there were 2,228,000.[41] The industrial cities of the North were rapidly becoming a new location for the reworking of American race relations.

For many sociologists, this vast black migration northward was viewed with alarm. In part this was because many of them still considered city life to be morally inferior to rural life, but also because blacks were thought to be incapable of adjusting adequately to the complex demands of an urban existence. Clarence Ellwood, for example, believed that blacks were better suited to agricultural than to industrial labor, while John Gillin, Clarence Dittmer, and Roy Colbert argued that blacks were better treated in the South than in the industrial cities of the North, where they could not "find anywhere more bitter enemies." They described housing for blacks in the city as even worse than on the plantation, and urban life as possessing a stress and strain that produced insanity and mental breakdown, a high infant-mortality rate, and a death rate higher than in the South. John Commons, in turn, insisted that city life "works its degenerating effects" and that northern blacks are twice as likely to go to prison for a crime as were their southern counterparts.[42]

In 1928, however, two empirical studies appeared, which, though different from one another, had the same basic concern: residential segregation in northern cities. The first of these, *Negro Problems in Cities* by T. J. Woofter, Jr., a southern sociologist, stressed that the "urbanization of the Negro population . . . involves a profound cultural change and demands multiple adjustments." His analysis focused on a residential density that produced overcrowding, deteriorating housing, and moral decline. It also produced "strains on racial goodwill. The expansion of Negro residence areas has frequently occasioned intense friction similar to that which resulted in the Chicago riots." Such observations seemed much like those of Ellwood, Gillin, and Commons, but Woofter was more optimistic, suggesting there would be a long-run process of segregation, neglect, then self-improvement and amelioration. But his more significant point was that northward migration of blacks produced a new, urban form of racial segregation by residential areas, those "more or less solid colonies."[43]

The notion of an urban racial colony was an obvious extension of the idea of the immigrant colony, by now a well-established conceptualization of the clustering of immigrants in single-ethnic neighborhoods. The work on the ecological patterning of the city, which Robert Park and his colleague, Ernest Burgess, pioneered at Chicago, provided a new theoretical context for interpreting residential patterning. Burgess developed the idea that the expanding city became segregated into *natural areas,* functional for sorting out populations and diverse social activities and processes, and developed largely by competition for space. Such sorting out created both the slum and the ethnic neighborhood. Burgess developed his famous *zonal hypothesis* to give an ideal type expression to this patterning as processual growth.[44]

The second study was by Louis Wirth, a University of Chicago student, whose 1926 dissertation on the Jewish community in Chicago became his book, *The Ghetto.* While the book provided a detailed analysis of the Jewish ghetto in Chicago, it also noted the generalization of the term to cover any immigrant or racial group new to the city: "In our American population the ghetto refers particularly to the area of first settlement, i.e., those sections of the city where the immigrant finds his home shortly after his arrival in America. . . . Morever, there seems to be a tendency to refer to immigrant quarters in general as ghettoes." In the American context, then, ghetto also meant the "Little Sicilies, Chinatowns, and Black Belts in our large cities." Its spatial segregation protected it and secured its survival but also set it apart in persistent social differences: "The ghetto, therefore, may be regarded as a form of accommodation between divergent population groups, through which one group has effectually subordinated itself to another. It represented at least one historical form of dealing with a dissenting minority within a larger population. At the same time it is a form of toleration through which a *modus vivendi* is established between groups that are in conflict with each other on fundamental issues. Finally, from the administrative standpoint, the ghetto served as an instrument of control."[45]

Wirth had now formulated a conception of the urban ghetto, both ethnic and racial, for sociological analysis. Ghettos had no assured permanency in the shifting ecological pattern of the city. Their formation and dissolution over generations, their sustaining of a cultural life among a subordinate and even oppressed people, their fitting into an urban accommodation of differentials of power and status, provided a new accommodative basis for the working out of new processes of assmiliation. In a few decades, *ghetto* was to become the common designation for the black residential area in the larger American city, its European origins largely forgotten.

Completing the Vocabulary: Minority, Race and Ethnic

During the 1920s the concept of *minority* had been used only incidentally and without definition or specificity. But in Europe it had been used to refer to the suppressed racial and national groups in eastern Europe. In his *Races, Nations and Classes,* Herbert Miller quoted from the "Declaration of Independence of the Czechoslovak Nation": "The rights of the minority shall be safeguarded by proportional representation; national minorities shall enjoy equal rights." But *minority* had also been used by some American sociologists. As early as 1913, in analyzing the European situation, Park spoke of nationalities as "intractable minorities engaged in a ruthless partisan struggle." Reuter said that whites viewed blacks as a "culturally backward minority." Louis Wirth, in turn, referred to the ghetto as "one historical form of dealing with a dissenting minority in a large population."[46]

The change from incidental term to central concept, however, was the act of someone outside the Chicago school. In 1932 Donald Young, a sociologist at the University of Pennsylvania, titled his new text *American Minority Peoples.* In the foreword he stated his intention to give "a new perspective to academic discussions of American race relations." The already numerous literature, he pointed out, had conveyed the impression that "Negro-white relations are one thing, while Jewish-Gentile, Oriental-white, and other race relations are vastly different from each other." It was his view that "the problems and principles of race relations are remarkably similar, regardless of what groups are involved; and that only by an integrated study of all minority peoples in the United States can a real understanding and sociological analysis of the involved social phenomena be achieved."[47]

Young's choice of a new term was dictated, in part at least, by the discrepancy between scientific and popular usages of the term *race.* Popular beliefs, he noted, still lump "biological, language, cultural, political, and other groups under the one heading of 'race,' ": "There is, unfortunately, no word in the English language which can with philological propriety be applied to all these groups, that is, which includes groups which are distinguished by biological features, alien cultural traits, or a combination of both. For this reason, the phrases, 'minorities of racial or national origin,' 'American minorities,' or 'minority peoples' are used as synonyms for the popular usage of the word race."[48]

Young's introduction of the concept of minority was intended to create a conceptual category adequate for racial groups, on the one hand, and cultural groups, whether ethnic or religious, on the other. Because it suggested that sociologists could in time construct an encompassing theory accounting in general terms for biologically and culturally different groups, which appealed to their scientific and theoretical ambitions, the concept proved attractive and soon became a permanent part of the vocabulary of the sociologists of race relations.

Nonetheless, however ready sociologists were to make use of the concept of minority, there remained with them a sense of the historic uniqueness of the place of blacks in the generally homogenizing American culture, which led them to speak of race and something else: immigrants, nations or nationalities, or culture. Thus, there were two conflicting purposes apparent in the search for an appropriate vocabulary: first, to emphasize the theoretical commonality of the social relations being analyzed; second, to keep the focus on quite different historical trajectories of development of different peoples in the United States. The later European immigrants and the blacks had reached the United States at different historical times and under different circumstances, and in the 1920s and 1930s their futures also seemed to be different. Assimilation was already under way for one, but it was too far off for the other to be a matter of practical import.

In 1931 T. J. Woofter's essay entitled "The Status of Racial and Ethnic Groups" introduced a new set of paired terms. Woofter followed that in 1933 with a book entitled *Race and Ethnic Groups in American Life*.[49] As a term for the less precise one of cultural group or nationality, which obviously had other possible meanings than that of a subordinated group, *ethnic*, when paired with *race*, was soon to became the accepted term in a developing vocabulary of race relations. In time the paired terms were widely used as titles for books and college courses.

By the mid-1930s a vocabulary for a sociological perspective on race relations had been put into place. *Assimilation* was the central term, specifying what was assumed to be the inevitable and necessary outcome of the process of modernizing American society. Since "modern" was clearly desirable, as well as inevitable, assimilation always carried with it a normative component. *Prejudice*, in turn, served as the counterterm to assimilation; it defined the white population's conception of blacks (and other nonwhite peoples) as unassimilable, an inferior people not to be granted equality. Park's idea of *social distance* began the process of measuring prejudice by degrees toward a plurality of racial and ethnic groups, which was to lead eventually to the psychologizing of the term. *Ghetto* became a term to characterize the developing pattern of residential segregation of blacks in northern cities, though in the early 1930s, "ghetto" was not as widely used by sociologists as it would be after World War II.

The adoption of the term *minority* spoke to the theoretical impulse to incorporate race into a larger conceptual framework, one encompassing all people whose assimilation into a dominant culture was hindered by the prejudicial refusal by those of dominant status to accept them. *Race* and *ethnic,* in contrast, reflected the practical recognition that blacks and European immigrants were too different in social origin, historical development, prejudiced definition (the visibility of skin color did make a difference), and contemporary status to subsume them wholly under an encompassing concept like minority. There seemed still to be a need to speak separately about blacks; what sociologists thought of as America's distinctive race problem required its own conceptual organization—a sociology of race relations—that spoke to the historical importance of race in the American experience. This ambivalence between an encompassing framework provided by the concept of a minority and the felt need to address race as a historically particular but crucial issue for Americans was to remain characteristic of American sociology from then on.

Segregation and Discrimination

Two terms that need special comment here are *segregation* and *discrimination. Segregation* was present and used in the new vocabulary, but neither frequently nor consistently, and unlike *assimilation* and *prejudice,* it was not a key term. That was primarily because segregation had not yet become a political or legal issue; it was widely practiced, still constitutionally sanctioned, and largely taken for granted as a settled feature of relations between the races. Park spoke, not of segregation, but of isolation, while Reuter spoke of cultural isolation; both were concerned primarily with the effect of isolation on the social development of the black population. But Reuter also spoke of segregation, as in the "segregation movement" and "enforced segregation and cultural exclusion." In his book on blacks in the city, T. J. Woofter titled a chapter "Racial Separation," wherein he made reference to forces attempting "to segregate Negroes from white neighborhoods, though the separation is seldom entirely complete." He also provided a discussion of "segregation ordinances." In his study of the ghetto, Wirth said that *ghetto* referred to "any segregated racial or cultural group," though, like Park and Reuter, he was primarily interested in the effects of the ghetto's isolation on its inhabitants.[50]

In the early 1930s, then, at the outset of the new sociology of race relations, terms like racial isolation and separation were used as much as racial segregation. Not until the fact of segregation was a political and judicial issue, and its practice morally condemned, would segregation become a central concept in the sociology of race relations.

If *segregation* was at least present in the sociological vocabulary, though not yet a central concept, *discrimination* was rarely evident in sociological discourse. It had not yet been paired with *prejudice*. The latter was a concept for the set of beliefs held by whites that defined blacks as unassimilable and unworthy of equal treatment. The details of the behavior that prejudice explained seemed unnecessary to delineate from other behavior; even in the North, little of such prejudicial behavior was illegal. What was later called discrimination was widely practiced and largely regarded as normative by white people. The idea of equal opportunity, for which discrimination was a violation, had as yet no place in white thought, except perhaps for some very few, and was not an issue of public discussion. That was to come later; only then would *discrimination* enter the sociological vocabulary and be paired with *prejudice*.

Race Relations: An Interpretive Consensus

By the mid-1930s the emerging sociology of race relations had a vocabulary that expressed a perspective on race that differed from that of the race problem. It did so in two significant ways: first, it no longer defined blacks as innately inferior and therefore unassimilable; and second, by the importance it attached to the concept of prejudice, it opened the way to shift the responsibility for the status of blacks onto the prejudiced whites, instead of placing it wholly on the incapacities of a presumably inferior people. This was a bold break with past interpretation, particularly in a decade when racial intolerance was widely and sometimes punitively expressed.

But the new sociologists of race relations did not break completely with the past. Instead, they retained the idea of the race problem, though modifying it to eliminate the biological assumptions on which it had rested for so long. They replaced biological inferiority with cultural inferiority, and in doing so they sustained the older, denigrating image of black people they had inherited from the social-problems sociologists. Furthermore, in the face of an implacable white prejudice, they offered no strategies of intervention and kept their distance from those who did. Yet they also believed that racial progress for black people was being made, if very slowly, and that the order of racial domination created after slavery could not persist. The new sociology of race relations, it would seem, did not replace the race problem but redefined it.

All of this was indicative of an interpretive consensus growing among the sociologists of race relations. They now shared a newly formulated vocabulary and an interpretive perspective that vocabulary provided. Less apparent though no less significant in the shaping of that interpretive consensus were two other matters: first, the exclusion of Park's concept of racial conflict from the sociology of race relations; and second, the use of science as a protective haven in a world unsympathetic to any new interpretation of race relations.

Park and Racial Conflict

The shaping of an interpetive consensus is always a selective process, one of including and excluding from among the ideas and themes offered for consideration. Accordingly, what is excluded from consideration can be as significant as what is included. This proved to be the case in selecting concepts for the sociology of race relations. What was not included in the emerging perspective was recognition of racial conflict as anything but an early phase of race relations, succeeded in time by accommodative and assimilative processes. But defining racial conflict in this way simplified and distorted the seminal thought about racial conflict offered by Robert Park in a number of essays from both early and late in his career.

Despite his late arrival on the academic scene, Park shared with the sociologists of the first generation the theoretical conviction that explanatory primacy should be given to struggle and conflict in the effort to explain social change and societal development.[51] From the beginning of his sociological work, Park's basic position was that race relations were relations of conflict among race-conscious groups, and he never deviated from or modified that position. Conflict, for Park, was inherent in the very nature of race relations. A full reading of his essays on race relations reveals that he continuously stressed the significance of racial struggle.

Park believed that black Americans were a race-conscious people struggling to create a world of their own out of the constrained circumstances of their lives. As early as 1913 he noted that "the world of the black man is silently taking form and shape" and that the black "has begun to fashion his own ideals and in his own image, rather than in that of the white man."[52] But for other sociologists, there was not a race-conscious black, there was only a black peasant, too culturally backward to be capable of rational, self-interested action. Unlike Park, they could not envision blacks reshaping the dominant white culture to express meanings derived from their own experiences, and, in doing so, constructing a cultural life of their own within the oppressive circumstances of racial segregation. Not until about 1970 did sociologists come to recognize the existence of a culture expressive of a distinctive black experience in the United States.

Park's comparison of a budding race consciousness among American blacks to the struggles of submerged Slavic nationalities in eastern Europe was intended "merely as an indication of similarities, in the broadest outlines, of the motives that have produced nationalities in Europe and are making the Negro in America, as Booker T. Washington says, 'a nation within a nation.' " One consequence of this, Park thought, was the emergence of "a vertical organization in which all classes of each racial group are united under the title of their respective nationalities."[53] From such an organization came the basis for effective struggle. Though circumstances for blacks changed over time, struggle continued in altered form. The movement of blacks northward into cities and into urban politics, the growth of a black middle class, the establishment of a black press, the expressive writing of black intellectuals and artists, all these contributed to a race-conscious context for a continuing racial conflict.

Given Park's emphasis on assimilation as the end point of race relations, sociologists influenced by Park, including his students, seemed to think that this nationalistic imagery of racial conflict was only a minor or an earlier and eventually surpassed theme in Park's work. But the rhetoric of racial struggle evident in Park's first paper in 1913 continued over the next thirty years, until his last essay on race relations in 1943, a few months before his death. He asserted there that "the races and peoples which fate has brought together in America and within the limits of a larger world economy will continue, in the emerging world society, their struggles for a political and a racial equality that was denied them in the world that is passing." He also claimed that "we may expect, therefore, that no matter how great the changes the war brings, that racial and cultural conflicts will continue in some form or other in the future as in the past."[54]

This concern for racial struggle was not, in Park's mind, a contradiction or repudiation of assimilation, which he always thought to be the ultimate outcome of a long process of cultural evolution. But the struggle of a racial group, and the conflict that struggle produced, was always a necessary process in achieving assimilation. Park possessed a sophisticated sense of the relations between conflict and assimilation that his colleagues seemed to lack. They saw racial assimilation as eventually producing black Anglo-Americans. They also read the race relations cycle quite literally as a series of steps or stages, in which conflict was an earlier one and assimilation the final one. If assimilation was already an ongoing process, then conflict was no longer a serious factor, or so they were predisposed to believe.

While his colleagues and students concentrated almost exclusively on race relations in the United States, Park viewed race conflict as a worldwide process, of which the American case was but a historical instance. That process was but one dimension of a modern world "which seems destined to bring presently all the diverse and distant peoples of the earth together within the limits of a common culture and a common social order." There will be "a diversity of peoples in the modern world," based "in the future less on inheritance and race and rather more on culture and occupation. That means that race conflicts in the modern world, which is already or presently will be a single great society, will be more and more in the future confused with, and eventually superseded by, the conflicts of classes."[55]

By the time Park retired in 1934, however, conflict was no longer a central concept for a new generation of sociologists. Even in the mid-1920s, there seems to have been no one among Park's younger colleagues and students to take up his concern for the significance of conflict in race relations. Influenced less by the first generation so steeped in evolutionary ideas, they absorbed the intellectual atmosphere created by John Dewey and the other pragmatic philosophers, who shunned ideas of struggle and conflict and put their confidence in the reforming potential of education and the reasoning mind.

In 1930, when Howard Odum was president of the American Sociological Society, social conflict was made the thematic topic at the meetings of the society, as it had been in 1907. But this time, as Lewis Coser noted, "the proceedings gave the distinct impression that the study of social conflict was no longer considered a central concern by the members of the Society." Coser contrasted a first generation of sociologists focusing on conflict because they were interested in change and "progress" and were reformers addressing a reform-minded audience, to a later generation oriented to "purely academic and professional audiences" or attempting "to find a hearing among decision-makers in public and private bureaucracies." Instead of conflict, they centered attention on problems of adjustment, on "the maintenance of existing structures," and on "maladjustments and tensions which interfere with consensus. Where the older generation discussed the need for structural change, the new generation dealt with adjustment of individuals to given structures."[56]

Beginning in the 1920s, then, a newly professionalizing sociology, seeking to establish itself as a science and also to secure its acceptance as a legitimate discipline within the university, neither of which came easily, discarded the reform interests of its first generation and turned its efforts to the establishing of a different relationship to American society. In such an effort, there was little value to be placed on the study of social conflict.

Race: Still the Intractable Problem

The efforts of sociologists to study race relations, according to Donald Young, was a "thankless task," arousing suspicions of minorities sensitive to observations not reflecting credit on them and resented by a majority both contemptuous and fearful of the minorities:

> Man is an impatient animal, eager for solutions of social ills and disdainful of academicians' surveys, hypotheses, analyses, and theories. Action, not cautious and laborious research, is demanded of those who would lead the populace. Thus, a Chamberlain, a Gobineau, or a Stoddard attracts myriads of followers of a pseudo-scientific program based on a doctrine of God-given white supremacy—each with its favorite subdivision of the white race— while the very names of Franz Boas, Eugene Pittard, Frederich Hertz, and other scholarly students of the peoples of the world are unknown outside of a small intellectual circle.[57]

It was not that race did not attract attention. "Few subjects," noted Edward Reuter, "have claimed a larger amount of attention in the magazines of general circulation." Nor has any issue been more widely debated. But whatever the point of view, it has been "prevailingly doctrinaire and the discussion impressionistic," and the numerous writings provide "remarkably little of practical significance or scientific value" (*American Race Problem*, 2–3).

More than that, the race problem did not fit the usual distinction so comfortable to academicians, that between an educated class, which accepted and absorbed scientific knowledge, and an uneducated class, which, instead, seemed to so many academicians to interpret the world from a perspective shaped by superstition, religion, and a commonsense unleavened by any significant degree of learning. But on matters of race, the uneducated included the educated. Prejudice seemed an insurmountable barrier just because it was so tenaciously exercised by almost all whites, not just the uneducated.

Because they viewed race as an intractable problem sustained by a fixed, prevailing prejudice, and because they perceived a compelling need for cultural assimilation to complete the modernizing of American society, and also because they recognized that the analysis of race relations was still a thankless task, the sociologists of race relations developed a self-conscious assessment of the difficult intellectual task required of them, of their own relations to society, and, accordingly, a rationale for their particular enterprise. To understand that rationale requires an understanding of how they made use of the concept of science.

The sociologists of race relations shared with other sociologists a profound commitment to science and a claim to be shaping sociology into a new science. The appropriate stance for the sociologist of race relations, as for all sociologists, could only be the scientific one, not that of reformer or special pleader, and nothing must budge the sociologist from presenting the dispassionate analysis. Indeed, the scientific interest, noted Reuter, was the "only practical one: to discover the mechanisms, the causal relations, in social phenomena and to provide a basis for social and administrative techniques" (18). Here, of course, was an echo of the Progressive movement: reform was to be an administrative responsibility.

Sociologists could also understand but not make common cause with racial movements or groups, for the objectives of such groups were too partisan, and they did not comprehend how their struggles fitted into the process of modernizing society. But neither had the sociologists any natural allies among the prejudiced majority. If, then, one were not partisan with the minority but did not share (at least fully) the prejudices of the majority, the standpoint of objective science provided perhaps the best defensible position for a sociological analysis of the race problem.

Always assiduously apolitical, sociologists put a safe distance between themselves and the passions of racial conflict and partisanship. Yet, within the posture of scientific objectivity, they purported to know what had yet to be done and the cost of not doing it. Their target of scientific persuasion became the better educated members of society, for they, however prejudiced, were presumed to be potentially persuadable by the logic and evidence of science. A careful reading of both Reuter's and Young's books, for example, reveals them to be making cautious arguments directed toward white college students— the future educated class—whose prejudice was assumed but not criticized, and who were presumed to be persuadable. Young readily acknowledged that his book was "written for the native white majority."[58]

Whatever assumptions about the persuadability of white people existed among the sociologists of race relations in the 1930s, one commonality of thought was evident: none of them believed that racial assimilation was anything but a distant and ultimate goal, not at present a practical issue. All of them, accordingly, believed that white domination, solidified by an unyielding prejudice, was a reality unalterable by any feasible measure or by the challenge of a militant minority. Such a perception of the reality of race relations in the United States meant that sociologists were able to offer nothing programmatic beyond what had been suggested since Booker T. Washington—namely, a little more training and somewhat less oppressive treatment. They often spoke disparagingly (as did Reuter) of black activists and white reformers, or at the most, viewed reform as accomplishing only the correction of injustices so outrageous as to be unacceptable even to the prejudiced (as did Young).[59]

Despite this pessimism about the possibilities of racial change, most sociologists (Park included) still insisted that progress was being made, however slowly. Gains in education and income, the growth of a black middle class, a decline in lynching, and some evidence of a developing racial tolerance, for example, were offered as modest but real evidence of progress. Even Reuter, one of the more pessimistic about the possibilities of racial progress, and believing that further racial exclusion was possible, anticipated "an increased tolerance in intellectual and cosmopolitan circles." Young, in turn, argued that the only feasible adjustment was to recognize the impossibility of racial equality but to provide genuine opportunities for blacks to develop their potentialities within a compromise between absolute caste and absolute equality.[60]

By the early 1930s, a new perspective on the unsettled matter of race in American society was taking shape among the sociologists of race relations. A new vocabulary was the basis for an interpretive consensus that centered around the concepts of assimilation and prejudice. The former stated what had to be done with minority populations to shape a modern society, while the latter expressed the implacable opposition of the white population to the assimilation of nonwhites. In the face of what sociologists saw as an insurmountable barrier of white prejudice, they counted racial progress in terms of small, incremental gains, while putting assimilation off into some distant future.

Yet the emergence of the sociology of race relations in that period did not fully eliminate the older conception of the race problem, which stayed alive among those sociologists who were still trying to build a newer case for notions of innate inferiority, though such a case was becoming harder to develop and increasingly less acceptable to their sociological colleagues. But it also stayed alive because, except for Park, sociologists believed that black people were culturally inferior, incapable of acting rationally on their own behalf. Race was still the white man's burden.

Postscript: A New Negro

During the 1920s the sociologists of race relations were fully aware that blacks were moving northward into the cities. Yet they remained reluctant to examine that critical process beyond the limited treatment offered by T. J. Woofter in his *Negro Problems in Cities*. But black intellectuals, social scientists, and artists understood full well that here was more than a migration; it was a transition bringing about a "new Negro," an urban black freed from the bondage of the rural South, far more hopeful and expectant, living in a new milieu from which was coming forth a new black identity, not an absorption into white identities.

In 1925 this sense of a new Negro in a new world found brilliant expression in *The New Negro,* an anthology of essays and literary work that exemplified the spirit and talent of the Harlem Renaissance. The aim of the volume, according to Alain Locke, its editor, was "to register the transformations of the inner and outer life of the Negro in America that have so significantly taken place in the last few years. There is ample evidence of a New Negro in the latest phases of social change and progress, but still more in the internal world of the Negro mind and spirit."[61]

In *The New Negro,* Charles Johnson, then still in New York as editor of the Urban League's journal, *Opportunity,* offered an insightful sociological commentary on what changes had occurred in a black people only recently removed from the rigid structure of southern race relations. He followed this with an exploration of the changes underway in the economy of the industrial city, in which he saw the coming of a new Negro:

The workers of the South and the West Indies who have come to the cities of the North with vagrant desires and impulses, their endowments of skill and strength, their repressions and the tell-tale marks of backward cultures, with all the human wastes of the process, have directed shafts of their native energy into the cities' life and growth. They are becoming a part of it. The restive spirit which brought them has been neither all absorbed nor wasted. Over two-thirds of all the businesses operated by Negroes in New York are conducted by migrant Negroes. They are in the schools—they are the radicals and this is hopeful. The city Negro—an unpredictable mixture of all possible temperaments—is yet in evolution.[62]

Johnson, later at Fisk to become the sociological student of race relations trained by Robert Park, understood better than did Edward Reuter the meaning of the Garvey movement underway in that decade, and he appreciated its significance:

The Garvey movement itself is an exaggeration of this current mood which attempts to reduce these vague longings to concrete symbols of faith. In this great sweep of the Negro population are comprehended the awkward gestures of Negroes for an independent status, the revolt against a culture which has but partially (and again unevenly) digested the Negro masses—the black peasants least of all. It finds a middle ground in the feelings of kinship with all oppressed dark peoples, as articulated so forcefully by the Negro press, and takes, perhaps, its highest expression in the objectives of the Pan-African Congress.[63]

The New Negro provided a clear indication that a black person marked by race pride and self-respect had created a new atmosphere in such a place as Harlem and was doing the same in Chicago and other cities. Blacks were now northern and urban and were remaking their racial identity in terms of new aspirations and possibilities found in the metropolis. But sociologists were proving to be slow to grasp the meaning of this development. As Alain Locke observed, "The Sociologist, the Philanthropist, the Race-leader are not unaware of the New Negro, but they are at a loss to account for him. He cannot be swathed in their formulae."[64] Indeed, the sociologists' formula did not allow for more than a temporary and dubious race consciousness, seen (except by Park) as hindering the path to ultimate assimilation. Yet, in the decade of the 1920s, there began the formation of a new black urban culture, a black urban community, and an urban experience that St. Clair Drake and Horace Cayton were to describe so brilliantly some twenty years later. All of that would become fully manifest in the black rebellion of the 1960s.

Notes

1. In 1928, for example, the noted historian Charles Beard produced a volume of essays for which he chose an anthropologist to provide one on race. See George Dorsey, "Race and Civilization," in *Whither Mankind: A Panorama of Modern Civilization,* ed. Charles A. Beard (New York: Longmans Green 1928), 229–63.

2. Park's ideas about evolution are explicated in the first three chapters of his *Race and Culture,* ed. Everett C. Hughes et al. (New York: Free Press, 1950).

3. For a full-scale, sympathetic biography of Park, see Fred R. Mathews, *Quest for an American Sociology: Robert E. Park and the Chicago School* (Montreal: McGill-Queen's University Press, 1977). See also Winifred Raushenbush, *Robert E. Park: Biography of a Sociologist* (Durham, N.C.: Duke University Press, 1979).

4. Floyd Nelson House, *The Development of Sociology* (New York: McGraw-Hill, 1936), 310–11.

5. See Robert E. Park and Ernest W. Burgess, *An Introduction to the Science of Sociology* (Chicago: University of Chicago Press, 1921), 506–10.

6. Park, *Race and Culture,* vii–viii.

7. Ibid., vii.

8. Robert E. L. Faris, *Chicago Sociology, 1920–1932* (Chicago: University of Chicago Press, 1970), 131.

9. James T. Carey, *Sociology and Public Affairs: The Chicago School* (Beverly Hills, Calif.: Sage Publications, 1975), 154; Mathews, *Quest,* 176–77.

10. Mathews, *Quest,* 176; Chicago Commission on Race Relations, *The Negro in Chicago* (Chicago: University of Chicago Press, 1922), 640–51, 520–94.

11. Mathews, *Quest,* 80–81.

12. Ibid., 188–89.

13. Park, *Race and Culture,* 150.

14. Ibid.

15. George Eaton Simpson and J. Milton Yinger, *Racial and Cultural Minorities: An Analysis of Prejudice and Discrimination* (New York: Harper and Brothers, 1953). For a later critique of the race relations cycle, see Amitai Etzioni, "The Ghetto—A Re-evaluation," *Social Forces* 37 (Mar. 1959): 255–62.

16. Park, *Race and Culture,* 138–51; Romanzo Adams, *Interracial Marriage in Hawaii* (New York: MacMillan, 1937).

17. Park, *Race and Culture,* 194–95.

18. Ibid., 186.

19. Ibid., 217–19.

20. Ibid., 218–20.

21. Ibid., 243.

22. Ibid., 144.

23. Edward Byron Reuter, *The American Race Problem: A Study of the Negro* (New York: Thomas Y. Crowell, 1927). Further references to this work will appear in the text.

24. For Park's far greater appreciation of black literature, see his essay, "Negro Consciousness as Reflected in Race Literature," *Race and Culture*, 284–300.

25. Floyd House, "Viewpoints and Methods in the Study of Race Relations," *American Journal of Sociology* 40 (Nov. 1935): 449.

26. For a discussion of the early interest in assimilation in the United States, see Stow Persons, *Ethnic Studies at Chicago* (Urbana: University of Illinois, 1987), chapter 1.

27. Sarah E. Simons, "Social Assimilation," *American Journal of Sociology* 6 (1900–1901): 790–822; 7 (1901–2): 53–79, 234–48, 386–404, 539–56.

28. Park, *Race and Culture*, 204; Park and Burgess, *Science of Society*, 735; Park, "Assimilation, Social," in *Encyclopedia of the Social Sciences*, ed. Edwin R. A. Seligman and Alvin Johnson (New York: MacMillan, 1930), 2:281.

29. Milton M. Gordon, *Assimilation in American Life* (New York: Oxford University Press, 1964), 85. For the origin of the term "Anglo-conformity," see Stewart G. Cole and Mildred Wiese Cole, *Minorities and the American Promise* (New York: Harper and Brothers, 1954), chapter 6.

30. Horace M. Kallen, *Culture and Democracy in the United States: Studies in the Group Psychologies of the American People* (New York: Boni and Liveright, 1924).

31. Herbert A. Miller, *Races, Nations, and Classes* (Philadelphia: J. B. Lippincott, 1924), 168.

32. For a highly critical discussion of the use of the concept of assimilation in American society, see Harry Bash, *Sociology, Race and Ethnicity: A Critique of American Ideological Intrusion upon Sociological Theory* (New York: Gordon and Breach, 1979), especially part 2.

33. W. I. Thomas, "The Psychology of Race Prejudice," *American Journal of Sociology* 9 (Mar. 1904): 607, 609–10; see also W. I. Thomas, *Source Book for Social Origins*, 4th ed. (Boston: Richard Badger, 1909), 156.

34. Park, *Race and Culture*, 226–27, 259.

35. Hamilton Cravens, *The Triumph of Evolution and the Heredity-Environment Controversy* (Philadelphia: University of Pennsylvania Press, 1978), chapter 6.

36. Park, *Race and Culture*, 231, 237–38. For a discussion of the controversy over the concept of instinct, see Cravens, *Triumph of Evolution*, chapter 6.

37. Park, *Race and Culture*, 233–34.

38. Ibid., 227, 260.

39. Reuter, *American Race Problem*, 432.

40. Park, *Race and Culture*, 256–57; see also, Emory S. Bogardus, *Immigration and Race Attitudes* (Boston: D. C. Heath, 1928).

41. T. J. Woofter, Jr., "The Status of Racial and Ethnic Groups," in President's Research Committee on Social Trends, *Recent Social Trends in the United States* (New York: McGraw-Hill, 1931), Table 5, 567.

42. Charles A. Ellwood, *Sociology and Modern Social Problems* (New York: American Book, 1924), 262; John L. Gillin, Clarence G. Dittmer, and Roy J. Colbert, *Social Problems* (New York: Century, 1928), 220, 225–26; John Commons, *Races and Immigrants in American Life* (New York: MacMillan, 1920), 172.

43. T. J. Woofter, Jr., *Negro Problems in Cities* (New York: Doubleday, Doran, 1928), 17–20.

44. Ernest W. Burgess, "The Growth of the City: An Introduction to a Research Project," in *The City*, ed. Robert Park, Ernest W. Burgess, and Roderick D. Mackenzie (Chicago: University of Chicago Press, 1925), 47–62.

45. Louis Wirth, *The Ghetto* (Chicago: University of Chicago Press, 1928), 4, 6; 4–5.

46. Park, *Race and Culture*, 218; Miller, *Races, Nations*, 191; Wirth, *The Ghetto*, 4; Reuter, *American Race Problem*, 2.

47. Donald Young, *American Minority Peoples: A Study of Racial and Cultural Conflicts in the United States* (New York: Harper and Brothers, 1932), xii–xiii.

48. Ibid.

49. Woofter, "Status of Racial and Ethnic Groups"; T. J. Woofter, Jr., *Race and Ethnic Groups in American Life* (New York: McGraw-Hill, 1933).

50. Reuter, *American Race Problem*, 149, 154; Woofter, *Negro Problems*, 37, 69–72; Wirth, *The Ghetto*, x, 9.

51. For brief citations from members of the first generation, namely, Cooley, Small, Ross, Sumner, and Park and Burgess, on their central emphasis on conflict in social life, see Lewis Coser, *The Functions of Social Conflict*, (Glencoe, Ill.: Free Press, 1956), 18–20.

52. Park, *Race and Culture*, 214–15.

53. Ibid., 218.

54. Ibid., 315.

55. Ibid., 116.

56. Coser, *Social Conflict*, 15, 16, 20.

57. Young, *American Minority Peoples*, x, 578.

58. Ibid., xiii.

59. Reuter, *American Race Problem*, 423–27; Young, *American Minority Peoples*, 589.

60. Reuter, *American Race Problem*, 434; Young, *American Minority Peoples*, 580–85.

61. Alain Locke, ed., *The New Negro: An Interpretation* (New York: Albert and Charles Boni, 1925), ix.

62. Charles S. Johnson, "The New Frontage on American Life," in Locke, *New Negro*, 294.

63. Ibid., 296.

64. Locke, *New Negro*, 3.

4

Folk, Peasant, and Caste: The Retreat from Racial Change

By the 1930s the sociologists of race relations were beginning to stake out a claim as the social scientists who were most concerned with race relations, taught college courses on the subject, and wrote extensively on the matter. No monopoly or proprietary interest was ever claimed, however, and other social scientists, particularly anthropologists, contributed to the published research on race relations, often in sociological journals. Nonetheless, race was more and more to become a sociological issue and to be defined both as race relations and the race problem.

Despite the well-known facts about the movement of blacks from the rural South to the urban North, the image of the black American held by sociologists in the 1930s remained that of the rural Southerner, in most cases an agrarian laborer or tenant farmer. There was an evident reluctance to shift the focus of race relations to those cities of the North that were the target of the migrating black population. That would have required sociologists to recognize in their scholarship what they knew to be so in principle: that race relations no longer concerned only the South. Throughout the decade, therefore, and despite the conceptual work of Park, Wirth, and Young, which made possible a new framework for redefining race as a national and urban issue, sociologists maintained a persistent focus on the rural South where a racial caste structure seemed still to be firmly in place.

In contrast to this, Park had developed a conception of race-conscious blacks emerging from the breakdown of the caste system and developing a new national identity like that of the national minorities in eastern Europe. In this conceptualization, Park gave to his fellow sociologists an image of a racial future marked by militant action, conflict, and possible violence, instead of one of gradual, peaceful change leading to increased tolerance and social acceptance. The Park of the race relations cycle ending in peaceful assimilation was acceptable to sociologists, but the Park of national minorities struggling for new racial accommodations was not. Most sociologists were ideologically uneasy with an image of collective action and group conflict as a way of altering the segregated pattern of race relations. That was to prove to be so for the next three decades.

But there were three other reasons for rejecting Park's most provocative idea. The first was the conviction that the implacable opposition of white Americans to racial change sustained caste relations and firmly controlled behavior while allowing only such gradual change as they accepted. Many sociologists, therefore, saw no serious threat to the established racial order. A second reason, in contrast, had to do with how most sociologists saw black people: too culturally backward to be able to organize and act effectively in their own interests. They were not capable, therefore, of altering caste relations. Such an image of black social incompetence was to remain dominant in sociological thought until the 1960s.

The third reason for rejecting Park's provocative notion was also rooted in the way sociologists saw black people: as a primitive people from Africa who had lost language, culture, and identity and possessed no collective memory of their social origins. To compare them, as Park did, with Europeans who possessed an ethnic identity derived from their culture and history seemed inapt and fruitless. This, too, was an image that was to remain strong among sociologists until the 1960s. Because of it, sociologists insisted that blacks had no culture but the American culture; they were Americans in dark skins, and for that reason the distinction betwen race and ethnicity was useful. Blacks were a racial category, but people from Europe possessed ethnic status. Lost from sight, therefore, was Park's effort to transcend this parochial American view of race relations by providing a cross-cultural, comparative perspective. Not until the 1960s would another effort be made.

But few other sociologists made the point, as Park did, that caste could not be sustained much longer. One who did was the southern sociologist, Guy Johnson, who wrote that "Any attempt to solve the race problem by a caste arrangement merely postpones the day when the white man must face the issue squarely and settle it, not according to his own convenience, but by making concessions to the powerful and race-conscious blacks. The progress of the negro since emancipation should be warning enough against the caste method."[1] A steadily emerging racial consciousness, a heightened intolerance in the North in the face of black masses arriving in its cities, and a search for a new adjustment suggested increasingly unstable relations between the races.

But most white sociologists were apparently not ready to accept the full implications of these developments, or even to acknowledge their existence. Nor did they abandon their belief in the unassailable power of caste. Perhaps only Herbert Miller, a student of and coauthor with Robert Park, thought that black racial consciousness possessed the potential for successful militant struggle, though he put emphasis on Park's idea of the feasibility of an educated class within the black population creating a vertical national organization.[2] For other sociologists, the presumed cultural incompetency of blacks as well as white prejudice as an immovable blockage to assimilation seemed to imply a definition of the race issue as the "white man's burden," to be analyzed and understood by white people and, finally, to be managed and controlled, if not solved, by the actions and policies developed by those same white people. That, too, was to remain for three decades a comfortable assumption of the sociologists of race relations.

Folk Culture and Black People

During the late 1920s a small body of sociological work provided ethnographic analysis of the folk character of rural, southern blacks and invoked the concept of a folk culture as a living remnant of a past soon to disappear before the relentless march of modernity. The idea was hardly new. That rural blacks might be seen as a folk people, carriers of a folk culture, had been suggested by Howard Odum and Robert Park early in the century.

Odum undertook the study of black folk culture even before he studied sociology. In 1909 his doctoral dissertation at Clark University in psychology (he was later to earn a doctorate in sociology at Columbia University) was about the folksongs and poetry of southern blacks, some of which he published in the *Journal of American Folklore* under Franz Boas's editorship. Robert Park, in turn, had developed an interest in peasants and folk culture while studying in Germany from 1899 to 1903. His later experience in the South while working for Booker T. Washington at Tuskegee Institute from 1905 to 1913 convinced him that the rural, isolated black was a peasant in a folk culture.[3] Besides Park and Odum in those early years, W. I. Thomas also developed an interest in folk culture after his exposure in Germany to the new field of ethnology and to the "folk psychology" of Lazarus and Steinthal.

His *Source-Book for Social Origins* (1909) presented material on the culture and life of premodern peoples.

Odum returned to his interest in a black folk culture in the 1920s and, in collaboration with Guy B. Johnson, incorporated the early material into two published volumes in 1925 and 1926. In the next five years, Odum, Johnson, Newell B. Puckett, and T. J. Woofter, Jr., published a total of seven folk studies of southern blacks. These works came at a time when the study of American folklore, white and black, was already well under way, and anthropological interest in ethnology and the study of folk culture was a source of both concepts and methodology. The anthropologist Robert Redfield, for example, had already begun his renowned work on folk culture and had noted that "the Southern Negro is our one principle folk."[4]

The study of black Southerners as a folk people, however, flourished too briefly to have a significant effect on the developing sociology of race relations. With increasing urbanization and northern migration of blacks, studying them as a folk people seemed to have no other value than to place in the scholarly record the story of a soon-to-vanish culture (and Odum voiced that intent). Like the study of mulattoes, the study of blacks as a folk people was soon to fade out as an object of sociological study. Before it did, however, it was to have an influence, though not one the folklorists intended.

Viewing blacks through the prism of folk culture could be read as descriptive of a people still beyond the reach of modern life, of being not far beyond the "primitive" state in which they had presumably arrived as slaves. Indeed, Robert Park called them a "marginal people" because, he said, they "live on the margin of our culture" and "occupy a place somewhere between the more primitive and the urban population of our modern cities."[5] From Park's viewpoint, and Odum's, too, there was no attempt to judge by modern standards, to denigrate the folk culture, or to make invidious comparisons, while yet observing how far such people were from being modern.

But it was also possible to read this literature with far less appreciation for the persistence of a folk people into the twentieth century. Educated blacks recognized this reading and were disturbed by the image of cultural backwardness it supported. They thought that, however sympathetic Odum may have been to the people he studied, his work was guilty of "glamorizing crudity and immorality."[6] Even though not intended by the folklorists, such a view supported an already dominant image of blacks as culturally inferior, an image to which Reuter gave such strong expression. It helped to set the stage for the condescending psychological interpretation of blacks as a childlike people that John Dollard was to provide only a few years later. And there was another unintended message as well: these black peasants so un-prepared for modern life were now pouring north in a great internal migration.

One among the educated blacks who was sensitive to the often denigrating image derived from the folk literature was Charles Johnson. Yet he had also contributed to that literature with his seminal study, *Shadow of the Plantation,* wherein he defined black people on the plantations of the "Black Belt" as a folk people and "perhaps, the closest approach to an American peasantry." However, he also tried to make the case that black culture was derived from the white culture of the early colonists, a culture later discarded and forgotten by ed-ucated white people: "Many crudities of manner, now largely aban-doned by the white population, were at one time accepted rules of conduct and still survive deeply imbedded in the modes of social life of Negroes, modified only as they have been able to escape their cultural isolation."[7]

Not all blacks in the South, however, were a folk people, and in 1934 Robert Park saw fit to remind sociologists of that by distinguish-ing between the folk and the "proletariat" of the city: "So the Negro of the plantation—though the two are closely related and the history of one goes far to explain the existence of the other—is not to be identified with the mobile and migratory Negro laborers who crowd the slums of southern cities, or, like the hero of Howard Odum's *Rainbow Round My Shoulder,* go wandering about the country cel-ebrating their freedom and their loneliness by singing 'blues.' "[8] Never-theless, the folk literature supported the reluctance of most white sociologists to move beyond the frame of reference set by postslavery adjustment.

Debating Change and Stability

If most sociologists seemed reluctant to recognize the coming of significant racial change, or to admit that caste was not going to remain firmly in place much longer, two black sociologists, Charles Johnson, by now firmly ensconced at Fisk, and E. Franklin Frazier were not. In a chapter at the end of a rather melioristic and benign textbook he coauthored with Willis D. Weatherford, a renowned white activist of that day, Johnson offered a more challenging interpretation. Northern migration had released blacks from traditional southern expectations and life-styles, Johnson claimed, and had created a new sense of in-dependence, which had affected even the white South. Race pride had increased, and though changes in attitudes were not revolutionary, "the vanguard had unquestionably shifted forward."[9]

Later, Johnson contributed an essay to a volume edited by Edgar T. Thompson for a series celebrating Duke University's centennial. While the essays in the book concentrated on the South, on slavery and its consequences, and on the postslavery adjustment characterized by racial caste, Johnson put forth Park's little-cited expectation that class conflict would eventually replace race conflict. The economic changes of the Great Depression, he argued, including the emergence of the new industrial unions and the rise of black union membership, as well as the consequences of changes in technology, were producing a new environment for race relations, one in which the older order could not be sustained, whether anyone wanted it to or not:[10]

> Further changes in race relations in America will depend not only upon fundamental domestic economic readjustments but also to some extent on world economics. Increase of education, which is now inevitable as a phase of general cultural development, will make a fixed status for the Negro improbable. New technical developments will continue to disturb the social and racial mores, creating new situations in which the racial etiquette will be undefined. Urbanization and industrialization will continue to shift the basis of race relations from a caste to a class structure. In the end there will be less emphasis on the significance of race differences than upon the solidarity of class interests.[11]

When Johnson said that increased education and technological developments would alter old racial patterns, he was merely affirming a proposition generally agreed upon by the sociologists of race relations. They also agreed that urbanization and industrialization were irreversible processes eroding the old order of race relations and making assimilation ultimately inevitable. Such ideas were the intellectual buttress of a perspective then beginning to crystallize, a conception that the basic trends of modern society were gradually but necessarily reshaping the society's traditional race relations. But these same sociologists expected and wanted these changes to come gradually and peacefully. And they were tone deaf to messages of class solidarity.

Johnson's assertion that "racial etiquette" would be "undefined" came from a book by Bertram Doyle, a colleague of Johnson's at Fisk and a student of Park's, who took a proposition by Herbert Spencer to the effect that ceremonial observance was the earliest form of government and developed from that a historical analysis of the etiquette of relations between the races as a powerful mode of social control.

Despite the change from slavery to the present, and the potential for conflict that always accompanies change, Doyle believed that the persistence of racial etiquette had preserved peaceful relations between the races and also preserved the differences of racial status.

From the period of slavery to the present, Doyle noted, "we find a remarkable resemblance in the forms and observances that have been, and still are, common to the contact and association of the two races." The black, who "has learned, through two hundred years of slavery, to accept the superior status of, and defer to, white people in most situations," has, said Doyle, "a sentimental attachment for the *status quo,* and, in general, expects no cataclysm to change conditions overnight, if indeed he thinks of such things at all."[12] Though it was not his intention, Doyle's widely cited book provided assurance that race relations were only slowly changing and that most blacks had no serious expectations of anything else. It also provided a comfortable antidote to any message about class conflict and solidarity. Johnson, however, was insisting that change would inevitably disturb the old order of race relations.

But an even more forthright assessment of the emergence of class conflict and a black proletariat was offered by E. Franklin Frazier, who had completed his doctorate in 1931 under Park and had published two books on the black family (one from his dissertation) in 1932. These and a number of sociological articles had established him as a rising sociologist of first rank. In an article not often cited, perhaps because it did not appear in a sociological journal, Frazier traced the historical development of the American black from slavery to the northern urban migration. That last movement, he argued, had produced an "industrial proletariat" and this class "is changing the character of the struggle for Negro status." Indeed, observed Frazier, "a degree of group solidarity has become a powerful force in the Negro's struggle for status":[13]

> But so far, the power of the Negro masses has not been utilized to improve their economic status which is at the foundation of their social status. The Negro is gradually learning that the status of a group is dependent upon social and economic power, and that "good will" on the part of sentimental whites will not help him. In the urban environment he is showing signs of understanding the struggle for power between the proletariat and the owning classes, and is beginning to cooperate with white workers in this struggle which offers the only hope of his complete emancipation.[14]

Whatever the adequacy of these assessments by the nation's two most prominent black sociologists, most white sociologists were not going to be lured into an analysis of race relations as class conflict. They were not, in fact, yet ready to confront fully the transition from agrarian caste to urban class. To a large extent, the South was still seen as the place of caste and the shaper of race relations; slavery and the events of Reconstruction remained the historic action defining the status of black people.

Most white sociologists were also apparently not ready to find any critical significance for race relations in the vast social changes that were the political consequence of the Great Depression and the New Deal. They did not seem to attach importance to the inclusion of voting blacks in the new political coalition formed within the Democratic party and based primarily in the industrial cities. Viewed in terms of a large migration of blacks to the urban North, this wrenching transformation of the American political structure shaped anew the social context within which the black struggle took place.

To be sure, the extent of the economic hardship experienced by blacks during the depression was duly recorded, particularly in *Social Forces.* A number of articles and several books examined black labor in terms of discriminatory treatment by employers, but also in relation to unions, which had a history of both deliberate noninvolvement and also deliberate exclusion; the new industrial unionism of the 1930s suggested possible changes in these practices. In the rural South, the sociologist Arthur Raper provided a soberly factual but sympathetic portrayal of the poverty and hardship suffered by plantation-dwelling peasants in two Black Belt counties during the depression. He included in that study an examination of the presence and significance of New Deal agencies among a people hard-pressed to meet their most minimal needs. Later, Raper and a black sociologist, Ira De A. Reid, portrayed in some detail how the depression affected the impoverished lives of sharecroppers, both black and white.[15]

Yet, the assessment of the depression's effect on race relations seemed only to reinforce existing conceptions of unequal economic status and opportunity. It broke no new theoretical ground, nor did it discover in this painful decade any anticipation of future possibilities beyond the possible inclusion of blacks in the new industrial unions. (In 1937 Donald Young, in the beginning of a long research memorandum on minorities and depression prepared for the Social Science Research Council, admitted that "practically nothing of scientific value is known about American minorities in depression.")[16] Charles Johnson's previously cited comment on the future "solidarity of class interests" and E. Franklin Frazier's positive reference to black and white workers uniting in class struggle clearly fell outside the range of theoretical discourse in which race relations were then encompassed.

Instead, the sociologists of race relations showed far more interest in the work of two anthropologists, W. Lloyd Warner and Melville Herskovits. Warner's influence on the sociologists of race relations was the greater, since his concepts of caste and class gave a new conceptual direction to work still largely based in the South. Herskovits, in turn, argued strongly that New World blacks had retained significant elements of their African cultures, a matter strongly disputed by E. Franklin Frazier. (The influence of Warner is the concern of this chapter; Herskovits's quarrel with Frazier will be examined in chapter 5).

The re-emergence of anthropologists as central figures in the development of the sociology of race relations in the 1930s deserves comment. Thomas Pettigrew believes that, in part, this was because both Warner and Herskovits were well known to American sociologists, who were always interested in "their work on American topics." They also published in sociological journals, which, Pettigrew claims, reflects "the fact that the social sciences in the 1930s were far less differentiated than they are now," and that sociologists were more open to the work of others, especially that of anthropologists.[17] Pettigrew is correct, but that does not explain why Warner was able to rekindle interest in race relations as an enduring caste structure. The problem, then, is not why Warner sought to develop a conception of race relations as a system of caste and class, but why sociologists responded so favorably to such an idea during the volatile decade of the 1930s.

Race Relations as Caste and Class

W. Lloyd Warner first advanced his conceptualization of caste and class in the Deep South in a brief note in the *American Journal of Sociology* in 1936, followed later by an extended discussion written collaboratively with Allison Davis for Edgar Thompson's volume on southern race relations.[18] He also directed an anthropological study of a community in the Deep South, and he profoundly influenced John Dollard, who undertook a study of the personality of the southern black by the method of the life history. Later, Warner applied his concepts to the study of personality among urban blacks in Chicago. In all three instances the efforts produced influential books.

Warner's anthropological research in the United States began with his Yankee City study, where he found a "well-elaborated class system in an old New England community." Several years later he extended his investigation "into other areas of the United States where our cultural traditions had had the longest time to produce an organized and settled order of community life—the Deep South." There he had to revise his original class hypothesis to include "a fundamental caste social grouping which separated the so-called Negro and white 'races' into two castes," with a separate class system within each caste. While caste and class are both forms of social rank found widely in human communities, the distinction between them, he asserted, is that a caste system practices endogamy and forbids exagomy, while a class system allows both. Caste prohibits upward or downward mobility, while a class system permits such mobility.[19]

For Warner, caste and class were systems of social control, specifically, means of regulating unequal social relations. Caste, in particular, "tends to maintain a stable equilibrium in the outward lives of the generations which occupy the system at any given time." There are always rules to maintain social distance between the castes, the most important of which "is the rule preventing whites and Negroes to perform the social ritual of eating together." Other controls are "the legal restriction upon mixed seating of Negroes and whites in public gatherings and in public carriers, the barring of Negroes from certain residential areas, and the deferential behavior demanded by whites of Negroes in all face-to-face relations, except that of white merchant and colored customer."[20]

From Warner's perspective the existence of social classes within a caste system constituted a modification of the horizontal barrier between upper and lower castes. Since Emancipation there had developed a class structure within the lower caste of blacks, so that some small number of blacks were able to rise to class positions superior to those of some whites. This concept of a black class structure modifying the caste system was hardly a new idea. The existence of a black middle class was common knowledge, and Robert Park had already described the emergence of biracial structures, each with its own class system. But for Park this had been a development toward an eventual new accommodation between the races, rather than further evidence of the firmness of caste.

In his research project in a small southern town, Warner's objective was to present a detailed analysis of how caste and class constituted an interrelated system of social controls and organized a stable though unequal pattern of race relations: "Once the strength of this system is perceived, only the superficial observer, who must also be an incurable optimist, can argue against the generalization that the Negroes form a lower caste in the South."[21] The power of such a caste system, it would seem, could be but little affected by piecemeal reform:

> As soon as the methods by which the caste system operates in the South have been understood, those groups interested in a more efficient social system will be in a position to look at the system *as a whole*. They will not speak merely of "prejudice," nor of lynchings, nor will they hope to make any efficient reorganization of the society by dealing with one symptom at a time, even though this symptom may be the educational subordination or the political disfranchisement of Negroes. Caste is too powerful an opponent for such a peripheral attack. It is an interrelated system of controls, and its effects appear all along the line.[22]

Since the caste system systematically maintained the many social disabilities of blacks—illiteracy, illegitimacy, broken families, and delinquency, for example—Warner thought that there had been little improvement in the previous twenty years: "Those social and relief agencies concerned with orienting the Negro family have learned by grim experience the hopelessness of effectively reducing illegitimacy and desertion, and of thus making the Negro lower-class family a more efficient training center for the Negro child. Such a social change would involve gradual but basic changes in the economic, occupational, educational, and class status of the majority of Negroes."[23]

Warner's theory of caste relations promoted a social scientific stance that insisted that relations between the races had changed but little, that efforts at social reform were largely futile, and without denying that change would inevitably come, that there was still a stable ordering of caste relations.

To this claim, there were contrary voices, those of the black sociologists and Robert Park. Park contended that blacks "had gradually ceased to exhibit the characteristics of a caste," and were now "a racial or national minority." They had changed their status from "that of a caste to minority group."[24] Yet, for the few years of the late 1930s, it was Warner's conception of a still persisting racial caste that seemed most compelling to sociologists. The question then becomes: Why did Warner's conceptualization of caste and class appeal to so many sociologists?

Why Caste and Class?

Park's race relations cycle had been a comfortable framework within which to interpret race relations as long as it predicted a peaceful, gradual assimilation of the races in a world increasingly civilized, that is, secularized and rational, liberated from parochial cultures. But the racial accommodation on which that assimilation presumably depended had been threatened, if not broken, by the eventual development of race consciousness on the part of southern blacks. The later migration of blacks to the urban North further altered the familiar pattern of caste relations and provided a new, uncertain, and potentially disruptive context. There were other changes, too, most importantly those brought on by the depression. Its severe economic dislocation, its wave of industrial unionism, and its new dominant electoral coalition, which included urban blacks, placed a renewed emphasis upon the significance of social class as the experiential basis for collective organization, for social movements, and for social conflict.

If one were to locate the study of race relations within the ongoing struggles brought on by the depression, and within the industrial cities where blacks had gone to stake out a new place and a new life for themselves, then one could see a sociological basis for focusing on the possibilities of racial and class conflict. Both Charles Johnson and E. Franklin Frazier, Park's two most accomplished students, and by then leading sociologists of race relations, offered suggestions for such a focus. Park, in his last theoretical essay, ended with a discussion of the cultural and racial conflicts among "we groups" and "other groups" (the terms were Sumner's), conflicts which, in an increasingly single great society, "will be more and more in the future confused with, and eventually superseded by, the conflicts of class."[25]

But American sociologists were not yet ready to redefine so radically their conception of race relations. Suggestions of group conflict and of racial conflict increasingly becoming class conflict did not provide an alternate conception that was ideologically palatable. Few of them had any conception of change that gave significant place to social movements or other forms of collective behavior. Instead, most of them saw change as a gradual, incremental trendline toward a more structurally complex society, one more secular and rationally guided, less separated by regional, local, and ethnic or other subcultures, and thus, more integrated. To put an emphasis on conflict, furthermore, would have been to deny the possibility of slow, steady progress toward an assimilative conclusion that was the basic postulate of the sociology of race relations. It would have contradicted the emphasis upon enlightened, intelligent leadership from the middle class—in both races, the educated leading the uneducated—and it would have assigned the capacity for collective, self-interested mobilization and militant action to a presumed "backward" people. But very few sociologists besides

Park believed that the vast majority of black people possessed any such capacity to act effectively in their own interest.

The sociologists of race relations, it is evident, were not conflict sociologists. Though they learned much from Park, who was a conflict sociologist, they did not accept his evolutionary-based conception of struggle and conflict as a basis for social change. They were not prepared to envision a racial situation that was unstable, unpredictable, and conflict-ridden, let alone to account for it sociologically. Instead, they returned to a conception of racial caste and to an analysis of its pyschological consequences for human personality. The message that the southern caste system was still largely intact seemed to provide the reassuring word that racial disorder was not likely in the near future.

No student of the period can fail to note the paradox of a renewed emphasis upon the stabilty of southern caste during a decade in which rapid, unsettling change was altering the American social order. Stanford Lyman, for example, has called this renewed emphasis "justified" on the grounds that the "vast majority" of blacks lived in the South and that racial control there was better codified, while in the North only race prejudice, not caste, prevailed.[26] But it was to the North that millions of blacks had migrated by the 1930s, thus providing a better symbol of the future, if one more threatening of violence and disorder. However, as shall be evident in subsequent discussion, W. Lloyd Warner was already asserting that at least a caste-like pattern of race relations prevailed in the North, and that the difference between North and South was one of degree, not kind.

Warner provided American sociologists with a comfortable assurance that change would not occur too abruptly, that racial disorder was not imminent, and he affirmed the "hopelessness" of efforts to intervene with well-intentioned programs of social betterment. He gave sociologists theoretical reason to doubt that biracial confrontation at several class levels at once, in short, the dynamics of vertical opposition taking over from horizontal domination, was at hand. Caste still prevailed. One can only believe that sociologists found in this refurbished theory of caste a reason to avert their sociological eyes from the emerging reality of urban race relations.

John Dollard: The Psychology of Caste Relations

One of those strongly influenced by Warner's theory of caste was the psychoanalytically trained John Dollard, whose *Caste and Class in a Southern Town* was to become a study of enormous influence in sociology. Dollard wanted to study the personality of southern blacks

through the method of life history. The anthropologist Hortense Powdermaker introduced Dollard to the small town she was studying, and
he chose the same small community as the site of his research. But it
was W. Lloyd Warner and his student, Burleigh Gardner, who taught
Dollard about caste as the basic social structure of a southern community. Consequently, the intent of Dollard's study was to explore the
emotional structure that both sustained and was reproduced by the
relations of caste.

To relate emotional structure to community structure, Dollard argued, one had to know about the advantages and disadvantages of
membership in caste: "... and in particular, we wish to state these
advantages and disadvantages from the standpoint of the types of direct
personal, ultimately organic, gratification derived." For middle-class
whites, there were three gains from caste: economic, sexual, and prestige. Economically, they avoided the hard manual labor, especially the
onerous task of picking cotton; and they earned substantially more
income. The sexual gain was "the fact that white men, by virtue of
their caste position, had access to two classes of women, those of the
white and Negro caste." And "in the South one has prestige solely
because one is white. The gain here is very simple. It consists in the
fact that a member of the white caste has an automatic right to demand
forms of behavior from Negroes which serve to increase his own self-
esteem."[27]

That an upper caste gained much from the caste system was obvious,
but that the lower caste also did so was not. Dollard noted that Northerners believed that these subjugated and exploited lower-class blacks
gained nothing from subordination to caste, yet southern whites insisted that blacks "have the best of it." He therefore set out to show
that the southern white had a valid point: "The 'gains' of the Negroes
are the compensation of the slave who has become a caste man." This
compensation is "the relatively indulgent behavior permitted to Negroes in lieu of the struggle to achieve higher social status." There are
three gains: "first, greater ability to enjoy sexual freedom possible in
his own group; second, greater freedom of aggression and resentment
within his own group; and third, the luxury of his dependence relationship to the white caste" (391–92). And since blacks were incapable
of altering their caste situation, it made sense for them to accept the
gratification offered:

> The Negro makes the best of his situation and exploits his free-
> dom from onerous responsibility and renunciation; as a realist
> there is nothing else he can do. This does not mean, however,

that he is biologically anchored to the gains which we shall discuss. It does mean that he has accessible pleasure possibilities which are abandoned by the better socialized, in particular by white middle-class people. His impulse expression is less burdened by guilt and less threatened by his immediate social group; the essence of his gain lies in the fact that he is more free to enjoy, not merely to act in an external physical sense, but actually freer to embrace gratifying experiences. (391)

To make the case that lower-class blacks gain in sexual pleasure, Dollard found it necessary to draw a contrast between acculturated whites practicing "impulse renunciation" and unacculturated blacks free of the "inner barriers against sexual enjoyment." He utilized a Freudian conception of culture as repressive of biological nature and as producing in white people "dimininished actual sexual gratification" and a secret envy of blacks: "Interpreters of the caste system in the South often indicate very directly their sense of the correlations between sexual freedom and low status, and sexual limitation and higher status. The future of the Negro is then said to be bound up with the acquisition of personal restraints on the white model and the rejection of impulse freedom. It is clear that an envious attitude is displayed here, and the claim of the Negro to have both high status and impulse freedom is rejected" (392, 393, 398–99).

Blacks, claimed Dollard, are also freer to act aggressively to one another, and this greater capacity for being aggressive, often to the point of violence, was a distinctive feature of lower-class life. Such aggression was a consequence of the frustration generated by white caste controls, but since it could not be safely directed at white people "the hostility properly directed toward the white caste is deflected from it and focussed within the Negro group itself." Dollard saw two advantages to such a procedure: "First, it is expressive from the Negro standpoint; Negroes are able to react in a biologically satisfying manner. Second, it is safer than taking up the hopeless direct struggle against the white caste which is so severely sensitive to all hostile expressions from Negroes" (267–68).

Dollard spent one chapter (chap. 13) describing the forms of aggression blacks directed against one another. If such aggression flowed from a white-created frustration, the relative freedom of aggression among blacks "is undoubtedly linked to the weakness of the monogamous family among lower-class Negroes. . . . Seen from the standpoint of the white-caste mores, the lower-class Negro family is much less tightly organized to control impulse expression." The greater vi-

olence among blacks, Dollard noted, was supported by the existence
of different standards of justice for whites and blacks. Blacks were
dealt with "more indulgently" as long as their victims were other
blacks. But this also meant that blacks received less protection from
the law than whites did: "the result is that the individual Negro is, to
a considerable degree, outside the protection of white law, and must
shift for himself" (275, 279).

In attempting to assess the significance of the toleration of black
aggression by the dominant whites, Dollard was impressed with how
functional this was for the white caste: "One cannot help wondering
if it does not serve the ends of the white caste to have a high level of
violence in the Negro group, since disunity in the Negro caste tends
to make it less resistant to the white domination." This is not, Dollard
added, necessarily a conscious policy; "instead, it would seem to be
pragmatic, unformalized, and intuitive, but nonetheless effective." The
greater freedom of agressive expression among blacks, he concluded,
would exist as long as the caste system did, "since it seems to be
functionally related to white superiority and Negro subordination"
(280, 285).

Though greater freedom of aggression was one of the putative gains
blacks got from the caste system, Dollard's analysis of aggression
among blacks only weakly supported such an argument. While he
claimed that blacks had the advantage of being able to react "in a
biologically satisfying manner," he also acknowledged that the white
caste gained more from their tolerance of violence among blacks, and
that blacks as a group lost: "It may be indulgent in the case of any
given Negro, but its effect on the Negro group as a whole is dangerous
and destructive." Later in the book, however, he again made the claim
that blacks gained a freedom of aggression from the caste system and
whites paid a psychic price for giving up such freedom: "We shall note
only two things, that such freedom is a luxury in social life and that
those who lack it must do something else with their renounced aggression. Very often the result is that it hangs like a noxious mist in the
personality and cripples the expressiveness and spontaneity of the individual. . . . To give up freedom of open resentment is not a small
price to pay for a civilized life. Negroes are the gainer, in that it is not
socially disadvantageous or necessary for them to renounce this freedom" (280, 400).

In arguing that blacks had sexual freedom and a freedom to be
violent, though in both cases only with other blacks, Dollard seemed
unaware that the pattern he was analyzing psychologically had an ideological history in white myth making about black people. Southern

whites had long been drawn in prurient fascination to the issue of sexuality, both in their imagery of black males and in relations between white and black people. As Hamilton Cravens demonstrated, an image of the black male as driven by exceptional sexual prowess and unrestrained lust emerged as public ideology in the South after the Civil War and reached its peak in the decades just before and after 1900. It served to justify, if not, in fact, to stimulate the southern white's practice of racial lynching and to advance the South's reassertion of full control over the black population.[28] What Dollard found in the 1930s was the last vestige of a once fearful imagery of black males, a less fearful, somewhat diluted, and now more envied view by whites of black sexuality and sexual freedom.

Dollard also duly noted but left unanalyzed another "advantage" of the caste system: the white male's sexual access to both black and white women. Here Dollard was equating advantages and disadvantages of caste entirely in male terms. Compared to white men, white women and black men were sexually restricted to their own caste, were severly punished at even the hint of crossing caste lines, and black males suffered from being unable to protect black women from sexual aggression by white males. Finally, it could not be called an advantage for black women to be sexually available to both black and white males when this was not a matter of personal choice.

Economic Dependence

Since the demise of slavery, a system of tenant farming had held blacks in a grip of economic dependence from which few could ever escape. But according to Dollard this was one of the advantages the caste system offered them: it provided blacks with economic security while excusing them from any responsibility for long-range planning and financing. It was this freedom from economic responsibility, said Dollard, that whites were referring to when they said "that Negros get the best of it." And responsible individuals, he added, "recognize justice in the white-caste claims" (401).

Under the tenant system, black tenants were dependent on white owners for housing and a cash advance until the cotton crop was harvested and sold. But what the tenant farmer earned was never sufficient to carry him and his family through the year, and he needed to borrow from the owner before the next season. Each of them, in fact, was trapped in a system of perpetual debt. But, as Dollard also noted, the system worked to the advantage of the white caste in that "it guarantees a secure labor supply, one of the prime considerations in cotton farming" (402).

Despite the recognizable exploitativeness of the tenant farming system, Dollard readily accepted the claims of white landowners that blacks benefitted more from the system. If Dollard was not out to prove that blacks did "get the better of it," he at least attempted to make the case that blacks did gain from the system. The gain of the black from tenant farming, Dollard said, was not economic, it was psychological: "The furnish system is a kind of permanent dole which appeals to the pleasure principle and relieves the Negro of responsibility and the necessity of forethought." But the economic dependency and permanent indebtedness of tenant farmers could only be called a gain if one accepted as legitimate the act of relieving blacks from any need to be responsible for economic decisions, even for their own life situation. Yet this was exactly the argument Dollard was making as evidence of a gain for blacks from the caste system: "The bountiful commissary and the Santa Claus planter offer all that is needed to live until the next year. The human organism is such a thing that under these circumstances it will accept the immediate pleasure gain and avoid the rigors of impulse renunciation. It must be noted that this dependence of Negroes is not regressive, but seems, on the contrary, a straight gratification of an infantile wish, a gratification continuing without break from childhood on" (404, 401).

The key word in the above quotation is "infantile," and Dollard built upon that concept: "The effect of the social set-up seems to be to keep Negroes infantile, to grant them infantile types of freedom and responsibility, and also to exercise the autocratic control over them which is the prerogative of the patriarchial father." Though it may be slightly traumatic for children to shift from their dependence on parents, Dollard noted, nonetheless, parents encourage their children to grow up. But not so the lower-class black: "The southern caste set-up, on the other hand, encourages the lower-class Negro to 'act like a little boy'; and this in fact he does" (404–5).

An image of biological adults who were psychologically infantile was offered by Dollard as evidence of a gain that blacks obtained from the caste system. Two comments are warrented. First, why a system-created inability to develop adult maturity can be deemed a gain is difficult to answer. Dollard thought of it as a gain because his functional argument needed to balance off some gains that each party to the caste system—the dominant and the subordinate caste—were accorded by the functioning of the system. But such a form of argument enabled him to deemphasize the sheer oppressiveness of the caste system and to fail to recognize that what was functional for the system could be hardship and denial for its lower-caste members. Then, too, Dollard was projecting a conception of bourgeois society as repressive of the natural impulses of the human being and the pleasure of being free of the burden of adult responsibilities. It was a way of turning loss into reward.

Second, Dollard's assertions about the infantile black were drawn entirely from his analysis of the black male role; he never systematically observed or interviewed black women. While he pointed out that black women were more economically independent than white women were, and were more dominant in the family, he never accorded women and children the detailed attention that the anthropologist Hortense Powdermaker did in studying the same community, or that Charles Johnson did in analyzing blacks in the same economic circumstances. The work of Johnson and E. Franklin Frazier would suggest that whites did not treat black women as "little girls" or try to keep them infantile, nor did they pretend to see them in such a way.

"Negroes Are a Happy People"

"The matter of gains," Dollard commented, "is often summed up in a single statement: Negroes are a happy people." He then tried to demonstrate that there was truth in this "romantic image." His attempt to project personality structure from the structure of caste rested upon a Freudian notion of civilization as repressive of natural impulses, albeit a necessary repression if modern life was to be sustained. This led him to project a two-sided view of the modern middle-class personality, against which he compared a two-sided view of the rural, lower-class black personality. The first of these stressed the disciplined capacity for impulse management characteristic of middle-class persons, but a discipline that is experienced as repressive and self-denying: "What poisons life for so many people in Western European society is internalized taboos which make it impossible for them ever to enjoy a spontaneously expressive biological life. Sexual acts, for example, may be performed but without gratifying abandon and release. Many people are torn between personal ideals and wishes, such as those for dependence, which must be rejected if feelings of adequacy are to be achieved" (405, 407).

Lower-class blacks, however, were spared such frustrating denials of spontaneous expression: "But in the case of lower-class Negroes, no such extraordinary demands are made on the body, and it is theoretically quite intelligible that such Negroes should be more comfortable, cheerful, and positive than the more culturally battered whites." There was also, claimed Dollard, a lack of sublimated expressive patterns among lower-class blacks. Such behavior was substitutive and occurred at the expense of more direct forms of gratification. Dollard briefly noted a number of these gratifications, including a highly expressive religious behavior. He went on to note that "there is much behavior that is sheer gratification of indolence tendencies, the mark of a relaxed and aimless existence in exact contrast to the intense 'time is money' attitude of the mobile middle-class people" (407, 410).

But there was another side to this view of the relation between biological impulse and social life, which Dollard equally upheld. Control of the impulse life, or impulse management, as he called it, was an essential aspect of modern life. It was necessary if there were to be competitive, striving, mobile persons, for they possessed the personality formation fitting the requirements of a capitalist economy. Lower-class persons could not become mobile unless they learned to practice impulse control.

The problem of impulse control suggests the importance of the family as society's socializing agent. Here Dollard noted the weakness of the conventional patriarchal family among lower-class blacks, their less stable family life, and their lessened capacity to exercise coercive controls over children. He also noted the existence of the black middle-class family, marked by its adoption of effective impulse controls and its frustrating pursuit of middle-class life—frustrating because white people refused to recognize or acknowledge the ability of middle-class blacks to practice impulse control (413, 420–27).

Dollard readily acknowledged that the gains attributed to lower-class blacks—the freedom of impulse expression and the freedom from typical adult responsibility—were outcomes of the caste system and the plantation and had begun under slavery. Such character formation was functional for the caste system, noted Dollard, but not for the economic world beyond caste: "Negro habits of life could not survive in an independent competing economy." Blacks, then, could not forever escape the absorption of all Americans into a competitive, middle-class life and in time they would of necessity give up their "gains" for restraint, independence, and personal maturity (431–32). But Dollard did not suggest how this was to come about or that such changes were to come soon.

The Significance of the Study

Two issues emerge from Dollard's study of racial caste in the South in the 1930s: first, his effort to demonstrate that blacks as well as whites gain from the caste structure; second, his delineation of the childlike, even infantile, character structure of lower-class black males. Both issues are fundamental to understanding the enormous influence that Dollard's study was to have among American sociologists of race relations.

In asserting that blacks received gains or advantages from the caste system not available to whites, and that whites paid a price for their obvious caste advantages, Dollard was postulating a conception of caste as a functioning social system. The logic of the argument was clear enough: any social system, including caste, endured because it offered some advantages, even to its lowest-ranking members. These advantages were positive functions serving to sustain the caste order as a coercive system of racial accommodation.

There was also implicit in Dollard's argument a conception of human nature, namely, that domination and control over human beings will always have necessary limits if individuals are to be motivated to perform some tasks within the system's division of labor. There are limits to what physical coercion can accomplish. For even the lowliest and most despised members of any social system, there must be some small degree of reward or advantage, some small return, if their participation is to be assured on a stable and continuing basis. These advantages must be both material and emotional.

Dollard's point was evident enough: however much the southern caste system contradicted the democratic values of American life, it had sustained itself as a functional system because it offered sufficient advantages to blacks to assure their continued participation; it had persisted since slavery; it was functioning effectively now; and it was not going to collapse in the near future. Caste was still the basic pattern of race relations in American society. And there was no great impetus to change, no swelling demand for racial reform: "There is some pressure for status change, but not at all to the degree that a northerner would imagine when he tries to put himself in the broken shoes of the field Negro. The wearer of these shoes has his own compensations, and there is some evidence that he is not a little envied by white people. The fact of white envy makes all the clearer the equivalence between mastery satisfactions and direct impulse satisfactions we have been discussing" (431).

Claiming an "equivalence" between the "mastery satisfactions" of the dominant white caste and the "direct impulse satisfactions" of the lower black caste carried Dollard's argument beyond that of merely asserting that there were gains for each caste sufficient to render the system functional. An argument for equivalence became a denial of the very inequality inherent in the very meaning of caste. Dollard, however, bolstered his claim by his insistence that the gains of the dominant caste were offset by the heavy psychic price they paid for impulse renunciation—thus, the white envy of the impulse freedom presumably enjoyed by blacks—while no case was made for any heavy cost paid by blacks. They had their own "compensations" and envy seemed to run in only one direction. It must be noted, however, that by Dollard's own analysis the cost that whites were said to pay— impulse renunciation—was not something peculiar to caste; instead, it was an asserted characteristic of Western bourgeois life, in short, an attribute of class.

It was in this psychological analysis of a caste-bound black lower class that Dollard sought to break new ground. That effort, however, must be regarded as sociologically unsatisfactory as well as ideologically conservative. The image of the black lower class that emerged from Dollard's analysis gave sociological credence to the popular white myth of a happy-go-lucky, primitive people, thoroughly contented with their lot in life. The thesis that impulse freedom and relief from any social responsibility rendered blacks "infantile," never to be required to or allowed to become psychological adults, to be confined instead to an aimless, relaxed existence, and able to pursue unrestrained biological gratification, suggested a way of life little mediated or organized by a culture—"a straight gratification of an infantile wish, a gratification continuing without break from childhood on" (401). This image of the black as infantile, effectively prevented from developing adult abilities and status, must surely have seemed to some perceptive readers to be an enormous cost to pay for some proclaimed biological freedom.

The whole of Dollard's study, however, offered much internal evidence to contradict this imagery. For example, though the coercion of caste was greatly frustrating, blacks could not direct their resultant aggression at whites; instead, they were allowed the "freedom" to vent their aggression on one another (this was specified as one of their gains). The result was a record of systematic, interpersonal violence, including homocide, among a lower-caste people reported by Dollard to be armed with knives and razors. But such a description hardly sustained the image of a happy and contented people.

Perhaps more significant was Dollard's recognition of the development among blacks of a sophisticated dual personality, a mask of smiling and subservient behavior presented to whites, behind which hid another person known only to other blacks. Such a complexity of personal development would seem to imply something critical about the primitive, infantile version depicted as a consequence of impulse freedom. Dollard acknowledged this when he said that "Negroes are quite adept both at concealing their feelings and dealing with white people." Near the end of the book, Dollard returned to his conception of "whiteness" as symbolizing "personal maturity and dignity," that is, the white person as responsible adult and the corresponding white assertion that blacks were children. Again, he found reason to qualify: "Lower-class Negroes are not always so childlike, in fact, as their social role would make them out to be. A statement of his social role always indicates what is desired of the individual, but not always what is delivered by him. The deference, subservience, and dependence of the lower-class Negro are often a social mask which he wears because he must and which conceals a well-fibered character capable of assuming adult status, did the social organization permit" (257, 439).

If the language of this statement is somewhat equivocal—"are not always," "are often"—the thrust, nonetheless, is to contradict the conception of personality that Dollard saw as a direct projection of caste requirements. Basic to his contradictory analysis was a conceptual issue: a failure to distinguish between the black role as shaped by the caste dominants, that is, enacting a prescribed role as one was taught by authority figures, and a Meadian conception of role as role-making, an interactive shaping of role from perspectives shared with others.[29] Dollard seemed to think that black personality was shaped entirely by the oppressive demands and controls of the dominant whites. As a consequence, he ignored the extensive interaction within the segregated confines of the black community as a role-shaping and personality-making process.

An additional conceptual difficulty arises from the fact that Dollard devoted very little discussion to the black family, other than emphasizing the failure of the black lower-class family to socialize children to the middle-class standards of disciplined behavior and orientation to achievement. He did not ask what such a family did accomplish as a socializing force. If he had, he might have seen the family as both an agency for the reproduction of the black lower class and a free space in an otherwise white-controlled environment where attitudes about white people were cultivated and taught to an oncoming generation.

Lastly, Dollard discussed the real and imagined aggression directed by blacks at whites. While outright aggression was infrequent, white anticipation of it was ever present: "Southern white people . . . show the greatest sensitivity to aggression from the side of the Negro, and, in fact, to the outside observer, often seem to be reacting to it when it is not there. Still, it is very convincing to experience in one's own person the unshakeable conviction of the white caste that danger lurks in the Negro quarter. Only constant watchfulness, it is believed, and a solid white front against potential Negro attack maintain the *status quo*" (286). The white people of Southerntown, apparently, knew only too well that behind the masks of smiling, obsequious blacks lurked other persons, quite capable of recognizing the proper target of their countless frustrations and indignities.

From the day of its publication in 1937, Dollard's book was universally lauded by sociologists and widely cited in the literature. Furthermore, it was cited, quoted, and recommended long after many other works of the 1930s had receded from early prominence and were little read. A second edition followed in 1949 and a third in 1957. In an introduction to the third edition, Dollard expressed a concern about the fact that blacks had not yet moved into the black middle class: "The *evolutionary* change which can now occur, and be furthered by human resolution, is to move larger and larger numbers of Negroes into the middle class *of their caste*." For Dollard, all those "who realize that change is inevitable but wish to bring it about in an orderly manner" must press government to be "even-handed and neutral in its treatment of Negro citizens." Nevertheless, thought Dollard, black Americans had still to be patient about their impending assimilation: "In the American evolutionary scheme, every ethnic group has had to stand in line, to endure the cruel paring of cultural habits, to work and wait for assimilation. In one sense, therefore, the Negro has met the same fate as every other ethnic group which has been introduced to the society."[30]

Three years after *Brown v. Topeka*, with southern whites in open, often violent resistance to school desegregation, and after the emergence of Martin Luther King, a charismatic southern leader of black resistance and bold action, Dollard's advice to a nation undergoing difficult racial change seemed, at the least, anachronistic.

Other Perspectives

Though Dollard's analysis of caste relations in a southern community became one of the most widely read and influential studies in race relations in the 1930s and for at least a decade after, there were other community studies during that same period that offered other perspectives on race relations in the South. Three of the more renowned were: *After Freedom, Shadow of the Plantation,* and *Deep South.*

Though replication of prior studies are sometimes done in social science, it is rare that the same community is independently studied at the same time by two social scientists. Dollard had been introduced to the small Mississippi community that became the site of his study by the anthropologist Hortense Powdermaker, who had already begun her own anthropological study. Her "Cottonville" was Dollard's "Southerntown." Her study, *After Freedom,* was published in 1939, two years after Dollard's *Caste and Class in a Southern Town.*[31]

A parallel reading of the two studies provides an instructive and sobering contrast between two social scientific interpretations of the same way of life. Instead of Dollard's analysis of the emotional and material "gains" for blacks in a caste system, Powdermaker offered a thorough anthropological depiction of life in a black community. Dollard seemed to find little redeeming quality in blacks on the plantation and ranged from condescension to dislike in his attitudes toward them—he said that the lower-class black "seems to deserve the low opinion of the whites" (85). Powdermaker's work, in turn, was characterized by an appreciative understanding of lower-class blacks as human beings and offered a sensitive and insightful account of what it meant to be black in a small southern town in the 1930s.

Furthermore, while Dollard emphasized the failure of the black family on the plantation to socialize their children to middle-class values, Powdermaker presented a compelling portrait of the familial adaptations of blacks and the varied patterns of family life to be found among them. In doing so, she refuted Dollard's unsubstantiated account of the black family as disorganized and unsocializing. Finally, unlike Dollard, Powdermaker did not persistently seek "truth" in and take seriously white claims and assertions about blacks. Instead, she noted how little whites really knew about blacks and the "somewhat unrealistic picture of the other part of the community" they held.[32]

In the last pages of her book, Powdermaker took up the issue of "gains" and "freedom" developed by Dollard, without, however, mentioning his name: "it is often felt and said that the Negro is more free with himself and other people. The popular conception of the Negro as a 'child,' a 'spontaneous creature,' unrestrained and living fully in the moment, implies an inner freedom that comes from lack of conflict and inhibition. . . . This is the Negro familiar in most of our fiction up to very recent times and, somewhat less idealized, on our musical comedy stage. . . . Our material contradicts it repeatedly, at least for certain blacks."[33]

The lower-class black, Powdermaker observed, feels restraints imposed from without, not the internal restraint that results "in decorous behavior, thrift, sobriety, and adherence to a strict code of sexual behavior." Yet, even this does not apply to all, such as the tenant farmer who, by hard work and thrift, became a landowner. Nonetheless, "that the appearance of full abandon and participation is not merely fancied will be attested by anyone who attends a church social or a religious service in Cottonville." While the behavior can be readily observed, she noted, one must be cautious about interpreting it: "To develop the capacity for present enjoyment at the expense of the more dreary virtues would seem a plausible accommodation to the conditions that have surrounded and dominated the Negro. The appearance of abandon and relaxation is, however, an index not fully to be trusted, since it depends so much on culturally determined habits of expression."[34] Powdermaker's last comment on the matter provided a direct challenge to Dollard's thesis: "Such possible mitigations as have been mentioned of the personal problems common to all Negroes in Cottonville are hardly to be viewed as major compensations. They are at best variable and minor as against the grave and constant lacks and denials that face every Negro inhabitant of the community."[35]

In equally sharp contrast to Dollard was Powdermaker's account of generational differences and the insistent processes of acculturation steadily going on among the lower-class blacks. She documented a generational drift away from an acceptance of the white-dominated racial pattern and an increasing acculturation of the young to dominant values and aspirations, including education.[36] Dollard, in contrast, had not observed generational differences or even noted whether the younger generation held any newer ideas or values.

Charles Johnson's *Shadow of the Plantation* predated the work organized by Warner around his conception of caste and class. It was based on research carried out in the early 1930s on six hundred black families in Macon County, Alabama. Johnson began by describing a way of life little changed since slavery, even to farming methods and machinery, and with memories of slavery still alive in the last generation of those born to it. The traditional life had a strength "magnified because of the low level of literacy and consequent imperviousness of the area to the modifying influence of news and the experiences of other communities." The economic life of an area where the crop was cotton had, by the 1930s, become one of stagnation, debt, and decline. Nine out of ten Negro farmers were tenants, a few were owners, the rest were sharecroppers, farm laborers, and casual laborers. Work was hard and economic gain was little or none; it was a "dreary cycle of life," inducing a sense of resignation and hopelessness, even despair.[37]

Nonetheless, even if slowly, change was coming. "Much of this study," Johnson observed early in the book, "will be concerned with the social tradition and how it is being modified, even though slowly, by various outside influences." Even older members of the community were aware of change: "The community is being affected at present by at least four factors: migration of a portion of the younger generation away to other states and to the North; return of a small number of younger members who have been sent away to school in Tuskegee and Montgomery; the gradually increasing literacy of the group, beginning with the children; and the introduction of certain programs of welfare from the outside."[38]

Education was basic to this change, and younger parents made evident "a zeal for more education for their children in the desire to escape a dismal economic plight." What was happening in Macon County was a gradual decline of the cultural isolation that had sustained the system since slavery. As Johnson noted, "there had been definite cultural penetration through the medium of the school, the church, the influence of persons educated outside the community, the exposure to demonstrations in health and agriculture, and through returned migrants. Throughout, the weight of tradition, as might be expected, had resisted these changes."[39]

Reflecting his training with Park, Johnson did not denounce either the economic system or its cultural conditions, but his factual, objective description made abundantly clear the exploitative character of the system. Interspersed with that description were the voices of black men and women speaking for themselves about their struggle to make a living and a life (again, the influence of Park). Nothing more effectively destroyed the myth of an unrestrained and spontaneous creature, free to enjoy organic gratification, than the testimony of these often illiterate people about the harsh conditions of their existence. In writing about *Shadow of the Plantation* forty years after its publication, Richard Robbins stated, "Its historic importance is that it took on a racial myth, the conception of the easygoing plantation and the happy Negro, and replaced the myth with the objective truth: Macon County was a twentieth-century form of feudalism based on cotton cultivation."[40]

The anthropological study, *Deep South*, published in 1941, was the last of the several community studies undertaken during the decade of the 1930s in the South. It was organized and directed by W. Lloyd Warner as further anthropological research on American communities and was offered as "but one more example of the almost infinite variety of social systems which man has devised to maintain ordered relations with the rest of nature and with his fellow-beings."[41] The fieldwork was carried out from 1933 to 1935 by five anthropologists (an interracial team) and written by three of them—Allison Davis, Burleigh

Gardner, and Mary Gardner—with an introductory first chapter by Warner.

The conceptual structure of the book, delineating a system of caste and class as the basic organizing process of social life in the Deep South, had already been made by Warner in published articles and by John Dollard in *Caste and Class in a Southern Town*. What *Deep South* had to offer was a sober anthropological account, devoid of Dollard's efforts to analyze the psychological character of lower-class blacks, of the way in which an economic system was interwoven with a system of caste relations between the races.

In studying Old City and the surrounding Old County, where cotton was the dominant crop, Davis and the Gardners focused on the coercive force of economic and caste power in maintaining an oppressive system of race relations. Caste and economy largely reinforced one another in a system of mostly white landowners and mostly black farm tenants and workers, in which deliberate intimidation was a constant factor assuring the racial stratification of daily life. It was also a harsh system, in which hard labor was a constant, but little economic reward could be earned; a debilitating poverty was the fate of most blacks. As if deliberately contradicting Dollard, the authors took pains to dispel the myth that "the cotton-farmer worked during only one-half of the year and the labor required is both light and unskilled." The cultivation of cotton, instead, "demands more prolonged and intensive labor than does that of any other crop, with the possible exception of tobacco." But if a hard workload persisted throughout the year, observed the authors, "most tenant-families in Old County, between 1933 and 1935, lived in semistarvation."[42]

If caste and economy reinforced and sustained one another, however, they did not do so perfectly. In perhaps the most insightful chapter in *Deep South*, Davis and the Gardners examined the contradictions between social caste and an economy operating on the principles of private property and free competition. What resulted was a modification of caste sanctions, so that economic relationships were less governed by caste than were any others. There were a few black landowners with higher incomes, for example; merchants competed for black customers; and blacks were often preferred for employment (in part, because of lower wages), to the disadvantage of whites seeking employment. In such fields as storekeeping, contracting, farming, and professional services, economic competition was able to offset the otherwise rigid application of caste sanctions and taboos.[43]

Though the authors of *Deep South* pursued the issue of contradictions between caste and economy, they did not see in this any significance for social change. Neither did they do so when viewing Old City as "an economy in decline." Though economic decline had begun well before the depression, and the future of farm tenancy as a system had already been threatened by possible migration and industrialization, Davis and the Gardners did not seem to see in this (as Charles Johnson did) the possible decline and fall of a racial caste system rooted in the remainders of the plantation economy. In the very last words of the book, they noted that, though the caste and class systems were subject to change through time, "Both are persisting, observable systems, however, recognized by the people who live in the communities; they form the Deep South's mold of existence."[44] In the end, then, an assurance of stability and persistence was the basic message.

The Appeal of Warner's Claim

Each of the community studies was widely read and appreciated by sociologists. Probably *Caste and Class in a Southern Town* and *Deep South,* in that order, were the more influential. They were widely read throughout the next two decades and were seen as classics of the field. Their widely praised and often cited material became part of the sociological knowledge about race relations transmitted in sociology's classrooms. The appeal of these several studies (but especially Dollard's) to the students of race relations was impressive.

To understand why this could be so, one has to appreciate the sociological perspective on race relations prevalent in the 1930s. The dominant factor in that perspective was the commitment to assimilation as the basic process that was going to reshape all migrant and minority peoples into middle-class citizens of modern society. And still taken as gospel was both a conviction about the psychological unreadiness of prejudiced whites to accept blacks and accord them any rights or opportunities, as well as the cultural unreadiness of the majority of blacks, not far removed from the conditions of slavery, to make that move. The assimilation and absorption of black people could not be hastened, furthermore, by programs of intervention or even social movements. Neither the political changes brought about by the New Deal nor the rapid urbanizing of millions of blacks were acknowledged as factors that might soon change that.

A generation of sociologists who had succeeded the eugenicists and biologists as the society's major students of race, and who had followed the leadership of Robert Park in developing a politically neutral and seemingly objective analysis of an often unpopular subject, now seemed hesitant to move on intellectually and explore the newly emerging racial patterns in the unsettled milieu of northern cities. To such a sociological mindset, the return to the rural South and to the solidity of caste was attractive. An anthropologist like Warner, therefore, could give new substance to a faltering perspective.

It is not difficult, therefore, to understand the pervasive and long-lasting appeal of Warner's thesis about caste. First, Dollard and then Allison and the Gardners strongly affirmed the power and stability of racial caste as the still definitive form of race relations, despite other social changes, and Dollard reinforced that with an apparently appealing conception of the psychological advantages gained from caste by both whites and blacks. He also portrayed the mass of blacks as relatively contented, free and irresponsible, ignorant, and incapable of acting in the disciplined manner required of middle-class life. If there was no biological hindrance to blacks entering the mainstream of American life, they were, nevertheless, still seen as incapable of doing so. The abiding irony here is that those white sociologists who had thoroughly rejected the concept of racial inferiority in biological terms still largely accepted the culturally inferior portrait of the black long projected by the same biological determinists.

Through these studies, then, Warner reassured another generation of sociologists that assimilation was still a gradual, long-run process. Whatever else had changed, the structure of American race relations was still intact; racial progress was still measured in inches and precipitate change or conflict did not seem likely in the near future.

Dissenting Views on Caste

Influential as the work of Warner and his associates was, not all sociologists accepted his thesis on caste as a framework for interpreting race relations. Robert Park had argued for two decades that caste was breaking down and being replaced by a race-conscious national minority. Guy Johnson, E. Franklin Frazier, and Charles Johnson had supported Park's position, though none of them sought to develop a detailed critique of Warner's argument for caste as the basic stable form of American race relations. However, in the closing pages of a book on rural youth in the South, Charles Johnson denied that the race system of the United States could be called a caste system, despite some obvious resemblances. A caste system, he insisted, did not require legal sanctions and the threat of physical violence, as did the system in the American South. Blacks, furthermore, were not accepting their inferior caste status; instead, they were struggling against it.[45]

But there was one sociologist who, alone among his contemporaries, undertook a thorough challenge to the idea that the concept of caste best fitted American race relations. Oliver Cox, then a little-known black sociologist at a small black college, published an uncompromisingly severe critique of Warner's argument. He focused first upon what he saw as the conceptual and theoretical inadequacies of generalizing the concept of caste to American race relations, particularly by comparing it, as Warner did, to the East Indian system. Cox quoted Alfred Kroeber's conclusion "that a caste system is not possible in western society," and he also invoked Kingsley Davis's distinction between "racial caste systems," as in South Africa and the United States, and "non-racial caste systems," as in India. He then criticized the conception of race relations that emerged from Warner's caste perspective: first, its undue emphasis upon the physical basis for membership in an enduring caste structure; and second, its conception of race relations as an integrated and thoroughly controlled caste system. American race relations, Cox insisted, existed in a different social reality, one—here he drew upon Park—made up of two societies, or two racial or national groups. There is not a status, he argued, but there is subordination and conquest, and there is antagonism: "Unlike the permanence of caste, it is a temporary society intended to continue only so long as whites are able to maintain the barriers against their assimilation."[46]

The analogy between American race relations and the Indian caste system, noted Cox, dates back to the middle of the last century. Now it had again become fashionable, but without adding anything new; it was "old wine in new bottles." While there was not any of the "anti-color complexes" of earlier theory, he observed, "Its leadership merely lacks, as Robert Park might say, a sociological tradition."[47]

Several years later Cox pursued the issue further in a book in which he explored critically and in detail the concepts of caste, class, and race both historically and from his own socialist perspective on a racially exploitative capitalism. Despite this radical perspective, however, Cox insisted that black people were not radical and were neither nationalists nor separatists; instead, they tended to be "conservative and forgiving, though not resigned," and had "an abiding urge to assimilate." Consequently, their group solidarity was "defensive and tentative." Black struggle, he believed, would accomplish little; any revolutionary change would come about through a white-led class struggle: "The problem of racial exploitation, then, will most probably be settled as part of the world proletarian struggle for democracy; every advance of the masses will be an actual or potential advance for the colored people."[48]

Cox also criticized much of the contemporary social scientific thinking about caste, class, and race, including a severe criticism of Robert Park's conception of race relations, calling it "weak, vacillating, and misleading."[49] But he never addressed the difference in his and Park's thinking about black Americans. Unlike Cox, Park spoke about the emergence of a long black struggle to overcome racial oppression, which he likened to the nationalist struggles in eastern Europe, and believed in its ultimate success.

The interest in racial caste declined steadily in the late 1940s as new work and new postwar concerns shifted the attention of sociologists to other issues. But the matter remained unsettled. In the first edition of their textbook in 1953, George Simpson and Milton Yinger stated that American sociologists and cultural anthropologists "are divided on the applicability of the term 'caste' to the United States." They repeated that statement in subsequent editions of their text in 1958 and 1965 and cited work that demonstrated a continuing if lessened interest in making use of the concept of caste in the study of American race relations. Such a lessened but persistent conceptual argument was also now less heated.[50]

Addendum: Sociology and the Topic of Race

Though the sociologists who studied race relations were reasonably consistent in their understanding of race and racial differences, it could not yet be said that such an understanding was shared by all their sociological colleagues. A committee appointed by the American Sociological Society in 1931 to examine the conventional introductory course in sociology departments recommended that race be one of the terms treated in the course. When Brewton Berry examined twenty introductory textbooks in sociology (not texts in race relations) published between 1930 and 1938, he found that all of them included the topic of race, however briefly in some cases. But he also found no consistent conception or definition of race, while strong residues of earlier biological thinking were prevalent among some of them.[51]

There was, it seemed, confusion over the very concept of race. Groups identified as races included, besides the black, a wide range of cultural and national categories, such an Anglo-Saxons, Greeks, Italians, Poles, and Jews. "As far as the nature of race is concerned, therefore," Berry noted ruefully, "these twenty books betray all the vagueness, inconsistency, and confusion that one finds in newspapers, Nazi primers, and popular folklore." A text by L. A. Boettiger, for example, still promulgated the idea of great differences, both intellectual and temperamental, among the races, while both Frank B. Hankins and L. C. Hayes still insisted on racial differences in intelligence, though now asserting that racial traits were a cultural acquisition. Berry was willing to grant that some confusion was pardonable in view of what was known about race, "but there is no excuse for some of these books in their abuse of the concept of race."[52]

Nevertheless, Berry found that most of the textbooks were at least closer to the newer sociological understanding of race than they were to Boettiger's, which for Berry apparently served as the epitome of the older, biological perspective, still alive and being taught in college classrooms, though no longer dominant. There now seemed to be emerging an agreement that "the innate intellectual and temperamental differences between the races are small, insignificant, and doubtful," and there was "considerable agreement that there is nothing instinctive about race relations."[53] As a whole, then, the sociological discipline was still catching up with Franz Boas and Robert Park.

Notes

1. Guy B. Johnson, "The Negro Migration and Its Consequences," *Social Forces* 2 (Mar. 1924): 408.

2. Herbert A. Miller, *Races, Classes, and Nations* (Philadelphia: J. B. Lippincott Co., 1924), 151–56. The coauthored work was by Robert E. Park and Herbert Miller, *Old World Traits Transplanted* (New York: Harper and Brothers, 1921).

3. On the development of Park's interest in peasants and folk culture, see Fred B. Mathews, *Quest for an American Sociology: Robert E. Park and the Chicago School* (Montreal: McGill-Queen's University Press, 1977), 71–76.

4. Robert Redfield, *Tepoztlan, A Mexican Village* (Chicago: University of Chicago Press, 1930), 6.

The seven folk studies of rural black people were: Howard W. Odum and Guy B. Johnson, *The Negro and His Songs: A Study of Topical Negro Songs in the South* and *Negro Workday Songs* (Chapel Hill: University of North Carolina Press, 1925, 1926); Howard W. Odum, *Rainbow Round My Shoulder: The Blue Trail of Black Ulysses; Wings on My Feet: Black Ulysses at the Wars;* and *Cold Blue Moon: Black Ulysses Afar Off* (Chapel Hill: University of North Carolina Press, 1928, 1929, 1931); Guy B. Johnson, *John B. Henry: Tracking Down a Negro Legend* and *Folk Culture of St. Helena Island* (Chapel Hill: University of North Carolina Press, 1929, 1930); Newell B. Puckett, *Folk Beliefs of the Southern Negro* (Chapel Hill: University of North Carolina Press, 1926); T. J. Woofter, Jr., *Black Yeomanry: Life on St. Helena Island* (New York: Henry Holt and Co., 1930).

5. Robert Park, Introduction to Charles S. Johnson, *Shadow of the Plantation* (Chicago: University of Chicago Press, 1934), xii.

6. Katheriner Jocher, Guy B. Johnson, George L. Simpson, and Rupert B. Vance, *Folk, Region, and Society: Selected Papers of Howard Odum* (Chapel Hill: University of North Carolina Press, 1964), xi.

7. Johnson, *Shadow of the Plantation,* 5–6.

8. Park, Introduction to *Shadow of the Plantation,* xiii–xiv.

9. Willis D. Weatherford and Charles S. Johnson, *Race Relations: Adjustment of Whites and Negroes in the United States* (Boston: D. C. Heath and Co., 1934), 542.

10. Charles S. Johnson, "Race Relations and Social Change," in *Race Relations and the Race Problem,* ed. Edgar T. Thompson (Durham, N.C.: Duke University Press, 1939): 271–303.

11. Ibid., 303.

12. Bertram Wilbur Doyle, *The Etiquette of Race Relations in the South: A Study in Social Control* (Chicago: University of Chicago Press, 1937), 169–70.

13. E. Franklin Frazier, "The Status of the Negro in the American Social Order," *Journal of Negro Education* 4 (July 1935): 305–6. Frazier's two books on the family were: *The Negro Family in Chicago* (Chicago: University of Chicago Press, 1932) and *The Free Negro Family* (Nashville: Fisk University Press, 1932).

14. Frazier, "Status of the Negro," 308.

15. For a brief review of articles on black labor, see Thomas F. Pettigrew, ed., *The Sociology of Race Relations: Reflection and Reform* (New York: Free Press, 1980), 88–89.

On black workers and unions, see, for example, Ira De A. Reid, *Negro Membership in American Labor* (New York: Negro Universities Press, 1969 [1930]); Sterling D. Spero and H. L. Harris, *The Black Worker: The Negro and the Labor Movement* (New York: Columbia University Press, 1930); and Horace R. Cayton and George S. Mitchell, *Black Workers and the New Unions* (Chapel Hill: University of North Carolina Press, 1941).

On economic hardship during the depression, see Arthur F. Raper, *Preface to Peasantry: A Tale of Two Black Belt Counties* (Chapel Hill: University of North Carolina Press, 1936); Arthur F. Raper and Ira De A. Reid, *Sharecroppers All* (Chapel Hill: University of North Carolina Press, 1941).

16. Donald Young, *Research Memorandum on Minority Peoples in the Depression,* Bulletin 31 (New York: Social Science Research Council, 1937): 11.

17. Pettigrew, *Race Relations,* 89 n. 7.

18. W. Lloyd Warner, "American Caste and Class," *American Journal of Sociology* 42 (Sept. 1936): 234–37; W. Lloyd Warner and Allison Davis, "A Comparative Study of American Caste," in *Race Relations,* ed. Thompson, 219–45.

19. Warner and Allison, "Comparative Study," 224–25, 229.

20. Ibid., 228, 232, 235.

21. Ibid., 244.

22. Ibid. (emphasis in original).

23. Ibid., 245.

24. Park, Introduction to Doyle, *Etiquette,* xxii.

25. Robert Park, *Race and Culture* (New York: Free Press, 1950), 116.

26. Stanford Lyman, *The Black American in Sociological Thought: A Failure of Perspective* (New York: G. P. Putnam's Sons, 1972; Capricorn Books, 1973), 91–92.

27. John Dollard, *Caste and Class in a Southern Town* (New Haven: Yale University Press, 1937), 98. Further references to this work will appear in the text. All italics appear in the original work.

28. Hamilton Cravens, *The Crucible of Race: Black-White Relations in the American South since Emancipation* (New York: Oxford University Press, 1984), chapters 4, 5, and 6.

29. For an explication of role-making, see Ralph H. Turner, "Role-Taking: Process versus Conformity," in *Human Behavior and Social Processes: An Interactionist Approach,* ed. Arnold M. Rose (Boston: Houghton Mifflin, 1962): 20–40.

30. Dollard, *Caste and Class,* 3d edition (Garden City, N.Y.: Doubleday Anchor, 1957), x–xi.

31. Hortense Powdermaker, *After Freedom: A Cultural Study in the Deep South* (New York: Viking Press, 1939).

32. Powdermaker, *After Freedom,* 41–42.

33. Ibid., 364.

34. Ibid., 366.

35. Ibid., 368–69.

36. Ibid., chapter 17.

37. Charles S. Johnson, *Shadow of the Plantation* (Chicago: University of Chicago Press, 1934), 16, 23–25, 104–14, 125–26.

38. Ibid., 17.

39. Ibid., 28, 132–33.

40. Richard Robbins, "Charles S. Johnson," in *Black Sociologists: Historical and Contemporary Perspectives,* ed. James E. Blackwell and Morris Janowitz (Chicago: University of Chicago Press, 1974), 68.

41. Allison Davis, Burleigh R. Gardner, and Mary R Gardner, *Deep South: A Social Anthropological Study of Caste and Class* (Chicago: University of Chicago Press, 1941), 14.

42. Ibid., 324–25, 379.

43. Ibid., chapter 21.

44. Ibid., 255–57, 539.

45. Charles S. Johnson, *Growing Up in the Black Belt: Negro Youth in the Rural South* (Washington, D.C.: American Council on Education, 1941), 325–27. I address Johnson's study of black rural youth in the South in chapter 5.

46. Oliver C. Cox, "The Modern Caste School of Race Relations," *Social Forces* 21 (Dec. 1942): 219–20, 224.

47. Cox, "Modern Caste," 226.

48. Oliver Cromwell Cox, *Caste, Class, and Race: A Study in Social Dynamics* (Garden City, N.Y.: Doubleday and Co., 1948), 545, 571, 583.

49. Ibid., 474.

50. George Eaton Simpson and J. Milton Yinger, *Race and Cultural Minorities: An Analysis of Prejudice and Discrimination* (New York: Harper and Brothers, 1953), 327; in 1958 edition, 355; in 1965 edition, 244.

51. Brewton Berry, "The Concept of Race in Sociology Textbooks," *Social Forces* 18 (Mar. 1940): 411–17. The report of the committee to examine the introductory course became the entire issue of the *Journal of Educational Sociology* 7 (Sept. 1933); for the recommendation concerning race, see 78–82.

52. Berry, "Concept of Race," 414, 417. The texts referred to were L. A. Boettiger, *Fundamentals of Sociology* (1938); Frank H. Hankins, *An Introduction to the Study of Society* (1935); and L. C. Hayes, *Sociology* (1930).

53. Berry, "Concept of Race," 415–16.

5

Discovering the Black American

The compelling interest in racial caste in the Deep South, whatever its theoretical drawbacks, did at least focus sociological attention on the lives of black people. Other work undertaken in the 1930s explored more fully and in greater scope the meaning of being black in the United States. Studies were carried out on the personality development of black youth, in the persistence or loss of an African heritage, on the black family, and on the new urban community, where black life was being reshaped. There was another significant dimension to this: much of the new work was carried out by black sociologists, marking for the first time a collective black presence in sociology recognized for its contribution to the study of race relations. That presence made possible a decade rich in sociological studies of black people, many of which were to become classics in the field; some were to remain in print for another two decades or more. Most of these works, all begun in the 1930s, were published between 1935 and 1945.

Black Youth

In 1935 the American Council on Education established the American Youth Commission to examine the needs of American youth and to devise plans and programs to meet youth's problems. A division of the commission, Studies of Negro Youth, directed by the sociologist Robert L. Sutherland, funded four research projects around the question "What are the effects upon the personality development of Negro youth of their membership in a racial minority group?"[1] The studies were then published by the American Council on Education under its own name in 1940 and 1941. Their publication was preceded in 1940 by a short work by the black sociologist Ira De A. Reid on the general

conditions of black life that served as the shaping environment of black
youth in the United States.[2]

Children of Bondage

The first book in the series—which became the best known—was
a study of black urban youth in New Orleans and in Natchez, Mississippi. Allison Davis, the black anthropologist who had coauthored
Deep South, and John Dollard, by now already renowned for *Caste
and Class in a Southern Town,* collaborated in the research for and
writing of *Children of Bondage.*[3] Davis acknowledged that the study
was a continuation of their earlier work on caste and class in the South
within the conceptual framework developed by W. Lloyd Warner.
Perhaps reflecting such renown, the book found a wide audience and
by 1947 was in its fifth printing.

Dollard seems to have been less directly involved in the field research
than Davis was, but his collaboration in the analysis of the materials,
his instruction of Davis in Freudian and stimulus-response psychology,
as well as his sharing in the writing, shaped the resulting document
into the most distinctively psychological of the four in the series. What
was psychologically new in the work was Dollard's exposure since
1937 to the behaviorist psychology of Clark Hull and Neal Miller; as
a result, a reward-punishment orientation to learning dominated the
analytic perspective for interpreting the interview materials.[4]

Most of the book was devoted to eight case studies of Negro adolescents between the ages of twelve and sixteen, selected from a pool
of thirty, and differentiated by the lower-, middle-, and upper-class
status of their families. The conception of social class was Lloyd Warner's, as developed in the Yankee City studies. The shared-class cliques
and the family were defined as the social environment in which "class
learning is instilled and maintained." Such class learning was presented
largely as the reinforcement of habits developed through parents' and
other's rewards and punishments, but particularly punishments:

> The child learns the more complex habits of class training by
> being punished for disapproved acts and rewarded for desired
> ones. In this process, he may be reinforced in new habit formation
> either by biological pain or gratification, or by the praise or scowls
> of his parents and other teachers. He may also be motivated to
> learn new behavior and to maintain his approved habits by an-
> ticipating rather than actually experiencing reward and punish-
> ment.... Since punishment is still the most frequently used
> method of training children, the anticipation of punishment be-
> comes the most constant reinforcement of human behavior.

In addition, anxiety, "a deeply internalized expectation of punish-ment," serves further to reinforce the lessons taught within the family and cliques.[5]

The analysis developed for the study culminated in a basic distinc-tion between the lower-class socialization of children and that of all other classes. Lower-class children were viewed as growing up inef-fectively supervised and as learning at an early age what is acceptable behavior in their own social class through unsupervised involvement in the daily life of the community. Unlike other children, they were not kept close to home—often, having no father and a working mother prevented that—and "protected" from such influences. Furthermore, since lower-class people were unprotected by white law, their children became "fighters, cutters, and shooters, and they were reinforced in this behavior by their parents" (270).

Lower-middle-class children, in turn, were seen as supervised by their parents and were sternly punished for any violations of rules and expectations; their behavior was always under parental control. They were required to do as well as they could in school, stay out of trouble, not fight with anyone, and strongly avoid the temptations of sex. At the same time, they received rewards: praise, privilege, and material possessions. Both punishment and reward reinforced the pattern of behavior that would ensure some class mobility within the limited possibilities of social caste.

Lower-class parents taught their children much, punished them often, yet failed to instill in them the social habits that would promote a middle-class life. Davis and Dollard suggested that there could be a difference in what parents wanted to teach their children and what in fact they did teach. These lower-class parents, they asserted, taught by example behaviors other than what they taught by precept. That, and less control over the lives of their children, left them unable to socialize their children to social values and aspirations other than what already existed in their social class. In contrast, there were "two crucial reasons for the effectiveness of lower-middle-class restraints upon the sexual, aggressive, and school behavior of children." These were "(1) constant, detailed supervision, and (2) threats of loss of status if the child is not a 'good' boy or girl" (274).

As Davis and Dollard made the case that lower-class child training usually failed, they also seemed to be greatly impressed with the suc-cessful child training carried out by middle-class parents. Here, ap-parently, there was no gap between what parents hoped to and did teach. Constant supervision and the threat of loss of status was ap-parently sufficient to build a conforming personality.

Yet Dollard's prior Freudian training had taught him that there had to be some negative consequences for such highly controlled behavior. In discussing how lower-class people vent their anger in various forms of aggressive behavior, the authors observed that lower-class children escaped "the necessity of continually repressing the aggressive impulses," which, in turn, "middle-class and upper-class people learn to inhibit only at the expense of great strain and anxiety." The lower-class person, they noted, "does not have to endure in his class world the feeling of incoherent rage and helplessness which result from the chronic suppression of aggressive impulses" (272).

This brief Freudian excursus, however, did not lead to any detailed probing of the anxieties and supressed rage of middle-class people, whether parents or children. Instead, the authors focused on their image of successful socialization. Yet, in the case studies they presented, there was evidence of pain, fear, anxiety, rage, and examples of behavioral consequences. There was also evidence of the fragility of lower-middle-class status; it could easily be endangered or even destroyed, as by a male parent's desertion or alcoholism. The "success" Davis and Dollard proclaimed was at least qualified by the reading of the case studies they presented.

Davis and Dollard, however, put the emphasis of their analysis on this presumably successful socialization, and the reason seems apparent. They wanted to demonstrate that between lower class and lower-middle class was a basic dividing line—a great chasm—separating those socialized successfully to the pursuit of status and achievement and those not so socialized. Among the more than three-fourths who were lower class, socialization had failed to produce behavior and attitude other than that already evident in the life-style of class members (264–65). In effect—though not in Davis and Dollard's language—lower-class socialization served only to reproduce the lower class.

In their emphasis upon socialization to the demands of middle-class life, Davis and Dollard were expressing an assumption common to the sociologists of race relations, that gradual assimilation was the only satisfactory solution to the race problem in the United States. As a consequence, they were always concerned about the processes of education and socialization necessary to accomplish that. Yet, no one seemed to know how to overcome the fact that by the socialization of its children the lower class could only reproduce itself: "The ineffectiveness of the usual middle-class stimuli upon lower-class people and the resultant waste of potential social and economic energy in the lower classes are the perpetual concerns of middle-class and upper-middle-class legislatures, social workers, and educators" (265).

Finally, Davis and Dollard turned from family to school to locate a basic source of the failure to socialize lower-class children to middle-class behavior and attitude. They posed a question: " 'Why do lower-class Negro children usually fail to develop and maintain habits of study in graded school, and why do children of upper-middle-class and upper-class status usually maintain such habits?' " To answer, they cited "the discovery of behavioristic psychologists" that rewards and punishments are necessary to form habits: "If there are no effective reinforcements for a child, he does not learn" (280).

For lower-class children there was, apparently, enough punishment, but that alone would not suffice: "Punishment and the anxiety it establishes may not alone maintain complex human learning, however. Apparently, a simultaneously biological or status *reward* is also useful." But in the schoolroom, they observed, teachers tend to bestow rewards on the children of the middle and upper classes, not on those of the lower class. These children were stigmatized because of their clothes, their dialect, the darkness of their skin, and their "ignorant" parents. Their response to such treatment was to become sullen, sometimes hostile: "If there is no reward for learning, in terms of privilege and anxiety-reduction, there is no motive for work." Lower-class adolescents learned that neither their parents nor their teachers expected them to "go far" in school, and they did not (281, 285).

In support of their thesis, Davis and Dollard described how interviewers for their study had accomplished some "therapeutic results" by developing nonpunitive, open relationships with two of the adolescents in the case studies, resulting in greatly improved school performance. Here, they thought, was a possible means to improve learning "with the great majority of retarded Negro children." But, being careful scholars, they added the necessary caveat: "Long and detailed research on this problem is needed" (289).

Children of Bondage, then, was not primarily a study of the development of black personality under the oppressive conditions of racial caste. Instead, its primary concern was how social class shaped socialization and learning, and it focused upon that large majority of blacks who were lower class and whose socialization and education failed to develop a person capable of achieving a middle-class way of life. In *Caste and Class in a Southern Town,* Dollard had asserted that "the dominant aim of our society seems to be to middle-classify all its members," and blacks were no exception; they, too, must eventually "enter the competition for higher status."[6] Whatever its stated scholarly purpose, then, *Children of Bondage* was an effort to analyze the difficulty in "middle-classifying" the vast number of lower-class blacks.

There was, then, a consistent theme that linked both books and was basic to their being widely read and highly praised: how to change the mass of black people so as to create the conditions necessary for eventual assimilation. That message, to be sure, was apolitical and conservative: changes in person were to precede changes in social institutions. As stated in *Children of Bondage,*

> the stubborn economic, political, and war-ridden habits of our society make it increasingly clear that neither government nor social reformers can change the behavior of human beings overnight, even when their biological survival seems to demand a change. In order to change an individual's familial, sexual, economic, or educational relationships, the social engineers must first know what his present class-typed habits are and how they are being reinforced. They will then be in a position to use this knowledge for the establishment of new modes of behavior in our society. But there can be no new learning with regard to war, economic relations, education, or family life, unless old habits are first broken down and old rewards and punishments withdrawn. (279)

Such a message re-echoed an old theme: change would not come quickly and not by social reformers. Nonetheless, undesired behavior could be altered. In a new psychology, it seemed, and in the controlled environment of education, social engineers could innovate new modes of learning and deliberately, not hastily, reshape human personality to produce en masse the middle-class striver. Such a gradual process of personality change also promised to contribute significantly to the eventual solution of the race problem.

A vision of social engineering accomplishing what government and social reformers by other means could not reflected a middle-class desire to take control over the lives of lower-class blacks, to use the school to retrain and resocialize a class of children whose social environment beyond the school would remain unaltered. It was also perhaps the first evidence of what was to become commonplace in the sociology of race relations after World War II: the support of sociologists for modes of intervention into the race problem.

At the Crossways: Youth in the Middle South

The second volume in the series, much different in method and message, was E. Franklin Frazier's *Negro Youth at the Crossways.*[7] By

1940 Frazier, who by then headed the Department of Sociology at Howard University, was coming into prominence as a sociologist of the first rank. His historical study of the black family in the United States, destined to become a classic of the discipline, had been published the year before. The "crossways" in the title meant the border or middle states, to be contrasted with the Deep South and the urban North. Accordingly, Washington, D.C., and Louisville, Kentucky, were selected as representative research sites.

Frazier's study was different from Davis and Dollard's in a number of ways. He did not make use of Warner's concepts of caste and class, he did not invoke the use of behavioral psychology, and the final product was not a series of case studies of presumably representative personalities of black youth. Instead, Frazier undertook a sociological exploration of the effect of community, class, family, neighborhood, school, church, and job-seeking on a generation of black youth. There were only two case studies presented—one with a brief commentary by the psychiatrist, Harry Stack Sullivan—and Frazier did not claim that either was representative. *Negro Youth at the Crossways,* then, was less a study of personality, more an analysis of the experiential basis for youthful attitudes and expectations. But it was also a community study, and in its sequence of topics, it gave evidence of Frazier's reading and appreciation of a neglected classic in sociology, W. E. B. Du Bois's *The Philadelphia Negro* (1899).[8]

Based largely on a ranking of seven occupational categories of the census, Frazier's description of the black community utilized a three-tiered system of social class: lower, middle, and upper. Though the lower class was predictably the largest of the three, there were still more persons of the middle and upper classes in Washington and Louisville than in any of the communities studied in the Deep South. The middle class, according to Frazier, contained "the most energetic and ambitious elements of the Negro community," a class careful not to be identified with the lower class and resentful of the upper class. The upper class, in turn, seemed always to have been more than an occupational category. A large part of it was a set of "first families" of long residence in the community, with white ancestry and color, and of free ancestry in contrast to those of slave ancestry. Many of these families had long been in the employ of prominent white families as valets and servants and had taken over "the manners and ways of living of these white families."[9]

A segregated but class-divided community cannot easily escape interclass resentments, hostilities, and derogations, and Frazier did not hesitate to explore this dimension of the black community. In Washington, he noted, the upper class "was accused with much justice of extreme snobbishness and discrimination against the blacks when it was in their power to discriminate in regard to jobs" ("black" here meant those of darkest color). With a growing race consciousness and the rise of some darker-skinned persons to higher status, however, such snobbishness was being modified or at least concealed. But Frazier's harshest comment was reserved for the upper class for possessing essentially a middle-class outlook "with an emphasis on pretension and display" and much talk about "culture":

> It generally turns out that "culture" is restricted to the social amenities, since it is difficult to find among this group many who read good books or have a genuine appreciation of literature or art or music. Rather it is in the matter of conspicuous consumption that the upper class expresses most explicitly its position and role in the social stratification of the Negro community. . . . High standards of consumption are often made possible by the fact that upper-class married women in the border states, unlike those in the South, engage in professional and clerical occupations. . . . Though the upper class is relatively small in numbers, it is important in the Negro community because it provides the standards and values, and symbolizes the aspirations of the Negro community.[10]

It was these pretensions, conspicuous consumption, and standards and values that Frazier was later to criticize so unsparingly in *Black Bourgeoisie.*[11]

Despite the obvious fact that even a black upper class could not escape the prevalence of racism, Frazier described the upper-class family as protecting its children from direct contact with discriminating whites, while also providing them with security in both family and economic relations. Upper-class youth were also insulated in their neighborhood activities, though never enough to escape totally the "contact with whites in the neighborhood which makes them race conscious."[12]

For the lower class, life was always and in every way harsh and unrewarding. Frazier noted carefully the ambivalence of lower-class youth toward the white world: on the one hand, the tendency to reject parental attitudes of accommodation to inferior status and to display hostility to whites, while on the other hand, taking over derogatory stereotypes of blacks. Yet, there was no single type of lower-class family. While a prevalent disorganized family life displayed a proneness

to fighting, other families possessed a Christian faith that inspired hope
in their children and even goodwill toward whites (41–55).

In the middle class, the family taught a complex pattern of behavior:
not to be servile to whites, but also to act in conventional, middle-
class ways; that meant, in addition and most importantly, to avoid
acting like the lower class. These family influences reflected an increasing race consciousness and race pride, but they also produced
among middle-class youth a resentment toward whites for treating all
blacks as the same. Similarly, in the neighborhood, these middle-class
youth were embittered by the tendency of the police to treat all blacks
as if they were lower-class and criminal (55–61, 83).

Besides family and neighborhood, Frazier looked carefully at the
school and the church as institutions significant for the development
of youth. When he discussed the public schools his emphasis was not
upon the fact of racially segregated schooling. White and black schools
in Washington, he observed, were not greatly different in equipment
and teaching competence, and blacks were proud of the quality of
their schools. Instead, it was in the social classes of the black community where Frazier found the major influence on the education of
children. In the schools, as in those Davis and Dollard studied, darker-
skinned children reported experiences of discrimination and favoritism
based on gradations of color. Here, as elsewhere, skin color was correlated with class position. As a consequence, Frazier observed, "Only
the upper-class pupils appear to experience the full opportunity for
success in school adjustment." Those who did succeed, however, became "dissatisfied with an inferior social status," for, having demonstrated academic achievement in schools comparable in quality to those
for whites, and having made good scholastic records in predominantly
white colleges, they knew that there was no "innate disabilty of intellect" to hold them back (91, 111).

If the problem of the schools was one of unequal treatment, the
problem the church posed for black youth was different. Like the
family, the church was a black-controlled institution, yet it did little
to promote racial self-respect among black youth and largely ignored
the race issue. For that reason, many youths, even those who were
religious, were highly critical of the church (112–33).

Beyond school and church was the world of work. Here, the youth
of all social classes recognized the reality of job discrimination, and
lower- and middle-class youth placed equal opportunity as first among
the changes in race relations they desired to see. Most lower-class youth
expected only unskilled jobs to be available to them, and, noted Frazier, "because of the lack of opportunities, many lower-class youths

are becoming convinced that illegal and anti-social means of making a living must be resorted to and are justified." But ambitious middle-class youth hoped to rise in status, while upper-class youth were confident about the future, yet "respectful of the many limitations under which they worked" (166–67).

Despite the daily reality of discrimination, Frazier found no significant social movement mobilizing blacks for efforts at social change, though he did find considerable support among the young for the campaign of the New Negro Alliance to picket a drugstore chain to get blacks employed as clerks. More generally, there was a belief that blacks did not "stick together," a position within the upper class that meant that other blacks should support black-run businesses. Youth of the lower and middle classes displayed a racial consciousness that focused on outstanding blacks as racial heroes; prominent among them was the heavyweight boxing champion, Joe Louis. Furthermore, the color consciousness of the thirties made brown the ideal color—Joe Louis was the "Brown Bomber"—and the black skin so common in the lower class was least desired or valued (170–73, 177–80).

Frazier brought to his study of black youth a keen sense of structure and institutions. The black border communities, in his acute analysis, were in each instance a complex and variegated social order undergoing generational change. If they were significantly removed from the black communities in the Deep South, they also lacked "the ferment of ideas and movements which ceaselessly agitate metropolitan communities in the North." The border community, then, clearly stood "at the cross-ways" between South and North. These black communities, according to Frazier, suffered a "social pathology" of poverty and dependency, family disorganization, criminality, and disease and death (287, 290–92). Frazier's attention to social pathology and disorganization, concepts so basic to the sociology of his day, and his location of the lower-class black family in such a social context, was later to become a source of criticism of his work.

This concern for social pathology, however, was but one dimension of Frazier's effort to analyze black urban life. Indeed, in this study the pathological features of lower-class life were secondary to his emphasis on the segregated, isolated world inhabited by blacks, one that necessarily developed its own cultural and institutional features. Within this isolated social world, black youth encountered a shaping social reality and experienced a constraining environment. For Frazier, this was basic to forming personality: "The sociologist recognizes that every human being is born into a pre-established society or group with its particular language, customs, behavior patterns, and ideas. As a result of his participation in a social world, the individual's behavior—what he perceives as well as what he does—is defined by the responses of other members of the group. In this manner the behavior of the individual acquires meaning in terms of the particular culture in which he is born" (273).

In order to understand a particular culture, Frazier said, "the sociologist focuses his attention first upon the social and cultural context in which the personality takes form." This statement appears late in the book, in an appendix on culture and personality, in which Frazier developed a conception of personality formation as the outcome of an interactive acquisition of culture. In support, he cited Herbert Blumer, George Herbert Mead, and Gordon Allport. Frazier made it clear that the relation of the individual to culture had to be seen as "the highly complex responses of the individual to the social world where meanings are the essential elements" (283, 276–77).

In insisting upon a cultural interpretation of personality, Frazier acknowledged the existence of other, noncultural explanations and found them inadequate. He briefly reviewed arguments for the domination of biological factors in personality, for example, and rejected them. From the same perspective he also challenged the behavioristic formulation that John Dollard was employing, but without mentioning his name. The "relation of the individual to his social and cultural milieu," he asserted, "is much more complex than is represented in such mechanistic formulations as *conditioning* and *stimulus* and *response*" and "it is impossible to reduce behavior to such simple mechanisms" (277).

But the personality of black youth was not a major concern of Frazier's study of the border communities. Instead, it is not difficult to see that *Negro Youth at the Crossways* provided him with an opportunity to advance his basic thesis that American blacks were not to be understood in terms of a culture of African survivals, and certainly not in biological terms, but rather in terms of a particular set of experiences within a social world relatively isolated from that of the white world. American blacks, Frazier kept insisting, could only be understood as a people shaped by their particular American experience: "The institutional life of the Negro community, especially where it is an expression of Negro enterprise and leadership, as, for example, the church, reflects in its organization and aims the various cultural heritages and traditions of Negro life in America. Social values and social distinctions stem from the experiences and actualities within the Negro world" (263).

Among white sociologists, however, there was strong resistance to such an idea. Frazier was fully aware of this resistance and acknowledged that there were "conflicting opinions concerning the existence or non-existence of a so-called Negro culture in America." But he made his own position clear: "the very fact that we have felt it necessary to describe the social and cultural world of the Negro indicates that we do not share the opinion of those who assert that the social and cultural world of the Negro is identical with that of the whites simply because the Negro wears the same clothes and speaks the same language as the whites." Instead, Frazier argued, American blacks live in a "more or less isolated world," and it is in this world "with its peculiar social definitions and meanings and with its own social evaluations and distinctions, that the personality of the Negro takes form and acquires a meaning" (277).

Grounded as it was in the daily realities of social interaction and experience in an urban black community, Frazier's was the most sociologically impressive of the four studies on black youth in the 1930s.

Growing Up in the Black Belt

The study that covered the more familiar territory was Charles Johnson's study of rural black youth in the Deep South, *Growing Up in the Black Belt*.[13] Like Frazier, Johnson was a student of Robert Park and at the time of the study was director of the Department of Social Sciences at Fisk University. In the world of sociological scholarship he had already achieved considerable recognition. His *Shadow of the Plantation* had become a widely cited sociological analysis of rural black life; he was a trustee of the Julius Rosenwald Fund, a first vice-president of the American Sociological Society, and he had been a member of the executive and planning committees of the White House Conference on Children in a Democracy.

In an effort to examine the varied breadth and range of black life in the South, Frazier and his staff selected eight counties in five states: Alabama, Mississippi, Tennessee, Georgia, and North Carolina. Six of the counties were plantation-cotton counties (half of the rural black population still lived in such counties), but differed in the extent to which the system of single-crop cotton economy either still flourished or was in some degree of disintegration. The eight counties in the study were chosen to represent 80 percent of the rural black population in the South (xx–xxii). Johnson made it clear at the outset that the rural South was not to be seen as a homogeneous and relatively unchanged racial system.

In its methodology this study reflected the contemporary interest of sociologists in collecting data in quantitative form. A sample of more that two thousand youths between the ages of ten and twenty were given an intelligence test and five tests developed at Fisk to test personal attitudes, color ratings, personal values, occupation ratings, and race attitudes. This was followed up with intensive interviews with about 20 percent of the sample. In addition, these same tests were given to samples of youths in both northern and southern cities to provide some comparative data for the analysis of three issues: intraracial attitudes, attitudes about color, and attitudes about whites (xxii, 254, 266, 308).

Like Frazier, Johnson studied such institutional structures as school and church, as well as recreation, and focused strongly on the family. Also, like Frazier, he used a three-tiered model of social class, but he subdivided the lower class into an upper-lower of "rank-and-file" blacks, a lower-lower category defined culturally rather than economically, as well as a "folk Negro," whose cultural attributes were developed under slavery (72–76). Consequently, much of the description and analysis Johnson provided differed little, except for the focus on youth, from that found in *Shadow of the Plantation*. The grinding poverty of rurul blacks, on the one hand, and the severe limitations of social development allowed in a racially oppressive system, on the other, accounted for a people poorly educated, little skilled, and culturally undeveloped.

What came through as the central message of *Growing Up in the Black Belt* was that even rural black youth were seriously discontented with their lot and with the racial system that defined their status. If the educational system served them badly, they nonetheless maintained a faith "in the power of education to confer prestige and to facilitate racial and occupational change." If rural youth did not reject the church and religion, they did look critically at the rural clergy and did not look for leadership from this most conservative institution. If in fact their occupational expectations were so unrealistic as to border on "fantasy," those expectations reflected a strong desire to escape farming and to achieve an occupation that offered security and greater material gain. By the same token, if sexual promiscuity was still common, both sexes looked for a more stable family life, and girls were in revolt against common-law marriage and easy separation, wishing to avoid the large families and hard work their mothers had had to endure (134, 146–54, 223, 240–41).

Rural black youth in the South did not see any virtue in those qualities that white people most appreciated in blacks: being "loyal, tractable, happy, and hard working." Yet, by and large, their capacity for pride in their own race had little to draw upon in the South's biracial environment, and consequently, compared to other black youth, they rated low on measurements of racial pride. The tests Johnson used revealed that racial pride increased substantially among those with higher education and higher intelligence. Also, urban black youth in the South possessed more race consciousness and had more race pride than did rural youth, while northern urban youth, by the same measure, were more race conscious and possessed more race pride than southern youth, urban and rural (242, 246–65).

Johnson's most crucial data dealt with the attitudes of black rural youth toward white people. After a review of the conventional stereotype of the "folk Negro" that originated in slavery, he pointed out that "the present generation of Negro youth presents somewhat different social and psychological characteristics than those of the stereotype of the Southern rural Negro." Though black youth varied considerably in their attitudes, "none of the youth, however, were without some measure of criticism of the bearing upon their lives and aspirations of the restricting institutions of the white world." In the interviews, Johnson reported, "The most frequent complaints were that white people try to keep Negroes down economically, and that whites insult and ridicule Negroes" (280, 282, 285).

One common response to insulting treatment was to avoid contact with whites as much as possible. Early adolescents between the ages of ten and fifteen tended to withdraw from all contact with white people, though after that, employment made such contact unavoidable. Furthermore, almost two-thirds of rural youth expressed a desire to move away, in most cases to northern cities like Chicago and Detroit. Among those who lived on plantations, where relations had changed least and economic status for blacks was most depressed, attitudes toward whites were the most unfavorable (294–95, 289, 325).

Though Johnson presented a quite varied body of data about rural black youth, revealing often inconsistent attitudes, and though there was no evidence of racial militancy, there could be no mistaking the message: the younger generation of southern blacks provided no reason for complacency for those whites, including sociologists, who still saw in racial caste a long-enduring system of social relations. In the future, Johnson concluded, "If one cannot safely predict progress in race relations, he can at least predict change" (327).

Color and Human Nature

The final volume of the series, Studies of Negro Youth, was *Color and Human Nature*, written by Lloyd Warner and two associates,

Buford H. Junker and Walter A. Adams. Compared to other studies this one was an anomaly, for it was not primarily about youth and there was no reference to youth or children in the title. The study was based on an analysis of 805 persons classified according to personality types; only 280 were young people, and "young" meant anyone up to and including twenty-five years of age. Many of those identified as youth in the analysis were in their twenties, in contrast to the exclusive focus on adolescents in the other studies. The authors defended this by arguing that, to understand the problems of youth, they "needed to know more about adults who displayed the same general social characteristics as the young people but in a more fully developed form." To study "a 16-year-old darkskin boy from a lower-middle-class family," they claimed, would not reveal "the long-run effects of being a Negro of that type."[14]

The assumption underlying this methodological procedure was that "long-run effects" meant a stable continuity in the social relations of color and caste in Chicago, so that one could study an adult of a specific class and color in order to foresee the personality-shaping problems a youth would encounter. Such an assumption presumed more persistence than change in the social lives of Chicago blacks and (as Dollard did) discounted the generational changes in attitudes and behavior to which Frazier and Johnson gave such importance. It was also consistent with Warner's framework of racial caste, which he was now to argue applied fairly well to Chicago in the 1930s. Donald Young's concept of a minority group, he argued, was inappropriate for blacks; instead, it properly applied only to the situation of white ethnics. The concept of caste fitted better the "systematic subordination" of blacks to whites in the American system. If that system persists, the "children and grandchildren of Negroes will continue to be born into, live in, and only die out of the Negro 'caste.'... For the individual, the essence of caste is its permanence."[15]

But did such a conceptualization, developed from an analysis of the Deep South, apply as well to a northern city? Warner argued that an examination of *The Negro in Chicago* (about the 1919 race riot) made it clear that in 1920 all the familiar characteristics of race relations in the South were evident in Chicago. At the time of this study, almost twenty years later, racial segregation was even more pronounced: "There is considerable evidence (with respect to segregation, for example) to show that the Chicago system is becoming more like that of the Deep South. Although the position of the Negro is certainly different in Chicago from that below the Mason-Dixon Line, a study of the city's entire community life, including the white world, indicates that if caste, as the term is here used, is not present in Chicago, then something very close to it definitely is. The situation must be described as at least a caste-like system."[16]

Within the caste-like structure of the black community, color and class, according to Warner and his associates, were the dominant factors shaping personality. The use of a set of class categories was basic to Warner's now well-established analysis, but he now introduced distinctions of color, from lightest to darkest, as an equally stratifying element. The combining of these into a single system provided a set of personality types. There were four classes in the black community of Chicago—upper, upper-middle, lower-middle, and lower—and within each one people were categorized as passable, lightskin, brownskin, and darkskin. Dividing these by male and female produced thirty-two personality types (e.g., passable upper-class woman and darkskin lower-class man).[17] The book then became a series of chapters organized by color (e.g., chap. 2, "Darkskin Men"; chap. 7, "Brownskin People"). Each chapter presented brief case material of people of a given color from each social class. Class and color correlated, so that the great majority of lightskin people were above the lower class, while almost two thirds of the darkskin people were in the lower class.

The case material recorded the processes of adjustment and adaptation made by Chicago's black population to the basic fact of being black, and within that caste prescription, to the realities of class position and the evaluations of color. They coped with limited opportunities, economic insecurity, often poorly defined social situations (in contrast to the South), and the awareness of a shared racial status. Some criticized their fellow blacks in terms of white standards, while others defended blacks and expressed solidarity with their own kind ("race man" and "race woman").

The interviews were designed to focus primarily on personal experiences and daily adjustments, that is, how blacks individually coped with and adjusted to a highly constraining racial structure. As a consequence, very little information on attitudes about social change or politics emerged from the material. Such a focus was consistent with the study's basic assumption, namely, that a "caste-like" structure of race relations was firmly in place and was likely to remain in force for an indefinite future. The reader could not look to this study to find out whether the black people of Chicago had developed attitudes favorable to some form of social change or were becoming potentially mobilizable for political struggle; that was outside the scope of the study.

Studying Black Youth: Contrast and Comparison

The four studies funded by the American Youth Commission were intended to answer one question: "What are the effects upon the personality development of Negro youth of their membership in a minority racial group?" Though all of the studies provided answers, they by no means spoke in a common voice or developed a common analysis. This was not because of the varying social contexts, urban and rural, north and south, in which the studies were carried on, for that was the intended dimension of the project. Rather, there were basic differences in perspective, methods, and analysis. One difference was the extent to which these studies, carried out by sociologists and anthropologists, were primarily psychological in their analysis. Dollard's utilization of a behaviorist psychology put *Children of Bondage* in sharp contrast to the others, even Warner's, where a psychiatrist was a coauthor. Frazier and Johnson made specific a culture and personality framework for their studies, and Frazier's emphasis upon institutional forces made his study the most sociological.

Yet, even on its own terms, the project as a whole remained incomplete. The intent of commissioning the four studies was to provide urban-rural and southern-northern contrasts. But the individual authors could not do that, for their studies were carried out simultaneously. Logically, that was the task of the summarizing volume, wherein the analysis of contrasting data might explicate evidence of changes and differences in patterns of personality development and in attitudes. But Robert Sutherland's short volume did not do that; instead, he generalized about the status of black youth as commonly disadvantaged and failed to provide any contrast or comparison.[18]

The fundamental flaw in the project was the lack of a common frame of reference by which the separate studies could have been tied together, and from which significant comparisons of findings could have been made. Dollard and Warner carried out their analysis within the framework of caste and class, but Frazier and Johnson, as students of Robert Park, and more important, as black sociologists, viewed race relations differently. They observed an already developing breakup of the southern pattern of race relations, and they noted a more volatile situation emerging in the urban North, not an extension of Southern caste.

In advancing the concept of an American racial caste, Warner had taken specific issue with Robert Park. He explicitly rejected Park's view that blacks could no longer be defined as a caste, but instead were to be understood as a racial or national minority. The widespread acceptance of Warner's concept of racial caste was thus, in the short run, a rejection of the view sustained by Park and other sociologists, and meant, instead, a conception of race relations as stability and continuity, not immiment change. Within a decade, however, the concept of minority, instead of caste, was to prevail.

In contrast to Warner, both Frazier and Johnson had looked for and found changes in attitudes and behavior among the coming generation of blacks. Johnson took deliberate pains to reject the notion of caste as applicable to American race relations. Instead, in the last sentence of his text, he reasserted his longstanding conviction that blacks were struggling against racial oppression and did not willingly accept a subordinate position. As for the future, one can predict change.

Frazier, who earlier in the decade had done research in New York City for Mayor LaGuardia's Commission on Conditions in Harlem (following a race riot in 1935), was particularly sensitive to changes brought about by the great migration to the North. Though, unlike Johnson, he made no reference to the concept of caste in *Negro Youth at the Crossways,* the idea that racial caste had been transplanted to northern cities violated what Frazier knew and admired about cities with "a ferment of ideas and movements which ceaselessly agitate." Frazier also took issue with Warner, and therefore with most of his white sociological colleagues, by challenging one of the most basic assumptions underlying the dominant concept of assimilation, namely, that blacks shared with whites the identical culture. In *Negro Youth at the Crossways,* Frazier had rejected the idea that black and white people were culturally identical "simply because the Negro wears the same clothes and speaks the same language as the whites." The isolated world that segregation produced, he insisted, had "its peculiar social definitions and meanings and its own social evaluations and distinctions." Warner, in contrast, explicitly endorsed the dominant idea of assimilation. It appears, he said, "that the Negro society in Chicago represents a group with an American culture but organized on a caste-like or racial basis." It has "assimilated all the characteristics of the larger society."[19]

There was one commonality between Frazier and Warner, however: both recognized the importance that black people attributed to shades of color and, therefore, of the slowly changing relationship between color and class. The darker the skin, the more likely such individuals were lower-class. In this way, both Frazier and Warner gave recognition to the superior status, in the eyes of both black and white people, of the person of mixed ancestry. Frazier described the differential treatment accorded schoolchildren by teachers because of differences in shades of color. Warner, however, went beyond Frazier in treating color as a decisive and presumably permanent feature of black life. Yet the significance given to shades of color among black people, and the preference for lighter color, was to receive its last emphasis in the sociological literature published just before World War II. Even by then, the term "mulatto" was used less than before, and after the War the issue of shades of color gradually became less and less significant.

However the merits of these contending positions may look by historical hindsight, in the early 1940s the majority of American sociologists of race relations seemed to be more responsive to the analysis set forth by John Dollard and W. Lloyd Warner, but particularly by Dollard. While all four books in the series were readily accepted as serious contributions to the sociological literature, Davis and Dollard's *Children of Bondage* was far more widely read and cited, going through five printings in the next seven years. Its portrait of blacks as a culturally backward, mostly lower-class people focused upon the difficulties of family and school as socializing agents in turning blacks into middle-class strivers, a process Dollard saw as taking precedence over other efforts at racial change. Like *Caste and Class in a Southern Town*, *Children of Bondage* offered a reassuring sense that blacks were still well removed from any cultural readiness to challenge the existing racial order.

One question remains: Why should so much effort have been put into a series of studies of social adjustment and development, rather than into studies of demographic, structural, and cultural change? If the question asked in the project was sociologically legitimate—and it was—it was still not necessarily the most sociologically important question. The ferment of the black communities in northern cities (the great explosion of the 1943 race riot in Detroit was just ahead), the structural consequences of a great migration out of the South, the new political opportunities for blacks in urban politics, and the new potential for overt racial conflict—these and other issues were no less demanding of an answer than the question that led to the funding of these four studies.

To the extent that the question originated with the funding agency, it is necessary to recall that the parent and founder of the American Youth Council was the American Council on Education, and it was its imprint as publisher that appeared on the books. It had founded the American Youth Commission in 1935 to consider the needs of all youth and to plan and promote desirable programs of action. The studies of black youth were one facet of that mandate. The underlying assumption was that the established organizations of education, as well

as other public and community agencies, could and should devise programs to fit the needs of black youth. But the recommendations offered
by Robert Sutherland in his summary volume were innocent of offense
to established practice and rhetorically innocuous. They remain a measure of what those inside the established order thought it expedient
to say (and not to say) in 1942.

The Black Family

In 1939 the publication of E. Franklin Frazier's *The Negro Family
in the United States* marked the emergence of a major new figure in
American sociology. Frazier was not the first black sociologist to
achieve scholarly recognition—Charles Johnson had already become
widely recognized and respected—but Frazier's sustained effort to define the black American as a product of slavery and segregation was
to provide an impressive body of work and to make him one of the
discipline's most often cited sociologists. *The Negro Family in the
United States* won the Anisfield Award as the most important contribution to the study of race relations that year. By 1939 Frazier had
already published extensively on the black family, including the publication of his doctoral dissertation on the black family in Chicago and
a study of the "free" Negro family. From 1926 to 1937, Frazier published sixteen articles on diverse aspects of family life among black
people in a wide variety of publications.[20]

Even though Ernest Burgess was to hail *The Negro Family in the
United States* as "the most valuable contribution to the literature on
the family since the publication, twenty years ago, of *The Polish Peasant in Europe and America* by W. I. Thomas and Florian Znaniecki,"
Frazier's book was more than a contribution to the sociology of the
family.[21] Frazier saw in the transformation of the black family from
slavery through Reconstruction to the conditions of northern urban
life an explanation of the structural changes that had shaped blacks
as persons and had given form and content to the culture and institutions of black life in the United States.

Frazier had dedicated himself to the task of providing a sociological
explanation of the development of the black family to replace those
varied racial and cultural explanations that, in most cases, reinforced
conceptions of black inferiority. The publication in 1939 of *The Negro
Family in the United States* was the culmination of that long effort.

The Family as Formative Process

Frazier took as his starting point the issue about which he was
later to quarrel with the anthropologist Melville Herskovits: the degree

of Africanness of American blacks. It was always Frazier's position that the enslaving experience had so removed African culture from the black people that they had been remade as a people: "But of the habits and customs, as well as the hopes and fears that characterized their forebears in Africa, nothing remains."[22]

Enslavement and the removal from Africa created the first and perhaps the greatest adaptation that black people were forced to make. What emerged from that process of deculturation was a folk people and a folk culture adapted to the conditions of slavery and an isolated rural life. The dominance of the matriarchal role was a natural consequence of the insecurity of black family life under slavery; as Frazier noted, "Generally speaking, the mother remained throughout slavery the dominant and important figure in the slave family" (60).

After Emancipation there was a second major adjustment, this time to a legally free but hostile and unrewarding environment. Frazier saw two general tendencies emerging. First, those families already possessing a patriarchal household, where "the authority of the father was firmly established," made the transition to freedom without difficulty. These freed families joined the nearly half-million blacks who were free before the Civil War. Frazier credits the already free blacks with first establishing the black family on an institutional basis. Their ranks were characterized by the prominence of mulattoes, and as a group they were both skilled and possessed some degree of education (106, 181).

The second tendency was the one so often identified with blacks, both in sociology and in popular images: that of the matriarchate. According to Frazier, "the loose ties that had held men and women together in a nominal marriage relation during slavery broke easily during the crisis of emancipation ... men cut themselves loose from all family ties and joined the great body of homeless men wandering the country in search of work and experience ... more often the woman with family ties, whether she had been without a husband during slavery or was deserted when freedom came, became responsible for the maintenance of the family group" (106–7). Under such circumstances, reports Frazier, "casual" sexual contacts continued, and these black women found themselves the economic support of and source of parental affection for children: "Thus motherhood outside the institutional control was accepted by a large group of Negro women with an attitude of resignation as if it were nature's decree" (107).

In the twentieth century, the great movement of rural blacks to northern cities destroyed what family organization had evolved in the rural South. Frazier traced through what happened "in the city of destruction." In separate chapters he analyzed desertion by fathers, illegitimacy, delinquency among youth, and divorce as a response to desertion. A rural, still largely folk people were unprepared to cope with the demands and pressures of an urban life marked by poverty, slums, and what Frazier called "the influence of a vicious environment," where broken homes and working mothers signified a failure of parental control (375).

Yet, the city of destruction was also to become the city of rebirth. In three chapters that closed the book, Frazier noted already observable developments that foretold a better future. In particular, he explored the emergence of a "brown" middle class and a "black" proletariat. Class differences would separate blacks from one another and would draw them closer to whites of the same class.

Frazier labeled the emerging middle class "brown" because of its "mixed ancestry," giving emphasis to what was still a strong theme in the sociological analysis of race, namely, the superior class status of mulattoes and others of mixed blood. Yet, he also noted, this was changing. Whereas a light skin, membership in an established family, and pretensions of culture once marked a small elite that could claim middle-class status, this was now giving way to an emphasis on occupation and income. Even then, however, a successful black male would often marry "a fair daughter of one of these old mulatto families in order to consolidate his social status" (428).

This middle class was not to be defined by some criteria peculiar to social status in the black community but by occupational criteria; it included "those in business enterprises and white-collar occupations, men and women engaged in professional pursuits and employed in responsible positions in public services." Frazier utilized census data, particularly data measuring changes from 1920 to 1930, to demonstrate growth in the middle class. He found an increase in the black middle class that ranged from 4.3 percent in Birmingham, Alabama, to 12.9 percent in Chicago and 13.4 percent in New York City. Growth was greatest in the professions and clerical services, least in trade and business enterprise (421, 423; see also Table 52, 640).

To Frazier, this apparent beginning of a change in the composition of the middle class from small business to professional status, to those employed in public services, and to a range of white-collar occupations—a shift that paralleled that of the white middle class—was a significant development. He pointed back to the origins of the middle class in the establishment of the National Negro Business League under the leadership of Booker T. Washington in 1900, the resolutions of which "contained a naive profession of faith in individual thrift and individual enterprise in a world that was rapidly entering a period of corporate wealth." Consequently, "when the economic foundations of the Negro middle class are explored . . . they are found insubstantial and insecure" (420).

In this insubstantial foundation of the middle class, Frazier located those characteristics and behavior patterns of family life he found wanting and deserving of criticism. A relatively isolated middle class of business operators and professionals serving a largely segregated and low-income population, he felt, displayed undue conspicuous consumption, spent too much time on social life, and possessed a "superficial" culture devoid of serious intellectual, artistic, or literary interests. This pursuit of middle-class respectability was complemented by a conservative economic outlook, little different from that of the white middle class. And though this middle class was "the most race conscious element in the Negro group," many nonetheless resisted the elimination of segregation that would admit lower-class blacks into public places; they wanted to retain a monopoly over a segregated market that provided the basis of their economic position: "They prefer the overvaluation of their achievements and position behind the walls of segregation to a democratic order that would result in economic and social devaluation for themselves" (433, 436).

Yet, Frazier claimed, there was no future in this: "There are no grounds for the belief that this class will find a secure economic base in a segregated economy with its Negro captains of industry, managers, technicial assistants, and white-collar workers." There would be, then, no black capitalism. Instead, the growth of the black middle class would occur primarily by the entrance of blacks into white-collar occupations. The breakdown of racial barriers allowing blacks to compete on equal terms with whites was one factor in this change, and Frazier was clearly confident that such a gradual change would continue. He also presciently noted one immediate factor contributing to greater white-collar opportunities for blacks: the increase in white-collar positions in state and municipal governmental agencies: "In fact, the Negro middle class is increasing in the very northern cities where Negroes are permitted through political power to compete with other races for positions under state control" (445–46).

In such economic changes, Frazier saw evidence of both growth and decline in middle-class family patterns. A continuing assimilation into the status of salaried workers, he thought, would produce a family life reflecting such a change in economic status and outlook on life. In turn, middle-class blacks would "cease to think of themselves as a privileged and 'wealthy' upper Negro class" (ibid.).

Even more important to Frazier than the growth of the brown middle class was the emergence of a black urban proletariat. The migration northward and subsequent urbanization of the black population had produced such a social class, and it was growing. The existence of black workers, even skilled workers, however, did not begin with northward migration. Frazier traced back the solid if small group of skilled artisans long existent in the South. He also noted a long existing body of black longshoremen, miners, and steel and stockyard workers, and among them there was a history of unionism, of industrial struggle, and the development of working-class consciousness, which necessarily meant cooperation with white workers. (Here was evidence of Frazier's early socialist outlook. His use of "proletariat" was not for the first time and not for any shock effect on his white sociological colleagues, even though the large majority of them found any item of the Marxian vocabulary uncongenial to their way of thinking. In an earlier article, Frazier had argued for the primacy of economic organization in establishing status and described the emergence of an "industrial proletariat" as the most important new class among blacks.)[23]

Though the proletariat was a growing class, noted Frazier, its members experienced unemployment and decreased income during the depression. Even that setback, however, had a positive effect, for the black worker's experience of the depression "has done more than years of agitation to make him conscious of his position as a worker." Consequently, black workers cooperated more and more with white workers and less often saw their problems as only racial. In the emergence of a stable black proletariat, Frazier envisioned a black worker who assumed responsibility for the support of his family and acquired a new authority in family relations. For Frazier, a new black proletariat disciplined to modern industry was the "most significant element in the new social structure of Negro life . . . since the Negro was introduced into Western civilization" (475, 486).

Why would Frazier have seen in the emergence of the black industrial worker a development more significant than the growth of the brown middle class? For one thing, this was a development that "affected tremendously the whole outlook on life and the values of the masses of Negroes" and turned them away from crude imitations of middle-class standards, long so common to domestic workers. Secondly, the black's attainment of a disciplined family life with the father as breadwinner signified success "in adapting habits of living that have enabled him to survive in a civilization based upon laissez-faire and competition." The black had become assimilated to a new mode of life and in doing so had "found within the pattern of the white man's

culture a purpose in life and a significance for his strivings." Furthermore, the black proletariat was breaking from the old and ineffectual
race leadership and from the influence of its unsatisfactory life-style
and moving closer to white workers in values, ideals, and in collaborative behavior (486–87).

For Frazier, the development of a black proletariat as well as of a
middle class were processes of assimilation by which racial differences
would decline and class differences would increase. Here was a reminder of Robert Park's prediction that racial conflicts would be
superseded by class conflicts as the focus of human struggle. But perhaps more so than Park, Frazier emphasized the integration of the
black into the economy as basic to promoting assimilation. This was
evident in the last two sentences of the book: "But, in the final analysis,
the process of assimilation and acculturation will be limited by the
extent to which the Negro becomes integrated into the economic
organization and participates in the life of the community. The gains
in civilization which result from participation in the white world will
in the future as in the past be transmitted to future generations through
the family" (488).

Frazier on Family Disorganization

In the 1930s, when Frazier was writing on the black family, the
concept of social disorganization was a mainstay of the American sociological vocabulary, and Frazier made use of it in his work. Later,
however, when the concept was subjected to severe criticism, his own
work was criticized. In 1941 a critical assessment of the concept began,
instigated by two articles in the *American Sociological Review*. The
first was the classic essay by Richard Fuller and Richard Myers that
made a persuasive case for replacing the concept of social disorganization with that of social problems; the second was by Ernest Mowrer
on the methodological problems inherent in the concept.[24]

In 1943 William Foote Whyte entered the debate with a paper that
argued that to define a slum as disorganized failed to observe the
organization that the slum possessed. The publication that same year
of his classic study, *Street Corner Society*, then offered the most sustained argument for observing social organization under conditions that
sociologists had often taken to be disorganized. Also in 1943 C. Wright
Mills published his influential paper on the ideological nature of the
social pathologists, under which he included all those whose work
employed the concepts of social pathology, social disorganization, and
social problems.[25]

To locate Frazier's work within the context of this critique requires that two different uses of the concept of social disorganization in American sociology be identified. The most common use was in defining the sociological concern for a set of social problems defined as most characteristic of the urban poor. Animated by moral judgment and an impetus to social intervention, most sociologists had used both the concepts of social pathology and social disorganization to define this intersection of class and urbanism as a debilitating and societally threatening social condition. It was a condition inviting the social intervention of the state through its representative agencies, for the people inhabiting this social condition were presumed not to be able to rise above their debilitating circumstances. It was this use of the concept of social disorganization that was brought into question by Mowrer, Fuller and Myers, Whyte, and Mills.

But Frazier's use of social disorganization was conceptually different. Like other sociological concepts of the Chicago school, disorganization was not primarily a social condition but a dimension of the process of social change. Disorganization necessarily implied a prior state of organization, the breakdown of which under new conditions was disorganization. But disorganization was always temporary, to be followed by reorganization. Within that paradigm, disorganization was not pathology, as Ernest Burgess had said in 1925: "So far as disorganization points to reorganization and makes for more efficient adjustment, disorganization must not be conceived as pathological, but as normal."[26]

Burgess was not the first of the Chicago school to so define disorganization. Several years earlier, in the classic study of ethnic migration and assimilation, *The Polish Peasant in Europe and America,* W. I. Thomas and Florian Znaniecki spoke extensively of disorganization, but always as process, not condition. As James T. Carey noted, "It is clear from their discussion of social disorganization that Thomas and Znaniecki see society as on a continuum from organization to disorganization to reorganization. Disorganization is but one phase of a three-stage process; it is viewed not as a condition but as part of a process."[27]

Whyte also understood these two conceptions of disorganization in sociology, and though he did not clarify the distinction, the issue was central to his argument. He pointed out that it was fruitless to study only "the breakdown of old groupings and old standards; new groupings and new standards have arisen." The organization of the slums, he insisted, cannot be understood until sociologists "shift the emphasis from social disorganization in order to investigate the process of social reorganization."[28]

Most of the criticism of Frazier's work centered on his analysis of the disorganization of the rural folk family as a consequence of urban migration. The six chapters of part 4, "In the City of Destruction," gave a detailed examination of urban family disorganization. But that was followed by part 5, "The City of Rebirth," in which he described a new middle class that had come into existence, as well as an emerging black proletariat. Here was social reorganization. The poverty and disorganization so prevalent among urbanized blacks was not, for Frazier, a permanent condition.

Frazier's use of the concept of social disorganization was clearly that of process, not social condition. His use of the concept made evident his training as a Chicago sociologist and as a student of Park. He was not in the melioristic tradition of the social pathologists, nor did he share that tradition's moral judgments. He accepted, for example, the existence of common-law marriage as the basis of family life. Within his processual framework, he sought to reconstruct a history of the black family as one of evolution, dissolution, and reconstruction under changing circumstances from enslavement to urbanization.

Since his own time, however, Frazier has sometimes been read as if he were a social pathologist. A notable case was that of the anthropologist Charles A. Valentine, whose otherwise useful critique of the culture-of-poverty thesis was marred by a gratuitous and condescending reading of Frazier. In a section headed, "The Pejorative Tradition Established by E. Franklin Frazier," Valentine claimed that Frazier "creates an image of the black poor as so abysmally disorganized and so hopelessly infected with social pathologies that they lacked public opinion, social control, or community traditions."[29] This pejorative tradition, he claimed, was then carried on by Glazier and Moynihan in their *Beyond the Melting Pot* and culminated in Moynihan's *The Negro Family*. But no such pejorative tradition can be inferred from a careful reading of Frazier's work.

Perhaps the most fruitful yet appreciative critique of Frazier has been that of the late historian Herbert G. Gutman, whose own historical reconstruction of the black family in the United States is the best work on the subject since Frazier's study, and the only work to supersede Frazier's in both the range and depth of its historical data. In a critical review of the relevant literature, Gutman defended Frazier from identification with the interpretations offered by Moynihan and others. "Such views," he noted, "draw in a somewhat distorted fashion upon Frazier's major arguments." Denying they were "serious historical and sociological analyses," Gutman identified them as "mere diachronic speculation upon the relationship between slavery and twentieth-century Afro-American life."[30]

Despite his own criticism of Frazier's historical work, Gutman did not hesitate to accord him a status attained by no one else: "Despite my own quarrel with Frazier's work as a *historian* of the black family, his reputation as a distinguished sociologist and pioneer student of Afro-American family life remains secure—and for good reason. His scholarship and that of W. E. B. Du Bois were the most significant in refuting widely approved racial 'explanations' of Afro-American marital and family institutions."[31]

Gutman recalled Ernest Burgess's preface to *The Negro Family in the United States* and quoted his statement that the study exploded popular misconceptions about uniform behavior among blacks and showed, instead, the wide variation that black social classes brought to family life. "More than this," Gutman insisted, "when we search for comparative materials on the history of white lower-class families, we cannot find a single study that compares in scope and detail with Frazier's work on the black family. It remains the best single historical study of the American family, black or white, published to date." Not only had Frazier's work been outstanding and of pathbreaking significance, according to Gutman, but it had not been superseded: "In truth, historians and sociologists have said little new about the history of the Negro family since Frazier published his work thirty-five years ago."[32]

Whatever its shortcomings, Frazier's study of the black family remains a major classic of the sociological literature. It has suffered from an unwarranted identification with the controversy created by Moynihan's report on the present status of the black family and from a conceptual confusion among sociologists between disorganization as condition and as process. Still, its achievements are noteworthy. As Gutman pointed out, it effectively challenged once and for all the still prevalent racial conceptions of black marital and family institutions, and, as Burgess emphasized, it demonstrated variations in the black family, not the uniformity of behavior so often attributed to blacks.

The publication in 1939 of *The Negro Family in the United States* secured E. Franklin Frazier's status as a major sociologist. It became the definitive work for sociologists on the subject for at least the next three decades, and it buried forever a body of sloppy and inaccurate, and in some cases racially biased, explanations of black family life in the United States. Its publication was also the culmination of an interest in the black family that Frazier had sustained since 1926. He had felt that, since the appearance of W. E. B. Du Bois's *The Negro American Family* in 1909, there had been a "long neglect of this phase of Negro life," and he meant to remedy that and "apply the tools and concepts of modern sociological analysis to the study of this problem in the North" (xix). His accomplishment, which reached a far wider readership than Du Bois was ever able to attain, was notable in narrowing the range of error and misunderstanding that would characterize the thinking of white sociologists about black people. Ernest Burgess's preface to the book recorded that accomplishment as a turning point in the sociology of the family. It was also a major step forward in the sociological understanding of black Americans.

African Survivals: Frazier versus Herskovits

The major thrust of Frazier's long study of black family life was his basic proposition that black people had been thoroughly stripped of their African heritage and had, in effect, been remade into a new people by the life that slavery had imposed upon them. Black Americans were to be understood primarily in terms of the formative power of slavery and segregation, not biological heritage, and not their origins in African cultures. His historical analysis focused upon the adjustments that blacks made to varying circumstances beyond their control and to the resultant differences in modes of black social life.

Melville Herskovits, a student of Franz Boas, and one of the few anthropologists who studied New World blacks, believed that a significant degree of African culture had been retained among blacks in the New World, including those in the United States. Thus, during the 1930s, Herskovits developed a position that was self-consciously opposed to the position being argued by Frazier, and which he also attributed to W. E. B. Du Bois. In 1941, in his major work, *The Myth of the Negro Past,* he sought to demonstrate that the continuity and strength of African heritage contradicted any notion of social disorganization among American blacks. A scholar of wide learning, Herskovits looked for evidence of African cultural elements retained and alive even under radically changed modes of living. He did not expect culture to go unaltered when the lives of its carriers were so greatly changed, so he argued for evidence of "reinterpretations," as well as "retentions," and also "syncretisms"—those amalgamations of cultural elements resulting from joining one cultural tradition to another.[33]

Often Frazier and Herskovits brought different evidence to bear upon the issue: Herskovits on African cultural elements; Frazier on adjustment to economic and social conditions. But the two seemed to come together when each spent an academic year in the early 1940s in Bahia, Brazil: Frazier in 1941–42, Herskovits in 1942–43. In 1942

Frazier published an article on his observations on the black family in Bahia, and in 1943 Herskovits published an article critical of Frazier's findings, to which Frazier made a rejoinder.[34]

Herskovits had long argued that one could not study New World blacks without a "base-line" of African cultures. With that in mind, he criticized Frazier's very way of undertaking his study. Frazier, he claimed, had brought to his Brazilian study the "methodological blind-spot" characteristic of research on Negroes in the United States: "No reference to any work describing African cultures is made in his paper, and only oblique references to the forms of African social structure are encountered." He proceeded, therefore, with a short sketch of West African family structures to show their relevance for the study of family life in Brazil and to see "whether or not the picture of almost complete disorganization Frazier presents cannot be resolved into a series of recognizable patterns of both form and sanction." He followed that with a detailed analysis on forms of marriage, relations of children to parents, and related rituals and symbols in Bahia. In particular, he asserted what he called the "untenability of the hypothesis of the 'weakness of institutional controls' " in Frazier's argument.[35]

Frazier's response to Herskovits was brief but pointed: "the facts which I gathered in Brazil do not support his conclusions." Reminding his readers that in *The Myth of the Negro Past* Herskovits had placed Frazier "among those Negroes who accept as a compliment the theory of a complete break with Africa," Frazier asserted it to be "a matter of indifference to me personally whether there are African survivals in the United States or Brazil." He then drew the distinction between Herskovits and himself that he regarded as basic: "Professor Herskovits was interested in discovering Africanisms and I was only interested in African survivals so far as they affected the organization and adjustment of the Negro family to the Brazilian environment."[36]

Frazier was equally direct in responding to Herskovits's criticism that he saw only family disorganization among Bahian blacks: "It was not my intention to give a picture of complete family disorganization among the so-called Negroes. As I undertook to show in my article, the family among these people did not have an institutional character but grew out of association of men and women in a relationship which was based upon personal inclination and habit. Although it is customary for men and women to initiate family life in such a manner, I found no evidence that their behavior was due to African customs. White men and women of the lower class form exactly the same type of unions."[37]

By "personal inclination and habit," Frazier was referring to what in the United States was called "common-law marriage," and what his informants in Bahia called "maritalmente" or "marriedly," a relationship they regarded as conjugal, not "free-love," and in which a man assumed responsibility for the support of the woman and her children. It was this relationship that, for Frazier, was the basis of the family as a "natural organization" among lower-class people in general. After arguing with Herskovits over some details of interpretation of material in his article, Frazier closed with an unqualified reassertion of his basic position: "So far as the pattern of the family is concerned, I am still convinced that African influences have on the whole disappeared and that the type of family organization which we find among the Negroes whom I have studied has grown up in response to economic and social conditions in Brazil."[38]

The argument between Frazier and Herskovits was to continue on into the 1950s, but their positions remained unaltered. Among sociologists, Frazier was by far the more persuasive, as he was also among black intellectuals. Frazier articulated a widely shared position that evidence of African survivals could readily be found, but, as Thomas Pettigrew recently noted, Herskovits's Africanisms seemed largely to be "place-names, superstitions, dance steps, singing forms, speech patterns, and religious folk customs," while Frazier was interested in "the broad structural features of black American families."[39] The two adversaries did not always seem to be addressing the same issue.

The starting point of Frazier's argument—that blacks were now an American people, not an African one—was widely shared and had been made before Frazier had stated it. As early as 1918, for example, Robert Park had said that "the Negro, when he landed in the United States, left behind him almost everything" and that "it is very difficult to find in the South today anything that can be traced back to Africa." And almost a decade before the Frazier-Herskovits debate, Guy B. Johnson had boldly stated, "No sociologist maintains that the Negro in this country retains any African social institutions of significance." Most sociologists sided with Frazier over Herskovits because they had already come to believe that the black population had been stripped of all remnants of African culture during slavery and thoroughly remade into an American people, if an inferior one. But unlike Frazier, who argued that slavery and segregation had shaped the enslaved Africans into a distinctive people, most sociologists believed that black people had simply taken over the existing white culture. Again, Johnson expressed the common position when he said the black "had tended to adopt the various white institutional complexes in toto," and "this seems to hold good all along the line," including even "the minor customary modes of everyday behavior."[40]

But most sociologists also believed that black people had a limited grasp of white culture and often distorted it. Edward Reuter, for example, argued that blacks had developed "faithful" but "inferior" copies of white institutions. Both Guy Johnson and Charles Johnson argued that rural blacks still exhibited a white culture learned in colonial times and now largely forgotten by the white population.[41] Even the culture of the most isolated blacks, therefore, was seen as rooted in archaic forms of white culture, not in retentions of Africanisms. While Frazier was bound to be preferred over Herskovits on this issue, Frazier was being read in a fashion that did not do justice to his own view that adaptation had meant, not a simple copying process of cultural adaptation, but a formative process of shaping a new black people.

The Black Community

That black people lived a separate collective life, distanced from white people by the boundaries set by segregation, was a fact no sociologist would deny. But throughout the first half of the century, there was little effort made by sociologists to penetrate into these segregated communities in which blacks constructed their own social worlds. Instead they restricted their observations to statistical data or to blacks in public places, which meant white-controlled places. What they did record was the circumscribed place for blacks in the larger social structure; what they did not do was provide a description of the social structure created by black people for themselves as a consequence of segregation.

In 1899 W. E. B. Du Bois had pioneered the study of the urban black community in his book *The Philadelphia Negro,* and in the first decade of the century he had tried to organize a program of empirical research in Atlanta on all aspects of black life. However, his efforts at Atlanta received almost no recognition from white sociologists—the *American Journal of Sociology* did not review *The Philadelphia Negro* and reviewed only two of the Atlanta research studies—and in 1910 Du Bois abandoned the project and soon after left sociology. In the 1920s, Ira De A. Reid, a young black sociologist then with the Urban League in New York City, wrote a short description of Harlem for *Social Forces.* He noted that, in terms of social research, Harlem "offers a virgin field" and that "there is a great need for a systematic, exhaustive study of Harlem, not into its single problems, as housing, recreation, health, justice, etc., but an integrated study of it in all its phases."[42] But no such study was undertaken.

Despite the interest that Robert Park had generated in both race relations and the city, and despite the brilliant use that Chicago sociologists made of the city as an urban laboratory, nothing significant was done on the black community *as a community.* A very brief description of the black community of Chicago in about 1920 appeared in the study of the 1919 race riot, *The Negro in Chicago.* But during the 1920s no systematic study of Chicago's black community was undertaken by Park or by any of his students. Frazier was partly an exception to this; he used Chicago as an urban context in which to study the black urban family, and his study, *The Negro Family in Chicago,* contained a rich sense of the community, its institutions and social structure. Yet his was a study of the family, not a community study. Later, he studied Washington, D.C.'s and Louisville's black communities for *Negro Youth at the Crossways.* Again, this was a study keyed to a specific interest—black youth growing up in a segregated community—and was not a full-fledged community study, one in which the community was the object of study, not merely the necessary contextual setting for other research concerns. Then in 1945 came the publication of *Black Metropolis,* the work of two black scholars, Horace Cayton, a sociologist, and St. Clair Drake, an anthropologist.[43] It was to provide sociology with its first full-scale study of a black urban community in the North.

Black Metropolis

Frazier's chapters on the brown middle class and the black proletariat had been one of the few efforts to come to terms with the great northward flow of black people into cities like Chicago. The rapid growth of concentrated settlements of black people in large cities formed a new reality, one that white sociologists seemed hesitant to examine. No sociologist (nor any other social scientist) had tried to sketch out the configuration of the new urban community of black people until Drake and Cayton accomplished it in *Black Metropolis.*

Though not published until 1945, the book was the outcome of a research project funded by the Works Progress Administration for a four-year period in the 1930s. W. Lloyd Warner was instrumental in organizing the project, for he wanted a comparison with the southern community studied in *Deep South.* The original intention, according to Drake and Cayton, was to present the material "as a research report with emphasis upon methodology in the social sciences," but they decided, instead, to write a book that would reach a wider audience (xiv). A grant from the Julius Rosenwald Fund aided the authors in organizing the considerable body of research materials gathered by the Warner-Cayton project, and the authors then spent three years collecting new data. The book that appeared in 1945 provided a detailed description and analysis of black Chicago during the depression and World War II. Rich in detail, full in scope, unparalleled in the sociological literature, and with an introduction by the black novelist Richard Wright—an essay deeply moving in its superlative understanding of what the book was about—*Black Metropolis* was soon to become a sociological classic.

What stood out in *Black Metropolis* was not only a picture of black people struggling to cope with the realities of the "color-line" and pervasive discrimination, but a conception of a *black community,* an organized way of life distinctive in its basic attributes. It was here that Drake and Cayton shared with Frazier a sense of blacks as a people, a sense that differed from that of white sociologists. In the 1940s the latter still pictured blacks as an aggregate of dark-skinned, largely lower-class people, different from white people mostly in terms of being still too little removed from the "backward" conditions imposed by slavery. Their differences from whites were seen as a measurement of how far blacks fell short of the putative qualities of the white middle class. For black sociologists, such differences never got to the heart of the matter.

Drake and Cayton deliberately chose the term "Bronzeville"—a term extant in the area since 1930—rather than Black Belt or ghetto, "because it seems to express the feeling that the people have about their own community. They *live* in the Black Belt and to them it is more than the 'ghetto' revealed by statistical analysis." For the residents of Bronzeville, there was always more to it than the unfavorable comparisons provided by those statistics. Their community was a way of life, an institutional framework for surviving and even getting ahead in a world controlled by whites. Bronzeville, the authors noted, was a world within the white world, one belonging to black people. It was a world with its own institutions and culture: "The people of Bronzeville have, through the years, crystallized certain distinctive patterns of thought and behavior.... The customs and habits of Bronzeville's people are essentially American but carry overtones of subtle difference" (385, 396). The "dissimilarity" between Bronzeville's institutions and those of the white world "springs from" two facts: "Because the community is spiritually isolated from the larger world, the development of its families, churches, schools, and voluntary associations has proceeded quite differently from the course taken by analogous white institutions; and, second, Bronzeville's 'culture' is but a part of a larger, national culture, its people being tied to thirteen million other Negroes by innumerable bonds of kinship, associational and church membership, and a common minority status" (396).

Drake and Cayton gave full attention to the struggle for equality, to the effort to break the job ceiling, to black workers and the new Congress of Industrial Organizations, and to the competition between the Republican and Democratic parties to win the black vote. They also explored the "organization of discontent" to advance the race, the "ferment of ideas and movements" within Chicago's black population, including the influence of the Communist party, the interest of many young, educated blacks in radical ideas, and the shift away from the "safe" leadership of the past (chaps. 11–13, 23). Only Gunnar Myrdal was to give any comparable coverage to the politics of the black community and to its internal efforts to work out a line of strategy for dealing with the white world, but his treatment was less sympathetic.

In the final chapter of the book, Drake and Cayton wrote of "things to come." They wrote, not as social scientists who were black, but as blacks who were also social scientists. They spoke, not of white prejudice and gradual progress, but of America's "moral flabbiness," of it being "frozen and paralyzed before its Negro problem" (765–66). Blacks were more aware than ever of worldwide changes in race relations, they asserted, and had developed a new mentality that refused to accept segregation and to be satisfied with concessions and small gains:

> In trying to assess the situation, white people did not realize that in measuring 'gains' for the Negro they were using an absolute yardstick. At a time when entire peoples are being liquidated or given equality overnight, the theory of 'gradual gains' for Negroes has little meaning. With a world revolution in progress, Negroes refused to be held apart from the stream of thought and to be told to have faith in the long-time process of education and goodwill. To ask the American Negro to go slowly was to attempt either to slacken the international pace of change or to isolate the Negro from the world forces in which he is engulfed. (763–64)

White Americans, the authors noted, believe that all social problems are solvable without violence, but they are incapable of dealing with the moral problems of race and have become "confused and impotent" and look only to preventing a race riot: "So a society convulsed by fear found itself not only unable to act rationally but unable to act at all. Again America resorted to artificial techniques—to magic—in trying to meet the problem. Rather than face the moral issue, society places its reliance in 'planning'—in frantically organized committees to prevent race riots, in anything that would allow it to escape the reality of its confusion and impotence" (766). No white sociologist had ever rendered such a judgment, and not merely because sociologists were committed to an "objective" analysis that precluded any value judgments. In fact, white sociologists were not value-neutral on the matter of race relations, but none of them were capable of coming to a moral assessment of the kind that Drake and Cayton made.

Like Frazier's study of the black family, Drake and Cayton's study of black Chicago was soon to be recognized as a major contribution to the sociology of race relations. It had done what no other study had in exploring fully the complex dimensions of black life in the urban North. And in addition it was an accomplishment of black scholarship. It made evident to those white sociologists who would read and learn from Drake and Cayton that the black ghetto, whatever its deficiencies of poverty and deprivation, was an urban community within which black people had constructed the framework for an organized way of life.

Postscript: Black Sociologists and White Sociology

The effort to discover the black American as a person and as a people provided the opportunity for the best of what black sociologists had to contribute to the sociology of race relations. The bleak story of the disadvantages borne by blacks in academic sociology from the experiences of W. E. B. Du Bois until mid-century has been told elsewhere.[44] The point to be made now is that sociologists who were black made contributions to the sociology of race relations unlike those made by sociologists who were white.

From the turn of the century the experience of black sociologists was not only to live the segregated life of a black American (including academic segregation), it was also to struggle intellectually against the image of black people offered by white scholarship. At its worst, until the 1930s, that image was one of biological inferiority. After that it was still a distorted image of cultural inferiority and social disorganization, often patronizing and simplistic. For those few black sociologists who published and had their work read by white sociologists, their major task became that of trying to create a more adequate image of black people *as a people*.[45] If in doing so they sometimes reached for a wider audience, the fact remains that the primary target of their message was an audience of sociologists and their students.

Perhaps the significance of E. Franklin Frazier, the most talented and successful of the black sociologists of the first half of the century, was the extent of his single-minded commitment to demonstrating that American blacks were a people to be understood primarily by their life-shaping experiences from slavery to twentieth-century segregation. Frazier got this major intellectual interest first from W. E. B. Du Bois, though Robert Park was always a source of encouragement and support. For Frazier both the distinctiveness and the complexity of the structure of black people's collective existence was evident in the institutional organization of their communities and in the pattern of their class structure. By the same token, blacks possessed a cultural distinctiveness because they had long existed as a racially oppressed and thoroughly segregated people.

Unlike their white counterparts, who kept a considerable distance between themselves and white liberals, black sociologists were active participants in black intellectual and political life. Throughout the 1920s and 1930s, E. Franklin Frazier, Ira De A. Reid, and Charles Johnson were closely involved with black organizations and political leaders and were themselves significant as black intellectuals.[46]

E. Franklin Frazier was actively involved with the NAACP from 1933 on, and, through this, he maintained a close involvement with the internal black political struggles as well as the civil rights activities of the depression era. His location at Howard University kept him in close proximity to whatever political actions within the Roosevelt administration affected blacks and influenced race relations. At Howard, too, he was associated with the political scientist Ralph Bunche and the economist Abram Harris, and he served the NAACP as a consultant and expert witness in civil rights cases.[47]

Charles Johnson, in contrast, was more actively involved in the world of philanthropy and government. In the 1920s he worked for the Urban League (as did Ira De A. Reid) and edited its publication, *Opportunity,* before going to Fisk University. There, Johnson was clearly the student of Robert Park in upholding the standard of objective, disinterested scholarship. Yet his best work, *The Shadow of the Plantation,* was a powerful indictment of the constraining racism suffered by the black tenant farmer and concluded with Johnson's observation that the future of the black farmer awaited comprehensive planning. In the same vein, he brought *Patterns of Segregation* to a close by demanding strong civil rights legislation. He wrote *The Collapse of Cotton Tenancy* (with Edwin Embree and Will Alexander) in

1935 to affect governmental policy. He was also active in other ways; he was closely associated with the Julius Rosenwald Fund and later the Southern Regional Council, was a consultant to the Department of Agriculture, and, during World War II, served on the Committee on Fair Labor Standards of the Department of Labor. All this, and more, testified to his belief in there being a vital relationship between scholarship and public policy.[48]

By the end of the 1930s, black and white sociologists had come to hold differing perspectives on race relations in the United States. Both understood that black people wanted the opportunities now denied them; but black sociologists also understood that blacks did not want to disappear as a people. Race pride, on the one hand, and deep resentment at white oppression, on the other, fueled a pattern of attitudes among blacks unlike any held by white people. Black sociologists were familiar with the growing current of nationalistic, nonassimilative thought among the young, educated blacks in the 1930s. They also thought in terms of the possibilities for political action, for legislative reform, and for unbiased federal policies when white sociologists still regarded such ideas as mere fantasy. Black sociologists were also acutely aware of the power and pace of economic and demographic changes and their effects, not only on the lives of black people, but also on the prevailing relations between the races. And they scorned ideas about caste as an illusion of stability and sameness when the reality was one of great social change, including the rapid urbanization of black people.

Did white sociologists read and understand the message of the black sociologists? That they read them is beyond doubt; Johnson and Frazier reached a wide sociological audience with their work, were cited often, and were appreciated and respected for the quality of their sociological work; that was also true of Drake and Cayton for *Black Metropolis*. But white sociologists read black sociologists in a selective manner, absorbing what fitted their fundamental assumptions about American race relations and their still limited conception of blacks as persons and as a people. At the same time, they read other works, such as John Dollard's, that offered a different, if not contradictory, message. The sociological mentality so responsive to Dollard was not likely to grasp in full the message of the black sociologists. As a consequence, the subsequent development of the sociology of race relations after World War II maintained an inadequate and distorted image of the black American, despite the best efforts of black sociologists from W. E. B. Du Bois to Charles Johnson and E. Franklin Frazier.

Notes

1. This identical wording of the research question appeared in the foreword to each of the four volumes in the series.
2. Ira De A. Reid, *In a Minor Key: Negro Youth in Story and Fact* (Washington, D.C.: American Council on Education, 1940).
3. Allison Davis and John Dollard, *Children of Bondage: The Personality Development of Negro Youth in the Urban South* (Washington, D.C.: American Council on Education, 1940).
4. See Author's Note in *Children of Bondage*, xv–xvii and xix–xx; see also chapter 1, "The Mystery of Personality."
5. Davis and Dollard, *Children of Bondage*, 256–62, 263–64. Further references to this work will appear in the text.
6. John Dollard, *Caste and Class in a Southern Town* (New Haven: Yale University Press, 1937), 431–32.
7. E. Franklin Frazier, *Negro Youth at the Crossways: Their Personality Development in the Middle States* (Washington, D.C.: American Council on Education, 1940).
8. W. E. B. Du Bois, *The Philadelphia Negro* (Philadelphia: University of Pennsylvania Press, 1899); reprinted with an introduction by E. Digby Baltzell (New York: Schocken Books, 1967).
9. Frazier, *Negro Youth*, 20–28.
10. Ibid., 27–28.
11. E. Franklin Frazier, *Black Bourgeoisie* (Glencoe, Ill.: Free Press, 1957).
12. Frazier, *Negro Youth*, 61–69, 84. Further references to this work will appear in the text. All italics appear in the original work.
13. Charles S. Johnson, *Growing Up in the Black Belt: Negro Youth in the Rural South* (Washington, D.C.: American Council on Education, 1941). Further references to this work will appear in the text.
14. W. Lloyd Warner, Buford H. Junker, and Walter A. Adams, *Color and Human Nature: Negro Personality Development in a Northern City* (Washington, D.C.: American Council on Education, 1941), 27–28.
15. Ibid., 11–12.
16. Ibid., 12.
17. Ibid., 25–27.
18. Robert L. Sutherland, *Color, Class and Personality* (Washington, D.C.: American Council on Education, 1942).
19. Frazier, *Negro Youth*, 277; Warner, *Color and Human Nature*, 292.
20. E. Franklin Frazier, *The Negro Family in the United States* (Chicago: University of Chicago Press, 1939); E. F. Frazier, *The Negro Family in Chicago* (Chicago: University of Chicago Press, 1932): E. F. Frazier, *The Free Negro Family* (Nashville: Fisk University Press, 1932). According to one source, Frazier was the most cited author in race relations between 1944 and 1968. See H. E. Bahr, T. J. Johnson, and M. R. Seitz, "Influential Scholars and Works in the Sociology of Race and Minority Relations, 1944–1968," *American Sociologist* 6 (1971): 296–98.

21. Ernest W. Burgess, Editor's Preface, in Frazier, *Negro Family,* ix.

22. Frazier, *Negro Family,* 22. Further references to this work will appear in the text.

23. E. Franklin Frazier, "The Status of the Negro in the American Social Order," *Journal of Negro Education* 4 (July 1935): 293–307.

24. Richard Fuller and Richard Myers, "The Natural History of a Social Problem," *American Sociological Review* 6 (June 1941): 320–28; Earnest Mowrer, "Methodological Problems in Social Disorganization," *American Sociological Review* 6 (Dec. 1941): 839–52.

25. William Foote Whyte, "Social Organization in the Slums," *American Sociological Review* 8 (Feb. 1943): 34–39; W. F. Whyte, *Street Corner Society* (Chicago: University of Chicago Press, 1943); C. Wright Mills, "The Professional Ideology of Social Pathologists," *American Journal of Sociololgy* 49 (Sept. 1943): 165–80.

26. Ernest Burgess, "The Growth of the City," in *The City,* ed. Robert Park et al. (Chicago: University of Chicago Press, 1925), 54.

27. James T. Carey, *Sociology and Public Affairs: The Chicago School* (Beverly Hills: Sage, 1975), 101.

28. Whyte, "Social Organization," 38–39.

29. Charles A. Valentine, *Culture and Poverty: Critique and Counter-Proposals* (Chicago: University of Chicago Press, 1968), 20.

30. Herbert G. Gutman, *The Black Family in Slavery and Freedom, 1750–1925* (New York: Pantheon, 1976); H. G. Gutman, "Persistent Myths about the Afro-American Family," *Journal of Interdisciplinary History* 2 (Autumn 1975): 183.

31. Gutman, "Persistent Myths," 184.

32. Ibid., 184–85, 187.

33. Melville Herskovits, "On the Provenience of New World Negroes," *Social Forces* 12 (Dec. 1934): 247–62; M. Herskovits, *The Myth of the Negro Past* (New York: Harper and Brothers, 1941).

34. E. Franklin Frazier, "The Negro in Bahia, Brazil," *American Sociological Review* 7 (Aug. 1942): 465–78; Melville J. Herskovits, "The Negro in Bahia, Brazil: A Problem of Method," *American Sociological Review* 8 (Aug. 1943): 392–402; Frazier, "Rejoinder": 402–4.

35. Herskovits, "Negro in Bahia," 395, 397, 402.

36. Frazier, "Rejoinder," 402.

37. Ibid., 403.

38. Ibid., 403–4.

39. Introduction to part 3, *The Sociology of Race Relations: Reflection and Reform,* ed. Thomas F. Pettigrew (New York: Free Press, 1980), 91. For a review of the critiques of Herskovits's work by anthropologists, see Norman E. Whitten, Jr., and John F. Szwed, eds., *Afro-American Anthropology* (New York: Free Press, 1970), 25–30.

40. Robert Park, *Race and Culture,* ed. Everett C. Hughes et al. (New York: Free Press, 1950), 267; Guy B. Johnson, "Some Factors in the Devel-

opment of Negro Social Institutions in the United States," *American Journal of Sociology* 42 (Nov. 1934): 329, 332–33.

41. Edward B. Reuter, *The American Race Problem* (New York: Thomas Y. Crowell, 1927), 412; Johnson, "Some Factors in Development," 334; Charles Johnson, *Shadow of the Plantation* (Chicago: University of Chicago Press, 1934), 5.

42. W. E. B. Du Bois, *The Philadelphia Negro* (Philadelphia: University of Philadelphia Press, 1899); Ira De A. Reid, "Mirrors of Harlem: Investigations and Problems of America's Largest Colored Community," *Social Forces* 5 (June 1927): 634. On Du Bois's Atlanta experience, see Elliott M. Rudwick, *W. E. B. Du Bois: A Study of Minority Group Leadership* (Philadelphia: University of Pennsylvania Press, 1960), chapter 2; republished in paperback as *W. E. B. Du Bois: Propagandist of the Negro Protest* (New York: Atheneum, 1968).

43. St. Clair Drake and Horace R. Cayton, *Black Metropolis: A Study of Negro Life in a Northern City* (New York: Harcourt, Brace, 1945); revised and enlarged edition, 2 vols. (New York: Harper and Row, 1962). Further references to this work will appear in the text.

44. See, for example, Introduction, in *The Black Sociologists: The First Half Century,* ed. John Bracey, Jr., August Meier, and Elliott Rudwick (Belmont, Calif.: Wadsworth, 1971); see also Morris Janowitz, Introduction, and essays by Francis L. Broderick, Elliott Rudwick, Richard Robbins, and G. Franklin Edwards, in *Black Sociologists: Historical and Contemporary Perspectives,* ed. James E. Blackwell and Morris Janowitz (Chicago: University of Chicago Press, 1974).

45. The failure to understand black Americans is what Stanford Lyman called "a failure of perspective"; see his *The Black American in Sociological Thought: A Failure of Perspective* (New York: G. P. Putnam's Sons, 1972; Capricorn Books, 1973). But Lyman's analysis said very little about Frazier and Johnson, barely mentioned Du Bois, gave only a few lines to Drake and Cayton (though the book was dedicated to Cayton), and did not mention other black sociologists.

46. See John B. Kirby, *Black Americans in the Roosevelt Era: Liberalism and Race* (Knoxville: University of Tennessee Press, 1980), 197–202; see also Charles U. Smith and Lewis Killian, "Black Sociologists and Social Protest," in *Black Sociologists,* ed. Blackwell and Janowitz, 191–228.

47. See Edwards, "Frazier," and Smith and Killian, "Black Sociologists," in *Black Sociologists,* ed. Blackwell and Janowitz, 85–117, 191–228; for Frazier's militancy and cultural nationalism within the internal struggles of the NAACP, see Raymond Wolters, *Negroes and the Great Depression* (Westport, Conn: Greenwood Press, 1970), 222–25, 252, 255–56, 319–20.

48. See Richard Robbins, "Charles Johnson," in *Black Sociologists,* ed. Blackwell and Janowitz, 56–84.

6

An American Dilemma:
Race as a Moral Problem

If World War II had not come when it did, the period of the early 1940s would still have been a watershed between old and new sociological generations and their modes of analysis of race relations. The founding era begun by Robert Park in 1913 was over, and a new period in the sociology of race relations was beginning. Though the generation coming on had absorbed well the basic themes developed by Park, Reuter, Frazier, and Dollard, it was also ready to make some changes. Many in this new generation were interested in a model of social engineering cultivated by the interventionist practices of the New Deal. Others were eager to pursue the social psychological issue of race prejudice with the new tools of quantitative measurement. The situation, then, was appropriate for a book that would capture a sense of both generational continuity and change. Such a book was Gunnar Myrdal's *An American Dilemma*.[1]

The circumstances of the book's publication are worth noting. It was the outcome of an immense collaborative effort of American social scientists; it was funded by a foundation, the Carnegie Corporation; and it was directed by a European social scientist who had no prior scholarly experience with, or even much knowledge of, American race relations. In a manner intended to challenge, to rebuke, and to praise, the book summarized past work and pointed to directions for the future.

The Carnegie Project: Origin and Organization

An American Dilemma was an immense work produced by a large project initiated by the Carnegie Corporation in 1937. The intention was to provide a comprehensive study of the American race problem—"the Negro problem"—done dispassionately and objectively. The demand for dispassion and objectivity led the trustees of the Carnegie Corporation to seek a director for the project from outside the United States, "limited to countries of high intellectual and scholarly standards but with no background or tradition of imperialism which might lessen the confidence of the Negroes in the United States as to the complete impartiality of the study and the validity of the findings." A young Swedish economist, Gunnar Myrdal, was selected, and he began the project in late 1938.[2]

Comprehensiveness required a large volume to summarize and evaluate the already extensive literature on race relations in American society. Besides drawing upon the existing literature, the project utilized the advisory comments of many scholars, and thirty social scientists submitted one or more of their unpublished manuscripts. In this way, one basic characteristic of the project was its rootedness in the existing literature and its detailed reporting of that material. At a later stage, E. Franklin Frazier and Louis Wirth provided a detailed, critical reading of the manuscript for Myrdal.

But Myrdal also took seriously the intent of the trustees in seeking a director from abroad who "could see things as a stranger."[3] Some of the most distinctive features of the book, such as the emphasis on the "American Creed" and the "value premise," for example, were Myrdal's innovations, reflecting both his outsider's perspective on American society and his more European conception of social science. Because of Myrdal's own contribution, the finished product was far more than a summary and assessment of what American social scientists wrote and taught about race relations in the United States in the years before World War II.

Myrdal and his staff finished writing the book in 1942, but publication in a nation at war did not come until 1944. An immense book of almost encyclopedic scope, it contained 1,143 pages of text (including 10 appendixes), another 37 pages of bibliography, and 259 pages of notes. In organizing such an enormous volume, Myrdal relied upon detailed assistance provided by Richard Sterner, his Swedish associate, and by a young American sociologist, Arnold Rose. He acknowledged their assistance on the title page, putting after his own name as author the phrase, "with the assistance of Richard Sterner and Arnold Rose."

Large and encompassing as it was, *An American Dilemma* was not the only book to be produced by the Carnegie project. In the fall of 1940, with Myrdal having returned to Sweden because of the German invasion of Denmark and Norway, and with the future uncertain, the Carnegie Corporation decided to publish some of the book-length memoranda submitted by participating scholars. Four works were subsequently published. The first of these was Melville Herskovits's *The Myth of the Negro Past,* the work that provided the basis for the distinguished anthropologist's quarrel with E. Franklin Frazier over the significance of African origins in black culture. Myrdal made only brief mention of that quarrel in *An American Dilemma* and seemed unimpressed with it. Herskovits and others, he noted, tried to derive music, dancing, and art from Africa and also described peculiarities in religion and the mother-centered family as an African heritage, but he blamed crime and amorality on white pressure. For practical purposes, Myrdal thought, the issue was "irrelevant," and those who, like Frazier, regarded the African heritage as insignificant were "predominant in the sociological literature."[4]

The second of the four volumes was Charles Johnson's *Patterns of Negro Segregation,* which summed up in detail the prevailing patterns of segregative practices in both the North and the South.[5] Johnson provided a book-length study of American racial segregation, a summary of which constituted chapter 29 of *An American Dilemma.* What was innovative in Johnson's book was the attention he gave to the place of law in defining and sustaining segregation, as well as changing it. The book culminated in something quite unique to the existing sociological literature, a chapter on civil rights legislation.

Richard Sterner, Myrdal's Swedish associate and an experienced social researcher, was the author of the third volume, *The Negro's Share.*[6] The study focused on the level of living as measured by income, consumption, housing, and public assistance that was characteristic of the black population. The innovation here was in the extensive treatment given to the problem of public assistance for black people; the last third of the text provided the first detailed analysis in the sociological literature of the various forms of social welfare that were available to blacks.

The final volume, *Characteristics of the American Negro,* was a collection of papers edited by Otto Klineberg. It summarized tests and experiments on intelligence, personality, mental disease, race attitudes, and other presumed characteristics of the black population that set them apart from white people.[7] Klineberg had long been interested in the capacity of scientific research to refute the various claims of significant differences in psychological and physical qualities imputed to the two races. His work testified to a still strongly felt need to provide scientific evidence that blacks were not inferior to the white population in such characteristics. That there was still such a felt need was evidence of how little most white Americans seemed to have changed their views about black people in the decade before World War II.

None of these four works broke any significantly new ground, though two of them were at least innovative. Johnson and Sterner brought to bear a wealth of new material on the status of blacks; Johnson did so with his highly detailed analysis of the legal dimensions of segregation, while Sterner provided the same detailed analysis on the relation of the black population to social welfare. Taken as a group, the four studies can be seen as useful summaries and analyses of particular areas of concern about race relations; each of them, thus, was a valuable contribution to the literature in its own right. It remained only for Gunnar Myrdal to sketch out a new framework by which to interpret the troublesome issue of race relations in American society.

The Organization of the Book

An American Dilemma opened with an introduction and first chapter setting forth Myrdal's conception of American race relations as a moral problem, defined as the violation of a consensually accepted "American Creed." This served as a prelude to forty-two chapters of detailed analysis of blacks in American society, interspersed with commentary and analysis of white beliefs about black people and their life conditions. A final chapter returned to Myrdal's theme of an American moral dilemma. Ten appendixes took up issues dealt with more briefly in the text, or presented more detailed data, or discussed research issues. The result was the most detailed analysis of race relations in the United States that has ever been undertaken, before or since.

Though Myrdal defined race as a moral problem, that was not meant to imply that material factors were not important or not basic to any causative analysis. In fact, the section on economics was the largest in the book, 222 pages in eleven chapters, exploring every facet of occupation, income, and social welfare down to World War II. Even more innovative was a section almost as large devoted to leadership, protest, and the organized efforts of blacks to effect social change. Rarely had the previous literature given any treatment to concerted action by blacks in their own behalf, let alone specific descriptions of the National Association for the Advancement of Colored People, the Urban League, and others.

Undoubtedly, *An American Dilemma* is the single most renowned work in race relations in American sociology; its status as a classic is undisputed. But this is not simply because of its size and comprehensiveness; those features do not alone win a place of honor in any body of literature. Rather, its classic status is due to the considerable influence it had at a time of generational change. Myrdal reviewed, summarized, and confirmed many commonly accepted findings, thus reinforcing and legitimizing their status as knowledge. He also accepted much of the dominant perspective. But he also challenged some accepted ideas, provided considerable criticism, and offered support for the interests of a new generation.

Race and the American Creed

When Myrdal chose "An American Dilemma" as the title for the book, he was looking for a phrase that would capture his sense of the race problem in the United States: a conflict between the highest of American ideals and lower parochial interests and prejudices. Myrdal described this conflict as "between, on the one hand, the valuations preserved on the general plane which we call the 'American Creed,' where the American thinks, talks and acts under the influence of high national and Christian precepts, and, on the other hand, the valuations on specific places of individual and group living, where personal and local interests, economic, social and sexual jealousies, considerations of community prestige and conformity, group prejudice against all particular persons or types of people, and all sort of miscellaneous wants, impulses, and habits dominate his outlook."[8]

From Myrdal's perspective, Americans were far more moralistic and less cynical than other Western peoples; each American was a "practical idealist." For that reason, "the American Negro problem is a problem in the hearts of the Americans." The moral struggle is not only between persons, it is essentially within each person, wherein moralistic Americans rationalize their failure to abide by their own highest ideals. To do so, they "mutilate" their own beliefs about social reality and produce many popular beliefs that are false but also loaded with emotion. But they also want to be rational, and this makes them responsive to scientific knowledge, even when it challenges their beliefs. The prejudicial and rationalizing valuations that people make, Myrdal said, are supported by these beliefs, even as the beliefs emerged to protect their valuations. Thus, knowledge that undermines beliefs forces a readjustment of valuations. Indeed, "Scientific truth-seeking and education are slowly rectifying the beliefs and thereby influencing the valuations" (xlvi–xlix).

Compared to other Western countries, Myrdal claimed, the United States has "the *most explicitly expressed* system of general ideals in reference to human inter-relations"; they are "conscious to everyone in American society." Rooted first in Western cultural development, particularly in the philosophy of the Enlightenment, in Christianity, and in English law, the creed grew in the early American effort at national independence. Its ideals were written into the Declaration of Independence, the Preamble to the Constitution, and the Bill of Rights. These ideals provided "the essential dignity of the individual human being, of the fundamental equality of all persons, and of certain inalienable rights to freedom, justice, and a fair opportunity" (3–4). Myrdal thought of the American Creed as the national conscience; therefore, black people became a "problem" because of the obvious conflict between the creed and the actual status accorded them: "From the point of view of the American Creed, the status accorded the Negro in America represents nothing more and nothing less that a century-long lag in public morals. In principal, the Negro problem was settled long ago; in practice the solution is not effectuated" (24).

That there was a gap between ideal and practice was not to be explained, noted Myrdal, by the "peculiarities" of black people. Rather, it was the white majority who decided the black's "place" and whose greater power denied equal treatment to blacks. "In that sense," wrote Myrdal, " 'this is a white man's country.' " The dilemma between the highest ideal and self-serving prejudices was a dilemma for white people, not for black people; it was, in effect, a way of defining the white man's problem (li-lii).

In this summary appraisal, Myrdal seemed to be suggesting two things. First, as he acknowledged, it required that "primary attention" be given to "what goes on in the minds of white Americans," since it is their views that were strategic to the politics of racial change. Whites had power, blacks did not. This seemed to say that what went on in the minds of white people (prejudice) was the cause of their discriminatory behavior; whites, not blacks, would or would not change race relations. It also seemed to imply that the social psychological study of prejudice would be a major methodological and substantive concern for sociologists.

But it also said that, given their lack of power, blacks could only react to white people; their opinions were "secondary reactions" to pressure from the dominant white majority. The implications were evident enough. On their own, blacks did not possess the capacity to act, only to react; their destiny was not in their own hands. They could only play upon the conflicting values of whites and identify with the American Creed. To the extent that, with the help of white groups, blacks were to gain some "footholds of power," such as being able to vote in the South or getting into trade unions, only then would they be able to do more than react (ibid.).

The Unity of Culture

Perhaps the most basic assumption underlying Myrdal's analysis of race relations in the United States was his conviction that American society exhibited a unified culture. This unity of culture meant "that all valuations are mutually shared in some degree"; in short, there was a body of common values. Most Americans, Myrdal insisted, "have most valuations in common," though different individuals and groups arrange them differently and "bear different interest coefficients." Furthermore, the most general valuations—those of the American Creed—were agreed to be morally higher; the others were seen to be "irrational" or "prejudiced," even by those who held them (xlviii–xlvix). In such a hierarchy of valuations in conflict, the advantage obviously went to the morally superior ones.

Two comments are merited. First, identifying those values fundamental to American society became an absorbing concern of many sociologists in the following two decades. Perhaps the most influential effort was by Robin Williams, Jr., whose widely read text on American society contained a long essay on American values.[9] Williams identified a greater number of values arising from the historic American experience, including achievement and success, activity and hard work, efficiency and practicality, material comfort, and external conformity. Though there were many evident conflicts and contradictions within this constellation of "dominant values," according to Williams, American society possessed a basic moral orientation. Second, this conception of a culture unified in its basic values was to become a major tenet of Talcott Parsons and other sociological functionalists during the decades of the 1950s and 1960s. In turn, in the 1960s, when a criticism of functionalist sociology first appeared with the emergence of a newly radicalized generation of sociologists, one of the strongest criticisms was that the claim of a culture unified in its basic values was evidence of a conservative bias.

The Principle of Cumulation

It was not possible, according to Myrdal, to isolate the "Negro problem" from other matters, such as law, education, employment, politics, and so on, and neither was it possible to reduce the race problem to a subsection of the class problem. Rather, it was necessary to recognize a general interdependence of all factors bearing on the problem. This interdependence meant that there was no single causal factor, not even the economic, but, instead, a series of interconnected factors that mutually reinforced one another. This scheme of causation Myrdal called "the principle of cumulation."

He also called it a vicious circle, because, if prejudice and discrimination kept blacks low in health, education, and standard of living, these conditions, in turn, reinforced that prejudice. Thus, prejudice and low social conditions "cause each other"; any change in one factor would set off a spiral of reaction in the others. If discrimination tightened, there would be a downward spiraling, a vicious circle. A rise of employment for blacks, in contrast, would raise family income, nutrition, housing, and health, and these and other changes would further improve the black's chances for employment (75–76).

It was basic to Myrdal's argument that any one factor could set off the cumulative process of spiraling change. But he did not ask if there was any empirical evidence that all factors were equal to each other in the capacity to set off a spiral of change; the functional conception of an interrelated, interdependent system assumed this to be the case.

For those who would reform American race relations, then, the message was clear: the economic factor was not primary, and any factor, when improved, could set in motion an upward spiral of racial progress. There was reason, then, for sociologists to focus on any convenient factor and not to worry about there being some primary causal process, such as the economic. This encouraged those sociologists who believed in progress by education as well as those who were psychologically oriented and who wanted to focus on racial prejudice as one of the more readily changeable factors.

Not all sociologists were ready to accept Myrdal's sense of the race problem as a conflict between American ideals and lower parochial interests and prejudices. When they did not, it was because of their position on the familiar sociological dilemma of choosing between the relative importance of values and social structure in shaping social behavior. But few sociologists were likely to disagree with the claims Myrdal offered in behalf of his case about the American dilemma: first, an American exceptionalism (an American more moralistic than other Westerners and a nation with a national conscience expressed in its basic documents); second, that race was the "white man's problem" because this was the white man's country; third, that American society exhibited a unified culture; and fourth, that there was an interdependence of all factors bearing on the race problem, no one of which was causally primary, not even the economic.

The Image of the Black American

If what Myrdal consistently called "the Negro problem" was also the "white man's problem," what did that say about blacks as a people? What was the image of blacks presented in *An American Dilemma?*

It was an image that did not significantly differ from that found in the prevailing sociological literature. Myrdal accepted from Frazier the proposition that black people had been shaped by their American experience, not by biology or their African heritage. He also stressed the oppression and isolation so crucial to their particular historic experience, as well as the struggle of blacks against that oppression, a struggle always severely constrained by the brute fact of often unrestrained white power.

But despite the emphasis that he put upon the historic particularity of the black experience, Myrdal did not follow Frazier beyond the point of insisting that neither biology nor an African heritage were forces shaping black people. Instead, throughout the pages of *An American Dilemma* ran a constant theme: blacks were culturally assimilated Americans, not a people different because of African heritage or by virtue of separate cultural development. From the first chapter, Myrdal sought to include blacks within the American experience. They, too, had been taught the American Creed; and despite their full knowledge that the creed had not been lived up to in their case, they retained a faith in it: "With one part of themselves they actually believe, as do the whites, that the Creed is ruling America." Blacks, he concluded, accepted no future other than full integration into American life: "The only thing Negroes ask for is to be accepted as Americans" (4, 1007).

Yet a vast amount of material in the book provided contrary evidence of a cultural difference: a different historic experience beginning in slavery; an inability to win equal status; a persistent social and political subordination; much mistreatment and insult, which had to be borne passively; access to only inferior resources; and social and cultural isolation from the mainstream of American life. If blacks were to be explained only in terms of their American experience, there was much in that experience that was unique to them and quite different from the formative experience of white Europeans. That, after all, had been the message of Frazier's work on the black family.

Myrdal did not overtly acknowledge any contradiction between the claim that blacks were culturally assimilated Americans and the abundant evidence of cultural differences between blacks and whites. But he did so covertly by invoking three different factors to account for the seemingly contradictory evidence: expressions of protest, secondary reactions, and pathologies of black life. What was undeniably different about blacks, he claimed, could be accounted for while being discounted as evidence of a black culture or of blacks as a distinct people.

Three Factors of Difference

The efforts by black intellectuals, writers, and scholars to offset white neglect of and bias toward blacks, noted Myrdal, led to a movement to discover a cultural tradition for American Negroes, that is, to construct a respectable past. While much of this was "zealous dilettantism," there was increasingly a genuine black scholarship. Propaganda and scholarship, however, went on side by side, and despite excellent historical research, there was a purpose to it that distorted the truth. That distortion arose from an emphasis and perspective; mediocrities have become "great men"; cultural achievements "no better—and no worse—than others are placed on a pinnacle; minor historical events are magnified into crises" (751–52).

Though Myrdal was here echoing sociologists like Edward Reuter, not E. Franklin Frazier, he was not as harshly judgmental as Reuter. These distortions were excusable, Myrdal reasoned, given the distortions practiced by white historians. But, while black scholarship countered the false and belittling treatment accorded the race by white scholarship, there was not in fact a cultural tradition to be rescued from white neglect and bias: "In spite of all scholarly pretence and accomplishments, this movement is basically an expression of the Negro protest. Its avowed purpose is to enhance self-respect and race-respect among Negroes by substituting a belief in race achievements for the traditional belief in race inferiority" (752).

In similar fashion, Myrdal claimed that distinctive features of personality characteristics of blacks were to be understood not simply as the outcome of a different set of life experiences, but as a protest against those experiences. Since blacks comprised one-tenth of the nation and could never hope to win a democratic majority, their cause often seemed hopeless. Yet even the poorest of them "keeps a recess in his mind where he harbors the Negro protest" (757). There was the consolation provided by religion, and there was faith in the ultimate triumph of the American Creed. But individually, Myrdal insisted, blacks must struggle against a personal sense of defeat by developing a balanced personality. This meant being realistic about themselves and about the world and accommodating under protest. The difficulty of doing so explains the sensitivity of blacks, particularly upper-class

blacks, to the smallest of even unintended slights. It also accounted
for the many subtle behaviors that expressed an underlying anger.

That whites had power over blacks made their attitudes primary
and decisive; those of blacks were often a defense against white opinion, what Myrdal called a secondary reaction. "The Negro's entire life,
and, consequently, also his opinions on the Negro problem," he wrote,
"are, in the main, to be considered as secondary reactions to more
primary pressures from the side of the dominant white majority." The
attitudes blacks held about whites, in turn, and their affirmation of
race pride and rejection of racial amalgamation were for Myrdal, in
both cases, a reaction to white doctrine, "a derived *secondary* attitude
as are so many other attitudes of the Negro people." The prejudice
of blacks—better described, Myrdal thought, as fear or hatred—was a
secondary reaction caused by humiliation and deprivation and "a natural dislike of the dominant person by the subordinate" (li, 1143, 56).

Myrdal believed that these secondary attitudes, being largely defensive responses to white attitudes and actions, were relatively superficial
responses, not deeply rooted in the individual psyche or in cultural
memory, and could easily be altered if white attitudes changed: "If the
deprivation or humiliation were to cease, the hatred and fear would
also cease." Similarly, there was no basis for race pride among blacks
except as a reaction to whites: "After weighing all available evidence
carefully, it seems frankly incredible that the Negro people in America
should feel inclined to develop any particular race pride at all or have
any dislike for amalgamation, were it not for the common white opinion of the racial inferiority of the Negro people and the whites' intense
dislike for miscegenation" (1143, 56). Reuter and the majority of sociologists shared this view.

The separate institutions that blacks had developed under segregation, Myrdal observed, were similar to those of whites and dissimilar
to African institutions. Where there were divergences from the American culture among blacks, these were sometimes exaggerations, that
is, intensifications of general American traits. But in most cases it was
a pathological response: "*In practically all the divergences, American
Negro culture is not something independent of general American culture. It is a distorted development, or a pathological condition, of the
general American culture*" (928). In words reminiscent of Reuter and
the social-problems sociologists, Myrdal detailed the pathologies of
black life:

> The instability of the Negro family, the inadequacy of educational
> facilities for Negroes, the emotionalism of the Negro church, the

insufficiency and unwholesomeness of Negro recreational activities, the plethora of Negro social organizations, the narrowness of interests of the average Negro, the provincialism of his political speculation, the high Negro crime rate, the cultivation of the arts to the neglect of other fields, superstitions, personality difficulties, and other characteristics are mainly forms of social pathology which, for the most part, are created by the caste pressures. (928-29)

The reference to a plethora of Negro organizations reflected Myrdal's discovery that black people maintained more voluntary associations than white people did. In this sense they were "exaggerated Americans" and "the situation can be seen as a pathological one: Negroes are active in associations because they are not allowed to be active in much of the other organized life of American society" (952).

A Different People?

Throughout the book Myrdal seemed to maintain a consistent position: black people had assimilated to the dominant American culture, and any differences were to be explained as their response to white domination, whether as protest, secondary response, or pathology. Yet, in a number of places in the text, Myrdal seemed also to acknowledge that blacks were a different people. At the end of a chapter on black education, for example, he referred to the North receiving "untutored and crude Negro immigrants ... uneducated masses," for whom there needed to be instituted a program of adult education to teach them "the elements of American culture" (906-7).

If southern blacks lacked American culture, it could only mean that their isolation was so extreme that it diminished their assimilation of white culture and thus allowed for some degree of indigenous development, or it produced a very crude and inadequate version of American culture. Myrdal gave expression here to an unresolved sociological ambivalence about just how assimilated blacks were to American culture. The dominant theme in the sociology of race relations was that blacks were indeed assimilated, but many sociologists judged rural southern blacks as only partially so. (This thesis on the lack of culture ignored the argument by Guy Johnson and Charles Johnson that southern black culture was a retention, because of isolation, of a largely forgotten, somewhat crude American culture of the colonial period.)[10]

No less revealing was Myrdal's comment following his characterization of cultural "divergences" as "pathological." The historical origin of these divergences, he noted, was irrelevant for practical purposes.

Though Melville Herskovits had argued for the retention of an African heritage, Myrdal found Frazier more persuasive in providing an explanation in the circumstances of slavery and caste: "Here the interest is in the fact that American Negro culture is somewhat different from the general American culture, that this difference is *generally created* by American conditions even if some of the *specific forms* are African in origin, and that the difference is significant for Negroes and for the relations between Negroes and whites" (930).

Most white people, Myrdal acknowledged, thought that blacks were different. Though blacks were as diverse as whites, Myrdal maintained, there were cultural traits that, according to white people, differentiated the typical behavior of black people from that of whites. He then provided ten pages of explanation of the "peculiarities" of Negro culture and personality as seen by white people: aggressiveness; emotionality and spontaneous good humor; love of the gaudy, the bizarre, and the ostentatious; the eating of particular foods, such as chicken and watermelon; a lack of poise; superstitiousness; and a dialect strange to northern ears. For Myrdal, all these "peculiarities" were to be explained as the consequence of an isolated and deprived past. But that would change: "As more Negroes become educated and urbanized, it may be expected that they will lose their distinctive cultural traits and take over the dominant American pattern" (957–66).

The contradiction between the view of the black American as an assimilated people and yet a different people was one Myrdal inherited from the existing American sociology of race relations. He reproduced that contradiction in his work, but he did not overcome it.

Blacks and the Matter of Culture

From the beginning of the sociology of race relations the matter of black people and culture has been a troublesome issue. It was a problem that began with the study of slavery. There was no proposition more fully agreed upon by the sociologists of race relations than the idea that enslavement had removed all vestiges of African cultures. They also assumed that, having lost their cultural heritage, the slaves had to learn another culture, and there was only one other culture for them to learn, that of the white masters. In that way, beginning in slavery, blacks became culturally American, however crude may have been their version of the culture.

What comes into question at this point is what is included in the concept of culture. For too long a time American sociologists held a notion of culture limited to the concept of a social heritage transmitted from one generation to the next by the socialization of the young.

Both *heritage* and *socialization* were key concepts in the sociological vocabulary, and sociological discourse was replete with terms like assimilation, acculturation, and adaptation, all of which assumed some degree of learning and accepting an already existing social order. From that perspective, a culture was learned and acquired by a people in an essentially passive process of becoming socialized into already established ways.

But cultures are in the first instance created, and a people in new circumstances will create culture anew. An oppressed people, furthermore, will not be any less culturally creative than their oppressors, even if cultural creativity is largely confined within the larger framework of domination. They would still alter, redefine, reinterpret, and invent culture. That, of course, was Frazier's position. He and other black sociologists, and also Park, understood and appreciated that blacks had created their own existence within the oppressive confines of white domination.

Myrdal, to be sure, recognized that American blacks had been culturally innovative, but he tried to explain it away as largely a reaction, a secondary response of the powerless group to the primary action of the powerful. But this explanation does not provide an adequate conception of how a people, even an oppresed one, shapes and defines itself. The creative capacity of an oppressed people is not limited merely to responsive actions, such as sullen anger, hidden resentment, or second-rate imitations of the dominant people's way of life. The black writer Ralph Ellison said it best: "But can a people (its faith in an idealized American Creed notwithstanding) live and develop for over three hundred years simply by *reacting*? Are American Negroes simply the creation of white men, or have they at least helped to create themselves out of what they have found around them? Men have made a way of life in caves and upon cliffs, why cannot Negroes have made a way of life upon the horns of the white man's dilemma?"[11]

But the constant reference to an entity labeled "the American culture" speaks to another underlying assumption: that there was a solid, undifferentiated culture shared by all Americans. Only those immigrants not yet fully assimilated or those whose racial status left them segregated from the mainstream of cultural life did not fully share in that culture. In either case, the exceptions were thought to be only temporary, as assimilation would incorporate the immigrants, and a lessening of racial segregation would give to blacks the opportunity to learn more fully the culture.

But a more basic issue was the taking for granted that American culture was a single, undifferentiated entity. Absent from Myrdal's book was any recognition of variation by region, by class or race, by ethnicity or religion, by gender, or by any other significantly differentiating factor. Yet a few years later Robin Williams's study of American society documented both diversity and change in American values. The image of American culture incorporated into *An American Dilemma* reflected well the sociological literature of the time that identified as universally American the culture attributed to an idealized conception of the middle class; John Dollard's work provides a case in point.

As a consequence of a static and undifferentiated conception of American culture, the image of the black American that emerged from the pages of *An American Dilemma* was that of a people who in their daily lives exhibited an impoverished version of American culture. In this classic study the portrayal of blacks remained that of a culturally inferior people. That portrayal was to influence Myrdal's approach to the issue of social reform, a matter on which he had much to say.

What Is to Be Done? Politics and Policies

Though Myrdal had been scathing in his critique of an earlier generation of what he called "do-nothing liberals," and though he was a forthright advocate of social engineering, his own recommendations for political action and for social policy provided neither surprises nor challenges. Instead, they remained fully within the acceptable sphere of action staked out by the New Deal generation; his program could be comfortably labeled American liberal.

Assimilation and the American Creed were the bedrock of Myrdal's recommendations for racial change. "*We can assume,*" he wrote, "*that it is to the advantage of American Negroes as individuals and as a group to be assimilated into American culture, to acquire the traits held in esteem by the dominant white Americans.*" Attaining that assimilation required removal of the barriers of caste, though not the distinctions of class. The American Creed, Myrdal asserted, demanded only equality of opportunity, not equality of economic and social rewards. On that basis, he held forth as value premise "*the American ideal of free competition and full integration*" (671–72, 929). His specific recommendations were about education, economic planning, and policies for the South alone.

That education can be a force for significant social change has long been a basic article of faith for Americans, and Myrdal seemed to share that faith when he said that "scientific truth-seeking and education" were "rectifying beliefs" and "influencing valuations." There was a clear implication in his argument that the race problem could be effectively changed by education, and Myrdal recognized and accepted the logic of his own argument: "A legitimate task of education is to attempt to correct popular beliefs by subjecting them to rigorous examination in the light of the factual evidence. This educational objective must be achieved in the face of the psychic resistance mobilized by the people who feel an urgent need to retain their beliefs in order to justify their way of life" (1030–31). If an educational effort is successful, "the illogicalities involving valuations" become evident to the people who hold them, which is then a pressure on them to change: "When supporting beliefs are drawn away, people will have to readjust their value hierarchies and, eventually, their behavior" (1031).

Myrdal made it clear that he did not share "the skepticism against education as a means of mitigating racial intolerance" characteristic of the sociologists of race relations (48–49). That skepticism was rooted in an image of a deeply ingrained prejudice in the white population, which had discouraged even educational efforts, let alone other modes of reform. But a new generation of sociologists was not to be so skeptical. For the next two decades there would be extensive efforts to educate Americans to the scientific truth about race and the social facts about racial discrimination, and sociologists were to share in that effort. The educational materials of such an organization as the Anti-Defamation League, for example, sought to promote a better understanding of the meaning of race and to appeal to the hearts of Americans in which the American Creed was enshrined. What was probably the most commonly expressed argument for racial justice in the 1940s and 1950s was the assertion that change had to come first in the hearts and minds of people. The prejudiced must unlearn their own prejudices.

This is not to presume that *An American Dilemma* alone initiated the development of the postwar educational programs; the rationalization for education was already an ingrained component of American culture. But the book did give support to the idea that racial change could only follow, not precede, the reduction of racial prejudice.

Myrdal never believed that education alone was sufficient to effect change. As a social democrat he believed firmly in the intervention of government to resolve difficult social problems. The time was past, Myrdal believed, when race relations could be changed only by "natural" developments like migration to the North. Rather, "governmental intervention is rising, and this trend means . . . a complex of intentional policies affecting . . . all the spheres of the problem" (201). Yet, Myrdal offered no bold, systematic program for changing race relations. Instead, scattered throughout the book, almost happenstance, were a number of limited policy suggestions, few very challenging, all acceptable to liberals, some even to conservatives. A number of these were about economic planning.

Gunnar Myrdal was a Swedish social democrat committed to rational planning and social engineering, which was evident in his most ambitious recommendation: that there be a planned policy of federal agencies to increase employment among blacks. (Almost alone among sociologists, Charles Johnson had called for comprehensive planning by the federal government a decade earlier.)[12] A basic aspect of this would be a deliberate, extensive campaign of popular education. Such a policy, Myrdal felt, had become a necessity, since the government had the choice of increasing employment among blacks or supporting them on relief. One element of such rational planning would be an investigation of the possibility of settling some blacks in smaller northern cities where their numbers were few; another would be the curbing of racially exclusive practices by labor unions. Lastly, Myrdal saw in President Roosevelt's executive order on fair employment the most definite break in the long federal indifference to racial discrimination and thus a promise for the future (387, 408, 416).

In the 1940s, while economic planning for the benefit of black Americans was not yet politically acceptable, these recommendations nonetheless carried considerable weight for liberals. They gave support to the principle that there was a necessary federal responsibility for employment policies beyond that of unemployment. If race was now a national problem, then it seemed to liberals that action at the national level was necessary. In a few years the assumption that race relations was necessarily a federal responsibility was to become a cornerstone of liberal strategy, bringing on a major political campaign to turn Roosevelt's wartime executive order into federal legislation. Sociologists were to share in such ideas and to support such actions.

Policies for the South

Throughout his analysis, Myrdal had made a sharp distinction between the caste-rigid South and the less rigid North. Often, in effect, he overstated the degrees of freedom available to blacks in the North because their blacks had the vote, there was no intent to deprive them of it, and there was *"no special problem of getting justice"* outside the general one of *"equal protection of the rights of poor and uneducated people."* It was a fact, he insisted, that in granting legal rights to black people, there was a sharp division between North and South: "In the North, for the most part, Negroes enjoy equitable justice" (528–29).

Accordingly, Myrdal offered several recommendations for effecting change in the South.

The most important of these had to do with the historical denial to blacks of the right to vote. Myrdal reasoned that disenfranchisement had become untenable and could not be sustained for much longer. It would be better, therefore, to make changes "in gradual steps," not by "sudden upheaval." In keeping with this concept of gradualism, and agreeing that the mass of blacks were too ignorant to participate responsibly, he offered what he called a "truly conservative" policy: that the South was *"to start enfranchising its Negro citizens as soon as possible."* The process was to begin by allowing the "higher strata of the Negro population" to participate in the political process soon, while speeding up the civic education of the ignorant masses. However, Myrdal gloomily acknowledged that the chances were small that southern conservatives would accept such a policy (518).

The large number of blacks too uneducated to participate in the electoral process, Myrdal argued, revealed the severe deficiencies of southern education. His response was like that of a New Deal liberal. Local control of education, he insisted, should be preserved, but the federal government should pay certain basic costs, such as original building costs, to meet the severe need for new buildings, and a teacher's basic salary, as a step to improve the quality of black teachers. However, it was important that absence of discrimination be made a condition for federal aid (904–5).

In responding to problems of poverty and health in the South, Myrdal turned away from any liberal program and, instead, proposed an intensive campaign to win acceptance of birth control practices among poor, rural blacks. The disease and high illegitimacy rates found among such blacks, he felt, warranted such a program. But since most blacks shared the prejudice against birth control common to the poor and ignorant, an intensive educational emphasis was needed: "adult education before clinical consultation." In one way, this was a daring proposal, in another way, it was not. The legal status of birth control was far from secure in 1942; a federal law banning dissemination by mail was still in force, and most states put some limits on the dissemination of birth control information. The Catholic church, furthermore, was adamant and influential in its opposition. Blacks, though, were suspicious of any program they saw as being directed specifically at them. On the other hand, as Myrdal noted, the otherwise conservative South led the nation in supporting birth control, in part because the region had fewer Catholics, but also because white Southerners, as black people fully understood, wanted to reduce the birthrate of the black population (178–81, 1226 n. 61).

The idea of birth control to ameliorate poverty among the lower classes, even if presumably voluntary, had overtones of the eugenics program that had only recently died out. It was Myrdal's most conservative position, in which he seemed to regard the nation's poorest blacks as beyond salvage by any social program. In the South, Myrdal argued, there were "a greater number of Negroes . . . so destitute" that it would be desirable "that they did not procreate." Many of them "are so ignorant and so poor that they are not desirable parents" and the chances of their children dying at an early age are much greater than those of other children. No social policy, however radically framed, would be able to lift the standards of these people immediately. By "not taking account of the value premises in the American Creed," Myrdal reasoned, the "most direct way of meeting the problem would be sterilization." But sterilization was "repugnant" even to the average white Southerner; for all practical purposes, therefore, birth control as population policy was restricted to contraception (175–76).

What Should Blacks Do?

If Myrdal's comments on limiting the reproduction of poor blacks harkened back to the most conservative position to be found in the sociological literature, he also stepped ahead of most sociologists in supporting the efforts of racial organizations and black leaders to advance the cause of civil rights. He pointedly defended the NAACP and other organizations against criticisms like those from Donald Young, who likened the NAACP's efforts to applying ice to a fever, that is, to doing battle with symptoms. But Myrdal also defended the NAACP against young black intellectuals, such as Ralph Bunche, who wanted a program of radical economic reform.

Myrdal was here seeking a ground between sociologists who doubted that blacks could act effectively in their own interests and young black radicals who demanded far-reaching economic reform. In doing so, he made a prediction about the future far bolder than any sociologist was willing to make. There was every reason, thought Myrdal, that blacks would increase their efforts for racial justice. Never again should they be regarded as a patient, submissive minority, and they will continually become less well " 'accommodated.' " But the force of that prediction was weakened by his limited conception of what blacks could strategically do (831–36, 1004, 1404–5 n. 66).

There were two key points to Myrdal's conception of a strategy for blacks. The first was the need, not for a single, united organization, but for several organizations dividing up the field; in that way each could apply "a different degree of opportunism or radicalism." It made sense that the NAACP and the Urban League did not overlap; each could gain the support of different constituencies, black and white, and accomplish useful goals. Second, it was in the interest of blacks to get the support of as many white groups as possible. Only through collaboration with whites had there been organizations capable of doing something practical; purely black organizations had been a disappointment. A people who were poor, lacked a political culture, and were without power needed to have allies among the powerful (835, 853–54). Myrdal, however, never acknowledged the other side of this strategy for blacks: that a people lacking a unifying mass base and dependent on their oppressor for allies were severely limited in the actions they could undertake and the goals they could pursue.

There was, nevertheless, some point to these arguments for interracial collaboration. Blacks did suffer from an imbalance of power and were indeed too poor to provide generous funding for any organization. But the lack of a political culture was a far more complex issue. The clear import of the phrase was that blacks lacked the political skills and the leadership abilities to function politically without the collaboration of whites. But there was never any discussion of how blacks were to gain the abilities of leadership if they were to be constantly subjected to the benign guidance of their white allies. Neither was there any recognition that black leadership might pursue other racial goals than those agreed upon when there was interracial collaboration.

But these practical reasons were subordinate to an ideological one. The need for white collaborators was an issue within the larger issue of what whites believed to be the preferable form of political mobilization of the black population. Collaboration with white allies and separate, specializing organizations was a strategic choice that precluded any effort to develop a broad, inclusive organization of blacks with a mass base. Myrdal clearly recognized the choice: "It is a peculiar trait of the discussion of Negro concerted action that it usually proceeds upon the assumption that one unified Negro movement is a desideratum." But such an assumption was "unrealistic and impractical" because it would not appeal to the masses "except by an emotional, race-chauvinistic protest appeal"; because it would estrange black intellectuals and the black upper class; and because it would also estrange whites (853). Myrdal seemed to be invoking the memory of

Marcus Garvey's Back to Africa Movement, with its powerful appeal to the masses of blacks but its rejection by the existing black leadership.

It was acceptable, Myrdal conceded, to appeal to race, but cautiously, and it was acceptable to appeal to the black masses, but only "by movements with specific and limited practical aims." And if that cautious, limited appeal did not work? "If, because of these reservations," he continued, "the Negro masses are not reached within the near future to the extent as would be possible in a race-chauvinistic, united Negro movement, that is the price that will have to be paid" (ibid.).

Ralph Bunche: A Radical Challenge

Myrdal did not arrive at this position without exposure to quite contrary arguments. Ralph Bunche, then a militant young political scientist and a member of the Carnegie project's working staff, had provided Myrdal with a detailed critique of existing organizations like the NAACP. Bunche labeled the interracial makeup of the NAACP as a weakness, for black leaders had to keep a "weather eye" on how their white sponsors reacted to any innovation. These white sympathizers were "cautious liberals or mawkish missionary-minded sentimentalists on the race question." Neither was there much good to be said about the black leadership: at best, "cautious, racially minded liberals and not infrequently, forthright reactionaries," who suffered from an "intellectual myopia toward all but narrowly racial problems" (*American Dilemma*, 1405–6 n. 72). The anger and contempt of a young black intellectual of that time came through in this comment: "The liberal, white or black, northern or southern, recoils from the shock of class conflict. Yet the twitchings of liberalism within him seek release; lacking the courage and conviction to face the harsher realities, he seeks to find release and solace in counterfeit substitutes, in political and social *ersatz*. He recognizes and revolts against injustices, but seeks to correct them with palliatives rather than solutions; for the solutions are harsh and forbidding, and are not conducive to spiritual uplift" (1406).

Myrdal recognized some merit in Bunche's criticism of existing organizations and racial practices, even if he did not accept it. A lack of mass support, he conceded, was an "indisputable weakness" of the NAACP, and seeking white allies was not reason to neglect the organizing of the masses of blacks. He invoked the words of the militant black leader, A. Philip Randolph, that "Negroes and the other darker races must look to themselves for freedom," that freedom is never granted but won, and that there must be a continuous struggle for it.

He also quoted Randolph as saying that blacks must not fight alone but must join "broad, liberal, social movements" (835, 857).

Randolph's concept of interracial unity with the working class and other progressive forces was not the same as the strategy of collaborating with white, middle-class liberal allies in a series of specialized organizations working for limited goals. The range of goals covered by that set of existing organizations did not match the broad social movement that Randolph had envisioned.

A vision of black organizations under a black leadership struggling for racial progress was appealing to many blacks, but, except for Robert Park, it had never won support from white sociologists. They never accepted Park's conception of a black people evolving politically into a race-conscious nationality and engaging in constant struggle for racial progress. Myrdal's insistence that blacks should have white collaborators, with the limits on strategy that implied, was a rejection of Park's notion of an independent black struggle. Accordingly, Park's idea did not survive the transition to a new generation of sociologists always resistant of encouraging notions of conflict.

In addressing the issue of strategy, Myrdal was not simply speaking for himself; he was also giving expression to the assumptions of American sociologists about the organizational structure that would control the pace and direction of racial progress. It was an ideological choice evident in three underlying premises, the first of which Myrdal brought into the open: that white, middle-class liberals were to collaborate in the controlling leadership of organizations for racial change. The other two were less open, at least in the 1940s: that as a consequence of the first, interracial programs were limited to what was acceptable to their white supporters; and that these same white liberals, social scientists included, feared greatly the consequences of the black masses becoming emotionally aroused over the matter of race. Restrained by the shackles of racial caste, the masses of ordinary black people had been objects of pity and contempt. Now released from southern bondage and moving North, they became, in their yet unassimilated presence, a force greatly feared.

Fact and Value in the Study of the Race Problem

Gunnar Myrdal was not only a European coming to examine with fresh eyes the American race problem, he was also a European social scientist who did not accept the dominant American model of a positivistic social science. His famous Appendix 2, "A Methodological Note on Fact and Valuation in Social Science," was a thirty-page essay advancing a severe critique of American social science and its high susceptibility to bias despite pretensions to scientific objectivity; the appendix also offered a way to mitigate such biases (1035–64). The issues at stake in his essay, however, were not confined to the race issue, but to how American social scientists studied all of social life.

There were, argued Myrdal, a classification of biases common to writings on race relations, each category being a continuum. There was first a scale of *friendliness to blacks,* most evident on the question of racial traits but also in such other efforts as the writing of history. White scholars had not escaped being effected by the dominant prejudices in judging black people: "Even the friends of the Negro people were moved by the dominant public opinion to assume, without much questioning, views which were unduly unfavorable to the Negroes. They were, in other words, 'friendly' to the Negroes only when compared with the very unfriendly general public opinion, but not when compared with what disinterested scholarship should have demanded" (1036). The observation was insightful; perhaps it could have only come from a dispassionate foreign observer. Edward Reuter's *The American Race Problem* serves as an example of Myrdal's point: what at the time was a work friendly to blacks when compared to the prevailing prejudices nonetheless offered an unredeemingly dismal image of blacks as a people and seemed to appreciate nothing about their cultural or political efforts.

Besides that of friendliness, there were five other biases. One was *friendliness to the South;* northern writers as well as southern ones had been mostly pro-southern. About a scale of *radicalism-conservatism,* Myrdal said that "in a sense it is the master scale of biases in the social sciences." A more radical view would be more favorable to blacks, but given the "heavily prejudiced" opinion of the white group, "even a radical tendency might fail to reach an unbiased judgment." Another scale, *optimism-pessimism,* measured the tendency of Americans to want happy endings and to be tempted to play down facts that offered little prospect of being changed. On the other hand, pessimism may fit a conservative bias. A scale of *integration-isolation* spoke to the "opportune interest and factual circumstances" that made social scientists treat the race problem "in isolation from the total complex of problems in American civilization." But an absence of bias required that race be interrelated "with the total economic, social, political, judicial, and broadly cultural life of the nation." Lastly, the scale of *scientific integrity* marked the degree to which a scientist could study unpopular subjects and state unpopular conclusions. The South, observed Myrdal, was still "not very favorable" to disinterested study of the race problem, though in the North, "and particularly at the great and famous institutions, such inhibitions were not found" (1038–41).

The significance of Myrdal's scales of bias was not in recording the persistent forms of bias "apparent on the surface," that is, those not difficult to recognize and readily evident in the work of social scientists studying "the Negro problem." Instead, it was in his emphatic point that the social scientist "is part of the culture in which he lives, and he never succeeds in freeing himself entirely from dependence on the dominant preconceptions and biases of his environment" (1035). Bias, then, was more than a methodological sin, correctable by peer criticism; it was an unavoidable aspect of being human: "Keeping in mind the actual power situation in the American nation, and observing the prevalent opinions in the dominant white group, we are led, even by superficial examination, to expect that even the scientific biases will run against the Negroes most of the time. This expectation has been confirmed in the course of this study" (ibid.).

That the sociological study of race relations was largely biased against blacks was possibly Myrdal's most important finding about American social science. Though Appendix 2 was to be widely read, the focus of the debate it aroused was largely around Myrdal's more general claims about the place of values in social research. Values, argued Myrdal, "permeate" research and are concealed within it; they cannot be edited out or offset by illusory efforts at a balanced picture. Neither can they be erased by sticking to the facts and using refined methods of statistical analysis. Nor was science protected against bias "*by the entirely negative device of refusing to arrrange its results for practical and political utilization.*" We cannot rid ourselves of bias: "the attempt to eradicate biases by trying to keep out the valuations themselves is a hopeless and misdirected venture" (1041, 1043). If bias were to be overcome, it had to be done in another way.

Myrdal pointed to another way, though not one consistent with the positivist assumptions of American sociology: valuations had to be confronted and acknowledged for their place in social research: "*There is no other device for excluding biases in social science than to face the valuations and to introduce them as explicitly stated, specific, and sufficiently concretized value premises.*" But the value premises to be introduced would not emerge from the facts, nor could they be left to the arbitrary choice of individual researchers. Rather, they would be selected "*by the criterion of relevance and significance to the culture under study*" (1043, 1045). That being so, alternative sets of value premises were possible and should be utilized.

It seemed not to occur to Myrdal, however, that white sociologists, as biased against black people as he had indicated them to be, and believing confidently in their own capacity for unbiased study, might have difficulty recognizing their own value premises as well as selecting value premises "of relevance and significance to the culture under study." Sociologists saw the race problem in terms of the particulars of their own national history and were not concerned with a broader comparative view that might have led them to develop a more critical, or even detached, perspective on American culture. As a consequence, they possessed little if any insight into their own values as a source of bias in their study of race relations.

The Conservatism of American Social Science

Myrdal understood full well that most American sociologists would resist taking seriously his value-based conception of social science, that they believed passionately in the existence of objective knowledge, and that some of them would be offended by his assertion that man, as Aristotle said, is a political animal and "social science is a political science, in that sense" (1043). For that reason, he looked back into the historical development of American social science to find the reasons for its commitment to a value-free discipline and to construct a case for discrediting that commitment.

A uniquely American social science developed, in the first place, he claimed, from a "particularly violent" reaction against an earlier highly normative social science uninformed by social facts. The avoidance of practical involvement in public affairs was further heightened by a high degree of specialization that led social scientists to feel "incompetent before the broad social tasks." Then, too, until the New Deal, scholars had been isolated from political agencies; indeed, in the United States the public did not look to academics "for the leadership of national thought in the broader issues" (1042). This last reference was an implied contrast to Europe, where scholars and intellectuals enjoyed greater public respect and played a far more influential role in the making of public policy than did their counterparts in the United States. Myrdal's own experience in Sweden was that of a university professor actively involved in the making of public policy.

But these moderate comments were but a prelude to a short essay within Appendix 2, "The History and Logic of Hidden Valuations in Social Science," in which Myrdal mounted a more serious charge of deeply rooted conservative bias in American social science. He found its origin in the influence of the philosophies of natural rights and utilitarianism on the development of the social sciences. That there is a common welfare and that human interests are in basic harmony were ideas developed by a conservative wing of Western liberal thought into a social science that possessed "a static and fatalistic political bias, a do-nothing liberalism" (1047).

Myrdal cited William Graham Sumner, Robert Park, and William Ogburn as influential social scientists who manifested such a bias. Sumner's famous concepts of folkways and mores, for example, had been used to ridicule the possibilities of human intervention into social life. To Myrdal it was significant that the folkways and mores had become the political credo of educated Southerners by which to demonstrate that change toward racial equality was not possible: "stateways cannot change folkways." Unlike Sumner, Park wanted social change in race relations, Myrdal acknowledged, but he did not look to planned intervention as a way to achieve it. Instead, his writings demonstrated "a systematic tendency to ignore practically all possibilities of modifying—by conscious effort—the social effects of natural forces" (1050). Park's vocabulary of competition and accommodation, the latter as "necessary internal adjustments" (Park's language), signified to Myrdal the do-nothing implications of Park's assumptions. Ogburn, in turn, was cited for his theory of culture lag, including his thesis about technology as the innovator of unplanned changes to which human beings must adjust.

Common to the work of all three—and of the many others for whom they served as models of scientific work—and despite the fact that all three made "monumental contributions to knowledge," there was a specific error "of inferring from the facts that men can and should make no effort to change the 'natural' outcome of specific forces observed. This is the old do-nothing (laissez-faire) bias of 'realistic' social science" (1052).

Myrdal rounded out his criticisms by citing the vocabulary, increasingly functional, that was becoming so common to American sociological discourse: balance, harmony, equilibrium, adjustment, organization, accomodation, and function. Such terms, he pointed out, implicitly evaluated a situation as "good," while terms such as disharmony, disequilibrium, maladjustment, disorganization, and culture lag described undesirable conditions (1055).

Myrdal made little distinction between Sumner and Park in his indictment of a conservative social science. Though he acknowledged that Park, unlike Sumner, did not desire to maintain the status quo in race relations, that in itself was inadequate to an understanding of Park's theoretical stance. If competition and accommodation were basic social processes for Park, no less so was conflict; it was conflict that brought about social change. Furthermore, as his biographer Fred Mathews noted, Park assumed that "the dynamic forces must come from the oppressed themselves." Park conceived of group struggle as a basic part of human history, admired the racial self-consciousness and solidarity that made disciplined struggle possible, and disavowed any notion of conflict as damaging or undesirable. In a book review, he once asserted that "the struggle to rise of the peoples who are down is one of the most wholesome exercises in which human beings can be engaged."[13]

Yet, from Myrdal's perspective, Park was conservative because he was committed to an ideal of objective, scientific scholarship, opposed to taking an active political role, and deplored the obvious trends in sociology away from detached, apolitical research. During the 1930s more sociologists were employed in public agencies, noted Fred Mathews, and "as they became more involved in the practical problems of the depression era and the challenge of Fascism from abroad, an open commitment to social engineering and political involvement replaced the Parkian image of the concerned scholar as detached observer and midwife to attitude change."[14] From Park's perspective, there was no virtue in that, but Myrdal saw planning and policymaking by the state as the way to achieve racial change. Park, in contrast, saw racial progress coming from the struggles of the subordinate race.

Whether Myrdal's charge of a conservative bias applied adequately to Park or not, it did apply to most sociologists of race relations, including Park's students. Most of them saw any change only as a gradual, incremental process, and they strongly preferred that it be that way. While they believed racial change to be a consequence of such complex processes as urbanization and industrialization, they expected these processes to be slowly moving trends, not rapid alterations in the established institutions. Park was undoubtedly speaking of these sociologists, among others, when he charged liberals with not wanting change so rapid as to produce disorder.[17] That fear of disorder was rooted in a conception of black people unprepared for a place in modern society. A vast migration of such people to the urban North then seemed a social threat, not a release of blacks from an oppressive situation. Indeed, Myrdal also made a similar judgment of southern blacks, and a number of his more conservative policy recommendations came from such an assessment.

But there was another reason why sociologists had assumed an apolitical stance on the matter of racial change. Until the 1940s, they had not looked to political activities, particularly those that sought governmental intervention, as useful efforts because they were convinced that the implacable opposition of the large majority of white Americans rendered impossible any directed change in the established pattern of race relations. They had often given such a reason for not making common cause with white liberals and with the leaders of black organizations. Indeed, some of them, such as Edward Reuter, had ridiculed the very idea of such an effort.

But a new generation, inspired by the interventionist policies and practices of the New Deal, was now prepared to work toward the possibilities of producing racial change. Myrdal's compelling case for social planning and interventionist practices by the state, as well as for a sociology openly committed to research relevant to such planning and practice, was no less a factor in legitimating an interventionist perspective in the sociology of race relations.

Nonetheless, Myrdal's influence on American sociology was limited. He did not succeed in altering the dominant conception of science held by most American sociologists, and he did not convince them that values as bias were to be acknowledged and made specific. Nor did they embrace social engineering in place of a "value-free" social science.[15] Yet Myrdal did provide one influential voice among several in support of those who were seeking an alternative image of social science.

Arguments about the place of values in sociology were not new when Myrdal's Appendix 2 projected him into the debate. That had been going on for at least two decades. In the face of an increasingly dominant model of sociology as quantitative, value-free, and apolitical, a vocal minority within the discipline criticized the positivistic paradigm and offered alternative visions of a social science. Louis Wirth, for example, in his preface to Karl Mannheims's *Ideology and Utopia*, stressed the centrality of values for social science and the value-rooted character of the social scientist as observer of social life. So, too, Robert Lynd in *Knowledge for What?* argued for a social science committed to a critical assessment of American culture.[16] Myrdal acknowledged Wirth and Lynd in his footnotes. His own essay, in effect, was a contribution, not only to the often heated controversy over the place of values in social science, but to the very meaning of social science as a human activity.

Assessing a Classic

To assess the place of *An American Dilemma* in the sociology of race relations is both easy and difficult. In its own time the book was well, even enthusiastically received and widely reviewed, discussed, and read well beyond the academic community; perhaps no sociological work ever became so well known to the general public. But not surprisingly, it was often roundly condemned in the South, even by southern liberals. Also, Arnold Rose's condensation was widely used as a textbook or as collateral reading in sociology courses in race relations.[18] The praise and wide readership it earned make it easy to acknowledge that this huge book is a classic of American sociology.

Yet, its reception among sociologists was usually more critical than praising. Some sociologists thought it too optimistic, others were unconvinced by its argument that the race problem was a dilemma of American values, while still others quarreled with its dictum on methodology. Only a few of them, like Robert Lynd and Maurice Davie, found reason for high praise. It should be noted, however, that the sociological reviewers were mostly of the older generation that Myrdal had so severely criticized; thus, Edward B. Reuter, whom Myrdal had criticized in the book, wrote a particularly harsh review.[19]

It is more difficult, however, to assess the book's lasting contribution. In part this is because it drew its material from the existing literature; it was not a report of original research. Ordinarily, one would not expect that a summary of existing literature, however useful at the time, would be a lasting contribution. A large number of American social scientists contributed to the volume, and a smaller group played a decisive role in its organizing and editing; it was never a one person project. Yet, it also bore the unmistakable stamp of Gunnar Myrdal; he was, quite rightly, listed as principle author and responsible for its contents.

It is also true that the book was published at a fortuitous time, when a major generational change was occurring among the sociologists of race relations. A younger generation of social scientists with a more interventionist perspective was arriving; a number of them participated in the small groups that worked closely with Myrdal. Though not planned to be such, *An American Dilemma* became a vehicle for releasing new directions and invoking a critique of the established one. A case can be made that one measure of its contributions was its ability to assess and evaluate the existing literature in such a way as to support new directions in the sociology of race relations while not abandoning the underlying perspective.

It would be difficult to show that *An American Dilemma* generated any significant amount of new research in race relations. Myrdal made suggestions for research throughout the book—three appendixes were devoted to aspects of research—but usually in areas in which there was already an established pattern of ongoing work. His one recognized contribution was the "rank order of discrimination," namely, the hypothesis that whites possessed a descending order of discriminatory standards from intermarriage and sexual intercourse at the most forbidden, to personal relations, segregation of public facilities, political disenfranchisement, discrimination in legal processes, and, least supported, discrimination in economic opportunities, including public welfare. The strategic implication was that the low-ranking discriminations were the most open to challenge. In turn, blacks were presumed to hold an inverse rank order, being most concerned about economic and legal discriminations, least about intermarriage. The hypothesis provided a good deal of discussion and a modest amount of research, not all of it supportive.[20]

The most significant new development in research after the publication of *An American Dilemma* was the onset of social psychological studies of prejudice. Myrdal could not be credited with initiating them, though the book ended with Appendix 10, "Quantitative Studies in Race Attitudes" (1136–43). Myrdal's thesis that race was primarily a white people's problem gave practical relevance to attitude studies, for such studies presumably could reveal possibilities for altering discriminatory behavior.

A Basic Perspective

For probably two decades after its publication, Myrdal's *An American Dilemma* continued to be a force within the social sciences and the discipline of history; it was both praised and made use of in scholarly work, as well as criticized and rejected.[21] If it generated only a modest amount of empirical research, it stimulated considerable debate on the question of values as fundamental in shaping race relations in the United States. But it also encouraged a new development in the sociology of race relations: an applied research into practical questions about removing both prejudice and discrimination in the relations between whites and blacks.

Yet it was not in encouraging specific forms of research but in sustaining a basic perspective that *An American Dilemma*'s influence on a new generation can be found. Five elements were central to this perspective: assimilation; cultural unity; race as "the white man's problem"; interracial collaboration in the pursuit of racial change; and race as a solvable social problem.

In reaffirming the ultimate social goal of assimilation, Myrdal maintained continuity with the sociological generations. The assimilation of diverse racial and ethnic groups into a homogeneous society had been a central principle of the dominant ideology in the United States and the most basic assumption of American social scientists concerned with race and ethnicity. However critical a young generation might be over other issues, they accepted assimilation wholeheartedly, and it became an overt value premise in Myrdal's American Creed. Even with the changing generations, then, there would be no radical break with past theory and, in fact, there was more continuity than discontinuity.

The ideal of the American Creed was Myrdal's unique expression of the American value system, but even before Myrdal, sociologists and others had noted the discrepancy between democratic principles and racial practices. Myrdal found a unity of values because he presumed that the American Creed was accepted as the nation's ideal; it was the country's national conscience. As the creed acted as a social trend, greater compliance reduced unjustified social differences and moved the nation toward full acceptance of its own moral standards. Such a nation then became a less differentiated, more homogeneous society. Assimilation and national unity, therefore, were reciprocally enforcing principles.

Not all sociologists, however, accepted Myrdal's particular formulation of the issue of national unity, but they did accept the principle of assimilation into an increasingly homogeneous society. For the older generation, such a society was an ultimate but still distant goal; for a newer generation, there was an optimistic sense that it was somewhat more approachable. In continuing and reinforcing the goals of assimilation and cultural unity, there was sustained across the sociological generations a basic American outlook, which then singularly narrowed the terms on which race relations could be interpreted and developed. That narrowing, however, retained the idea that race was still "the white man's problem," both in the older sense that only whites had the power to solve it and in the newer sense that the irrational prejudices of the dominant whites were a key to the problem. Myrdal clearly encouraged the notion that these prejudicial attitudes were changing, and were changeable, which to him meant that there were real possibilities for movement toward racial equality.

Optimism for Change

From the outset Myrdal argued that there was reason to be optimistic about the prospects for racial change, but being optimistic required taking issue with what he called "the defeatist attitude toward the possibility of inducing social change by means of legislation." He identified as one factor in that defeatist attitude the "do-nothing" tendency so prevalent in American social science—"stateways cannot change folkways"—but another was the pessimism, even among blacks, about effecting any political or legislative change in race relations against what seemed the entrenched opposition of the white population. But Myrdal insisted that there were promising developments, chiefly "the growing cultural homogeneity and the increasing social and political participation of the masses" (19–20). His major argument, however, rested on the power of the American ideals. Throughout the book he constantly insisted that the ideals encapsulated in the American Creed were a powerful force for change; their weight was on the side of racial justice.

Myrdal had made clear his own commitment to bringing about racial change in a rational and gradual manner, particularly by planning and social engineering. The perspective of a Swedish social democrat could not, in itself, be persuasive to a majority of Americans, even liberal ones raised on the values of the New Deal; America was not Sweden. Yet Myrdal did have an effect. It was not in any specific recommendation for rationally planned change, but in his constant assurance about the possibilities of achieving reform by deliberate measures. Strategies for social change, Myrdal recognized, must be developed within a social context, with full recognition of the nation's values, history, and conflicting forces. Consequently, he used the American Creed as his constant point of reference, and he persistently praised, even extolled, the promise to be found in the American experiment. He looked for trends and developments that supported the possibility for further change. His was a constant appeal to the American liberal's sense of reform as gradual, rational, and nonviolent. (Myrdal denounced the Marxian concept of class struggle as "a superficial and erroneous notion" [676].)

A new generation of sociologists, then, did not get from Myrdal any specifics of strategy or particular changes to advocate. They did get support for their own conception of a more applied form of the sociology of race relations and a developing commitment to a national legislative solution to the inequities of racial discrimination. Myrdal helped to supplant the inherited sociological pessimism about the short-run possibilities of racial change with the confident idea that the race problem was there to be solved.

The idea that social problems, however difficult, were nevertheless solvable fitted the American pragmatic temperament. But the application of this idea to race relations, however, was not yet a matter of full consensus. Before this point, sociologists saw the race problem as without solution in the present (as Reuter did), or as changing only in incremental steps by the forces of urbanization and industrialization, and believed that effective intervention was still sometime off. But a new generation, accustomed to governmental programs designed to solve difficult social problems, was ready to assume that race was now also a solvable problem.

To that readiness, *An American Dilemma* gave full support. Throughout the pages of the book, Myrdal always spoke of "the Negro problem" as a difficult matter and progress in solving it as necessarily gradual. But that did not alter the fact that rational action was possible, and changes could be deliberately created. From then on, the issue was settled; race in the United States was a social problem now amenable to rational effort. What was significant about this development was that it pressed sociologists in a new direction without disavowing the most settled assumptions.

An American Dilemma, in fact, sustained an essential continuity with the interpretive consensus developed over the preceding quarter century. Myrdal's polemical attack upon the apolitical, objective stance of American sociologists tended to obscure how much basic agreement was sustained and strengthened. Only in the idea that sociologists could support black and white collaborative efforts to intervene in the established racial order did Myrdal break with the past generation, and on this he was only advocating what a younger generation was ready to do.

Notes

1. Gunnar Myrdal, with the assistance of Richard Sterner and Arnold Rose, *An American Dilemma: The Negro Problem and Modern Democracy* (New York: Harper and Brothers, 1944).

2. See both the Foreword, v–viii, and Author's Preface, ix–xx, for the origins of the project. A more detailed history of the organization of the project can be found in David W. Southern, *Gunnar Myrdal and Black-White Relations: The Use and Abuse of An American Dilemma, 1944–1969* (Baton Rouge: Louisiana State University Press, 1987).

3. Myrdal, *American Dilemma*, xviii.

4. Melville Herskovits, *The Myth of the Negro Past* (New York: Harper and Brothers, 1941); Myrdal, *American Dilemma*, 929–30.

5. Charles S. Johnson, *Patterns of Negro Segregation* (New York: Harper and Brothers, 1943).

6. Richard Sterner, *The Negro's Share: A Study of Income, Consumption, Housing, and Public Assistance* (New York: Harper and Brothers, 1943).

7. Otto Klineberg, ed., *Characteristics of the American Negro* (New York: Harper and Brothers, 1944); for Klineberg's own work on differences between blacks and whites, see his *Race Differences* (New York: Harper and Brothers, 1935).

8. Myrdal, *American Dilemma*, xlvii. Further references to this work will appear in the text. All italics appear in the original work.

9. Robin M. Williams, Jr., *American Society: A Sociological Interpretation* (New York: Knopf, 1951), chapter 11.

10. Guy B. Johnson, "Some Factors in the Development of Negro Social Institutions in the United States," *American Journal of Sociology* 42 (Nov. 1934): 329, 332–33; Charles S. Johnson, *Shadow of the Plantation* (Chicago: University of Chicago Press, 1934), 4–5.

11. Ralph Ellison, *Shadow and Act* (New York: Random House, 1964), 315–16.

12. On Johnson's call for planning, see the statement on the last page of his *Shadow of the Plantation*.

13. Fred H. Mathews, *Quest for an American Sociology: Robert E. Park and the Chicago School* (Montreal: McGill-Queen's University Press, 1977), 188; review by Park of *Races, Nations, and Classes* by Herbert J. Miller, *American Journal of Sociology* 31 (Jan. 1926): 537.

14. Mathews, *Quest*, 183.

15. See, for example, Kimball Young's response in his review of *An American Dilemma* in the *American Sociological Review* 9 (Apr. 1944): 326–30.

16. Louis Wirth, Preface to Karl Mannheim, *Ideology and Utopia* (New York: Harcourt, Brace, 1936); Robert S. Lynd, *Knowledge for What?: The Place of Social Science in American Culture* (Princeton: Princeton University Press, 1939).

17. Mathews, *Quest*, 189.

18. Southern, *Gunnar Myrdal*, chapters 4 and 5; Arnold Rose, *The Negro in America* (New York: Harper and Row, 1948).

19. Southern, *Gunnar Myrdal*, 80–87.

20. Myrdal, *American Dilemma*, 60–61. For examples of work on the rank order of discrimination, see citations of articles in *The Negro in America: A Bibliography*, compiled by Elizabeth W. Miller (Cambridge: Harvard University Press, 1966). For a discussion of the rank order of discrimination as an aspect of strategy, see George Eaton Simpson and J. Milton Yinger, *Racial and Cultural Minorities: An Analysis of Prejudice and Discrimination*, 4th ed. (New York: Harper and Row, 1972), 663–66.

21. For a review of the treatment of *An American Dilemma* within the social sciences and history from 1945 to 1965, see Southern, *Gunnar Myrdal*, chapter 8.

7

Race Relations as Intergroup Relations

Prior to World War II, the academic study of race relations had been separate by intention from the work of the small group of liberal activists. By the end of the war, however, the sociologists of race relations, sometimes reluctantly, sometimes not, had begun to cohabit with an enlarged and professionalizing body of practitioners. An area of practice variously labeled "human relations," "community relations," and eventually, by professional choice, "intergroup relations" was in the making. This partial conjoining of two groups, academic and practical, neither of which had yet been able to effect much influence on race relations, was, in the first instance, a consequence of a new generation of sociologists more committed to the possibilities of social intervention. It was also a matter of finally placing race on the liberal agenda.

Race Relations as Liberal Reform

Despite the integration of black voters into the political coalition supporting the Roosevelt administration, few New Dealers in Washington had much interest in the race issue. But a small group within the administration, supported strongly by Eleanor Roosevelt and Harold Ickes, worked hard to influence those policies that most affected blacks. In working out their ideas, they emphasized three points: the need for economic reform from which both blacks and whites would benefit; the importance of education for blacks; and the need to educate whites in order to lessen the force of racial prejudice. The belief that economic reform would benefit blacks along with whites and that prejudice and racial hostility would decline as a consequence of both economic recovery and the education of both races provided a basis for a liberal optimism that was to carry over into the 1950s. At last the liberal reformer's interest in solving America's social problems had been extended to the issue of race.[1]

An even greater impetus to liberal reform, however, came from two events controlled by neither the Roosevelt administration nor white liberals. The first of these was the famous march that did not occur, the March on Washington Movement of 1941; the second was the explosive race riot in Detroit in 1943. The first of these events testified to the consciousness of blacks that their incorporation into the New Deal's political coalition had not provided much racial progress; the second spoke to the potential for racial conflict in the urban North.

In 1941 an effort to organize a massive march on Washington to demand action from what seemed to blacks still to be a largely indifferent government touched the consciousness of the black masses as few other such efforts had done. A. Phillip Randolph, president of the Brotherhood of Sleeping Car Porters, organized the movement and enlisted the support of the established civil rights organizations, such as the NAACP and the Urban League, while also generating mass enthusiasm within the black population. Eventually taking seriously the threat of 100,000 black people marching on the nation's capitol, President Roosevelt, under his emergency wartime powers, on June 25, 1941, issued Executive Order 8802, which forbade racial discrimination in defense industries and established a Committee on Fair Employment Practice.[2]

During the week of June 20, 1943, the city of Detroit was rent by a severe race riot, the largest urban racial disturbance since the Chicago riot of 1919. Thirty-four persons died in the rioting and federal troops were brought in to restore to the city its place as the "arsenal of democracy" for the war effort.[3] A lesser and more effectively contained riot occurred in early August in Harlem, while in Los Angeles that same summer there was a series of violent outbursts between Mexican-American youths, whose distinctive "zoot-suit" set them off from others, including soldiers and sailors stationed in the area.

To both of these events, the liberal response was similar: to seek legislative remedy and to create local groups committed to programs of racial change, preferably with official status. Efforts of congressional passage of permanent fair employment legislation began in 1942. In 1943 the National Council for a Permanent FEPC was organized to pressure for the creation of a Fair Employment Practices Commission patterned after the National Labor Relations Board. The National Council then enlisted a body of cooperating organizations and also organized local councils to provide local pressure for fair employment legislation. By 1949 thirty-four states had from one to ten such councils.[4]

The interest of some members of Congress in fair employment legislation prompted the introduction of several bills; however, they died in committee or, when reported out, failed to come to a vote. In early 1946, at the opening of the second session of the Seventy-ninth Congress, a move by senatorial supporters to bring a bill to the floor of the Senate produced a twenty-three day filibuster by southern Democrats. When a vote on cloture failed, the bill died with the Seventy-ninth Congress. The failure to achieve fair employment legislation at the national level then encouraged an alternate strategy of focusing primarily on the local and state level. That effort was modestly successful; by 1948 six states had enacted legislation and three northern cities had enacted local ordinances.[5]

The shock of the 1943 race riot in Detroit also stimulated the organization of local groups, both official and unofficial. A year after the riot the Social Science Institute at Fisk University reported the existence of 224 committees formed to deal with racial tensions. Of the 166 about which the institute received information, 135 were local organizations and another 16 were statewide. Thirty-two had offical status, appointed by mayors, governors, and state legislators. By 1945 an estimated four hundred such groups had been established.[6]

While many groups faded out as fears about race riots subsided, some of them became permanent agencies. Though almost always understaffed and underbudgeted, and rarely possessing adequate resources or effective authority, they nonetheless provided the basis for the emergence of a new professional role, that of the intergroup relations practitioner. Most of these new professionals were white, male, and college educated. While many came from social work, education, psychology, and sociology, still others came into the new profession from a wide range of other occupations and academic backgrounds.

Conscious of a new and as yet poorly accepted status, the new practitioners formed the National Association of Intergroup Relations Officials (NAIRO). Its membership consisted of the new professionals in the new state and local agencies, as well as those in the older civil rights organizations (NAACP, the Urban League, the Anti-Defamation League, the National Council of Christians and Jews, and the like), besides others employed in federal and state agencies who could apply a knowledge of race relations to specific programs. NAIRO established a national office, an annual convention, a journal, and sought to define the role and the training adequate to its tasks. In short, it soon exhibited all the characteristics of a profession.

Intergroup Relations and Sociology

The new profession of intergroup relations was a response to racial tensions and disturbances, but it was the kind of "rational" response that social scientists, among others, had recommended. Once in existence, however, it had a considerable effect on the sociology of race relations. There was first the recruitment of some of the new professionals from among the sociologically trained, and, second, the consequent development of a liason between practitioners and academics. Louis Wirth of the University of Chicago, for example, was actively involved in 1944 in the founding of the American Council on Race Relations, which served as a coordinating and advising agency for local groups dealing with race relations. He also founded the Committee on Education, Training, and Research in Race Relations at the University of Chicago. A number of other sociologists and social psychologists became involved in the activities of NAIRO. In the same year that Wirth was helping to found the American Council on Race Relations, Howard Odum and Guy B. Johnson were actively involved in the organization of the biracial Southern Regional Council, which revitalized and expanded the former Commission on Interracial Cooperation. Johnson, in fact, served as its first executive director.

Another effect of these professionally organized efforts was to shift the emphasis in sociology from the "objective" study of race relations to race as a reformable social problem and, consequently, to stimulate a greater interest in applied research. Such a shift was aided and abetted by the interest that the foundations began to take in intergroup relations. The founding of the American Council on Race Relations, for example, was made possible by grants from the Julius Rosenwald Fund and the Marshall Field Foundation, and in 1945 the Social Science Research Council established a Committee on Techniques for Reducing Group Hostility; and the Rockefeller Foundation commissioned Robert MacIver, one of sociology's distinguished scholars, to write a book on strategies for controlling intergroup relations.

This greater interest in race relations on the part of some foundations, evident in increased funds for research, conferences, and related activities, spoke to a concern for racial change on the part of some members of the American elite. If the efforts of those seeking racial change had not yet found any support by reaching downward into the white citizenry, a reaching upward touched and drew upon an elite consciousness of an issue that compelled examination and could be left unchanged only at peril to social stability. In the 1930s, foundation involvement in race relations had begun with grants from the Julius Rosenwald Fund, the Phelps-Stokes Fund, and the Rockefeller Foundation, but also from the American Council on Education's commissioning of the several studies of black youth, and the Carnegie Corporation project, which culminated in Myrdal's *An American Dilemma*. In the years after 1945, there was to be considerably more such support from foundations for programs in race relations.[7]

Invigorated and made ambitious by such financial support, the realm of intergroup relations grew rapidly, shaped by intentions of moderate, cautious, but professional intervention into the prevailing racial structure of American society. That self-conscious intention was evident, not only in the messages of tolerance and equal opportunity found in its literature, but also in its recognition of the ideological latitudes lying just beyond its range: the power of conservatism, always hesitant to disturb practical interests; and a radicalism demanding more militant action and more sweeping social changes. Beyond even that was the mass of ordinary people, defined as prejudiced and ignorant, whose resistance to equal treatment of the races was soon to be defined as the core of the problem.

Some twenty years earlier, the sociologists of race relations had advanced an argument against biological racism to which there was little approving response. Though there had been a small cadre of practicing liberals, there had been no concerted social power pressing for racial change, and an Anglo-Saxon Protestant establishment had been slow to abandon an intolerant view of "lesser breeds." But within a new generation, there had emerged some who no longer accepted the earlier racial ideologies; instead, they recognized the reality of a new situation in race relations and felt there was a need to change the nation's racial posture. They responded favorably, therefore, to new ideas about racial change and to newer scientific information about race. The slow spread of scientific knowledge about race eventually had some real effect, particularly among the college educated.

A liberal constituency for race relations now existed, and its vantage point was that of the better-educated liberal activists seeking to change a recalcitrant world sustained, they felt, by ignorance and prejudice. Sociologists were readily drawn into that liberal constituency, helped to shape its distinctive view on race relations, and came increasingly to support its activism. One consequence, already evident by 1950, was the proliferation of workshops and conferences on intergroup relations and intercultural education in which sociologists and social psychologists became increasingly involved with community activists and professional practitioners.[8]

Sociologists were not yet ready to claim that they possessed answers to the nation's racial problems, but they were confident that sociological research could enable social-action agencies to be more effective. There seemed to be a need, therefore, to synthesize existing knowledge as well as to accumulate new knowledge. What was new in this was the proposition that knowledge had to be sorted into what was most and least useful to practitioners. A new professional constituency of knowledge users had now come into existence and was to have an effect on what new knowledge was sought and how the accumulation of knowledge was assessed. In 1947 and 1948 three publications illustrated this first effort on the part of sociologists to move into closer relations with social practitioners: Arnold Rose's memorandum summarizing studies on attitudes toward minority groups; Robin Williams's monograph on the reduction of intergroup tensions; and Robert MacIver's book on controlling intergroup discrimination.

Studies in Intergroup Prejudice

Arnold Rose's memorandum, *Studies in Reduction of Prejudice,* typified the new relations between sociologists and practitioners; it was prepared for and published by the American Council on Race Relations in 1947, with a second edition in 1948. With slightly over one hundred pages of typescript, Rose briefly summarized and assessed a large number of social psychological studies, ranging from those on the effectiveness of propaganda, attitude-testing techniques, prejudice among children, public opinion polls on attitudes toward minorities, the psychology of prejudice, and audience studies.[9]

Rose found little to commend in an array of psychological and sociological studies. There were contradictions between the results of various studies, frequent lack of specificity in measuring variables, weak testing techniques, and a lack of carryover from studies on children and college students to the mass of the population. Studies of attitudes differentiated by region, ethnicity and religion, sex, intelligence, social class, and community size were also often inconsistent and contradictory. A discussion of various techniques for measuring ethnic attitudes concluded that all tests had at least one major defect, and a criticism of them all was that "they were pencil-and-paper tests which did not measure 'real life' situations."[10]

A survey of theories and empirical studies of prejudice revealed "a most bewildering array of contradictory thought and evidence." Perhaps only the literature on children showed some consistency, namely, that prejudice commonly appeared at age five; it was never instinctive, however, but was learned, especially from parents. Though all but one of the theories agreed that education could reduce or eliminate prejudice, there was diverse opinion "as to what that agreement should consist of." According to all the theories, prejudice was not fixed and inevitable, but was changing and reducible. Among the several schools of contemporary psychology, Rose felt that "only psychoanalysis has proved to be of any assistance." Prejudice, he concluded, is "of a more complex character than many of the things that psychologists are accustomed to studying."[11]

Empirical data that contradicted one another, faulty testing techniques, and theories poorly grounded in evidence did not provide a body of social psychological findings useful to those intergroup relations practitioners who were intent on devising programs that would reduce racial and ethnic prejudice. More than anything else, Rose's memorandum suggested that social psychological theory and empirical research had little as yet to offer social practice when the central concern was prejudice. There were, of course, many sociologists who believed that prejudice should not be defined as the central concern.

Reduction of Intergroup Tensions

Robin Williams's small monograph, commissioned by the Social Science Research Council's Committee on Techniques for Reducing Intergroup Hostility, was an influential step in linking social science to social practice.[12] That was so, not only because the monograph bore the imprimatur of the prestigious Social Science Research Council, but because its careful enumeration of more than one hundred testable propositions set out an agenda for social research that was intended to reduce the gap between academics and practitioners. The very publication of the monograph was a commitment by the social scientific establishment to a greater interest in the applied problems of intergroup relations.

The committee's three distinguished members—Leonard S. Cottrell, Jr., of Cornell University, the chairman; Charles Dollard of the Carnegie Corporation; and Carl I. Hovland of Yale University—set out in a brief foreword the political context within which the monograph was set. "Implicit in democratic theory," they pointed out, "is the fact of the acceptance of conflicting interests and even the positive encouragement of the expression of divergent views, aims, and values." But there is also the assumption "that conflicts can be resolved or accommodated by nonviolent means and that intergroup hostilities can be kept below the point where the basic consensus of the society is threatened." That being so, the "survival of the democratic nation, therefore, depends on the invention of techniques for resolving its internal group conflicts in such a way that the welfare and interests of all elements of the community are given adequate consideration in the community" (vii).

Williams, too, pointed to the threat that intergroup hostility posed to the common value system, to the recognized need for national unity accentuated by World War II, to the international imagery of the United States, and "to a pervasive strain of optimism, belief in progress, and faith in the perfectibility of human society which have deep roots in American culture." But he also asserted a functional need for intergroup tolerance: "The varied cultures from which our population stocks have come have made intergroup tolerance, at least, not just a virtue but in some senses a societal necessity" (3).

A focus on reducing intergroup tensions, as the title specified, seemed to Williams to require explanation, for it appeared to rest on an implicit value premise "that the reduction of hostility is in itself a desirable goal regardless of other considerations." No such assumption need be made, he argued, for there is also the possibility that a measure of intergroup hostility is unavoidable, and there are also instances "in which temporary intensification of conflict" has led to changes that are improvements. Nonetheless, Williams insisted, "much intergroup hostility is extremely costly" and there is "the possibility that adequate solutions can sometimes be achieved at less social cost through avenues other than conflict." Williams then assigned world-historical significance to finding such a solution to intergroup hostility: "The extent to which techniques can be developed and utilized to reach such solutions will have much to do with the whole future of American—and world—society" (5-6).

Here, then, was the basic premise for the social scientific contribution to intergroup relations practice: the peaceful resolution of intergroup hostility and conflict was essential for both the democratic character and the unity of the nation. Progress in intergroup relations, therefore, was to be defined in terms of the national interest. Despite Myrdal's emphasis on the American Creed, the idea that a racial minority was entitled to equal treatment as a matter of simple justice had not yet become an explicit rationale for racial progress.

The emphasis that Williams gave to hostility and its opposite, tolerance—not respect, liking, or brotherhood—originated in his conception that, not only had full assimilation not occurred, but there were serious questions about both the likelihood of actually accomplishing assimilation in the near future and about the value of such a goal: "To many the melting pot has begun to represent flat uniformity imposed by the dominant group." But the opposite of assimilation, a society of culturally distinct and socially separate groups with only minimal contact among them was impossible to maintain "in an industrial, urban, secular, mobile society." This produced a compromise, cultural pluralism, which "envisions an end-situation in which (1) a considerable portion of the cultural distinctiveness of various groups will be retained, but (2) there will be extensive interaction among all groups, and (3) at least a minimal body of *shared* values and traditions will be emphasized" (17).

Having set forth a context of values and national interests for studying intergroup tensions, Williams then proceeded to establish a sociological approach to intergroup relations. First, he distinguished between prejudice as negative attitude and discrimination as differential behavior. Second, he noted three "realistic" bases of conflict: conflict of interests, of values, and of personality. But, he added, group hostility also involves "unrealistic" components: ignorance and error, deflected hostility, and historical tradition. This suggested that no one single factor was sufficient to explain conflict; rather, there was a "strong presumption that a main source of intergroup hostility is precisely the *interlocking and mutual reinforcement* of cultural differences, other visible differences, realistic interests, deflected aggression, and other factors" (39). Furthermore, factors like the early socialization of children, important in producing hostility, were not the same as those important for purposes of control.

By invoking Myrdal's conception of society as an unstable equilibrium and his theorem of cumulation in social change, Williams buttressed his argument that intergroup hostility was bound up by a complex process of mutually reinforcing factors in a social system; therefore, "*to be effective, research on approaches for reducing intergroup hostility must be oriented in terms of the social system in which it operates.*" In addition, since many causes, like early socialization, cannot be directly attacked, and some actions produce hostile reactions that intensify conflicts, the principle of indirection is then applicable. When efforts to change attitudes or behavior are perceived as an attack on the group, "the most promising approach is often that of instituting processes which undercut the basis of the undesired behavior," for example, "a long-term program of industrialization and improvement of facilities for communication and mobility might do more to reduce hostility between Negroes and whites in these areas than elaborate attempts at education and propaganda" (46–47). The emphasis upon the principle of indirection revealed how cautious sociologists still were about confronting directly the deeply ingrained prejudices of the white population.

At a time when emphasis on the psychology of prejudice had become significant in intergroup relations, Williams argued for the necessity of a basic sociological analysis. That was made clear in his critical assessment of prior work in intergroup relations. Most early research, he noted, was "static, descriptive, and atomistic," seeking to measure "the degree of incidence of prejudice of individuals," as if individuals "were the only significant units in social systems." Their difference from sociological work, then, was noted by the fact that such studies "were almost wholly divorced from social surveys, from analyses of economic conditions, legal structure and power relations, and other broad formal types of investigation" (47).

Within this sociological approach, Williams then offered 102 propositions at varying levels of generality as working hypotheses. Many were only "educated guesses," while others were supported by some degree of evidence. Many dealt with prejudice and with psychological processes, and a number dealt with the efforts to educate the prejudiced. Those dealing with strategy emphasized attacking discrimination at one point in time and stressed the danger of a boomerang effect in direct attack, and therefore, advocated the strategy of indirection.

Buried among the total set of propositions were a few about stratification and authority; these were to move to the center of the sociology of race relations in the 1950s. Four of them dealt with the relation of social class to group hostility. One argued that the American Creed was most strongly sustained "among small groups of professionals and upper class persons," for only such persons had "sufficient security to work actively for innovation in the direction of greater privileges for minorities." As a consequence, the universal values of the American Creed circulated from the top down. Another proposition, in contrast, identified the lower middle class as the most psychologically insecure about its place in the stratification order, and this class, therefore, may "be expected to exhibit a maximum of free-floating hostility" (59–61).

Two other propositions dealt with the prejudice of immigrant groups toward other immigrants and toward blacks. One asserted that in the lower class, where there were successive groups of immigrants, each class level "could thus control and subdue those still lower by displacing its aggression on lower groups as a means of maintaining its own sense of status." But the "cessation of large-scale immigration has thus removed an important element of flexibility in the balancing system for controlling intergroup hostilities." Of these immigrant groups, according to the other proposition, those most recently "Americanized" and attempting to be mobile were likely to be "especially vigorous and vocal" in their prejudice against blacks and other minorities (60–61).

For Robert Park's generation, even the educated were prejudiced. And even if many still were, it now seemed that the message of tolerance was increasingly being accepted by the better educated and those of upper status. A conception that liberalism on race was in inverse relation to class—the lower the class, the greater the prejudice—was now becoming a sociological truism. In the 1950s this was to become a basic dimension of a sociological strategy for racial change.

Two other propositions hypothesized that a firm exercise of authority and a judicious display of force, even its minimum use, would decrease the likelihood of open conflict (74). This idea was to become increasingly attractive to sociologists and to undergo a subtle redefinition. What was first meant to apply to tense crowd situations with a potential for violence later came to be applied to circumstances of directed change, as, for example, for the purpose of desegregating large organizations, where firm authority was presumed to reduce the likelihood that resistance to change would become effective.

Williams put the sociology of race relations and the new field of intergroup relations firmly within the framework of postwar thought in discussing racial progress in terms of national unity and the peaceful resolution of conflict. The war just completed, and the ethnic and racial tensions so evident in the 1930s and carried over into the war—after all, in 1943 there had been a major race riot—were matters of concern to those among the educated elite who held strongly to a belief in a national consensus of values and also in the rational and peaceful resolution of conflict.

Of the abundance of sociological ideas, hypotheses, and propositions Williams offered in his monograph, three of them were readily incorporated into the postwar sociology of race relations and became decisive to the sociological definition of the race problem: the distinction between prejudice (attitude) and discrimination (behavior); the inverse relation between prejudice and social class; and the firm exercise of authority in desegregating situations. These ideas also became central to the professionals of intergroup relations, because they seemed to bear on the matter of strategy.

The More Perfect Union

Robert MacIver was not of the new generation; he was a senior and distinguished scholar who had not previously specialized in matters of race and ethnicity. But his work had long manifested a theoretically sensitive concern for the nature of modern, large-scale society, in contrast to and evolving from the earlier traditional community. For those for whom the issue of intergroup relations was the threat to societal (i.e., national) unity, MacIver's analytic skill and theoretical grasp of the issues seemed most appropriate.

The very title of his work—*The More Perfect Union*—made clear that the thrust of its concern was national unity. At the outset, MacIver defined his issue as the serious challenge of group cleavage to that unity: "What we are pointing to is the danger inherent in the multiplicity of compartmented groups unless some way is found of evoking the primary sense of unity that far transcends them." Such compartmentalization, MacIver believed, strengthened the "natural tendency to group-bound thinking, the gravest peril in the social stratification of modern man." But the answer to this threat was not simply an uncritical acceptance of either assimilation, defined as "conformism" and "an undifferentiated common," or cultural pluralism, "in which each group cultivates its particularism in a kind of federated community." He objected to both these alternatives because "both, though in different degrees, reject the spontaneous processes that from the beginning have built up community life."[13]

Despite some small differences in vocabulary, Williams and MacIver were in agreement. MacIver rejected assimilation as "conformism" and as "an undifferentiated common," while Williams with equal firmness rejected assimilation as a "flat uniformity imposed by a dominant group." Both of them also rejected the opposite, an aggregate of culturally differentiated and separately existing groups. MacIver labeled this "cultural pluralism," while Williams used the term to define his conception of the tolerance of a degree of cultural distinctiveness within a larger cultural whole.

Not since the work of Horace Kallen more than twenty years before had there been as strong a critique of assimilation as goal and as normative standard. In part this was a recognition by both Williams and MacIver that the melting pot had not yet melted all groups into one homogeneous mass and was not likely to do so in the near future. But more important than that, it was a political recognition that, with the emergence of a newly professionalized intergroup relations rooted in the reality of existing racial, ethnic, and religious groups, and in the racial politics of urban communities, academic social science could no longer advance the idea of full assimilation as the only goal or even as the desired solution.

There was a quite practical reason, then, for Williams and MacIver to acknowledge a place for pluralism and thus to modify a long-standing support for full assimilation. The burgeoning profession of intergroup relations brought together for common action the long-established ethnic groups, others devoted to racial progress, and the new public agencies. The ethnic groups, but especially the Jewish agencies, resolutely opposed any notion of an ultimate assimilation of all groups in an Anglo-Saxon model of what was American. Instead, they insisted on the right of each group to retain its cultural identity, and that meant pluralism, not assimilation, and a tolerance of cultural differences, not acculturation. A sociology that intended to assist in the development of effective practice, therefore, needed to accept at least a modicum of cultural pluralism. Not to concede the value of pluralism would have meant that the sociology of race relations and the profession of intergroup relations would have had too little in common, and the sociological message would have been interpreted as ideological support for the effort to enforce a homogenizing assimilation on all ethnic and racial groups.

The time was also past when sociologists of race relations had reason to turn away from liberal social practice; a new generation was committed to the social intervention that an older generation had avoided. Furthermore, the new profession of intergroup relations provided sociology with a new clientele of professionals who could put knowledge to use. The possible uses of sociology would now inevitably affect empirical research and the theoretical organization of knowledge.[14]

While Willams's monograph was addressed primarily to other sociologists, MacIver's intended audience included (besides sociologists) professional practitioners, educators, and the educated public. Yet he was no less intent on setting forth a distinctly sociological analysis, evident in an explicit distinction between prejudice and discrimination—the one is the psychological attitude, the other the social act—and his assertion that the basic issue was discrimination, not prejudice; more precisely, it was the social control of discrimination. In its more public form, discrimination "can be the object of legal and other institutional restraints"; prejudice cannot be similarly controlled. Discrimination and prejudice, to be sure, are interactive and "breed" one another, but prejudice can exist "without specific discrimination." The emphasis on the public form of discrimination led to its definition as "the denial of equal access to public opportunity."[15]

It is fair to say that *The More Perfect Union* was a work inspired by Gunnar Myrdal's *An American Dilemma*. Myrdal was cited frequently in the text, and his model of social research in the service of social engineering was acclaimed by MacIver, who, like Myrdal, provided an appendix explicating the relation of research to social policy. Myrdal's influence was also evident in MacIver's use of the concept of caste to define race relations in the United States. As a consequence of caste, according to MacIver, discrimination and segregation were complex processes, difficult to assess accurately and revealing no single trend: "It is quite possible that discrimination may be decreasing in some directions and maintaining itself or growing stronger in others." Nonetheless, the caste system was being undermined by forces having "a broad base," though that very erosion was prompting new discrimination, such as "restrictive covenants and the resort to additional voting restrictions in some southern states" (44–45, 273–80).

In a work devoted to controlling racial discrimination, MacIver made it clear he was not going to undertake an elaborate analysis of causation. He had already made the point that prejudice and discrimination interacted in complex ways, and he followed that with a brief analysis of "balance"—the equilibrium between dominant and subordinate forces—and "circles"—the interlocking of forces—including a discussion of Myrdal's "vicious circle" (chap. 4). The lesson for social policy was that, since policy measures could not change basic drives but could affect social institutions and economic conditions, that is where the effort should be directed. That was MacIver's starting point in pursuit of an effective strategy.

Myrdal had emphasized the power of the American Creed and the appeal to moral values in which all Americans had a stake. With this MacIver agreed but with an important proviso: the power of moral force must be directed by a strategy. His basic principle of strategy was that "there are great advantages in attacking at points, where, if success can be achieved, the gain can afterwards be stabilized." There is no assurance that an attack on prejudice can maintain ground once won; it is too volatile and fluctuating. But an institution perpetuates itself, and a law is harder to repeal than to pass. It is, therefore, more important to attack discrimination than it is to attack prejudice. Furthermore, the scale of any effort at changing discrimination is important: "Some forms of discrimination cannot be effectively attacked by local controls; they require statewide, regional, or possibly even national programs" (89, 91).

MacIver thought that minority groups also needed to consider the issue of strategy. But his resultant discussion focused largely on arguments against blacks pursuing "radical programs" and making "aggressive demands," much as Myrdal had done in *An American Dilemma*. While radical demands, noted MacIver, call attention to matters often neglected, they also evoke an equally aggressive opposition, and they divide and weaken the forces fighting discrimination. What must be done, instead, is to carry out a gradual forward movement, a step by step advance, where each movement, once stabilized and having become customary, prepares the ground for the next one (95–98).

According to MacIver's strategy, taking the next step forward was often a matter of resolute leadership capable of acting decisively in situations where there was an ambivalence about what to do next. Like Myrdal, MacIver saw innovation and new movement as depending to a great extent on the quality of leadership in the existing institutions and organizations, especially the leadership of churches, corporations, and trade unions. In ending discrimination, therefore, the firmness of management in moving a step forward was of crucial importance (108–11).

The struggle against discrimination, maintained MacIver, must be won on three fronts: the economic, the political, and the educational. The economic front offered four advantages: there was less resistance to demands for economic opportunity; discrimination was economically wasteful, and people could be made conscious of that; it was also more bitterly resented by and more significant to blacks than other forms of discrimination; and economic objectives had a greater effect on the "vicious circle" of discrimination (here MacIver went beyond Myrdal's comfortable assertion that changing any factor was equally useful). When it came to a strategy of economic advance, however, MacIver was unable to go beyond the level of generality he had maintained to this point; the strategy must be "flexible and opportunistic" by adapting itself to conditions "that are everywhere variant and always changing." Opportunities created by the war, by technological advance, and by legislation were to be utilized to move into new economic areas. In this process, blacks stood to gain much by admission to labor unions (113–33, 136).

On the matter of the political front, MacIver was cautious about government coercively mandating behavior, yet he felt that government should establish civil rights. In that light, the FEPC experiment, for MacIver, was a successful one, despite its obvious failures in many particular instances. Its results did not depend on resorting to direct coercion but on settling complaints in conference, not by summons to court. What to practitioners was often a strategy of cautious action dictated by limited support for civil rights was here elevated by MacIver to a principle of compliance by persuasion over compliance by legal coercion. But he also noted critically that the FEPC only acted on complaints brought to it; it did not initiate investigations of discriminatory practices (145–68).

Given the structure of the political party system in the United States, MacIver saw good reason for blacks to be educated to take advantage of greater opportunities to vote; already underway, he noted, were changes removing some impediments to registration. Sometimes, however, MacIver did not understand how political structures encouraged or discouraged blacks to vote. He noted that proportionately more blacks in Chicago voted than did blacks in Detroit, and he called that a "curious" difference, suggesting an inertia in Detroit that needed to be dispelled by leadership and education (181). That difference, however, was hardly curious. In Chicago blacks voted in partisan elections and voted by wards, thus maximizing the political consequence of residential segregation. In Detroit, in contrast, the nine members of the city council were elected at-large on a nonpartisan ballot, in effect diminishing the voting power of blacks. The political structure of Chicago enabled blacks to become part of the political process in a fashion not possible in Detroit.

When it came to the enfranchisement of blacks in the South, MacIver followed Myrdal in suggesting that "a gradual process of enfranchisement, accompanied by appropriate advances in Negro education and in economic opportunity, would be more feasible, and might be more desirable, than an all-at-once revolution of southern ways" (182). Like Myrdal, he saw illiteracy and poverty of the black population as a menace to democracy, bringing on corruption and boss rule. Once their vote was effectively marshalled, MacIver believed that blacks should constitute an interest group of moderate demands attached to no political party.

Even as Myrdal had, MacIver saw opportunities in education to combat discrimination, though he seemed to be more impressed than Myrdal was by the limitations and difficulties of the task. For one thing, he noted, there was no overall program to unify and sustain the educational efforts of teachers; most teachers were poorly prepared for intercultural education by lack of training and by their own attitudes; there was still much segregation in teaching staffs; and local political control often blocked educational efforts. And while there were many organizations carrying on educational programs, there was no coordination among them to make common cause and so to get the most out of their efforts. The educational strategy-maker, MacIver observed, was engaged in the difficult task of counter-indoctrination, working against the mores. In such efforts, social science knows more about what does not work—an appeal to facts will not rebut prejudice, for example—than what does work. Efforts at evaluation of educational programs, furthermore, can offer little conclusive evidence concerning their effectiveness; and many programs have proceeded without any evaluation (chap. 9).

But if educational programs had little to offer, MacIver pointed out, the existing sociological literature had little to offer practicing professionals. Consequently, he called for research that focused on combatting and controlling discrimination, as well as evaluation studies of the action programs conducted by various organizations. And as strongly as Williams did, he placed intergroup relations on sociological ground by emphasizing discrimination, not prejudice, as the necessary target of social action, a principle that was to become widely accepted among both practitioners and sociologists during the 1950s. Finally, his summary of the strategy he had enumerated suggested to sociologists how much *The More Perfect Union* drew upon and sustained the social engineering perspective of *An American Dilemma* (241, 244–53).

But even as Myrdal had, MacIver made common cause with the practitioners of intergroup relations by fitting his sociological analysis into the worldview of practicing liberals. This was evident in his assertion that combatting discrimination should be primarily viewed in terms of the welfare and unity of the nation, not of a particular group. It was even more evident in his conception of strategy: moderate in demands, gradual in pace of change; attacking discrimination at its weakest points; and adapting to the mores, that is, avoiding "radical" demands that might provoke a backlash.

Domestic Peace and the National Interest

Williams and MacIver undertook two related tasks: first, to define a sociological research program to advance the process of desegregation and the reduction of discrimination; and second, to ground such sociological research in the moral values of American society. The first task would put the sociology of race relations into serving the practical interests of intergroup relations, thus making it an applied field. The second, in seeking to place such research on moral ground, made visible the underlying premises of a new generation of sociologists of race relations. In some respects, these goals were continuous with those of the previous generation, in other respects, not.

Robert Park's generation faced the seemingly impregnable reality of a white societal consensus about race; their arguments, therefore, were based on the scientific evidence against the assumption of racial inferiority and on their belief that the evolution of modern society would lead to assimilation at some future time. But a new generation now viewed the racial practices of the past as alterable by rational intervention, despite the still persistent prevalence of prejudice and discrimination. For them, the assimilated future seemed much nearer.

Williams and MacIver, however, added two further arguments to the new discourse being constructed by the postwar generation. The first, reflecting the sensibilities of a nation that had only just finished with a great war, argued that reduction in discrimination was in the national interest, for discriminatory practices detracted from national unity. In that sense they were like the previous generation in asserting reasons other than the principle of civil rights for reducing discrimination. It was a concern, however, that was to fade out over the next decade as the concerns of the war receded before the onset of postwar issues.

The second argument put the strongest possible emphasis on the necessity of using only nonviolent means to eliminate racial discrimination. In this, Williams and MacIver were giving expression to a widely shared liberal fear about the capacity of prejudiced whites to resist change by violent action, as well as the uncontrolled potential of the masses of uneducated blacks if aroused by "radical" leaders and programs. The avoidance of possible violent conflict was to become a fundamental premise of the postwar generation.

The Minority Group: Race and Ethnic Relations

The postwar emphasis on intergroup relations and the problems of social practice were accompanied by an increasing use of the concept, *minority*. Donald Young had introduced the term *minority peoples* in 1932, primarily as a term inclusive of both racial and ethnic categories. In 1945 Louis Wirth provided a sociological definition: "We may define a minority as a group of people who, because of their physical or cultural characteristics, are singled out from the others in the society in which they live for differential and unequal treatment, and who therefore regard themselves as objects of collective discrimination." If there is a minority group, then there is also "a corresponding dominant group enjoying higher social status and greater privileges." A minority, in effect, is excluded by the dominant group "from full participation in the life of the society. Though not necessarily an alien group, the minority is treated and regards itself as a people apart." But commmon to the definition was also the idea of prejudice, and Wirth noted that aspect: "The members of a minority group are held in lower esteem and may even be objects of contempt, hatred, ridicule, and violence."[16]

Wirth also brought to the fore characteristics of the minority due, not to factors of origin like skin color and alien culture, but to factors developed through the experience of being a minority: "One cannot long discriminate against people without generating in them a sense of isolation and of persecution and without giving them a conception of themselves as more different from others than in fact they are." A minority, therefore, may come to suffer from a sense of its own inferiority or develop a rebellious attitude and "clamor for emancipation and equality," thereby becoming "a political force to be reckoned with." For minority individuals, Wirth noted, "the most onerous circumstances under which they have to labor is to be treated as members of a category, irrespective of their individual merits."[17]

Until Wirth's essay, the distinction between these two sets of factors was largely absent from the sociological literature. The emphasis had always been on the originating factors of race and culture, not in how black people suffered under the burden of unequal race relations. Though Wirth did not use Park's term, race consciousness, he was calling attention to the sense of injustice that the members of a minority group felt and to their consequent efforts to overcome a deprived status. It was the beginning of what would in time be more frequently expressed in the sociological literature.

Though Wirth had opened up a long neglected matter—the historic shaping of a particular people under a system of subordination—his discussion pursued only a limited consideration of the issue. He advanced four types of goals pursued by minority groups: pluralistic, assimilationist, secessionist, and militant.[18] For his sociological readers—and the essay was widely read and cited—the first two were familiar and consistent with the American experience; the other two, however, seemed not to be a part of that experience and to be applicable only to situations elsewhere in the world. At a time when the American study of race and ethnic relations was only rarely comparative, Wirth's essay was read to support the already comfortable notion that pluralism and assimilation were essentially the only two goals pursued by minority groups in the United States.

The concept of minority proved useful for sociological analysis for several reasons. First, it allowed an analysis that placed such groups in relative positions of disadvantage within the social structure of a nation or community. But structural disadvantage could then be specified as discrimination. Second, it also lent itself to a social-problems approach, for the inequality of relations between minority and dominants could then be defined as the basic core of the problem. The inequalities of opportunity that defined being a minority became the focus of efforts at social change. But, third, though the concept was sociological, it nonetheless allowed for the social psychological analysis of prejudice as a phenomenon of group attitudes and of stereotypical images of minority groups.

The concept of minority, largely as Wirth had specified, soon became a central concept in the vocabulary of the sociologists of race relations. But the term that Wirth used as its conceptual opposite—dominant—did not become incorporated into that vocabulary. Instead, most sociologists spoke, not of the dominant, but of the majority. To pair together minority and majority had less critical force than did minority and dominant; it spoke primarily of numerical size rather than of power and domination. Nonetheless, minority and majority soon became the standard pairing of concepts in the developing vocabulary of the sociology of race relations.

For these reasons, the concept of minority group allowed sociologists to conceptualize beyond the particulars of a single category, such as race. The black people in the United States could be compared conceptually to immigrants and to other racial groups as sharing both the deprived status of a minority group and as displaying the social characteristics commonly generated by such status.

Racial and Ethnic

Despite the ready incorporation of the concept of a minority group into the sociological discourse, most sociologists still found reason to maintain a distinction between ethnic and racial groups. This division was not derived from a theoretically based distinction but from two basic assumptions about the American situation common to the thinking of most sociologists of race relations. The first was that black Americans possessed no culture of their own; that had long been lost by the circumstances of slavery. They were dark-skinned Americans, a minority set off only by racial differences. But ethnics, in turn, were immigrants who were carriers of a distinctive culture, one which had originated elsewhere. An ethnic, therefore, could be defined, as W. Lloyd Warner did, as "any individual who considers himself, or is considered, to be a member of a group with a foreign culture, and who participates in the activities of that group."[19]

The second assumption was based upon an assessment that sociologists made about what white Anglo-Americans considered the future prospects of European immigrants to be, in contrast to those of nonwhite people. Gunnar Myrdal had pointed out that most white

Americans believed that over time the minority groups would be assimilated into a homogeneous nation, except for those racial minorities
they defined as "unassimilable," blacks, Chinese, and Japanese: "The
Negroes ... are commonly assumed to be unassimilable, and this is
the reason why the characterization of the Negro problem does not
exhaust its true import."[20]

This distinction between racial and ethnic groups, between race and
culture, prevailed in sociological discourse well into the 1960s despite
E. K. Francis's effort in 1947 to define ethnic groups as a variation of
community, that is, a *gemeinschaft*.[21] In Francis's conceptualization,
racial categories would be viewed as ethnic groups, and, if sociologists
had found reason to accept this formulation, it could have provided
the basis for an enlarged exploration of the values and worldviews of
black Americans. But sociologists in the 1940s were not ready to seize
upon such a conceptual opening and move into new territory. Instead,
reshaping the sociology of race relations into a form more useful for
the practices of intergroup relations was the dominant consideration.

Race, Intolerance, and Authoritarianism

Immediately after World War II, social scientists became more
sensitive to the threat to democracy and to the stability of a free society
in the rise of fascism in Europe and in the many manifestations of
racial intolerance and bigotry both at home and abroad during the
1930s. Within such a perspective, the race problem took on an enlarged
significance. That significance was further enlarged with the realization
that the United States, as an emergent world power, contradicted in
its race relations its claims to be the model of a free and democratic
society.

Such concerns were evident in the Social Science Research Council's
Committee on Techniques for Reducing Group Hostility and the monograph that Robin Williams prepared for it. In the first paragraph of
its foreword to Williams's study, the committee pointed to the emergence after World War I of many groups characterized by aggressiveness: the Italian Fascists, the Nazis, the Communists in Russia, and the
Ku Klux Klan in the United States. Such groups, the committee asserted,
"thrived on hostility, intolerance, and the absence of practical effective
nonviolent means of dealing with conflict situations" and "explicitly
advocated methods of violence and suppression." Williams, too, immediately set the tone of his analysis by reference to widespread mass
violence and to "many disruptive movements based on systematic philosophies of hate and violence," such as the Nazi systematization of

"racialism." In *The More Perfect Union*, MacIver's concern for national unity was focused on the capacity for "group-bound thinking" to produce intergroup tensions and antagonisms, now a worldwide phenomenon. We do not, MacIver insisted, "so readily perceive the more insidious danger presented by the clash and tensions of ethnic groups, racial groups, culture groups, even though it is revealed in the red glow of the greatest of world wars."[22]

The threat to democracy posed by domestic and international forms of intolerance and bigotry brought to the sociology of race relations a new angle from which race could be defined as a social problem. To the previous generation of sociologists, the "backwardness" of blacks and the intransigence of white racism were each a hindrance to the process of assimilation so necessary to the evolution of the United States as a modern society. Assimilation was a slow, gradual process, the culmination of a long-run development; there was no sense of urgency about the pace of racial change. But to a new generation, race relations took on some sense of urgency; racial and ethnic intolerance constituted threatening evidence of the potential for antidemocratic forces to effect an authoritarian reality.

In such an atmosphere, the study of prejudice had a greater appeal. Not just the measurement of prejudicial attitudes in the general population, but the strong appeal of prejudicial myths and stereotypes suggested to many social psychologists that within the population there were individuals who had not simply learned prejudice from others, but had a deeply rooted need for ideas expressing racial hostility. Arnold Rose identified a number of newer theories—such as Dollard's frustration-aggression thesis, but also displacement theory, projection theory, and symbolic theory—that sought to explain these more deeply rooted aspects of prejudice. Most of the studies conducted within the framework of these new theories, however, were concerned with anti-Semitism, not with racial prejudice.[23]

Among the ongoing studies reported by Rose were several seeking to identify a prejudiced personality, again, an anti-Semite. Prominent among them were two early reports on an ambitious project, "Studies in Prejudice," begun in 1944 and sponsored by the American Jewish Committee. The publication in 1950 of five works in the series became a noteworthy event in American social science. One of the studies in particular—*The Authoritarian Personality* by Theodor W. Adorno and several of his colleagues—was to have an effect, however unintended, on the sociology of race relations.[24]

The Authoritarian Personality

In a short period of time, *The Authoritarian Personality* acquired the status of a classic of American social science. The project was the work of an unlikely combination of American social psychologists skilled in quantitative measurement and some major figures of the Frankfurt School of critical theory then in the United States. The resulting product brought together the methodological and interpretive styles of both, combining efforts at quantitative scaling and the analysis of personality through clinical interviewing. Furthermore, its analysis was psychological, not sociological; the "historical factors or economic forces" operating in society, the authors claimed, were beyond the scope of the study.[25]

It is not the purpose here to analyze in detail this remarkable study—that has been done in abundance—but to assess what significance it had for the sociology of race relations. Its primary concern was to define and describe the authoritarian personality, but it was in its efforts to define and measure ethnocentrism on a numerical scale (the higher the score, the greater the ethnocentrism) that the study had some implications for sociology. An Ethnocentrism (E) Scale included a Negro Subscale, which correlated highly with other subscales, suggesting "that ethnocentrism is a general frame of mind, that an individual's stand with regard to one group such as Negroes tends to be similar in direction and degree to his stand on most issues of group relations" (113).

The Ethnocentrism Scale went through several different versions, including a shortened one, and each produced somewhat different empirical results. Adorno and his colleagues correlated ethnocentrism with a large number of social and psychological attributes, some of which were the kind of social variables so common in sociological survey research: for example, age, class, political ideology, religion, IQ, and education. Given the fact that the samples used in the study were not randomly drawn from the population, the findings at best were tentative, as the authors acknowledged. And given the fact that the American psychologists built their scales upon other recent and equally tentative findings of social psychological research, there were few unexpected findings; that was particularly true of the social variables.

Perhaps the most significant finding of the study was how modest the statistical correlations often were. Age revealed only a "slight but consistent tendency for younger adults to be less ethnocentric than those of middle or old age." The factor of religious denomination, in turn, did not correlate significantly with ethnocentrism, nor did frequency of church attendance. But those without a religious affiliation scored as less anti-Semitic and less ethnocentric than those with an affiliation. Intelligence (as measured by IQ score) revealed "a very low but dependable relationship between intelligence and ethnocentrism," while ethnocentrism showed "a slight negative correlation with amount of education" (141, 209–13, 284, 287).

When political-economic ideology was measured on a scale from liberal to conservative, the result correlated with both the anti-Semitism and Ethnocentric Scales: "In everyday terms, we may say that conservatives are significantly more ethnocentric than liberals are." Strong political liberalism proved to be a good indicator of anti-ethnocentrism, "but political conservatism is less consistently related to ethnocentrism." Social class, however, proved to be an elusive variable when correlating it with ethnocentrism. At first, the authors declared that "socioeconomic class, as such, is not a major determinant of differences in ethnocentrism," while pointing out the wide variations in how different groups of the same class scored on the ethnocentrism scale. But the classes did seem to differ in their relation to both ethnocentrism and political ideology; working-class groups were more ethnocentric than conservative, while the middle class was more conservative than ethnocentric (137, 173, 180–81).

In a short, closing chapter, Adorno and his colleagues turned to the matter of treating "symptoms" and finding "cures" for this "disease," thus invoking the rhetoric of mental illness to deal with the highly ethnocentric, authoritarian personality. It followed from the findings, they claimed, that "it is not difficult to see why measures to oppose social discrimination have not been more effective," for neither reason nor sympathy will appeal to such persons. If not reason or sympathy, then perhaps appeals "to his conventionality or to his submissiveness toward authority might be effective." Similarly, it could be supposed that the potentially fascist personality "would be impressed by legal restraints against discrimination," and "that his self-restraint would increase as minority groups become stronger through protection." These measures, it was readily acknowledged, were symptomatic treatments, not a cure, but "some symptoms are more harmful than others, and we are sometimes very glad to be able to control a disease even though we cannot cure it" (973–74). More significantly, this was an anticipation of an idea that was to blossom among racial liberals in the 1950s: the use of law and formal authority to control the behavior of the prejudiced.

Then they turned to the larger question: What can be done about the disease itself? Their answer was not encouraging to those who thought that appeals to the American Creed would ensure progress. At the outset, they admitted that "the therapeutic possibilities of individual psychology are severely limited" and "the direct contribution of individual psychotherapy has to be regarded as negligible." If child training were the focus, "it would not be difficult to propose a program which ... could produce nonethnocentric personalities." But such a program "would have the aspect of being more easily said than done." Therefore, they concluded, "the modification of the potentially fascist structure cannot be achieved by psychological means alone. ... These are products of the total organization of society and are to be changed only as society is changed" (974–75).

Yet, if changing the fascist personality required changing society, "it is possible to have social reforms ... which though desirable in their own right would not necessarily change the structure of the prejudiced personality." For that to happen there must be an increase in people's capacity "to see themselves and to be themselves." But some people lack insight into themselves and are "least able to see the way the world is made"; they resist self-insight and resist social facts: "It is here that psychology may play an important role. Techniques for overcoming resistance, developed mainly in the field of individual psychotherapy, can be improved and adapted to use with groups and even for use on a mass scale" (975–76).

This was said on the last page of the book, and there was no further suggestion as to how psychology could provide therapy on a mass basis. But the very idea of efforts at mass therapy suggested something inappropriate for a democratic society. On the preceding page, in fact, the authors had made the point that changing the prejudiced personality "cannot be achieved by the manipulation of people, however well grounded in modern psychology the devices of manipulation might be." But the study as a whole had made a strong claim that personality as well as social structure needed to be considered, and that "where the problem is considered and action planned, the psychologists should have a voice" (ibid.).

In the following decade there was a great deal of research and much critique as social scientists sought to assess and evaluate an impressive work, to undertake further research that tested hypotheses derived from the study, and to duplicate its findings in other contexts with other samples of the American population. For the sociologists of race relations, the significance of *The Authoritarian Personality* was threefold: in the support it gave to the concept of the deeply prejudiced personality not necessarily "cured" by social reforms; in the correlations it found between ethnocentrism and selected social variables; and in the support it gave for the exercise of authority in strategies of racial change.

Prejudice and the Veteran

Another work in the American Jewish Committee's "Studies in Prejudice" series was an analysis of intolerance among war veterans.[26]

The study was carried out by Bruno Bettelheim, then an educational psychologist at the University of Chicago, and Morris Janowitz, a young sociologist at the same university. They studied the responses of a sample of 150 former army enlisted men under the age of thirty-five, largely working class and lower-middle class, to an extended interview. Blacks, Jews, Chinese, and Japanese were excluded. From the interviews, the authors found a pattern of hostility to both blacks and Jews, though blacks received proportionately more hostility than Jews did. The authors then concluded that the factors of subjective deprivation, downward social mobility, anxiety, and the absence of control of hostile discharge against ethnic minorities were the main factors explaining intolerance among veterans.

Like Adorno and his colleagues, Bettelheim and Janowitz drew implications for social action from their study. Since many of the veterans' anxieties were about employment, they suggested a program of security as well as changes in the economic ethos to divorce self-respect and respect for the community from upward mobility and the continuous incitement to consumption. These were admittedly remote goals, but more immediate action to reduce ethnic intolerance, they argued, should stress that a readiness to obey the law was common to the vast majority of veterans: "If the majority of the population, like the majority of the sample, submit to external controls, then the task at hand is to change the complexion of these external controls as they relate to interethnic practices." In a legalistic society such as ours, they emphasized, "the legal decision is still a basic and powerful weapon for social change."[27]

To create a society in which the psychological need to discharge hostility is eliminated, to provide a long-run education for tolerance that went deeper than merely factual information, and to improve child-rearing in order to shape integrated personalities in the milieu of the family—all of which Bettleheim and Janowitz advocated—was to offer unexceptionable goals, but devoid of any strategy. It was the immediate issue of law as external control that was to be incorporated into the strategy of intergroup relations. Like the authors of *The Authoritarian Personality*, Bettleheim and Janowitz became another voice in the social scientific community advocating the use of law to overcome the prejudicial opposition of the white majority to racial change.

Prejudice or Discrimination: The Problem of Strategy

For the sociologists of race relations, the emergence of intergroup relations as profession and as social action had established a new milieu for their own work. Now the focal point of reference for all work on race relations was the strategic possibilities suggested by research on the relationship of prejudice to discrimination. The sociologists had sought to make discrimination the basic issue—both Williams and MacIver had asserted that—and so to reassert the claim that the study of race relations belonged in the first instance to sociology. Still, there were persistent interests in the psychological aspects of the problem, and it was not hard to suggest to Americans that it was prejudice that provided the motives for, and thus was the cause of, discrimination. That was a conceptualization congenial to an American individualistic emphasis, and in a new era of expanded social action, the measuring of prejudice became an accepted and widely utilized technique.

At the outset this was a matter of defining prejudice as both a cultural and a psychological phenomenon. It was cultural because it expressed a set of commonly shared attitudes and stereotypes of and antipathy toward a minority. But it was also psychological because it was acquired by the individual in the normal process of socialization, and thus it was psychologically normal to be prejudiced. But in the 1940s a new direction of psychological research challenged this comfortable notion by suggesting that prejudice could also be a deeply rooted expression of psychological need, a projection of psychological hostility on the socially acceptable target. This newer conception of prejudice was not offered in place of the other—which was accepted as properly applicable to the larger part of the prejudiced population—but to suggest another category of persons whose prejudice would be more difficult to alter. In such a case, prejudice was viewed as but one dimension of an essentially antidemocratic, rigidly inflexible, power-admiring individual, an authoritarian personality.

Though the psychologists claimed a rightful place for their analysis in the study of race relations, they readily conceded that institutional change, not psychological therapy, was the necessary solution. Furthermore, they also pointed out that their often statistical measurements did not locate most people at the extremes of their scales as bigoted or liberal, but somewhere in between. In this fact, presumably, was strategic room for action.

It was in terms of this need to locate people in other than extreme positions and to differentiate strategy accordingly that Robert Merton offered a logical set of combinations of prejudice and discrimination in what was soon to become a widely cited contribution to the sociology of race relations.[28] The set was based on the premise that prejudiced individuals did not discriminate in every situation and unprejudiced ones sometimes did. It was not difficult to imagine an unprejudiced person not discriminating, though Merton took care to point out that such people were often ineffective because they so often talked only to like-minded liberals. It was also easy to recognize the prejudiced discriminator, consistent in belief and practice. But there were also inconsistent patterns, and Merton insisted that these were not merely logical combinations but were empirically evident. The prejudiced person who did not discriminate was one who conformed, however reluctantly or expediently, to nondiscriminatory practices when these were the norm or were required by law. Similarly, the unprejudiced discriminator was one who conformed to discriminatory practices when such was common practice and it was difficult to do otherwise.

There were different possible strategies for each of these types, taking into account the social situation and whether each was conforming or not to community practices and norms. But the basic message that sociologists drew from Merton's essay was that individual behavior did not directly follow from individual attitudes, and that most people behaved in conformity to norms or laws or established practices even when that behavior violated their own attitudes. Controlling discrimination, then, did not seem to require that attitudes first be changed.

Whether the emphasis was upon prejudice or discrimination, the focus in either case was on the dominant group, not the minority. As prejudiced persons or as discriminators, white people were the object of analysis. They were the target of any strategy for racial change, and it was they who had to change in attitude or behavior or both if any improvement in race relations was to be effected. Perhaps the most significant consequence, then, of sociology's response to intergroup relations and to the demand for strategies of social action was to find even less need to be concerned about the black minority and what it might bring to the struggle for racial change. Consequently, what white people regarded as the negative features of black people got the attention of sociologists—Myrdal, for one, spent ten pages on what whites saw as the "peculiarities" of blacks—for these negative attributes had to be denied by offering more accurate information, or, more usually, explained away as a consequence of deprived circumstances.

But in terms of strategies for racial change, blacks were given but a limited role in the ideas for social action developed by and for the established action agencies. After the war there was no more talk of such direct action by blacks as A. Phillip Randolph's March on Washington Movement. The issue of militant, collective protest by blacks alone, which Myrdal had at least acknowledged if not supported, was well out of the hearing of sociologists by 1950. Their thinking never went beyond the ideas Myrdal had reported in *An American Dilemma*, namely, that of junior partner in cooperation with white leadership.

At one time it seemed that a counteracting consciousness of this blindness to the actions and concerns of the black minority was possible. Jewish leaders recognized the same process in their own experiences when anti-Semitism was called a "Christian" problem, even though they insisted it was a "Jewish-Christian" problem. As one aspect of confronting such a concern, the Commission on Community Interrelations of the American Jewish Congress commissioned Arnold Rose to study the response of black Americans to their minority status. Rose traced the morale and group identification of blacks from slavery to the present, examined factors that both blocked and promoted group identification, and explored anti-Semitism among blacks. He saw the future as one of increasing group identification, with blacks becoming "a more group-conscious and effectively organized group," even as discrimination decreased.[29]

Yet this one small but prescient effort in sociological analysis did not significantly affect the restricted scope of the study of race relations that an emergent intergroup relations had imposed on sociology. A new decade was to carry to its logical development this conception of intergroup relations as "the white man's problem" and of social action as a strategy of moderate, gradual racial change.

Other Voices, Other Views

Not all sociologists shared fully in the new sociological interest in intergroup relations. Among them were those who had once accepted the earlier biological arguments about inherent racial differences. If, however grudgingly, they felt compelled to abandon or at least seriously modify those arguments, they did not feel compelled to accept in full the emerging sociological perspective on race. Others, especially some Southerners, approached race relations with a fuller appreciation of the depth of white resistance to racial progress and a better realization of how much racial antipathy still characterized many white Americans.

Among those with a different view were a number of sociologists still teaching and writing; if their voices were lesser ones, they were still voices heard in the land. Two of the more well knownwere Henry Pratt Fairchild and Thomas C. McCormick. Fairchild was an academic liberal who had once believed in the biological inferiority of blacks. While most of his generation had abandoned the field and were no longer heard from, Fairchild, now retired from his academic position, was still actively engaged in arguing the issue of race. If he no longer asserted the old biological arguments, he still did not identify with and, indeed, roundly criticized those "anti-racists" whom he accused of allowing "their zeal for human kindness and world brotherhood to lead them astray into very questionable statements and unscientific methods."[30] McCormick, a transplanted Southerner at the University of Wisconsin, reflected in his thinking a caution born of his deep familiarity with southern race relations. Though Fairchild and Mc-Cormick were hardly identical in their thinking, the two expressed viewpoints that were largely unaffected by the newer, postwar optimism about the future of race relations.

Fairchild and McCormick held firmly to the position so common in that period, that any claim to racial differences was unproven; science, it was always asserted, could not as yet either prove or disprove inherent racial differences. Fairchild, in fact, still believed in such differences, for he argued that it was "entirely logical that there are intellectual differences among the various races of mankind." He also criticized Franz Boas's efforts "in promoting the doctrine of the negligibility of intellectual race traits." However, he acknowledged, "there does not exist as yet any conclusive scientific evidence as to the actual genetic mental equipment of the various racial subdivisions of mankind." After reviewing the results of performances on IQ tests, Fairchild again pointed out that "no one has the right to assert categorically in the name of science that there are, or there are not, intellectual and emotional differences among the races of mankind, or at least to say what they are."[31]

Despite these assertions, Fairchild returned to his first point that "there would seem to be only one defensible conclusion, which is that there must be differences of greater or lesser significance in the mental, emotional and temperamental equipment of the different racial groups."[32] This insistence on innate mental and temperamental differences among the races was a singularly persistent retention of a position largely abandoned by social scientists some two decades earlier.

For McCormick, in contrast, there was no apparent need to demonstrate that there must be mental differences, let alone emotional and temperamental ones; but, like Fairchild, he also took the position that racial inferiority had not yet been proven: "The best tests that have been devised by psychologists to date fail to show that the Negro measures up to the white on the average in mental performance." However, he acknowledged, there is a "growing opinion among anthropologists that even the average innate inferiority of the Negro is not yet scientifically proven" and that the explanation may lie "wholly in economic and social disadvantages." But, he concluded, from a "rigorously scientific point of view," the answer is not known.[33]

Beyond the issue of racial inequality, Fairchild and McCormick pressed different themes. At a time when law and legal authority was becoming a central concern, Fairchild tried to find a position between laws enforcing discrimination—to be condemned—and laws preventing discrimination, on which he was exceptionally cautious. While justifying laws banning distinctions in voting, holding office, taxpaying, and governmental remuneration, Fairchild was dubious about most legislation: "Legislation cannot be pushed too far ahead of the public mind or the public conscience." He argued that "laws may do more harm than good" unless "liberals and progressives" were to work for "the humanizing of the heart of man."[34] This argument—that changes in law could only follow changes in attitude—was to become the countering argument to the position more common among the sociologists of race relations in the late 1940s and the 1950s about the use of firm authority and about changing behavior, not attitudes.

McCormick, in turn, was more interested in presenting data describing the present condition of black people, on changes in their status, and on the forces working against discrimination. These included such objective factors as improved education, a growing black middle class, the manpower shortages produced by war, and the tendency to close the gap between ideals and practice (an echo of Myrdal). But there was also reference to "the inclination of white politicians of every party in Northern cities to cater to the Negro vote, the zeal of white liberals, and the increasing strength of militant Negro organizations in the North." McCormick also thought that possibly the most decisive force "will prove to be the illicit crossing of the races," producing an "extensive population of mixed bloods." He dwelt at some length on this matter: on intermarriage as a white fear, on the taboos against intermarriage, the concern for racial purity, and the exclusion from the white race of all racially mixed persons.[35]

On the matter of policy, McCormick offered little optimism. He insisted that the "most general and fundamental of all white attitudes" was a belief in the biological inferiority of blacks, thus legitimating segregation and a "humbler role" for them. While there had been and would continue to be progress in education, the urban professions, and industrial employment, and even general enfranchisement soon, "no direct progress toward social equality and intermarriage has been observed." At the same time, McCormick warned against employing methods that went "much faster than the dominant white sentiments of any great section of the country approved," a position that would give a decisive voice to the South. He concluded on a cautious note: "Yet progress is not arrival. The realities that we have examined do not point to the disappearance of racial antipathies in the decades that lie ahead." Though these realities do suggest a gradual approach to equality, noted McCormick, he parted company with a whole generation of sociologists who were certain of the eventual outcome by asserting that "so little can be predicted about the long-time prosperity and destiny of American society as a whole that it cannot, of course, be said that such an outcome is certain or inevitable."[36]

By 1947 these views of McCormick and Fairchild were out of step with the new sociology of race relations. Each in his own way had yielded some ground to the newer thinking while holding stubbornly to a position resonant of older, once more dominant views. Though now less frequently given public voice by academics, these were views still widely shared in the middle class and even within the academic community. Needless to say, they were also views well in advance of those still openly expressed by many white Americans, especially in the South.

During the 1940s the sociologists of race relations were well aware that many of their sociological colleagues still held older, even discredited views of race, and that these views could be found in introductory textbooks. At the outset of the decade of the 1950s, therefore, they were heartened to learn from Chester Hunt that the introductory textbook in sociology no longer offered an outdated conception of race and race relations. In 1940 Brewton Berry had examined the treatment given the topic of race in introductory textbooks published in the 1930s and had lamented the strong residue of biological thinking still evident and the persistent confusion over the meaning of race. In 1951 Hunt did the same for introductory textbooks published in the late 1940s and found significant change, if not a wholly satisfactory treatment. By the late 1940s, he noted, the study of race was becoming more an investigation of social relationships, less one of biological variation. All the texts, furthermore, rejected any notion of biological determinism. They divided largely between those who, in the manner of Gunnar Myrdal, offered a definition of race as social and a matter of convention, and those who sought to provide a defensible racial classification, while denying biological causation of temperament, intelligence, and manipulative ability.[37]

Notes

1. For a detailed examination of racial liberalism during the years of the Roosevelt administration, see John B. Kirby, *Black Americans in the Roosevelt*

Era (Knoxville: University of Tennessee Press, 1980). For an analysis of the reform efforts of the NAACP during the depression, see Raymond Wolters, *Negroes and the Great Depression: The Problems of Economic Recovery* (Westport, Conn.: Greenwood Press, 1970), chapters 9–13.

2. See Herbert Garfinkel, *When Negroes March: The March on Washington Movement in the Organizational Politics for FEPC* (New York: Free Press, 1959).

3. For an analysis of the Detroit race riot of 1943 by a sociologist and an anthropologist who lived in Detroit at the time, see Alfred McClung Lee and Norman Daymond Humphrey, *Race Riot* (New York: Dryden Press, 1943).

4. For a history of the FEPC campaign, see Louis Coleridge Kesselman, *The Social Politics of FEPC: A Study in Reform Pressure Movements* (Chapel Hill: University of North Carolina Press, 1948). See also *The Dynamics of State Campaigns for Fair Employment Practices Legislation* (Chicago: Committee on Education, Training and Research in Race Relations, University of Chicago, 1950).

5. Kesselman, *Social Politics*, 227.

6. Ibid., 27.

7. John H. Stanford has written a study of foundation support for social scientific research into race relations during the 1920s and 1930s around the thesis that such support was evidence of how elites consciously created and controlled social knowledge. See his *Philanthropy and Jim Crow in American Social Science* (Westport, Conn.: Greenwood Press, 1985); also see, John H. Stanford, "The Cracked Back Door: Foundations and Black Social Scientists between the World Wars," *American Sociologist* 17 (Nov. 1982): 193–204.

For a very different and more complex view that argues for a far more limited influence of foundations on social scientific work, see Martin Bulmer, *The Chicago School of Sociology: Institutionalization, Diversity, and the Rise of Sociological Research* (Chicago: University of Chicago Press, 1984), chapter 12.

8. This point was duly noted at the time by Howard Odum; see his *American Sociology: The Story of Sociology in the United States through 1950* (New York: Longmans, Green, 1951), 338.

9. Arnold Rose, *Studies in Reduction of Prejudice*, 2d ed. (Chicago: American Council on Race Relations, 1948).

10. Ibid., 54.

11. Ibid., 61, 96.

12. Robin M. Williams, Jr., *The Reduction of Intergroup Tensions: A Survey of Research on Problems of Ethnic, Racial and Religious Group Relations* (New York: Social Science Research Council, 1947). Further references to this work will appear in the text. All italics appear in the original.

13. Robert M. MacIver, *The More Perfect Union: A Program for the Control of Inter-Group Discrimination in the United States* (New York: MacMillan, 1948), 2, 9–10.

14. For a highly revealing discussion of the development of sociology as a response to the potential uses of knowledge and of organizational clients

as the primary users of that knowledge, see the introduction to *The Uses of Sociology,* ed. Paul Lazarsfeld, William H. Sewell, and Harold L. Wilensky (New York: Basic Books, 1964), ix–xxxiii.

15. MacIver, *More Perfect Union,* 14–15. Further references to this work will appear in the text.

16. Louis Wirth, "Problems of Minority Groups," in *The Science of Man in the World Crisis,* ed. Ralph Linton (New York: Columbia University Press, 1945), 347–48.

17. Ibid., 348–49, 359.

18. Ibid., 354–64.

19. W. Lloyd Warner and Leo Srole, *The Social Systems of American Ethnic Groups* (New Haven: Yale University Press, 1945), 28.

20. Gunnar Myrdal, with the assistance of Richard Sterner and Arnold Rose, *An American Dilemma: The Negro Problem and Modern Democracy* (New York: Harper and Brothers, 1944), 53.

21. E. K. Francis, "The Nature of the Ethnic Group," *American Journal of Sociology* 52 (Mar. 1947): 393–400.

22. Williams, *Reduction of Tensions,* vii, 1; MacIver, *More Perfect Union,* 4.

23. Rose, *Reduction of Prejudice,* chapter 7.

24. The five studies sponsored by the American Jewish Committee and published in 1950 by Harper and Brothers were: T. W. Adorno, Else Frankel-Brunswick, Daniel J. Levinson, and R. Nevitt Sanford, *The Authoritarian Personality;* Bruno Bettleheim and Morris Janowitz, *Dynamics of Prejudice;* Nathan W. Ackerman and Marie Jahoda, *Anti-Semitism and Emotional Disorder: A Psycho-analytic Interpretation;* Paul W. Massing, *Rehesarsal for Destruction: A Study of Political Anti-Semitism in Imperial Germany;* and Leo Lowenthal and Norbert Guterman, *Prophets of Deceit: A Study of the Techniques of the American Agitator.*

25. Adorno et al., *Authoritarian Personality,* 972. Further references to this work will appear in the text.

26. Bettleheim and Janowitz, *Dynamics of Prejudice.*

27. Ibid., 174–77.

28. Robert K. Merton, "Discrimination and the American Creed," in *Discrimination and the National Welfare,* ed. Robert W. MacIver (New York: Harper and Brothers, 1949): 99–126.

29. Arnold M. Rose, *The Negro's Morale: Group Identification and Protest* (Minneapolis: University of Minnesota Press, 1949), 142.

30. Henry Pratt Fairchild, *Race and Nationality as Factors in American Life* (New York: McGraw-Hill, 1947), 96.

31. Ibid., 67, 72, 78, 96.

32. Ibid., 79.

33. Thomas C. McCormick, "The Negro," in *Problems of the Postwar World,* ed. Thomas C. McCormick (New York: McGraw-Hill, 1945), 257.

34. Fairchild, *Race and Nationality,* 96, 172–73, 191, 194–95.

35. McCormick, "The Negro," 256, 258, 260–63.

36. Ibid., 260, 265–66.

37. Brewton Berry, "The Concept of Race in Sociology Textbooks," *Social Forces* 18 (Spring 1940): 411–17; Chester L. Hunt, "The Treatment of 'Race' in Beginning Sociology Textbooks," *Sociology and Social Research* 35 (Mar.-Apr. 1951): 277–84.

8

Desegregation and Social Practice

By 1950 the redefinition of race relations as one form of intergroup relations had already won wide if not universal support, and the very term was increasingly accepted by academic social scientists. However, it was not yet evident that the subsumption of both racial and ethnic groups with divergent histories and different structural locations under such an inclusive rubric as intergroup relations could provide an adequate conceptual basis for social analysis or for planning social action. But it hardly mattered; in the 1950s race, not ethnicity, was the issue, and the conflict-ridden problem of racial desegregation dominated both public and scholarly concerns.

Sociologists, in turn, interpreted desegregation as evidence that social intervention in race relations was now possible. As a consequence, they undertook industrious efforts throughout the decade to contribute to attempts at social intervention by carrying out research on the military, industry, and housing. Their intention was to help a new profession of intergroup relations practitioners develop an effective social practice. Though not recognized as such, this was an early experiment in an applied sociology, one which lasted only about a decade and disappeared from sight and memory in the tide of black rebellion that swept over and out of the South in the 1960s.

Four issues were foremost among the concerns of sociologists during the 1950s: first, a complex of issues about race relations that were social psychological in nature; second, the possibilities for racial desegregation and for a sociologically guided social practice; third, the U.S. Supreme Court's decision on school desegregation in 1954; and fourth, the difficulty of trying to apply theory to practice and the thicket of complexities that emerged from the effort to work with practitioners.

The 1950s also provided a new social context that bore indirectly but effectively on thinking about race relations. While the optimistic assumptions about the possibilities of intervention that had emerged from the New Deal atmosphere carried over into the 1950s, sociologists were also chastened by a liberal mood of caution and constraint that emerged with the cold war and clearly influenced their work.

The 1950s: Caution and Constraint

A generation that had come to believe in the possibilities of social intervention was greatly encouraged by the desegregation of the armed forces by 1952 and the Supreme Court's decision invalidating school segregation in 1954. These events only sustained their conviction that the gradual breakdown of racial inequality was inevitable. But there was also throughout the 1950s a persistent theme of caution and constraint effecting the way that sociologists viewed the prospects for racial progress. The concept of an authoritarian personality found more abundantly among the less educated and those of lesser status provided a depressing image of people poor and poorly educated; they not only were not an ally in the effort to overcome racial inequality but were perhaps the source of the resistance to racial change, or at least a serious dimension of the problem.

Significant as is the work on the authoritarian personality, it cannot be given full credit for the sobering mood that so effectively served to check the optimism sociologists derived from the postwar desegregation. Instead, it is better seen as consistent with the politically chastened atmosphere of the decade and the modes of thought that appeared during that period. The United States emerged from war with a new national stance toward global affairs and an adversarial stance toward the Soviet Union. By the late forties, the "Cold War" and a virulent anticommunism were part of contemporary politics and ideology.

The end of hostilities in Europe and Asia, however welcome, produced no joyous expectation from the intellectual community; instead, there was a sober assessment of the threat to democratic institutions to be found in fascism and communism and in their antidemocratic ideologies. These, it was claimed, had appealed strongly to ordinary people under conditions of economic depression. Group hostility, racial and ethnic prejudice, class antagonism, and scapegoating—all these and more seemed to suggest that national unity and a consensus of values were essential to the survival of democratic institutions. This was the message already promulgated in the late forties by Robin

Williams and Robert MacIver. The sociologists of race relations, there-fore, found themselves in a wider intellectual context of cautious, worried reasoning, in which their own efforts to reduce prejudice and discrimination seemed to take on greater importance for the fate of democratic institutions.

One undertaking of the postwar sociological generation was to de-velop a political sociology, and from the outset the new sociological specialty offered a disenchanted view of politics. This was evident in the decision in 1949 to republish Robert Michel's classic study of the "iron law" of oligarchy, a work that raised serious doubts about the ability of ordinary people to sustain democratic processes in large or-ganizations. Contemporary work on the same theme soon followed. Philip Selznick's analysis of the Tennessee Valley Authority as a bu-reaucratic organization and Floyd Hunter's study of the power of a local business elite in a large city built upon the theme of elite dom-ination of social organization. Selznick's other study of how com-munists manipulated organization as a weapon in the struggle for power added support to the idea of a controlling power behind a democratic facade. A study of democracy in an American craft union by Seymour Martin Lipset, Martin Trow, and James S. Coleman was a direct effort to put to the test Michel's proposition in an American, twentieth-century situation. While C. Wright Mills's work was based on a dif-ferent worldview, his analysis of a national power elite also contributed significantly to the image of democracy thwarted.[1]

The nation's adversarial stance toward the Soviet Union in the late 1940s produced a wave of domestic anticommunism. Its virulence made possible the brief episode known as McCarthyism, when Senator Joseph McCarthy of Wisconsin carried on Senate committee investi-gations into various American institutions. The response by political sociologists was to identify those to whom McCarthy proved appealing and to locate in that appeal the emergence of a "radical right," a term that first surfaced in a book edited by Daniel Bell. Essays by Richard Hofstadter, David Riesman and Nathan Glazer, and Seymour Martin Lipset advanced the idea of "status politics" instead of class politics, proclaimed the exhaustion of liberal ideology, and set out to identify the various social groups and categories identified with the radical right and a politics of status.[2]

One of those Lipset identified with the radical right was the industrial worker, whose intolerance—political, racial, and ethnic—was explained by a lack of material and psychic security correlated with a lack of education and political sophistication. Lipset followed this by arguing that the working classes of modern industrial societies were possessed of "deep-rooted hostilities expressed by ethnic prejudice, political authoritarianism, and chiliastic transvaluational religion."[3] In this manner, the study of the roots of McCarthyism were interwoven with the extended discussion of fascist and democratic personalities set in motion by the publication of *The Authoritarian Personality.*

An array of other academic work offered a view of American culture and society that only added support to that provided by political sociology's study of McCarthyism and the radical right and the studies of political and racial beliefs found among the authoritarian-minded. In 1950, for example, David Riesman set off a decade-long discussion about conformity in American life with his seminal work, *The Lonely Crowd.* Such a popular work as William H. Whyte's *The Organization Man* drew upon Riesman's work to cultivate the idea of a conforming middle class in postwar America. This, in turn, provided the key to an interpretation of middle- and working-class movement to the suburbs, yielding an image of suburbia as a protected enclave from which blacks and other minorities, as well as the old and the poor, were excluded. The sociological literature emphasized the connection between the suburbs and such phenomena as familism, consumption, leisure pursuits, and new life-styles, on the one hand, and on the other, the suburban tendency to racial and class homogeneity, concerns for status and advantage, and a narrow, less challenging existence, what Riesman called "the sadness of suburbia . . . an aimlessness, a low-keyed unpleasure."[4]

This concern about conformity widened to become a concern about the loss of individuality, creativity, and authentic leadership, the fear of a mass society dominated by the intellectually unqualified and of a mass culture, destroyer of high culture. Philip Selznick opened the debate in the social sciences in 1951 with an essay on the "vulnerability" of institutions in mass society. The European origins of the issue, however, go back at least to Ortega y Gasset's *The Revolt of the Masses* (1932) and flourished in the European effort to explain the rise of a totalitarian social order. The threat to democracy posed by mass society prompted a rereading of Alexis de Tocqueville's *Democracy in America* and an extended discussion about a politically pluralistic society and the loss of autonomy on the part of elites and the loss of independent group life on the part of nonelites. The threat posed by mass society was complemented by a conception of mass culture; here, too, protection of creative elites and high culture from a manufactured, manipulative mass culture set off an often virulent debate.[5]

It remained, however, for Daniel Bell to provide a culminating assessment of an intellectual and political mood, one to which he only

partially assented by declaring his own perspective to be "anti–ideological, but not conservative": "In the last decade, we have witnessed
the exhaustion of the nineteenth-century ideologies, particularly Marx-
ism, as intellectual systems that could claim *truth* for their views of
the world. In reaction to these ideologies—and their compulsion to
total commitment of intellect and feeling—many intellectuals have begun to fear 'the masses,' or any form of social action. This is the basis
of neoconservatism and the new empiricism."[6]

These, then, were the several themes and ideas interwoven into the
texture of a dominant perspective for the cold war decade of the 1950s:
a worry about a radical right intolerant of political dissent; a concern
for a middle-class conformity; the fearful idea of American society as
a mass society and a mass culture; a notion that oligarchy, not democracy, prevailed in politics; the fear of an authoritarian-minded populace; and the not unwelcome notion of the exhaustion of the historic
ideologies. These several themes were evidence of a cautious, disenchanted liberalism, uncertain of its own future and turning away from
the collaborating politics that had been the basis of the New Deal.

The effect of all this on the sociology of race relations was indirect
and largely reinforcing of an already developing theory and practice.
It served to moderate the views of those who looked to a democratic
politics and equalitarian values for racial progress; its specter of an
authoritarian populace narrowed what was taken to be viable strategy;
and it helped sustain a view of the black American as ignorant, incapable of rational, self-interested action, and possibly susceptible to extre-
mist politics. Such a view of black people, combined with that fear of
the masses Bell noted, produced a neglect of the black struggle, indeed,
an ignoring of any evidence of such a struggle, and led to an equivalent
neglect of collective behavior, especially social movements, as a potentially progressive factor in race relations.

Race Relations as Social Psychology

If the social psychological perspective on race relations did not
come to dominate sociological work in the 1950s, and it did not, it
nevertheless came to be more significant in the sociological study of
race relations than at any previous time. There were three primary
concerns of social psychologists that guided the work they carried out
in the 1950s. The first of these was in the relation of prejudice to
discrimination; a second was on the correlates of authoritarianism believed to be attributes of the prejudiced personality; and a third was
on a psychiatric analysis of black personality. While the first of these

was a continuation of an interest that had developed earlier, the latter two were clearly new concerns of the 1950s.

Prejudice and Discrimination

For sociologists, the development of a commanding interest in examining prejudice posed a disciplinary threat to their insistent claim that the study of race was in the first instance a study of social relations in a structural context. Since W. I. Thomas's 1904 essay on prejudice, sociologists had accorded the phenomenon a place of conceptual importance—and they were still inclined to do so—but they had never defined prejudice as the determining factor in race relations. Their first response to the extensive involvement of psychologists in the study of prejudice, therefore, was twofold: first, to state a dynamic interdependence of psychological and social factors and to avoid an either/ or definition of the issue; but, second, to assert the significance of social factors in the origin of prejudice as well as in the problem of effecting change. Such an approach sought, not to deny the relevance of prejudice, but to incorporate it into a larger effort both to explain and change race relations.

Some psychologists shared in that effort. Gordon Allport, for example, in his highly influential study, *The Nature of Prejudice,* offered a detailed analysis of prejudice in all its known manifestations. Throughout his analysis, he gave full recognition to social factors, and in three chapters (14, 15, and 16), he specifically focused on the "sociocultural factors" that resulted in prejudice. Since prejudice and discrimination were "simultaneously present and formed parts of a single story," a multiple approach to a theory of prejudice was required, "including *historical, sociocultural,* and *situational* analysis," as well as psychological factors and actual group differences. An implication for effecting change was that, while legislation against discrimination would have only an indirect bearing on the reduction of prejudice, it "may be a sharp tool in the battle against discrimination." Though law only controlled outward expression, psychology knew that outward action "has an eventual effect upon inner habits of thought and feeling."[7]

But sociologists also pressed the issue. In an article drawn from the first edition of what was to become the leading textbook on race relations in the postwar era, noted for its encompassing range of relevant materials and its thorough treatment of all aspects of prejudice and discrimination, George Simpson and J. Milton Yinger argued that the prejudice-prone individual, for whom prejudice served basic personality needs, was but one explanation of prejudice. Another was in both prejudice and discrimination as manifestations of the struggle for power, prestige, and income between and within societies. Still another was that most majority group members of a society were taught, as part of their cultural equipment, the groups that it was appropriate for them to dislike or consider inferior. Prejudice, then, was to be understood as in the culture and in the economic and political structure of society. Furthermore, locating prejudice in the culture as an attitude learned in the normal process of socialization clearly distinguished that source of prejudice from the first, where prejudice met the psychic needs of the person.[8]

In an argument utilizing the recently emergent critical concept of mass society, Joseph Lohman and Dietrich Reitzes argued that explanation lies, not in the attitudes of individuals, but in the activities of deliberate groupings organized in response to specific interests. Since modern society was now a flux of changing patterns, it had the appearance of a shapeless mass; its "form and organization are achieved through deliberate and calculated association." The actions of individuals, therefore, are controlled by and consequently vary by the interests organized by different collectivities and "do not merely manifest their private feelings toward the races, for examples, Negroes." Therefore, they concluded, "it is more frequently the policy, strategy, and tactics of organized interest groups, rather than the folkways, rather than the individual dimensions of personal prejudices or racial amity, which control behavior in specific situations."[9]

In asserting the relative independence of behavior from prejudicial attitudes, Lohman and Rietzes were reaffirming race relations as social process, the cause of which was not psychological. Such a position contrasted with the psychological one that viewed discriminatory behavior as the result of prejudice, even though prejudice, in turn, was a consequence of social process. From such a perspective, prejudice and discriminatory behavior were necessarily interdependent phenomena. Yet Robert Merton had already questioned such a necessary interdependence by insisting that individuals could be prejudiced without discriminating and could discriminate without being prejudiced. Simpson and Yinger, furthermore, also pointed out that under certain conditions prejudice and discrimination could vary independently.[10]

Arnold Rose than carried the matter further by insisting "that it may be desirable to assume that patterns of intergroup relations (including prejudice and discrimination) are quite distinct from attitudes of prejudice in that each has a separate and distinct history, cause, and process of change." Thus, "patterns of intergroup relations" and "attitudes of prejudice and stereotyping are fairly unrelated phenomena, although they have reciprocal influence on each other, as they also have to seemingly extraneous phenomena, such as anxiety levels or class." In support of his thesis, Rose reminded his readers of LaPiere's famous report in 1934 of discrepancies between situational behavior and verbal statements. Furthermore, he pointed out, public opinion polls provided evidence of local opposition to desegregation, even as such desegregation proceeded without overt resistance. No theory of prejudice, claimed Rose, helped in predicting the desegregation process; the explanation must be sought in "legal, economic, political, and social structural forces." Even though prejudice and discrimination may go together at given times, "the laws of change—or origin, development and decay—which govern one are independent of those governing the other."[11]

Support for the argument that prejudice did not directly produce discriminatory behavior came from a series of empirical studies testing both attitudes and behavior in different social situations. In situations where whites were served by nonwhite sales clerks, where blacks were served in a white restaurant, where white schoolchildren were a minority in a mixed racial setting, and where the number of blacks increased, prejudice did not predict behavior. In observations on Washington, D.C., and Chicago, Lohman and Reitzes added further evidence. In Washington they found that it was not the prejudice of federal employees but the directives of authoritative personnel that decided differences in racial practices among the agencies. In Chicago they found that unionized workers displayed no prejudice in a work situation but did so quite strongly in their residential neighborhood, yet shopped in stores that also served black people. Further evidence was provided by a study of "unpatterned" situations where definitions of appropriate conduct were ambiguous and in process of change. In such unclear situations, it was found, individuals responded uncertainly and inconsistently and looked to others for clues to appropriate behavior. From even the most tentative responses could come new patterning to the situation.[12]

Studies such as these offered empirical evidence for the arguments put forth by Rose, Simpson and Yinger, and Lohman and Reitzes. These arguments were based on a conception of society undergoing such change that older patterns of caste could no longer persist, regardless of racial attitudes. For Rose, as for Simpson and Yinger, the origin of this change was the fairly rapid transformation of those social structures in which blacks were primarily located. The mechanization of southern agriculture dispossessed millions of blacks and in turn necessitated their northward migration, urban settlement, and industrial employment.

These developments, in turn, broke down caste relations and thrust blacks and whites into wholly new relations. Thus, structural changes in the economy forced changes in race relations, even though attitudes changed more slowly.[13]

To these interpretations can be added one by Herbert Blumer, who offered the thesis that "race prejudice exists basically in a sense of group position rather than in a set of feelings which members of one race group have towards the members of another racial group." Since prejudice was fundamentally a matter of relationships between racial groups, it presupposed that individuals thought of themselves as members of a racial group; thus, racial identification was necessary as a framework for racial prejudice. A dominant group defined itself in relation to a subordinate group in terms of a sense of group position, which produced a proprietary claim to certain areas of privilege and advantage and a fear or suspicion that the subordinate group was seeking to make a claim on those prerogatives: "The source of race prejudice lies in a felt challenge to this sense of group position."[14]

Sociologists, then, did not hesitate to respond to the ambitious claims often offered for psychological studies of prejudice, to reclaim race relations as essentially a sociological problem, and to dispute the importance of prejudice as a factor in accounting for discrimination. If some, like Rose, denied any independent role to prejudice, most others took a more moderate position, asserting that there was an interactive and cumulative set of forces influencing intergroup relations, which included the psychological. But however varied their positions, sociologists had responded to the surge of psychological theorizing by denying to prejudice the status of primary causal factor in the explanation of racial discrimination.

However, one social psychological concept that sociologists found particularly attractive was that of "equal status contact," which said that when interracial contact occurred among individuals equal in status as measured by income, education, and occupation, racial attitudes became more favorable. This proposition was the outcome of much research examining the commonsense idea that contact between racially different people, as Gordon Allport phrased it, "can thereby destroy stereotypes and develop friendly attitudes." Allport acknowledged, however, that "the case is not so simple." His summary of the relevant research concluded that in "a population of ordinary people," that is, those without deeply rooted prejudice, their prejudice "may be reduced by equal status contact between majority and minority groups in the pursuit of common goals." Such a reduction, he added, was "greatly enhanced if this contact is sanctioned by institutional support (i.e., by law, custom or local atmosphere), and if it is of a sort that leads to the perception of common interests and a common humanity between members of the two groups."[15] Because this contextually limited proposition suggested some possibilities for strategic action in such areas as housing, the supporting research was widely cited by sociologists in the literature on race relations.

The Correlates of Authoritarianism

Even though sociologists were quick to demonstrate that prejudice could not readily be used as the cause of discrimination, and that changes in discriminatory patterns of behavior were to be explained largely by structural factors, they were nonetheless strongly influenced by one dimension of the study of the authoritarian person: the social correlates of authoritarianism. During the 1950s a number of studies, some limited in scope, some drawn from large samples, found that authoritarianism was consistently correlated with age, education, and intelligence. Other studies also found authoritarianism particularly evident among members of disadvantaged minorities, members of certain religious organizations, and, most significantly of all, those of lower-class status. In one such study, Morris Janowitz and Dwaine Marvick found that those more authoritarian were usually older, less educated, and lower class. In a national sample that divided the population by income and education, Samuel Stouffer found those of lower rank more authoritarian and more intolerant. William MacKinnon and Richard Centers found that 88 percent of those with the least education were in the top half of measures of authoritarianism, but only 20 percent of college graduates were.[16]

Prejudice and authoritarianism, however, were not attributes that sociologists found only in the majority group; they were also evident within minority groups. MacKinnon and Centers, for example, found that 80 percent of respondents of Mexican descent and 77 percent of blacks were in the upper half on authoritarian scores. A study of students at seven predominantly black colleges recorded scores on the Fascism (F) Scale higher than those reported for most white college students. A study from a large stratified sample of Philadelphia residents produced similar findings.[17]

When sociologists looked for the social correlates of authoritarianism, their research often utilized the familiar social variables of so much conventional research: age, education, religion, and various indices of class and social status. On the basis of the empirical evidence their research generated, they advanced the general proposition that the educated and those of higher social status were more liberal and tolerant on matters of race than were those less educated and of lesser status. Their argument emphasized that those more tolerant held richer, more complex views of the world, in contrast to the simple, concrete images of reality held by the less educated. Limited social experience and contacts and a more isolated, parochial life were also said to contribute to authoritarianism. Those less sophisticated about the world and more insecure about their place within it, it was claimed, were more likely to be authoritarian and to see the world in black and white terms. Such people also were likely to be less educated and of lower social status.

It is worth remembering here that the origin of the search for an authoritarian personality was the effort to find the anti-Semitic, pro-fascist person whose very existence was a threat to democracy. To claim that the authoritarian person was to be found primarily in the numerically dominant lower strata only served to emphasize that threat to democratic practice. In turn, to claim for the college-educated middle class a richer, more varied experience and a more sophisticated worldview provided a flattering self-image for those who possessed such an education; that included, of course, those who had created the image.

It is also worth remembering that the studies of prejudice and authoritarianism, beginning with *The Authoritarian Personality*, were subject to both methodological and interpretive criticism. Some social scientists did not believe an authoritarian personality had been validated by the research, while others claimed that the high scores of many lower-status respondents could largely be accounted for by acquiescence, the tendency to accept a positively stated item on the test.[18] Nevertheless, a conception of prejudice and authoritarianism located disproportionately within the lower classes and the less educated, including the minorities, came to be widely accepted among sociologists, even when the methodological underpinnings of such an imagery were uncertain. One cannot account for the widespread acceptance of these tentative findings solely by the strength of the supporting research; there was also an apparent readiness of middle-class sociologists to accept a denigrating image of those of lower social status.

The Black as Psychological Cripple

Even as sociologists studied the correlates of authoritarianism to identify the prejudiced personality, they continued to present a thoroughly negative portrait of black people unrelieved by any redeeming features. Witness, for example, this statement by Arnold Rose:

The instability of the Negro family, the inadequacy of educational
facilities for Negroes, the emotionalism of the Negro church, the
insufficiency and unwholeness of Negro recreational activity, the
excess of Negro sociable organization, the narrowness of interest
of the average Negro, the provincialism of his thinking, the high
Negro crime rate, the cultivation of the arts to the neglect of
other fields, superstition, personality difficulties, and other "characteristic" traits are mainly forms of social ill-health, which, for
the most part, are created by caste pressure.[19]

The ensemble of these traits constituted a pathological portrait unrelieved by any offsetting modicum of positive features. It was drawn
from a selective perception of black people tacitly compared to an
idealized image of a white, middle-class culture not found in the real
world. Sociologists, to be sure, did not create this bleak portrait or its
tacit contrast; instead, it was the image of black people shared in
common with most white Americans. Sociologists differed from those
other white Americans only in their insistence on attributing the traits
to caste pressure. But if sociologists did not create this bleak image,
they nonetheless reinforced and legitimated it by systematically sustaining it in their writings.

When Arnold Rose mentioned "personality difficulties" among the
pathologies of black life, he touched upon an issue that had moved
into sociological consideration since John Dollard's efforts in the late
1930s to examine psychologically the plantation black. Even before
that, Herbert Miller had suggested that both blacks and immigrants
suffered from an "oppression psychosis," a condition he defined as
"those persistent and exaggerated mental states which are characteristically produced under conditions where one group dominates another." Such mental states included being "abnormally subjective . . .
a complete incapacity to view its own problems objectively," and a
tendency to be suspicious. Jews, he said, are "introspective, analytical,
aggressive, and conspicuous," and "the Negro has many of the same
characteristics." Edward Reuter and other sociologists of that day accepted oppression psychosis as a valid description of blacks, though
Robert Park disputed it: "It is very doubtful whether the mental state
of the most ardent national minorities in the United States can be
described as in any real sense pathological at this or any other time."[20]

Nonetheless, a notion of pathologies of personality as a consequence
of racial domination persisted in the sociological literature and required
only a psychiatric analysis of urban blacks to give it a central place in
the sociology of race relations. That came with the publication in 1951

of *The Mark of Oppression* by Abram Kardiner and Lionel Ovesey, both of whom were psychiatrists.[21]

The theoretical basis for their study was in a conception of a "basic personality structure," defined as the formative outcome of the adaptation of the human being to an institutional order. Kardiner had developed this approach in an earlier work and had tested out the thesis with the anthropologist Cora Du Bois.[22] In moving from the study of preliterate peoples to the study of American blacks, Kardiner and Ovesey saw their analysis, not as challenging or disputing the existing sociological literature, but as providing a knowledge of black personality lacking in American sociology. Their intention was to further buttress, not refute, the prevailing sociological image of the black American.

Consistent with that intent, Kardiner and Ovesey shared with sociologists the prevailing assumption that blacks lacked any culture of their own. An *"aboriginal culture,"* they asserted, had been *"smashed at the outset of enslavement."* The slaves were then forced to accept another culture, since, in losing their original culture, they could not create a new one: "The conditions of slavery were such that they not only destroyed the possibility of reciprocal interaction between master and slave, but in a large measure, free emotional interaction among slaves was seriously impaired. No *culture* can arise under these limitations." The psychological effects of this slave status produced, among other effects, a degradation of self-esteem, a "forced adoption of foreign culture traits," and destruction of the family unit, "with particular disparagement of the male." The inability to have their own culture destroyed social cohesion among blacks. Furthermore, the white master was idealized; "but with this ideal was incorporated an object which was at once revered and hated. They became incompatible constituents of the Negro personality."[23]

Beyond slavery, according to Kardiner and Ovesey, a persistent and pervasive experience of discrimination continued to have a destructive effect on the personality of black Americans. The need to adapt to discrimination produced low self-esteem as the self-referential component and agression as the reactive. But aggression cannot easily be expressed, and the effort to limit it, to control rage, often led to a suppression that produced submission and compliance. It could also be replaced with resentment. Rage could sometimes "ricochet back on its author" or produce psychosomatic reactions: "The two commonest end products of sustained attempts to contain and control aggression were low self-esteem and depression" (303–5).

This psychiatric profile found no positive or creative skills or achievements to compensate for the destructive consequences of discrimination. Kardiner and Ovesey even denied that blacks possessed any "genuine religiosity" and claimed that "they have invented no religion of their own." Instead, "compensatory activities" served to bolster self-esteem ("flashy and flamboyant dressing"), to narcotize against traumatic impact ("largely through alcohol and drugs"), to disparage other blacks ("vindictive and vituperative" actions "widespread among urban Negroes"), and to get magical aid for status improvement (chiefly gambling). For upper-class blacks, there were special problems. Their need to control their psychic life was so great that "they must be extremely cramped and constricted and unspontaneous" (385, 313–14, 316–17).

To Kardiner and Ovesey, all of this meant that there was a "basic personality" for the black American. In much the same manner as John Dollard in *Caste and Class in a Southern Town*, they took the white middle class as a "base line" and found a black personality that was a "caricature of the corresponding white personality." This occurred, they theorized, because blacks had to adapt to the same culture and accept the same social goals while denied the opportunity to achieve them (317).

Perhaps the most damning claim that *The Mark of Oppression* made was that black Americans "lack the capacity for social cohesion," which was "the ability of the individuals who compose a group to cooperate to the end of improving their common lot." Such cohesion had its roots in the structure of personality, not in leadership, and required a social ego, a capacity for "cooperative relatedness." But among blacks, Kardiner and Ovesey argued, the frustrations of childhood "create a personality devoid of confidence in human relations, of an eternal vigilance and distrust of others." Yet, the emotions most conducive to social cohesion were those that pertained to the categories of love, trust, and confidence (359, 308, 306).

This lack of social cohesion could be traced back to slavery, where neither the capacity for concerted thought nor the capability for action could be developed. Nor did Emancipation provide any significant opportunity to change before new oppressive conditions took hold. A depressed self-esteem, self-hatred, and identification with the white oppressor ("the bane of Negro cohesion from the very beginning of slavery") were basic to an inadequate social ego. Successful blacks displayed, paradoxically, a fear of success and a contempt for poor blacks, which came from a projected self-hatred (359–67).

For lower-class blacks, there was a particular factor, a basic condition of life, that provided other causes for the lack of social cohesion:

> They depend essentially on the lower effectivity potential that results from the broken home, the absence of dependable parental figures, the vanishing father, the working mother who has no time to care for her children, the loveless discipline to which the children are exposed, the inability to idealize parental figures who frustrate more than they satisfy dependency cravings, the distorted relations between the sexes, the female-dominance in a male-oriented society, the disparagement of the masculine ideal, the universal mistrust and essential isolation of the lower-class Negro—all this in spite of the fact that the Negro is an interminable joiner. (366)

Oppression, Pathology, and Social Change

The portrait of the black person projected from the pages of *The Mark of Oppression* was unrelievedly negative. It was the portrait of a mentally unhealthy individual, an incomplete and distorted human being incapable of even the slightest collective effort at self-liberation, in short, a psychological cripple. Kardiner and Ovesey seemed to recognize how bleak the portrait they drew was and offered a "word of caution": the documents "read much worse than they are," and some of those "unrelieved by the persistent failures and frustrations, nevertheless are able to salvage some happiness, now and then." Not depicting the "happier aspects of their lives" was "the result of the focus of the work." Despite such demurrers, however, Kardiner and Ovesey insisted that "the final result is a wretched internal life" (80–81).

It also occurred to the authors that their pathological portrait of black people could be used to support those who would draw from *The Mark of Oppression* support for a denigrating view of blacks. In an "Advice to the Reader" section that appeared at the outset of the book, they spoke of the "hard choice" to make between dispassionate inquiry and a moratorium on investigation to avoid misuse of the findings. They had chosen the former, they declared, and "elected to accept such misuses as may attend it." They further noted: "Anyone who wishes to quote from the conclusion of this book to uphold any other thesis risks doing injustice to the material in the book, to the intentions of the authors, and to the Negro people" (v–vi).

Notwithstanding their genuine sympathy and compassion for black people, and their willingness to label racial discrimination as oppression, the authors of *The Mark of Oppression* continued a line of analysis that ran from Edward Reuter and Herbert Miller to John Dollard and Gunnar Myrdal, buttressing a social and psychological portrait of black pathology with a psychiatric one. It was an analysis that denied that blacks had created anything culturally distinctive, or, in effect, that there was any such thing as a "black experience" except for adaptation and reaction. (One is reminded again of Ralph Ellison's protest of the notion that blacks developed only by reacting and did not help to create themselves.)

Kardiner and Ovesey's argument was that whites had so thoroughly oppressed and victimized blacks that only whites could undo the damage. While sociologists always stressed the need to educate blacks, Kardiner and Ovesey argued that what blacks needed was not education but "reintegration," while "it was the white man who requires the education." The "product of oppression" can only be dissolved by stopping the oppression, they said, and it was evident they meant that only the oppressor could be the liberator. In speaking of their "psychodynamic approach," Kardiner and Ovesey said that "to those disposed to social action, such studies can give particular indications. Whether we accept these indications or not depends on our willingness to see the mutilating marks that oppression leaves on the human mind, and our readiness to be moved by them" (387). The "we" referred to here are not those whose minds have been mutilated, but the mutilators, who, if they were but moved, could be the liberators.

The message of *The Mark of Oppression* about social change seemed fairly obvious. A people mentally crippled by oppression and lacking in any capacity for social cohesion were incapable of the coordinated action for self-liberation that might challenge an oppressive racial structure. In the same way that W. Lloyd Warner had earlier reassured sociologists that caste-enclosed blacks could not be seriously disruptive of the social order, Kardiner and Ovesey were now telling them that blacks could not organize adequately to be effective, independent agents of their own liberation, but were, instead, dependent on a white leadership. Such a people could at best, if at all, provide from within its own small middle class the junior leadership that would join with a white leadership to give direction to a program of social change.

While Kardiner and Ovesey made a powerful statement about the psychological costs suffered by an oppressed people, their analysis was nonetheless incomplete. One need not deny that oppression is destructive, that it represses and distorts, and that it leaves an indelible mark on the human psyche to deny also that oppression succeeds in permanently crippling the human spirit or forever renders a people incapable of mobilizing collective action to shape its own future. If a minority people suffer under oppression, they also survive, physically and mentally, except for those infrequent occasions of genocide. If their environment is punitive, they nonetheless learn to cope and to construct cultural and institutional resources for sustaining hope and a sense of their own humanity. Black people created cultural expressions of extraordinary quality, as in religion and music, that provided an enduring source of self-respect and a reservoir of strength and hope. And the black church became a significant institutional force for providing leadership and for sustaining family and community.

Yet little of this was evident in the sociological literature. While much sociological work documented the unmistakably destructive consequences of oppression, there was no comparable work identifying cultural and institutional resources among blacks. Instead, sociologists insisted on the lack of a distinctive black culture, and thus of cultural creativity, and saw only the pervasiveness of social disorganization. Consequently, they did not recognize any developed cultural response among blacks that might serve to cope with oppression or to provide underdog perspectives and life-styles, out of which in time some more positive political action might generate. Neither were they looking for evidence of a social movement among blacks; instead, they seemed not to envision any possibility for the emergence of forms of black-directed collective action. In 1951 that was late in the day to be unaware of the coming storm.

A sociological concern for a pathology of black personality continued steadily throughout the 1950s and flourished even more in the 1960s. Sociologists produced other studies to demonstrate that blacks suffered from a lack of self-esteem and from a propensity to self-hatred and self-destructive action. In a highly critical analysis of this theme, and of the research that supported it, John D. McCarthy and William L. Yancey noted that as late as 1971, despite a few tentative dissents, there was "a rather clear consensus: the black man's life and personality were disorganized as a result of white prejudice and discrimination."[24]

Race Relations and Social Policy

If a concern for the pathology of black personality represented a continuity with past sociological analysis, many sociologists of race relations were intent on breaking new ground by undertaking research on practical issues by which they could show possibilities for change. From the end of World War II and through the 1950s, sociologists carried out research on segregation in the military, in industrial em-

ployment, and in residential housing.[25] There were a number of factors
that accounted for these research efforts: the army's use of social scientists for studying the attitudes of soldiers during World War II;
President Truman's desegregation of the armed forces; the political
struggle to institute fair employment laws and to alter federal and state
policies and laws maintaining racially segregated housing; and the Supreme Court's decision on restricted covenants in housing (and later
on the desegregation of schools).

But even these developments must be seen in the context of a changing and volatile racial situation in the United States. The active challenge to discrimination and the changing position of blacks, Herbert
Blumer observed, "subjected previously established areas of racial discrimination to a great deal of stress. We can see this in the need for
Negro manpower in the war, in the pressure for housing and living
place as Negroes flocked into urban communities, and in the movement
of Negroes into industrial occupations."[26] Such stresses focused greater
public attention on race relations, but they also became the concern
of political and corporate elites. One consequence of a greater elite
concern was an increase in funds allocated by major foundations for
policy-oriented research on race relations.

An awareness of a changing race relations also provided the political
context for the emergence of a profession of social practitioners whose
strategic need for information and for knowledge about the control
and manipulation of human behavior brought them into a close working relationship with social scientists. The research that sociologists
carried out was largely a response to the needs of these practitioners,
as well as an effort to contribute to the making of policies that would
change race relations.

The use of social scientists in the making of policy about racial
practices gained impetus during World War II through research carried
on by the Research Branch, Information and Education Division,
United States Army. After the war the army turned the data over to
the Social Science Research Council, and an analysis was prepared
under a grant from the Carnegie Corporation. The first volume (of a
four-volume series) of *The American Soldier* concluded with a chapter
on the black soldier, analyzing in what way blacks defined the military
situation in racial terms, how they viewed their stake in the war, their
reaction to the prospect of overseas duty, their adjustments to army
life, their reaction to being stationed in the North and the South, their
attitudes toward racial segregation, and their opinions on leadership.
On particular issues, comparisons were made with the attitudes of white
soldiers.[27]

In 1948 (a year before *The American Soldier* was published), President Harry Truman issued an executive order requiring equal treatment of all races in the military, and by 1952 all branches of the armed services had been desegregated.[28] Social scientists were acutely aware that the army had been able to desegregate with little overt opposition because of its structure of authority, but that ending segregation and discrimination in industrial employment and housing was a more difficult problem, as the experience in seeking fair employment legislation had demonstrated. Ever since the wartime FEPC, however, there had been a widely shared interest in reducing job discrimination, particularly in the nation's industries, which employed so many semiskilled workers. The campaign for a federal law ensuring fair employment practices gave political expression to that interest, as did a comparable effort in some states and large cities. That, in turn, encouraged research on race relations in industry.

From the late 1940s on, a number of studies explored relations between black and white workers at the industrial workplace. A widely cited study by Everett Hughes found that informal relationships changed stereotypes, easing working relations, while Lewis Killian reported that southern whites would work alongside blacks without protest or opposition, although they did not change their racial views. Other studies reported on the use of managerial authority to upgrade blacks and to end discrimination, while yet attaining satisfactory relations on the job between white and black workers.[29]

These latter studies marked the increasing sociological interest in industrial employment as a structure in which management could successfully utilize its authority to require compliant behavior among workers despite contradictory attitudes. During the 1950s there was to be an increasing interest by sociologists in ways to overcome the resistance of the majority by the use of executive, legal, and judicial authority.

But in contrast to the army and the corporation, housing lacked an overarching structure of authority, and within any residential area there was no authoritative system of sanctions by which behavior could be controlled. Residential housing, furthermore, was a segregated area of social life about which the white public seemed to have no qualms. By 1950, however, a number of states had passed laws against racial segregation in public housing, and as a result some mixing of the races within previously segregated projects was underway. Sociologists were quick to seize the opportunity to study how race relations developed between white and black tenants. Most of the research tested the concept of equal status contact and found it valid when limited to specific conditions.[30]

In 1947 the Supreme Court decided that "restricted covenant" clauses in the deeds to residential property (forbidding any sale by whites to blacks or other designated peoples) were unenforceable in the courts. Among hopeful liberals, that aroused an expectation that in the near future the breakdown of segregated housing was possible. As a consequence, sociologists began to study racial housing patterns, to measure residential segregation in cities, and to describe trends in residential segregation over time. Such studies provided abundant evidence that black residents were largely concentrated in "black belts" and central-city ghettoes, that whites were strongly resistant to any change, and that those who supported racially segregated housing were going to offer effective resistance to the goal of an integrated neighborhood.[31]

The Desegregation of Public Schools

On May 17, 1954, in the case of *Brown v. Topeka*, the Supreme Court ruled against state-required segregation of public schools. The decision was of momentous significance in the struggle against segregation and culminated a long legal effort by the National Association for the Advancement of Colored People to compel the federal government to enforce the Fourteenth Amendment to the Constitution. The decision signified the end of legalized segregation in the United States and the beginning of a period in which the law as a social institution moved from being a supporter of segregation and discrimination to an active force for desegregation and equal opportunity.

But for social scientists, the significance of the historic decision was not only in a decisive legal victory over segregation, but also in their own participation in that decision. Their involvement in the legal process began in 1951 in cases before several federal district courts and one state court, at the invitation of the legal staff of the NAACP. As part of an effort to break through the framework of the "separate-but-equal" principle set forth in 1896 in the case of *Plessy v. Ferguson,* NAACP lawyers argued in these cases that, besides the obvious inferior educational facilities provided for black children, segregated schooling psychologically harmed them. For evidence to sustain such an argument, and to build a case around the "equal-protection" and "due-process" clauses of the Fourteenth Amendment, the lawyers turned to psychologists for testimony and for the evidence provided by psychological research. Led by the black social psychologist Kenneth Clark, psychologists testified that segregation taught black schoolchildren that they were inferior; it destroyed their self-respect and produced emotional turmoil; and its cumulative effect was damaging to the personality development of black children.

When several of these cases, including *Brown v. Topeka,* reached the Supreme Court in 1953 on appeal, the NAACP asked Kenneth Clark and others who had been involved in the cases to prepare an appendix to its brief to the Supreme Court. A short statement setting out the social scientific case against racial segregation was drawn up by Gerhart Saenger, Isador Chein, Stuart Cook, and Clark. It summarized the testimony given in these cases and offered as documentation a number of psychological studies; it also carried the endorsement of thirty-five noted social scientists. Among the studies cited was a survey published in 1948 offering the responses of 517 social scientists to questions about possible detrimental effects of segregation. Ninety percent thought "enforced segregation" harmed blacks and 83 percent thought it was harmful to whites.[32]

In the text of their decision, the justices acknowledged the "modern authority" of social science in asserting that segregation was harmful to black children and in a footnote cited seven social science documents as supporting evidence.

Implementing the Decision

When it issued its decision in May of 1954, the Court postponed to October a decision on implementation and, to prepare for it, required the parties to submit briefs on the process of desegregation, including evidence on whether the Court should decree that children be admitted immediately to schools of their choice or permit "an effective gradual adjustment." In anticipation, Kenneth Clark had developed a statement on implementation before the May decision; therefore, with the aid of other social scientists, he prepared a document for use by lawyers in the October hearing.[33]

Clark's document reviewed all known instances of desegregation under diverse circumstances and argued that immediate desegregation was to be preferred over a gradual process. Gradual desegregation, the document asserted, does *"not necessarily insure 'effectiveness' of the desegregation process or increase its chances of acceptance by those who were opposed to desegregation."* Nor does the time allowed for desegregation necessarily promote either effectiveness or smoothness of change, since that time may also provide an opportunity to mobilize resistance. Resistance, it was added, was not directly dependent on the degree of expressed racial prejudice, since prejudiced persons accommodate to racial change as well as less prejudiced ones. The possibility of active, disruptive resistance, even by a minority, could not be denied, though violent incidents in resisting desegregation were quite rare, it was claimed, and desegregation had been accomplished in instances of initially strong opposition. Active, even sometimes violent resistances, when they do occur, the report argued, were associated with ambiguous and inconsistent policy, ineffective policy action, and conflict between competing government officials. In contrast, opposition and overt resistance decreased, if it was not eliminated, *"when the alternative for the whites is a complete loss of a desired public facility or the imposition of a direct economic burden or some other important stigma."*[34]

These last statements drew upon what was now becoming a firm conviction of the sociologists of race relations that consistent policy and firm execution of authority were necessary to enforce desegregation. The document concluded, in fact, by underscoring what "desegregation with a minimum of social disturbance depends upon." Besides an appeal to brotherhood, fair play, and justice, these included "a clear and unequivocal statement of policy"; "firm enforcement" and "persistence . . . in the face of initial resistance"; and "a willingness to deal with violations . . . by a resort to law and strong enforcement action."[35] This insistence on the firm exercise of authority had developed among sociologists from their recognition of the way in which military and corporate authority could enact and carry out decisions without disruptive resistance. They were also convinced that, within the white population, there was now a racially enlightened minority, largely the more educated, who needed to act effectively to offset the unenlightened majority.

Social Science and the Courts

The use of social scientists to provide scientific evidence in judicial proceedings, whether as written statement or as verbal testimony, touched a raw nerve among both jurists and southern segregationists. Criticism, more learned and technical from the legally trained, while largely abusive and polemical from the segregationists, was loud and frequent after the 1954 decision. Some lawyers made the claim that the decision was illegitimate for being sociological, rather than being based on legal reasoning; others, that social science was not yet sufficiently scientific to provide valid propositions on which the courts could rely for sound legal decisions. As the key figure in preparing the brief and the later report on implementation, Kenneth Clark wrote an article for a law review to defend himself before lawyers against their criticisms, such as, for example, that he had exaggerated the contribution of social science and that the evidence offered was of little value.[36]

While such criticisms as these could be viewed as coming from lawyers unhappy with the presence of social scientists in major court decisions (even, in some cases, when they supported the decision on legal grounds), there were also critical judgments made by social scientists who did not oppose the Court's decision or even the effort of social scientists to support it. For the sociologist Morroe Berger, for example, the social scientific evidence used to buttress a decision made primarily on legal grounds was weak and inspired no great confidence. The data on harmful effects of enforced segregation were meager, Berger thought, for little research having a direct bearing on the issue before the Court had ever been carried out. However, noted Berger, "despite its weak role in the segregation cases, social scientists can play a useful part in the courts, both to enable judges to interpret legislation in the light of current social needs and to establish facts in dispute."[37] Though the critics were correct in pointing to the limitations of social science, conceded Berger, we do not have any more reliable knowledge than social science offers.

A similar strong critique was offered by a political scientist supportive of the Court's decision and of the use of social scientific evidence. In a careful, detailed effort to establish the relevancy and adequacy of social scientific research and theory for the validity of arguments offered in the 1954 case, Herbert Garfinkel acknowledged that the evidence for claiming that school segregation was harmful to children "is least securely derived from research findings." The weakness here, he noted, was in basing broad generalizations on meager evidence. Nonetheless, he concluded, "a persuasive case has been constructed but adequate research techniques are yet to be devised which can distinguish the broad effect of minority group status and the specific psychological consequences of institutionalized segregation."[38]

Besides the arguments among social scientists and legal theorists, there was another consequence of the Court's fateful decision in 1954. The order to desegregate public schools enraged segregationists and set in motion an effort to resist its implementation, even to reverse the decision. That, in turn, renewed debate on black and white intelligence and on innate and learned capacities of the races, which continued well into the 1960s. If psychologists led the social scientific effort to support the legal case for desegregation, other psychologists testified against the decision to desegregate and, after the decision, spurred the effort to restore legitimacy to racially separate schools. They were able to reach a large, responsive public, particularly in the South, so that presumptions of the inherent inferiority of blacks continued to be a defense of segregation in public education. As college teachers, sociologists had to refute such claims of racial inferiority, though as scholars and researchers they focused on other issues. By the early 1960s the issue remained important enough for both the American Anthropological Association and the Society for the Study of Social Problems to issue statements rejecting any scientific validity for claims about racial differences in such attributes as intelligence. In that same period, Melvin M. Tumin and Thomas F. Pettigrew wrote readable treatises on what was known scientifically about race and intelligence.[39]

In plunging into the thicket of judicial action, social scientists soon learned the hazards involved. When they intruded upon the monopolized terrain of the legal profession, their claims were subjected to critical and sometimes hostile scrutiny. The counterattack of prosegregationist psychologists forced them into a renewed educational effort to combat ancient claims about race and intelligence. And some social scientists, however sympathetic to their objectives, had to admit that the evidence offered the Court was too weak to sustain the argument.[40]

Few sociologists have ever written about such experiences at the state level in that same period. One who did is Lewis Killian. He conducted research in Florida to provide data useful to the state's attorney general, who planned to file a brief to require Florida schools to comply with the Supreme Court's decision. This was not social research as usual, but research carried out in the glare of publicity on a very controversial issue. In a brief paper in *Social Problems*, Killian reported on how the research was influenced by that heated environment, as well as on the advantages to educate both political officials and the public that flowed from having carried out the research.[41]

Studying Desegregation

Despite the recommendations that Kenneth Clark prepared for the hearing on the implementation of desegregation, the Supreme Court opted for a gradualist approach. But once the decision was made, the issue of desegregation as a practical problem was before the nation, and social scientists responded to it in different ways. Some, for example, exhorted educators and community leaders to carry out desegregation effectively and offered advice on the factors necessary to that end, usually setting forth some set of ideal conditions not likely to occur in the real communities facing desegregation. Herbert Blumer, for one, argued that the only way to achieve desegregation was to utilize "the weight of transcending prestige, authority, and power," backed by "organizational pressure and support," to control the functionaries responsible for the decisions and practices either sustaining or altering segregation in the community.

But such transcending prestige and authority had already been invoked, yet the implementation of the decision to desegregate faced enormous opposition. Blumer suggested that the dominant racial group "might be lacking in organizations to mobilize such opposition and convert it into action," though actual experience in the South suggested otherwise. More often, it was local forces for desegregation that lacked organizational strength and were less able to make use of what Blumer called "the potential of power and prestige available in a given situation."[42] Desegregation of the public schools remained a practical problem of large dimensions.

Some sociologists, however, were able to make reasonable predictions about how desegregation was likely to fare in the South. Particularly prescient was Guy B. Johnson, who, in his presidential address to the Southern Sociological Society just before the May, 1954, decision, made some predictions about the transition to a desegregated South. The early period, he noted, would be one of tensions, evasive actions, an increase in aggression against blacks, and some violence. Equal-status contact would be very rare, though official norms of "equal treatment" of all students would soon develop. Where black populations were sparse, desegregation would occur completely, but in urban areas where there were large black residential areas, blacks would choose to stay in their own schools. Desegregation, furthermore, would cost some black teachers their jobs. Predictions similar to these were also made by other sociologists.[43]

A different response was made by the official leadership of social science. The Committee on Social Behavior of the Social Science Research Council saw in desegregation a unique opportunity for basic research. A memorandum prepared for the committee and a summary article to interested social scientists put an emphasis on long-run scientific advancement, not on immediate applied aims. Accordingly, desegregation was not viewed as a theoretical issue: "Desegregation is an empirical problem-area, not a delimited scientific problem. What it does provide is a suitable context in which to study strategic intersections of interesting variables—interesting from the standpoint of growing points of development of theory."[44]

There are difficulties associated with trying to do "disinterested scientific research" in a "highly charged atmosphere," and there is also an interest in doing research of social importance, the authors argued, but not clearly recognized "is the opportunity the situation contains for basic research on scientifically important questions." While desegregation does not involve elements that could not be found in other settings, the significant point is that "it does involve *variables that are important from a scientific standpoint* and that these variables are present with very strong weights." Here was the key to the advantage of studying desegregation: "The context of desegregation is thus a major research opportunity to those social scientists, regardless of scientific field, whose interests require situations that embody high values of intensity, involvement, and social embeddedness of certain psychological and social system variables." Accordingly, the authors suggested, desegregation provided opportunities to study changes in attitudes, in personality, and in small-group processes.[45]

A research program that looked only to the opportunity that desegregation provided for pursuing conventional research interests was not likely to be imaginative or creative about research on the dynamics of the struggle to desegregate. The authors, for example, suggested that studies be made of differences in how communities carried out or resisted desegregation and how changes in one institutional area (education) affected other areas. Changes in the perception of law and legal institutions was another research topic suggested. Beyond references to some effects on both black and white people, blacks as research subjects were mentioned only twice. Under the study of normative conflict, it was suggested that "Negro groups obtaining advantages from segregation are one type under strong conflicting pressures"; on problems of institutional integration, it was then asked: "What are the effects on political behavior of Negroes not themselves directly involved in desegregation?"[46]

What was absent was as notable as what was present. Though there was a concern for studying normative conflict, there was no suggestion to study overt group conflict, or possible new struggles for power, or desegregation as a context for patterns of collective behavior. While there was an interest in attitude and personality changes, there was no similar interest in the effect of the Court decision on the collective expectations of blacks about educational opportunities, as well as the possible reactions if these expectations were not realized in a short time.

As it turned out, little research of any kind beyond descriptions of specific events was carried out in the South. Thomas Pettigrew claimed that the pressures by segregationists had deterred research on desegregation by creating such a "stifling atmosphere" that it led social scientists "to work in a less controversial area."[47] An unanticipated factor, however, was the sudden cessation of foundation support for research on race relations. The fury of southern segregationists found political expression in an attack by southern members of Congress on the tax-exempt status of foundations. The intimidated foundations responded by shifting funds to projects that did not anger southern segregationists. It would be ten years before they would return to the support of research in race relations.

The retreat of foundations and social scientists before the attacks of segregationists was but one small aspect of the struggle over desegregation, which proceeded slowly and unevenly over the rest of the decade. Southern resistance was formidable, and there was open conflict and serious disruption. Kenneth Clark blamed the slow pace of desegregation on token compliance, harassment of blacks, intimidation and immobilization of nonsegregationist whites, and a mood of moderation, retreat, and loss of initiative to the prosegregationists: "Generally, the social scientists underestimated the intensity and deviousness of the opposition, the effectiveness of prosegregationists' propaganda outside the South, the lack of deep effective moral commitment in the nation as a whole and particularly in the executive branch of the Federal Government, and the ease with which the initiative would be seized by prosegregationists."[48]

This was a shrewd and insightful observation about the difficulties of desegregating southern schools, made by a keen and deeply involved observer, but it was also an observation made six years after the Court's decision. Whether intended or not, it stood as a serious criticism of the work of sociologists and social psychologists, but particularly of sociologists. Though they claimed to be the students of societal change and development, no sociologist had provided such an assessment as Clark's, nor had any sociologist provided the systematic research needed to add flesh to the bare bones of Clark's observations.

Sociologists could not provide such research, not only because they could get no funding and because they had withdrawn from the conflict-ridden scene, but also because they had never developed a methodology, even a set of research techniques, to undertake research projects in an emotionally charged context of conflict and social disruption. As a consequence, they contributed little to the efforts to desegregate, and they learned little from the difficulties of the process.[49]

Readiness to Desegregate

One ambitious study on desegregation in the South was undertaken by Melvin Tumin and a group of associates at Princeton University. Tumin measured the attitudes of a sample of white males in

Guilford County, North Carolina, in 1956 to test the hypothesis that
formal education was the major factor responsible for differences in
readiness for desegregation. The study found that those most likely to
accept desegregation, though no less prejudiced than others, were better educated, of higher social status, and more exposed to the mass
media.[50]

What was distinctive in the study was its attempt to show that those
most ready to desegregate were not necessarily less prejudiced but,
when considering action, were better able to check their prejudices by
countervailing perspectives. Formal education contributed most to the
development of an individual's perspective that was not narrow or
localized, not immediate, but an enlarged perspective on time, place,
person, and value. Tumin characterized such an individual as having
been transformed by education "from a self-centered creature to a
balanced and mature citizen of a community." He also lauded the
"exemplary conduct of the legitimate leaders" of the county, who
encouraged the majority of residents to accept the decision to desegregate the schools. In following their leaders' model of behavior, they
exhibited "those qualities of character and conduct which insure peaceful change."[51] (One notable feature of the book was the remarkably
laudatory rhetoric used to describe the actions of an established white
leadership in a southern community.)

That a mature social perspective produced by education could effectively offset an individual's racial prejudice in deciding on possible
actions on desegregation was the innovative claim of the study. It went
beyond previous studies that sought to directly link attitude to behavior, but it still invoked the crucial role of the better educated in
undertaking movement toward a less segregated society. Like all such
studies, however, it raised questions for sociologists about the relation
of the ideational (attitudes, perspectives) to social action. Though most
sociologists of race relations were favorably disposed to the claims
Tumin made for the educated stratum, others were bound to disagree
that educated perspectives were so decisive. One who did was Leonard
Broom; he argued in his review of the book for the *American Sociological Review* that, not the attributes of leadership claimed by Tumin,
but situational factors were more likely to determine social events.
This study, he insisted, "does not describe the determinants of action."
However, what this study did do was reinforce the already accepted
idea that the fate of desegregation depended upon the better educated
white people, whose "mature and responsible" action, as Tumin saw
it, would provide a "legitimate and respected" leadership and prevent

the emergence of a "non-legitimate, ordinarily disrespected leadership."[52]

Theory, Practice, and Social Power

Though social scientists were sparingly involved in the desegregation of schools, that did not mean they were not interested in further research in race relations or in efforts to assist in the development of a more professionalized intergroup relations. They were, in fact, deeply interested in developing an early effort at an applied sociology of race relations. But this involvement of sociologists with intergroup relations was to occur mostly in the North, not in the conflict-ridden atmosphere of the South. Sociologists were obviously more comfortable working in the organized context of established agencies than in the embattled atmosphere of southern communities in open conflict over school desegregation.

Most sociologists accepted research in intergroup relations as legitimate, but sociological researchers experienced difficulty in relating their work to the practical interests of nonacademic practitioners, producing some tension and misunderstanding between them and social scientists. A cultivation of better relations seemed necessary. Robin Williams explored this problem of communication between researcher and practitioner by pointing out some problems: that of what he called "administrative anxiety," namely, the fact that program evaluation is "likely to be perceived in advance as implicit criticism and hence as a threat to the status and interests of the individual and the organization or group"; that the practitioner's commitment to getting things done is not "conducive to easy acceptance of the slowness of the research process, the qualified nature of its findings, or the frequent warning signals it raises as to the range of limited possibilities or as to the unanticipated consequences of action"; and that the committed practitioner "will react negatively to a complexity that seems to be immobilizing for action."[53]

Williams's answer to these problems of relations between social scientists and practitioners was better communication: "The evidence would seem to be convincing that research is most likely to be utilized, and to be utilized skillfully, when the practitioner has become meaningfully involved in the research process early in the development of the study." In support, he cited the observation of Morton Deutsch and Mary Collins that "to be used, social research must seem relevant to social decisions in the making," and for this to happen, "decision-makers must be directly or indirectly involved in the study."[54] Such forthright advice, however, posed serious problems that sociologists during the 1950s seemed not to have fully grasped: the constraints imposed on professionalizing practitioners by the social agencies in which they practiced; the significance of social power for the practice of intergroup relations; and the frustrations evident in the effort to relate theory to practice.

The Constraints of Professionalism

In 1953 the practitioners of intergroup relations were still shaping a new profession and were self-conscious about the extent to which their practices had yet to crystallize into a coherent pattern. As a consequence, there was considerable interest in defining professionalism in terms of roles and the agencies in which these roles were situated. This had the effect of confining race relations practice to a set of established agencies closely connected to and controlled by the established civic and political leadership of the community. Such a limiting circumstance produced a narrow definition of the realm of effective practice. Even in 1953, however, there were those who could recognize at least some of the implications. For example, George Nesbitt (a practitioner employed by the Federal government) acknowledged the problem inherent in locating practice in a particular structural context. He made the point that what a practitioner "can and cannot do . . . is affected by the racial attitudes and purposes of the agency, its personnel, and the practitioner's place within the organizational structure with respect to the work flow." Even the direct action organizations, he noted, placed inhibitions upon the professionals, "for such organizations also must raise money, and sometimes have powerful board members with low sights and vested interest in the status quo."[55]

That practitioners functioned in agencies largely controlled by political and civic elites defined a political constraint upon their practice, one that had much to do with what they derived from their reading of the social scientific literature and how they related that to the practices accepted by their governing boards. Public agencies, in particular, were likely to be directed by boards on which sat a diverse range of people representative of particular interests concerned with race relations, not all of whom were necessarily supportive of active programs to advance racial change.

Those same agencies also followed the unpublicized but widely accepted principle that the best persons to staff public intergroup agencies were white Anglo-Saxon Protestants. Only such a person, the practitioners believed, would be accepted as legitimate by the civic elite of the community. There were, of course, problems in publicly acknowledging such a belief. Charles Livermore, president of the National Association of Intergroup Relations Officials, reported that in 1952 the organization had adopted a statement endorsing such a belief as one of its basic assumptions, but it did not appear in the final printed report "because the editors apparently believed that it was subject to too much misinterpretation."[56]

The existence of such constraints on practitioners suggests that the apparent tension and misunderstanding between them and sociologists, which Robin Williams noted, were rooted in quite different interests, role constraints, and values brought to the study. That both parties wished to be "practical" did not necessarily provide a wide stretch of common ground on which to cooperate. To involve practitioners in the design of social research was to accept the political constraints under which they operated. It did not seem to occur to sociologists in the 1950s to examine the emerging role of the professionalized practitioners, as well as the public and private agencies in which they worked, to assess what limitations on practice, and thus on research, were a consequence of political constraints.

That practitioners read the social scientific literature from the constrained interest of agency and role becomes evident from an examination of material published by the National Association of Intergroup Relations Officials (NAIRO). In a list of "immediate assumptions," for example, there occurs the statement that prejudiced attitudes and behaviors are rooted in emotional needs, therefore rendering ineffective the usual educational approach; but this is followed by the proposition that discrimination cannot be changed without changes in attitudes, so that "the best approach in the long run is to educate for better attitudes." Considerable prejudice, it was also argued, "is grounded in the casual acceptance of stereotypes"; therefore, a popularizing of counter-stereotypes is needed. In this same list is a statement that discrimination is "nothing more" than conforming behavior, therefore, "the most progress can be made by organizing those who feel the issue most strongly"; "establish the right practice, and the vast majority will conform. We overestimate resistance." Supporting the conformity postulate was the assertion that law is valuable "in achieving climate, status, norm."[57]

Such apparent contradictory assumptions as these and others reflected differences in the roles professionals were playing, according to Charles Livermore, then president of NAIRO: "Some assumptions are basic to one role and others are basic to another, and I am not at all sure that there would be much general agreement among all professionals as to which were and which were not basic."[58] But the list of assumptions also reflected contradictory messages in the existing literature, especially that between sociologists and social psychologists. Practitioners, accordingly, were free to pick and choose those particular messages that suited their practice and did not violate the political constraints under which they worked.

Social Power and Intergroup Relations

In the early 1950s, political sociologists had begun to study power in the community, and sociologists like Robin Williams recognized that research in race relations needed to include that dimension. However, given the marginal position of intergroup relations in the community, the consideration of power and leadership was not motivated by a desire to challenge or alter the community's established mode of decision making. Instead, sociologists wanted to attain a better understanding of the existing power structure of the community in order to assess the limits to which it could be pushed or manipulated to make progress in race relations.

Beginning in 1949, the Social Science Research Center at Cornell University, under the direction of Robin Williams, undertook a research project of ongoing intergroup relations in a number of communities, including a study of power and leadership in the community as it affected intergroup relations. In 1955 the project published a manual written by John Dean, a sociologist and field director of the project, and Alex Rosen, a professional worker in community organization, that offered techniques for improving intergroup relations within organizations and in the community. The explicit rationale of *The Manual of Intergroup Relations* was to offer some tentative propositions about intergroup relations and to make their implications more readily applicable to social practice.[59]

Dean and Rosen began with the assumption that the climate of opinion was favorable to changes in race relations, that "fair practice" was an accepted goal, and that the only major issue was one of strategy. Accordingly, they noted that the main controversies "revolve around how much, how fast, and how far we should proceed." But no strategy could be effective unless it involved representatives of the power structure, since "community-wide action can go no further than local leaders are willing to move." The involvement of community influentials was always possible, since intergroup relations was an acceptable cause: "In many sections of the country, intergroup relations has become a good 'cause' for conservatives to be liberal about. It is not basically threatening to their own economic and social status in the community and meets all the requirements of moral rectitude."[60]

Once the involvement of key influentials had been secured, effective strategy required the development of further organization for specific objectives, including all the familiar organizational paraphernalia of urban middle-class life: committees, workshops, commissions, and boards. The professional's role was that of strategist in guiding a program from inception to acceptance by the power elite, thus to become a reality of community policy and practice. The role of professional practitioner, therefore, was not that of public leader but a "behind-the-scenes" operator. To give emphasis to this last point, Dean and Rosen argued that the overtly active professional incurs antagonisms; therefore, the professional should instead work through committees, letting others initiate the contacts, direct the negotiations, and invoke the sanctions. The basic aproach was to involve community influentials and an appropriate organizational structure in negotiations with "gatekeepers": "The basic strategy of negotiation has two facets: (1) interpreting the consequences of change as *less* threatening than the reluctant gatekeepers suppose, and (2) interpreting the consequences of not changing as *more* threatening by bringing sanctions to bear."[61]

Though the *Manual* provided little explicit discussion of a community power structure, what it did present looked much like the model offered by Floyd Hunter in his pioneering investigation, namely, a top leadership that effectively interlocked the various organized and institutional segments of the community and which "made most of the decisions on significant community affairs."[62] If influence over community affairs was not so centered in a civic elite, the strategy of selecting those community leaders more sympathetic to intergroup relations to be representative of the power structure would not work.

The fundamental premise of the strategy Dean and Rosen advocated was to operate within the existing power structure, not outside of, independent of, or as a challenge to it. There was no conception of a constituency to be organized among non-elite groups or a linking of the objectives of intergroup relations with other social causes. In asserting that intergroup relations was a "liberal" cause conservatives could embrace, Dean and Rosen were implicitly severing ties with other liberal causes not so acceptable to conservatives, such as social welfare and civil liberties. As a consequence, they extracted intergroup relations from the liberal frame of reference within which it had first developed; in that sense, theirs was a conservative strategy.

A conservative strategy also meant that there would not be efforts at alternate forms of organization, and the movement for racial change would go no further or faster than the community power elite would accept. For example, Dean and Rosen offered the hypothetical possibility of a small committee examining real estate practices in a community. In order to avoid uniting the real estate people in opposition, they suggested that some key realtors be involved in the project; as a consequence, from such involvement they *"may* become motivated to take a greater amount of responsibility for the intergroup injustices. . . . It is on this sense of deepened responsiblity that the action committee *must* rely for its leverage in future community action."[63]

Confidence in the viability of such a strategy, with its reliance on the goodwill of those long sustaining the existing pattern of discrimination, rested on Dean and Rosen's sense of the uniqueness of intergroup relations and "fair play" as a cause conservatives could support, but also on a climate of opinion favorable for changes in race relations. There was, they asserted, "an established and growing tradition of civil rights," so that those striving to perpetuate discrimination and segregation "find it difficult morally to defend their position."[64] The notion that a conservative power structure was capable of making such changes as it chose, that it easily embraced the liberal cause of intergroup relations, and that the prevailing climate of opinion was favorable, led Dean and Rosen to devise a strategy that gave to a body of professionalized practitioners and to a conservative civic elite the decisive roles in advancing the cause of race relations. Such a strategy had the consequence of linking theory and practice in such a way as to frustrate both sociologists and practitioners.

The Frustration of Theory and Practice

Throughout the 1950s intergroup relations grew as a professional field. By 1948 NAIRO listed 294 staffed agencies with about 1,400 professional workers; their combined annual budgets exceeded $21 million. Clearly, intergroup relations had grown and become established. Yet its achievements were modest at best, and its practitioners lacked a confident sense that their practice had been significantly enriched by social theory. Discussions in conferences and in print continued to debate why it was that, as Dean George Eply commented, "one cannot truthfully claim that great strides have been made in the development of a systematic body of theoretical principles validated by actual experience of practitioners in the field." Nonetheless, both sociologists and practitioners believed that sociological theory for effective practice was possible, and the failure to achieve it did not seem to diminish that belief.[65]

Both the sociologists of race relations and the practitioners of intergroup relations had their own reasons for believing so strongly that a relevant theory of race relations was possible. For the practitioners, to be recognized as a profession required there be a body of theoretical knowledge, the application of which constituted their professional practice. This gave them strong reason to need and believe in the possibility of a theory of intergroup relations; it was fundamental to their aspiration for professional status.

For the sociologists of race relations, theory was the ultimate validating mark of a scientific discipline. But the sociological effort to study race relations had long been perceived—even by those making such studies—as being historically particular and lacking in theoretical accomplishment. Many sociologists thought of race relations as belonging to the eclectic category of social problems, itself a sphere of sociological study lacking in an established theory. The strong impetus of many sociologists to make sociology a science brought into question the value of so much effort to study social problems; that seemed not to be the route to a science of society. The sociologists of race relations, therefore, were particularly anxious to develop an acceptable theory. They were attracted to the concept of intergroup relations rather than merely race relations, because it suggested the possibility of subsuming both race and ethnicity under an encompassing theory of minority groups. To include both race and ethnicity within a more abstract theory offered the possibility of a set of theoretical propositions that escaped the historical particularities peculiar to each category.

They were also anxious to develop a theory that would provide social practitioners with a reliable guide for effective social action. But such a belief was illusory. For one thing, knowledge in the form of theory is necessarily a set of abstractions, but practice occurs in a specific social context and unavoidably involves more factors than are accounted for by the abstractions of theory. Practice is also a political process; there cannot be more than the most general guiding relations between it and theory. This is not to deny the importance of theory for practice, but a strategy of practical action cannot be developed from theory alone. Rather, strategy must move down from theory's level of abstraction to the practical context of action, where a host of other factors must be accounted for in a political assessment of what can be done.

In this particular instance, furthermore, theory and practice began independently of one another and did not become well acquainted until the 1950s. At that point, to make them coherent to one another would restrict theory to the already existing modes of practice and to the organized context in which that practice was supported and controlled. That would then extend those political controls and their ideological rationalizations into theory itself. To narrow the relation of theory to practice to this established framework, morever, was an ideological choice, not an action dictated by theory. Such a choice denied any theoretical consideration of other modes of practice or of social actors other than professional practitioners and civic elites. Dean and Rosen, for example, had said that people dedicated to better intergroup relations, such as school teachers, clergy, social workers, and minority leaders, were rarely influential leaders of the community.[66] And the black community was still assumed to be not only unorganized but unorganizable. Thus, a constituency for a movement challenging established community power was presumed not to exist.

This presumption was not based on any significant body of sociological research; it came, instead, from a perspective on social change rooted partly in prevailing assumptions about social power in the local community and about the inability of black people to organize for effective action in their own interest, and from a widespread disinterest among sociologists in the study of collective behavior, particularly social movements.

Finally, whatever may have been the more general issues at stake in the relation of theory to practice, there was still the matter of the adequacy of sociology's mode of theorizing for any strategy of action in race relations. A sociology oriented to functional studies of social roles within stable structures was ill-equipped to analyze the dynamics of a changing race relations. In none of the existing literature of intergroup relations was there a conception of change in terms of social movements or collective behavior. The focus, instead, was on change achieved by the manipulation of variables in a controlled experiment, a model that fitted poorly the flux of less integrated social phenomena. Such a model was derived from a Comtean image of a world controlled for rational decision making by a scientific command of the statics and dynamics of modern society. No such control, of course, has ever existed.

Dissent and Doubt: Other Voices

Not every sociologist agreed fully or even at all with the development of a perspective oriented to a strategy for changing race relations. Some disagreed because they believed a concern for practice and application was not sociology's task; others did so because, despite Myrdal, they wanted to retain an "objective" approach that avoided value judgments.

The most common criticism that sociologists made of their own study of race relations was that it lacked a coherent theory. Morton

King, for example, while reviewing in 1956 a dozen textbooks published in 1948, complained of the lack of a "systematic and comprehensive set of sociological generalizations." The delay in developing a truly sociological approach, thought King, was due, first, to sociologists being preoccupied with "problems" and "what to do with them," and, second, to the lack of a "conceptual position" for interpreting minority phenomena. King urged the development of "minority-dominant" relations within the general conceptual orientation of a sociology of power, an idea that was soon to become more widely discussed.[67]

While most sociologists seemed to agree on the need to develop theory, they also wanted to provide guidance for social policy. That was Robin Williams's position and also that of the Social Science Research Council. What bothered many of them was the fact that theoretical development had not evolved sufficiently to support an effective set of policies and practices. Even Louis Wirth, who had provided both intellectual and organizational leadership in bringing sociologists and practitioners together, had serious concerns about the state of theory in race relations. Though he defined "racial and cultural relations" as "a distinctive body of knowledge" only in the sense that it dealt with a set of practical problems, and though he hoped it would "make significant contributions to the solution of urgent practical problems" while also enriching knowledge of human behavior, Wirth had concerns about the matter of theory: "What the field of racial and cultural relations, as it has developed in the United States, lacks, is an ordered system of underlying theory which could guide and enhance the value of the many disparate research projects and lead to the building of a cumulative body of tested knowledge. Viewed from one angle, the field of racial and cultural relations is as broad as the social and psychological sciences. From another angle it appears as a narrowly restricted miscellany of *ad hoc* information."[68]

Wirth likened race and cultural relations to industrial sociology or international relations, a distinctive body of knowledge only in the sense of dealing with practical problems. This implied that race and cultural relations would not constitute an object for theory, but would be an empirical area for the application of a more general sociological theory, which was what Wirth apparently meant in noting the lack of an "underlying" theory. The British sociologist, Michael Banton, asserted just such a position in arguing that race relations had no pure theory of its own and should be viewed as an applied science.[69]

Herbert Blumer also believed that theory was a problem in the study of race relations, but for quite different reasons. The existing pattern of race relations, he pointed out, was the outcome of particular historical processes: European colonialism, European industrial expansion, and economically motivated migration. These processes had produced a race relations that was a hierarchical order with a dominant racial group and one or more subordinate groups. The resulting theory of race relations has been concerned with explaining that hierarchical racial structure.[70]

Nonetheless, derived as it was from "a recent and special kind of historical setting," it was a "better theory" than those that tried to explain race relations in terms of prejudice or the authoritarian personality structure, or racial behavior in terms of attitudes, or racial tensions in terms of a blocking of motives and feelings by overt patterns of race relations, or racial opposition in terms of cultural differences. For Blumer, these were ideas "that would never be entertained if it were recognized that race relations are formed by complicated and varying factors in complex processes of historical experience" (12).

But the world was changing, and the old hierarchical order was giving way to a new pattern of race relations, one that, Blumer said, would be "a fluid, blurred, and variegated process of racial thrusts and accommodations." The new race relations would be like the emerging "technological mass society . . . organized intrinsically on the premise of change," and, by virtue of this, placing "a premium on innovation, pressure and counterpressure, the opening of new opportunities and the disappearing of old ones, and the realignment of groups in almost all spheres." Race relations could not be "segregated and insulated from these shifting and continuing forces that are integral to modern society." In such a society, a new and stable "accommodative order" of race relations could not emerge. Over time, a more fluid race relations would become less important but would not disappear, and there would remain reasons for people to retain racial identities (17–18).

Blumer saw changes in race relations coming, not because Americans were intent on living up to the American Creed and were thus susceptible to social intervention and manipulation, but because race relations "cannot avoid being incorporated to the full in the unsettling and dynamic changes that are part and parcel of the industrialized and urbanized mass society that is emerging in the world today" (17). The clear implication of his argument was that race relations would also be unsettling and dynamic. Here Blumer returned to a basic theme in the American sociology of race relations, that of racial change occurring within the pattern of industrial development of the society as a whole. But he did not see this as a slow, gradual process, as had an older generation and as many of his contemporaries still did; instead, he saw a quickening pace of social change necessarily affecting race relations.

Without saying so, Blumer was challenging perhaps the most basic assumption on which the existing theoretical perspective was built: that the further modernizing of industrial society would eventually have no place for race relations organized by prejudice and discrimination and would gradually become a nonracial society in which old racial identities would dissolve. Blumer saw a different outcome in race relations because he saw a different outcome in the development of modern society. His colleagues of the interpretive consensus saw modern society as an increasingly secular and rational social order—for them that was the very meaning of "modern"—in which such historic irrationalities as racial prejudice and privilege would gradually fade out in the face of the functional demand for social efficiency and the myth-destroying power of modern science.

But Blumer thought that the forces at work in the world were shaping a "modern industrialized mass society," characterized by such "central features" as: "increased diversification of groups and organizations; increased technological and occupational change; increased territorial movement of individuals; quickened vertical mobility; increased exposure to new definitions of objects and situations; rapid turnover in the objects of attention and interests; and intensification of the play of pressure groups and interest groups." He modestly acknowledged "the conjectural character of these sketchy views" of what mass society as a human future would be like (a compelling interest he shared with a number of thoughtful sociologists in the 1950s) and what the fate of race relations would be in such a society. Nonetheless, he insisted that "the dynamic forces inherent in modern and technological society" constitute a trend; "It is a trend toward fluidity in social relations, including race relations" (20).

A theory "suited to this emerging world is not too promising," Blumer thought, "if one seeks theory in the form of 'universals.'" More likely, theory here would be policy theory, "which is designed to analyze concrete situations as a basis for the revision of policy and the guidance of action." Blumer pointed out two attributes of "policy theory" not found in "scientific" theory: policy theory requires "an intimate knowledge of the given concrete situation, its people, their traditional views, their present run of attention, and the forces at work among them"; and it "seeks through analysis . . . to assess the possible consequences of alternative schemes of action." In race relations, Blumer thought, it was to policy theory, not scientific theory, that "racial experts" were likely to make contributions (21). On this matter he was in agreement with Louis Wirth and Michael Banton, even if he arrived there from a different route.

Blumer's commentary on the state of theory in race relations contrasted far more strikingly with those of other sociologists, such as Morton King and Louis Wirth, than his contemporaries then seemed to realize. King's criticism that the sociology of race relations lacked a body of empirically tested generalizations, and Wirth's argument that an "underlying theory"—a general sociological theory—was needed, in both cases resonated with sociology's positivist image of science characterized by an abstract theory of universal propositions. But Blumer pointed out to his fellow sociologists that there had, in fact, been theory and it had been reasonably coherent with its object of study, a historically particular racial order. The lack of theory was not the issue. Instead, a historically grounded theory was being rendered obsolete by the dissolution of the historical racial order it explained.

In this argument about theory and in his claims about the future of race relations, Blumer had provided an opportunity to open up two issues: first, whether a theory of race relations (or, by implication, any form of sociological theory) could ever be other than a historical construction; and second, whether the conception of a mass society was an adequate basis for rethinking the future of race relations. The implication of the first issue went beyond race relations to basic assumptions about sociological theory and to alternate models of scientific work. But there was not then any readiness to open up such an issue; that was to wait for a later day. The second issue simply died away as the concept of mass society remained entangled within the ideological concerns of that particular decade and failed to become a central concept in sociological theorizing. As a result, Blumer's intriguing potential for a new, fruitful way to anticipate the possible future of race relations in the United States was lost.

The 1950s was the last decade in which sociologists could hold confidently to the assumptions of their perspective and believe them to be congruent with the real world of racial events and actions. A perspective on race relations that had dominated sociological thought since the 1920s was coming to an end. Even before the decade was over there was evidence of a revolution of civil rights in the making. The Supreme Court's decision to desegregate public schools had begun the task of undermining the legal structure underpinning segregation so carefully built up in the decades after the Civil War, and new organizations and leaders, such as Martin Luther King, were already on the scene. A firestorm of protest and militant action in the South was gathering force, and before that force was spent not only would race relations in the United States be forever changed but the sociological perspective would no longer be intact and unchallenged.

Notes

1. Robert Michels, *Political Parties* (New York: Free Press, 1949); Philip Selznick, *TVA and the Grass Roots* (Berkeley: University of California Press, 1949); Floyd Hunter, *Community Power Structure: A Study of Decision Makers* (Chapel Hill: University of North Carolina Press, 1953); Philip Selznick, *The Organizational Weapon* (New York: McGraw-Hill, 1953); Seymour M. Lipset, Martin Trow, and Joseph S. Coleman, *Union Democracy* (Glencoe, Ill.: Free Press, 1956); C. Wright Mills, *The Power Elite* (New York: Oxford University Press, 1956).

2. Daniel Bell, ed., *The New American Right* (New York: Criterion Books, 1955).

3. Seymour Martin Lipset, "The Sources of the 'Radical Right,'" in *New American Right*, 197–99; S. M. Lipset, "Democracy and Working-class Authoritarianism," *American Sociological Review* 24 (Aug. 1959): 495.

4. David Riesman with Nathan Glazer and Reul Denny, *The Lonely Crowd* (New Haven: Yale University Press, 1950); William H. Whyte, *The Organization Man* (New York: Simon and Schuster, 1956); and David Riesman "The Suburban Sadness," in *The Suburban Community*, ed. William Dobriner (New York: Putnam, 1958): 375–408.

5. Philip Selznick, "Institutional Vulnerability in Mass Society," *American Journal of Sociology* 56 (Jan. 1951): 320–31. On the loss of autonomy and independent group life, see William Kornhauser, *The Politics of Mass Society* (New York: Free Press, 1959); see also Robert A. Nisbet, *The Quest for Community: A Study in the Ethics of Order and Freedom* (New York: Oxford University Press, 1953). For representative writings on mass culture, see Bernard Rosenberg and David Manning White, eds. *Mass Culture: The Popular Arts in America* (New York: Free Press, 1957). On individuality and identity, see Maurice R. Stein, Arthur J. Vidich, and David Manning White, eds. *Identity and Anxiety: Survival of the Person in Mass Society* (New York: Free Press, 1960).

6. Daniel Bell, *The End of Ideology* (New York: Free Press, 1960), 16.

7. Gordon W. Allport, *The Nature of Prejudice* (Cambridge, Mass.: Addison-Wesley, 1954), 476, 442.

8. George Eaton Simpson and J. Milton Yinger, "The Changing Pattern of Race Relations," *Phylon* 15 (Fourth Quarter 1954): 327–45. The textbook was *Racial and Cultural Minorities: An Analysis of Prejudice and Discrimination* (New York: Harper and Brothers, 1954).

9. Joseph D. Lohman and Dietrich C. Rietzes, "Note on Race Relations in Mass Society," *American Journal of Sociology* 58 (Nov. 1952): 241–42.

10. Robert K. Merton, "Discrimination and the American Creed," in *Discrimination and the National Welfare,* ed. Robert M. MacIver (New York: Harper and Brothers, 1949), 99–126; Simpson and Yinger, *Racial and Cultural Minorities,* 28–29.

11. Arnold M. Rose, "Intergroup Relations versus Prejudice: Pertinent Theory for the Study of Social Change," *Social Problems* 4 (Oct. 1956): 173, 176.

12. Gaerhart Saenger and E. Gilbert, "Customer Reactions to Integration of Negro Sales Personnel," *International Journal of Opinion and Attitude Research* 4 (1950): 57–76; Berhard Kutner, Carol Wilkins, and Penny Y. Yarrow, "Verbal Attitudes and Overt Behavior Involving Racial Prejudice," *Journal of Abnormal and Social Psychology* 47 (July 1952): 649–52; Joseph Rosner, "When White Children Are in the Minority," *Journal of Educational Sociology* 28 (Oct. 1954): 69–72; Lohman and Reitzes, "Note on Race Relations," 244; Melvin L. Kohn and Robin M. Williams, Jr., "Situational Patterning in Intergroup Relations," *American Sociological Review* 21 (Apr. 1956): 164–74.

13. Rose, "Intergroup Relations," 175; see also Simpson and Yinger, "Changing Patterns," 332–42, and Simpson and Yinger, "The Sociology of Race and Ethnic Relations," in *Sociology Today: Problems and Prospects,* ed. Robert K. Merton, Leonard Broom, and Leonard S. Cottrell, Jr. (New York: Basic Books, 1959), 376–99.

14. Herbert Blumer, "Race Prejudice as a Sense of Group Position," *Pacific Sociological Review* 1 (Spring 1958): 3, 5.

15. Allport, *Prejudice,* 250, 267. See chapter 16 for a review of the research on equal status contact.

16. Morris Janowitz and Dwaine Marvick, "Authoritarianism and Political Behavior," *Public Opinion Quarterly* 17 (Summer 1953): 185–201; Samual Stouffer, *Communism, Conformity and Civil Liberties* (Garden City, N.Y.: Doubleday, 1955); William MacKinnon and Richard Centers, "Authoritarianism and Urban Stratification," *American Journal of Sociology* 61 (May 1956): 610–20. For bibliography and summaries of the literature, see John P. Kirscht and Ronald C. Dillehay, *Dimensions of Authoritarianism: A Review of Research and Theory* (Lexington: University of Kentucky Press, 1967).

17. Mackinnon and Centers, "Authoritarianism," 61; G. A. Steckler, "Authoritarian Ideology in Negro College Students," *Journal of Abnormal and Social Psychology* 52 (May 1957): 369–99; Fillmore H. Sanford, *Authoritarianism and Leadership* (Philadelphia: Stephenson Brothers, 1950).

18. The most thorough critiques can be found in Richard Christie and Marie Jahoda, eds., *Studies in the Scope and Method of "The Authoritarian Personality"* (New York: Free Press, 1954).

19. Arnold Rose, *The Negro in America* (New York: Harper and Brothers, 1948), 294.

20. Herbert Miller, *Races, Nations and Classes: The Psychology of Domination and Freedom* (Philadelphia: J. B. Lippincott, 1924), 32, 35–36; Robert

E. Park, *Race and Culture,* ed. Everett C. Hughes et al. (Glencoe, Ill.: Free Press, 1950), 368.

21. Abram Kardiner and Lionel Ovesey, *The Mark of Oppression: A Psychological Study of the American Negro* (New York: W. W. Norton, 1951).

22. See Abram Kardiner, *The Individual and His Society* (New York: Columbia University Press, 1939); Cora Du Bois, *The People of Alor* (Minneapolis: University of Minnesota Press, 1944); and Abram Kardiner and Associates, *The Psychological Frontiers of Society* (New York: Columbia University Press, 1945).

23. Kardiner and Ovesey, *Mark of Oppression,* 39, 44, 47. Emphasis in original. Further references to this work will appear in the text.

24. John D. McCarthy and William L. Yancey, "Uncle Tom and Mr. Charlie: Metaphysical Pathos in the Study of Racism and Personality Disorganization," *American Journal of Sociology* 76 (Jan. 1971): 650.

25. For a review of studies in these areas after World War II, see St. Clair Drake, "Recent Trends in Research on the Negro in the United States," *International Social Science Bulletin* 9, no. 4 (1957): 475–92; see also Herbert Blumer, "United States of America," in *Research on Racial Relations* (Paris: United Nations Educational, Scientific, and Cultural Organization, 1966), 87–133.

26. Blumer, "United States," 98.

27. Samuel Stouffer et al., *The American Soldier: Adjustment during Army Life,* vol. 1 of *Studies in Social Psychology in World War II* (Princeton: Princeton University Press, 1949), chapter 10.

28. On the desegregation of the armed services, see James C. Evans and David A. Lane, Jr., "Integration in the Armed Services," *Annals of the American Academy of Political and Social Science* 304 (Mar. 1956): 78–85; Eli Ginsberg, *The Negro Potential* (New York: Columbia University Press, 1956); and Lee Nichols, *Breakthrough on the Color Front* (New York: Random House, 1954).

29. Everett C. Hughes, "The Knitting of Racial Groups in Industry," *American Sociological Review* 11 (Oct. 1946): 512–19; Lewis M. Killian, "The Effects of Southern White Workers on Race Relations in Northern Plants," *American Sociological Review* 17 (June 1952): 327–31. On the use of managerial authority, see, for example, John Hope, "Industrial Integration of Negroes: The Upgrading Process," *Human Organization* 2 (Winter 1952): 5–14; Jack London and Richard Hammet, "Impact of Company Policy upon Discrimination," *Sociology and Sociological Research* 39 (Nov.-Dec. 1954): 88–91; and Bernice Anita Reed, "Accommodation among Negro and White Employees in a West Coast Aircraft Industry," *Social Forces* 26 (Oct. 1947): 76–87.

30. See Marie Jahoda and Patricia Salter West, "Race Relations in Public Housing," *Journal of Social Issues* 7 (nos. 1 and 2, 1951): 132–39; Morton Deutsch and Mary E. Collins, *Interracial Housing* (Minneapolis: University of Minnesota Press, 1951); and Daniel A. Wilner, Rosabelle Price Walker, and

Stuart A. Cook, *Human Relations in Interracial Housing: A Study of the Contact Hypothesis* (Minneapolis: University of Minnesota Press, 1955).

31. See Robert C. Weaver, *The Negro Ghetto* (New York: Harcourt, Brace, 1948); E. F. Schietinger, "Racial Succession and Value of Small Residential Properties," *American Sociological Review* 16 (Dec. 1951): 832–35; Charles Abrams, *Forbidden Neighbors: A Study of Prejudice in Housing* (New York: Harper and Brothers, 1955); Donald A. Cowgill, "Trends in Residential Segregation of Non-whites in American Cities, 1940–1950," *American Sociological Review* 21 (Feb. 1956): 43–47; Otis Dudley Duncan and Beverly Duncan, *The Negro Population of Chicago* (Chicago: University of Chicago Press, 1956).

32. "The Effects of Segregation and the Consequences of Desegregation: A Social Science Statement." Appendix to Appellant's Brief, Supreme Court of the United States, October Term, 1952; reprinted in *Minnesota Law Review* 37, no. 6 (1953): 427–39; also as Appendix 3, Kenneth B. Clark, *Prejudice and Your Child* (Boston: Beacon Press, 1963), 166–84.

The survey referred to was reported in Max Deutscher and Isidor Chein, "The Psychological Effects of Enforced Segregation: An Appraisal of the Evidence," *Journal of Psychology* 16 (Oct. 1948): 259–87.

33. The full text of the report appeared as Kenneth B. Clark, "Desegregation: An Appraisal of the Evidence," *Journal of Social Issues* 9, no. 4 (1953): 2–77.

34. Ibid., 32, 43, 53. Emphasis in original.

35. Ibid., 54.

36. Kenneth B. Clark, "The Desegregation Cases: Criticism of the Social Scientist's Role," *Villanova Law Review* 5 (Winter 1959–60): 224–40.

37. Morroe Berger, "Desegregation, Law, and Social Science," *Commentary* 23 (May 1957): 476. Berger had a particular interest in race and law; see his *Equality by Statute: The Revolution in Civil Rights* (New York: Columbia University Press, 1952) and *Racial Equality and the Law: The Role of Law in the Reduction of Discrimination in the United States* (Paris: UNESCO, 1955).

38. Herbert Garfinkel, "Social Science Evidence and the School Segregation Cases," *Journal of Politics* 21 (Feb. 1959): 57–58.

39. Melvin M. Tumin, ed., *Race and Intelligence* (New York: Anti-Defamation League, 1963); Thomas F. Pettigrew, *A Profile of the Negro* (New York: D. Van Nostrand, 1964). For a full discussion of the opposition of some psychologists and other social scientists to the 1954 decision, see I. A. Newby, *Challenge to the Court: Social Scientists and the Defense of Segregation, 1954–1966* (Baton Rouge: Louisiana State University Press, 1967). A revised edition in 1969 contained critical responses by eight of those whom Newby had included under the term, "scientific racism."

For an anthropological response to the issue, see Juan Comas, " 'Scientific' Racism Again?" *Current Anthropology* 2, no. 4 (Oct. 1961): 303–40; see also "More on 'Scientific' Racism," *Current Anthropology* 3, no. 3 (June 1962): 284–305.

40. The use of social scientific evidence in the courts has remained an issue of contention and concern. For a more recent review, see Betsy Levin and Willis D. Hawley, *The Courts, Social Science, and School Desegregation* (New Brunswick, N.J.: Transaction Books, 1975).

41. Lewis M. Killian, "The Social Scientist's Role in the Preparation of the Florida Desegregation Brief," *Social Problems* 3 (Apr. 1956): 211–14.

42. Herbert Blumer, "Social Science and the Desegregation Process," *Annals of the American Academy of Political and Social Science* 304 (Mar. 1956): 141–42. See also Ira De A. Reid, "Desegregation and Social Change at the Community Level," *Social Problems* 2 (Apr. 1956): 198–200.

43. Guy B. Johnson, "A Sociologist Looks at Racial Desegregation in the South," *Social Forces* 33 (Oct. 1954): 1–10. For a review of these and other predictions, see A. Lee Coleman, "Social Scientists' Predictions about Desegregation, 1950–1955," *Social Forces* 38 (Mar. 1960): 258–62.

44. Robin M. Williams, Jr., Burton R. Fisher, and Irving L. Janis, "Educational Desegregation as a Context for Basic Social Science Research," *American Sociological Review* 21 (Oct. 1956): 580.

45. Ibid., 578–79, 583 (emphasis in original).

46. Ibid., 582.

47. Thomas F. Pettigrew, "Social Psychology and Desegregation Research," *American Psychologist* 16 (Mar. 1961): 106.

48. Kenneth B. Clark, "Desegregation: The Role of the Social Sciences," *Teacher's College Record* 62 (Oct. 1960): 14. This paper was an expanded version of Clark's presidential address to the Society for the Psychological Study of Social Issues.

49. For evidence of a decline in sociologists' interest in race relations from 1955 to 1959, see Richard Simpson, "Expanding and Declining Fields in American Sociology," *American Sociological Review* 26 (Aug. 1961): 458–66. For a summary of research in race relations undertaken in that same period, see Melvin Tumin, *Segregation and Desegregation: A Digest of Research* (New York: Anti-Defamation League, 1960).

50. Melvin M. Tumin, *Desegregation: Readiness and Resistance* (Princeton: Princeton University Press, 1958).

51. Ibid., 94, 203–4.

52. Leonard Broom, review, *American Sociological Review* 24 (Aug. 1959): 590; Tumin, *Desegregation,* 202–3.

53. Robin M. Williams, Jr., "Application of Research to Practice in Intergroup Relations," *American Sociololgical Review* 18 (Feb. 1953): 79–80.

54. Ibid., 79; Deutsch and Collins, *Interracial Housing,* xii. For a complementary discusion by a practitioner, see Oscar Cohen, "The Application of Social Research to Intergroup Relations," *Social Problems* 2 (July 1954): 20–25.

55. George Nesbitt, "What Are the Roles of the Intergroup Relations Worker?" *Intergroup Relations* 1 (1953): 33.

56. Charles Livermore, "The Basic Assumptions in Intergroup Relations," *Intergroup Relations* 1 (1953): 32.

57. *Intergroup Relations* 1 (1953): 30–31. The list that appeared in *Intergroup Relations* was an abbreviated list of assumptions taken from the *Proceedings,* Conference on Research in Race Relations, National Association of Intergroup Relations Officials, University of Chicago, July 26–30, 1952.

58. Livermore, "Basic Assumptions," 32.

59. John P. Dean and Alex Rosen, *A Manual of Intergroup Relations* (Chicago: University of Chicago Press, 1955). The influence of this book can be measured in part by noting that it won the Anisfield-Wolf Award in 1955 in recognition of outstanding influence in the field of race relations, that it went through four printings in the following eight years, and that in 1963 the University of Chicago Press issued a paperback edition.

60. Ibid., 125, 128. The following discussion deals only with the second half of the book, wherein the issue of intergroup relations in the community is examined. The first half of the book is concerned with intergroup relations within organizations. The discussion draws from my more extended comments on *A Manual of Intergroup Relations;* see James B. McKee, "Community Power and Strategies in Race Relations: Some Critical Observations," *Social Problems* 6 (Winter 1959): 195–203.

61. Dean and Rosen, *Manual,* 157–58.

62. Ibid., 124. For Floyd Hunter's model of a community power structure, see his *Community Power Structure: A Study of Decision-Makers* (Chapel Hill: University of North Carolina Press, 1953).

63. Dean and Rosen, *Manual,* 128–29 (emphasis added).

64. Ibid., 113.

65. Frances R. Cousens and John G. Feild, "Some Observations on the Nature and Scope of Intergroup Relations," *Journal of Intergroup Relations* 1 (Sept. 1958): 86; Dean George Epley, "Notes on the Nature, Scope, and Theory of Intergroup Relations," *Journal of Intergroup Relations* 1 (Sept. 1958): 2.

66. Dean and Rosen, *Manual,* 125.

67. Morton B. King, Jr., "The Minority Course," *American Sociological Review* 21 (Feb. 1956): 80, 81–82.

68. Louis Wirth, "Problems and Orientations of Research in Race Relations in the United States," *British Journal of Sociology* 1 (1950): 121, 125.

69. Ibid., 121; Michael Banton, "Sociology and Race Relations," *Race* 1 (Nov. 1959): 3–14.

70. Herbert G. Blumer, "Reflections on Theory of Race Relations," in *Race Relations in World Perspective,* ed. Andrew Lind (Honolulu: University of Hawaii Press, 1955), 13–14. Further references to this work will appear in the text.

9

The Failure of a Perspective

In the 1950s it seems not to have occurred to sociologists that their research and theorizing were not congruent with the world of ongoing race relations. They took it for granted that they were providing a realistic account of the state of race relations and also of the degree and direction of social change. Yet the racial events of the 1960s were soon to demonstrate that they were simply wrong and had probably been so for some time. Race relations in American society as they appeared in the reported events of a society in racial conflict and as they were analyzed in the writings of sociologists became increasingly divergent and incompatible.

If the decade of the 1960s was one of militant black action, of movements of black-directed protest, and of a growing black consciousness and a capacity to act, such a seemingly sudden development had not sprung into being unannounced. From the outset of his academic career, Robert Park had observed a growing race consciousness among southern blacks, but influential as his work was in establishing the sociology of race relations, he was never able to convince his students and colleagues that such a consciousness was steadily growing among black people. Neither Marcus Garvey's Back to Africa Movement of the 1920s nor the March on Washington Movement of the 1940s appeared to sociologists as evidence of a black potential for rebellion.

After World War II, that readiness of blacks for independent action was demonstrated first in 1955–56 in the boycott of public buses in Montgomery, Alabama, in the very heart of the still segregated South. Their success in that boycott proved to blacks that they were capable of carrying out a successful struggle against entrenched segregation and that they possessed a capacity to organize and direct a unified campaign without relying on white support and leadership. The action that followed in time, beginning with the lunch counter sit-in in Greensboro, North Carolina, on February 1, 1960, set in motion a vast black rebellion against the institutionalized segregation of the South.

But, however powerful the effects of the black rebellion, the landscape of race relations was also radically altered by a transformation of the law in the late 1940s and early 1950s. This was the consequence of an earlier black struggle, led by the NAACP, to get the federal judiciary to enforce the Fourteenth Amendment to the Constitution. A series of Supreme Court decisions, culminating in the school desegregation decision in 1954, began the process of dismantling the body of law and precedent that had legally sustained racial segregation in the United States since the Supreme Court decision of 1896. After that struggle was won, Congress began the process of building the concept of equal rights under the law into legislation. A civil rights bill was adopted in 1957, and subsequent acts were passed in 1960, 1964, 1965, and 1968.

After a century of a glacial pace of racial change, the social landscape of race relations had been irrevocably altered within a single decade. Never again would the pursuit of civil rights be carried out in a manner chosen by white people alone, nor would blacks be excluded from leadership positions in the struggle for racial equality. And never again would the federal government be the major force it had so long been in sustaining the historic structure of segregation and discrimination.

Racial inequality now had no legal basis, and the federal government was now legally committed, whatever the attitudes of its elected officials, to desegregation. The struggle for racial equality still had a long way to go, but now it had moved into a new, radically changed context. Not having anticipated such a change, sociologists were not immediately prepared to come to terms with it. Most of them still reasoned within the assumptions of their perspective; only a few had begun to recognize its failings. Nonetheless, by the mid-1960s the basic assumptions of the perspective seemed increasingly less applicable to a new racial reality; it was the beginning of a slow dissolution.

The Failure of a Perspective

The thesis of this study has been that the inability of the sociologists of race relations to anticipate the coming of a black rebellion cannot be explained away as a failure of their empirical research. Instead, it was a failure of the perspective within which research problems were defined. The fault lay with the assumptions and themes, the values and biases, in short, the worldview that gave direction and plan to research. The eight preceding chapters of this study have offered a detailed textual analysis of the development of the sociology of race relations produced by that perspective, and of its limitations and weaknesses, which did not become evident to sociologists until the 1960s.

Yet the sociologists of race relations would prove to be slow to recognize that the perspective on which the sociology of race relations had been constructed was now in a state of dissolution. Sociologists have never explicitly rejected the perspective, acknowledged its demise, or given strong voice to the need for a new and more adequate one. (Robert Blauner was an exception to this, but his call for a new theoretical perspective was in terms too radical for most of the politically moderate sociologists of race relations.)[1]

Four dimensions of the perspective merit some comment here. Two of them—the belief in modernization as the inevitable process for assuring assimilation and the image of the black American as culturally inferior—were part of the perspective from its beginning in the 1920s. The other two—the claim about a less prejudiced middle class and the attempt to make the sociology of race relations an applied study—did not become aspects of the perspective until after World War II.

Modernization and Assimilation

One fundamental assumption of the perspective that commanded wide consent among sociologists was the assured decline and eventual disappearance of separate ethnic peoples and their assimilation into a homogeneous modern society. It was one of the bolder components of the perspective that blacks, too, would eventually be assimilated, though that outcome was viewed as occuring in a more distant future. From the 1920s on, sociologists clung tenaciously to the idea that all that was not modern was incompatible with the functional requisites of modern society. The measurable decline of the separate ethnicities that originated from European immigration had provided the empirical evidence for their confidence that cultural assimilation was an inevitable consequence of the modernization of society. As late as 1964 that position was still dominant, as evident in Milton Gordon's statement in his widely acclaimed book, *Assimilation in American Life,* in which he not only restated the presumed necessity of social assimilation, but also incorporated that process into a functional theory of society:

The operation of modern urbanized industrial society is predicated upon the assurance of an easy interchangeability and mobility of individuals according to occupational specialization and needs. The fulfillment of occupational roles, the assignment of living space, the selection of political leaders, and the effective functioning of the educational process, among others, demand that universalistic criteria of competence and training, rather than considerations based on racial, religious or nationality background, be utilized. The subversion of that principle by ethnic considerations would appear bound to produce, in the long run, confusion, conflict, and mediocrity.[2]

Yet, one year later Herbert Blumer challenged this most fundamental assumption with the argument that the industrialization of societies with a strong, entrenched racial order did not lead to any racial change: "In such societies, the racial ordering of industrial organization and operations persists without difficulty and without change unless there are powerful outside influences which attack the racial order." Blumer chose the concept of industrialization, not urbanization or modernization, because, he said, it "is usually assigned the central role in the shaping of modern life." The beliefs about it, Blumer argued, "signify that the process of industrialization is the master force at work in modern civilization, fabricating its life and institutions and setting its peculiar mould."[3]

The industrial system, Blumer claimed, was conceptualized as a system marked by several structural requirements: commitment to a rational and secular outlook, contractual relations instead of status relations, impersonal markets, physical and social mobility, and an "inbuilt dynamic condition" that keeps the other characteristics in play. The consequence of these requirements is to undermine the established preindustrial order, set up new social relations for people, and consolidate a new industrial order in which "race vanishes as a factor which structures social relations." Blumer summed up the prevailing belief about the effect of industrialization on race: "The premium placed on rational decisions will relegate racial prejudice and discrimination to the periphery" (220–31).

This mode of thought, Blumer pointed out, has constructed an ideal type of industrialization "as it would be if it could operate freely according to its logical imperatives." But what he called a "sparse and uneven" array of historical evidence provided no confirmation of the claim that industrialization inevitably removes race as a decisive factor in social relations. To the contrary, it is, he insisted, quite rational for the industrial manager to adjust to the prevailing racial system; not to do so "would affront others and disrupt efficient operations." Therefore, "the rational imperative in industrial operations may function to maintain and reinforce the established racial order." In examining the record of the effect of industrialization on race relations in the American South, in South Africa, and in areas under colonial domination, Blumer pointed out that in such areas, "where a superordinate-subordinate racial arrangement was deeply entrenched, industrialization meant essentially a transfer of the established racial scheme to the new industrial setting" (230, 231, 233, 235).

Blumer was not arguing that racial systems do not change. His view was that "racial alignment is shaped in major measure by non-industrial influences, that resulting patterns of racial alignment permeate the industrial structure, and that changes in such patterns are traceable mainly to movements in social and political happenings." Such happenings, Blumer argued, are brought about by forces from outside the industrial system, and often, as in the case of the American South, from outside the region (239, 246).

Blumer recognized that many scholars believed that the conditions he described were true but that "with time, or in the long run, the industrial imperatives would gain ascendency, stripping the racial factor of any importance." But a half century of industrial experience in South Africa and the South of the United States, he noted, "brought no appreciable change in the position of the races in the industrial structure." Furthermore, "we do not know how much time is needed to constitute the 'long run.'" He was not, therefore, convinced by such an assumption: "We must look to outside factors rather than to a maturation of these imperatives for an explanation of the disintegration of the racial mould" (238–39).

But if outside factors, particularly politics, rather than industrialization, produce racial change, "Whence comes political change?" That was the question asked by Guy Hunter, the editor of the volume in which Blumer's essay appeared. While Hunter called Blumer's argument "incontrovertible," he answered his own question by asking another: "Is it not industrialization itself, or rather the philosophy which leads to it, which gives to politics their modern direction?" For an answer, Hunter reasserted the social scientists' faith in the process of modernization, referring to "the relationship between the deflection of human interest from theology to science in the seventeenth century, the rise of capitalism, the creation of a middle class, the growth of democracy and the appearance of industrialization." If industrialization, Hunter argued, is but one manifestation of a larger change, it "is not an originating cause. But if the industrialist only follows in the orbit of political change, he is today following it in a trajectory compatible with the natural gravity of the industrializing process, and perhaps accelerated by it."[4]

Hunter's response can be seen as a reluctance to surrender the long-standing belief in the capacity of modernization to rid society of racial inequality by seizing upon the one opening that Blumer gave him, namely, politics as the source of racial change. That a politics committed to racial change was solely an outcome of modernization, however, was here only a suggestion, and it lacked the detailed case that Blumer had constructed against the claim for industrialization. However one views Hunter's comment, Blumer demonstrated how intractable an entrenched racial order could be; even when the traditional social structure in which it had been embedded had been thoroughly dissolved, it could emerge as the racial order for the new industrial system.

A decade later Edna Bonacich's concept of the split-labor market, a term she used to designate a difference in the price of labor between two racial groups holding constant their efficiency and productivity, showed how capitalist labor markets acted, not to end racial differentials in employment, but to use black labor as a way to lower wage costs.[5] Though Bonacich shifted the argument from industrialization to capitalism and held a more radical perspective than Blumer did, her work nonetheless lent support to Blumer's case that industrialization does not inevitably weaken an existing structure of racial discrimination.

In the 1960s it was still possible to believe that such components of modernization as science, rationality, secularism, capitalism, and industrialism would assuredly bring about a progressively more enlightened society in which the inequities of race would disappear. But for at least two decades now, the intellectual currents that have flourished in the Western world have disabused most scholars of any such illusion. For sociologists, race relations become a more complex, more difficult matter, forcing them to abandon their once confident assumption of a steady trendline of racial progress.

The Sociological Image of Black Americans

This study has argued that the most fundamental assumption of the sociology of race relations has been the image of black people that sociologists maintained from the time they gave up the belief in racial inferiority. There were two components to this assumption. One was the early judgment that blacks, if not biologically inferior, were a culturally inferior people not yet fit to participate in modern society. The other was that blacks, unlike European immigrants, possessed no inherited culture of their own and therefore shared language and culture with the white population; they were, therefore, not an ethnic group.

In the 1920s the judgment of cultural inferiority was based upon an assessment of an isolated rural black population in the South, viewed as having developed but little beyond its African origins and barely able to function within American culture. By mid-century, when blacks had settled in the urban North, their cultural inferiority was perceived to be a distorted, pathological version of American culture, marked only by the peculiarities of their reactions to pressures from the dominant whites.

After World War II, sociologists acknowledged the existence of an acculturated black middle class, but the larger body of blacks were deemed still to be lower class. In the description of the life-style of such people, particularly that of family life, work, and moral standards, their cultural inferiority was always made evident, even if such an overt term was not used. Milton Gordon, for example, said it more delicately when he observed that "lower-class Negro life . . . is still at a considerable distance from the American cultural norm." This failure to be culturally normative, to be sure, was explained as a consequence of prejudice and discrimination: "The subculture of the Negro lower class testifies eloquently to the power of prejudice and discrimination to retard the acculturation process both in external behavior and internal values."[6]

The second component began with the assumption that blacks had lost all vestiges of their original African cultures and therefore, unlike the European immigrants, had no inherited cultural tradition and thus no ethnic status; their only culture was American. To make such a claim, however, did not easily fit with the previous claim that blacks were not yet a modern people, but sociologists never seemed to recognize the conceptual discrepancy. Nonetheless, sociology's fundamental distinction between race and ethnicity had been erected upon this historical conception of the black experience.

From the 1930s until 1970, therefore, sociologists were blind to evidence about a black culture and black identity and assumed that blacks had no other objective than to be integrated into American society and to disappear as a racially distinct population. In his 1962 presidential address to the American Sociological Assocation, Everett Hughes said that "the Negro Americans want to disappear as a defined group; they want to become invisible as a group, while each of them becomes fully visible as a human being."[7]

While Hughes's address was widely read and appreciated, a paper in that same year with an opposing theme was largely ignored. L. Singer pointed out that sociologists treated blacks as a category (a social aggregate without shared values or social relations), not as a social entity (possessing the attributes of a group or community). He then made the case that American blacks since slavery had been, and still were, undergoing a process he called "ethnogenesis," that is, the building of an ethnic group that possessed both a culture and an internal social structure. But in 1962 there were few sociologists who were receptive to such a redefining of the sociological conception of blacks in American society. (Singer's paper, furthermore, was not published in one of the mainstream sociological journals and, except for Lewis Killian, went unread and uncited by sociologists).[8]

Despite the ignoring of Singer's paper, however, only a few years later sociologists could not say without fear of contradiction what Hughes had said in 1962. By then blacks were openly asserting a cultural identity distinct from that of white people and also claiming a black culture and a black experience; they were, in short, presenting themselves as a culturally distinct people.

Still, sociologists did not easily accept these new manifestations of black life in the United States. Bennett Berger, for one, in a review of the anthropologist Charles Keil's *Urban Blues,* disputed Keil's impressive case that black Americans had a distinct culture. Instead, Berger thought that what was called black culture was only the black version of lower-class culture, which constituted no basis for developing either consciousness or solidarity.[9]

But in 1970 Robert Blauner made a strong case that black people in the United States had since the time of slavery been engaged in the building of a culture and the construction of a group. The strength of Blauner's paper was in his explication of the sources of that process: slavery, southern culture, the "promises, betrayal, and frustrations" of Emancipation, the consequence of being overwhelmingly lower class, and the "key reality" of white racism.[10] By that time a grudging acceptance of a new conception of black Americans seemed to be slowly seeping into the sociological consciousness.

If sociologists found it difficult to recognize the existence of a black culture, they also were slow to recognize that black people were capable of acting effectively on their own behalf. Throughout the 1960s the black-led civil rights movement provided convincing empirical evidence that blacks had the capacity to act effectively in their own interests and the sense of themselves as a distinct people with their own agenda of change.[11]

Bias and Social Class

Before World War II, a belief in the racial inferiority of blacks seemed to be equally shared throughout the social classes of the white population, and sociologists found little difference in racial prejudice among them. But in the 1950s they assembled a body of data from sample surveys that defined those of lower social status (designated variously as the lower class, the working class, the less educated) as the strongly prejudiced who always resisted, sometimes violently, any effort toward racial equality. In contrast, the image of the educated middle class was that of a less prejudiced class ready to eliminate discrimination. During the same period, the social psychological work on the authoritarian personality only reinforced that invidious class distinction.

However dubious the argument, it became a staple of liberal as well as sociological thought; only recently has it been subject to rigorous testing and serious challenge, as, for example, in work by Mary Jackman. The best summary and analysis of the available data is by Howard Schuman, Charlotte Steeh, and Lawrence Bobo, who found that on matters of principle, such as the right of blacks to live where they choose, more of the educated than the less educated will sustain that right. But when the question is one of implementation, the difference between the more and less educated decreases or even disappears. On social distance questions, the educated more readily than others accept integration when only a few blacks are involved, but difference by education declines when the proportion of blacks increases, and it disappears when whites are no longer the majority.[12]

This self-flattering belief in the moral superiority of the educated middle class must also be set aside. The differences in racial prejudice among the white social classes provide no basis for a workable strategy of change. Its demise only further dissolves the perspective.

Race Relations as Social Intervention

In the 1950s, for the first time, race relations appeared on the liberal agenda for social change, and sociologists were quick to accept the premise that now was a time for effective social intervention into the discriminatory practices of American society. They undertook research intended to guide the practical efforts of the new profession of intergroup relations professionals, and in doing that, whether intentionally or not, they moved the sociology of race relations toward being an applied study. The most important advice they gave the practitioners was to exercise firm authority in making decisions about racial change; the main finding of their research was the hypothesis of "equal status contact," which offered limited possibilities for racial change, given the economic differentials between blacks and whites.

The experiment was short-lived. It was a product of the particular environment of the 1950s, and it soon disappeared in the radically changed milieu of the next decade. Its value was in demonstrating how difficult it was for scholars and practitioners in an area as fraught with conflict as race relations to find a basis for effective partnership. With no previous experience in social intervention, sociologists were unprepared for the problems they were soon to encounter, particularly those of political constraints on the practitioners, of how to deal with social power in the community, and of their inability to provide practitioners with a theory applicable in community contexts. The advice they did provide was itself ideologically constrained and politically limited by their conception that progress would only come by a strategy that gave to the civic elite a monopoly of leadership in programs of social intervention. With the onset of the 1960s, and in the face of a powerful current of a black-led movement of racial change, the effort to create an applied sociology of race relations seemed to fade quietly away without acknowledgment or proclamation.

In fact, little of the sociological research on behalf of social intervention that sociologists carried out in the years after World War II survived the altered circumstances of the 1960s. That included the work undertaken for reducing job discrimination, where sociologists believed that the firm exercise of managerial authority offered the most promising means for significant racial change. Sociologists shared with liberals the belief that a major progressive step in race relations had been taken when various states and municipalities passed antidiscrimination legislation in the 1940s and 1950s. The process had been one that sociologists preferred: the legitimation of antidiscrimination by legal statute, and the authority given to a professional agency for enforcing the law. But the critical assessment made by various social scientists in the late 1960s and early 1970s made it clear that so little had been accomplished that the very process had to be suspect.

The first study to make that amply clear was Leon Mayhew's critical assessment of the Massachusetts Commission against Discrimination in 1968. A similar and equally critical study of the New York City Commission on Human Rights by Gerald Benjamin found a large agency with considerable legal powers, but few of its functions had been well performed, and it had not "substantially affected the patterns of discriminatory conduct in the city at large." Calling the agency more of a liability that an asset, Benjamin recommended that it be abolished.[13]

These two studies were each about a single agency, but Frances
Cousens in 1969 published an equally critical assessment of state and
municipal civil rights commissions. Her "sobering findings," she noted,
showed little improvement since 1945 and a dim prognosis for improvement in employment opportunities for minorities "for some time
to come." Civil rights commissions, she noted, "have been largely
ineffectual in aiding significant numbers of nonwhites to move into
nontraditional and better paying jobs."[14]

These three critical studies were published from 1968 to 1974, yet
they were assessments of a mode of reform that had been instituted
in the 1940s. The failure of the public agencies to reduce racial discrimination to any significant degree had already been even more
strongly proclaimed by the rise of the black rebellion, which offered
another mode of change in race relations. But the failure of antidiscrimination legislation to alter the pattern of discrimination also
brought about an effort to find new ways to attain equality of opportunity. An interpretation of Title 7 of the Civil Rights Act of 1964
brought into being the concept of affirmative action. As it became the
new liberal weapon to achieve equality of opportunity, it also became
enormously controversial, splitting the historic coalition of blacks and
Jews in the civil rights movement and failing to gain the support of
the majority of white Americans.

Race and Politics

In the years before World War II, sociologists did not include a
concern for politics in their perspective on race, convinced that blacks
were outside the political system. What little political study was done
was left to journalists and political scientists, but the latter also undertook very few studies of race. Even in the 1950s, sociologists gave
little thought to the politics of race, despite a national political effort
to pass fair employment legislation, the emergence of community relations agencies in larger northern cities, and significant judicial decisions by the federal courts. An exception to this neglect of politics
was Wilson Record's two studies of the attempt over several decades
of the American Communist Party to exploit the issue of race.[15]

But a far more significant neglect of the political has been the failure
of sociologists to recognize the growth since 1960 of the professionalization and bureaucratization of race relations. The failure of the
official intergroup agencies at the municipal and state levels to be effective did not prevent their further growth, nor that of professionally
staffed positions at the federal level, and, more recently, in the universities. Only Lewis Killian seems to have noted this phenomenon,

observing that "one of the greatest changes in race relations in the United States since 1960 has been the development of a network of professionals in the federal government with a vision of eliminating racial discrimination and producing equality of both opportunity and results." Borrowing a British phrase, he called this "the race relations industry."[16]

Killian undertook an assessment of the fact that a body of committed professionals had succeeded a once vital and challenging civil rights movement, the most militant phases of which had vanished. They were, Killian asserted, "engaged in one of the most extensive programs of social engineering in the nation's history."[17] Their positions in a civil rights bureaucracy gave them the power to promote selective programs of change, particularly those promoting educational desegregation and affirmative action, changes mostly beneficial to a growing black middle class, but of little value to the masses of black people trapped in urban ghettos.

The emergence of a "race relations industry," then, is, once again, the construction of a process of constrained and limited social change controlled by professionals, a "rational" process that sociologists, who see themselves as professionals, view as appropriate and preferred, leaving them insensitive to the shortcomings inherent in both professionalization and bureaucratization. As Killian noted, "The concept of the 'race relations industry' suggests, therefore, that to understand what is going on in race relations it is necessary to consider not only theory in race relations but also organizational theory and the history of bureaucracy." Contemplating the possibility that race relations might become an industry, he concluded, "sensitizes us to the fact . . . that the organizational structures within which even 'good works' are done may be constraining."[18]

But if sociologists have otherwise neglected the study of politics and race, so, apparently, did the political scientists. It was not until the middle of the 1960s that they gave the matter any significant attention.[19] Sociologists still have not.

Here then is a series of issues—the neglect of the politics of race relations, the failure of social intervention, the power of assumptions about modernization and assimilation that simply proved wrong, a distorted image of black Americans, and the myth of an unbiased middle class—that makes painfully evident the inability of sociologists to anticipate how American race relations would develop after World War II. But any critique of that inability must recognize two other issues that are generalizable beyond the issue of race relations: the constraining power of social context and the place of collegial consensus in the shaping of sociology.

Context and Consensus

In recent decades, with the decline of positivism and the increasing recognition of the social character of science, sociologists have been able to acknowledge the restrictions imposed by social context. No matter how creative, sociologists do not escape either the web of prevailing assumptions that people at a given time and place so easily take for granted or the seeming natural fixity of the particular social arrangements that then prevail. The power of social context to limit social thought testifies to the inability of scholars to see beyond the existing reality in which they are encapsulated, indeed, even to see possibilities in the present that are only recognized after they develop.

The record provided by the sociologists of race relations in the United States provides powerful testimony to the capacity of the social context to provide enduring assumptions that limit and constrain sociological thought. For longer than they should have, sociologists took for granted that racial progress was a steady trendline into an inevitable future of racial integration, that it could be accomplished without conflict, that race relations would remain under white control because black people lacked the capacity to act effectively on their own behalf, and that ethnicity was an element rapidly and permanently disappearing from American society.

No less a factor than social context was the interpretive consensus developed within the community of sociological scholars who studied race relations. Those who review the development of sociological theory seem most often to offer a series of accounts of the works of several theorists. In textbooks this comes out as a chapter devoted to each individual theorist deemed to be a theoretical star. While one cannot fail to acknowledge the work of the more creative minds of the discipline, it would be a mistake to assume that the final product is due entirely to their seminal contributions. At least, if the sociology of race relations is taken as a case in point, the community of scholars who read and interpret the works of the leading theorists exercise significant judgment in the shaping of an area of sociological study.

The name of Robert Park is usually cited as the sociologist most responsible for shaping the study of race relations. But as this work has pointed out a number of times, Park, while clearly entitled to be thought of as the founder of the sociology of race relations, did not by himself shape this area of study. If much of what he offered became incorporated into a new study of race relations, his own basic conception of the new emerging study of race did not. His thesis of a race-conscious black population becoming a people with a culture of their own, comparable to ethnic minorities in Eastern Europe, of their consequent increasing race consciousness, and of the significance of conflict in race relations, was never included in what became the sociology of race relations.

Park's contribution was filtered through the cultural lens of a group of like-minded sociologists who learned from and appreciated him, but who did not fully share his ideas and did not accept that with which they disagreed. By selectively choosing from Park what they found intellectually agreeable and discarding what they did not, and then building into the new study of race relations their own assumptions about race, about black people, and about racial change, they developed a sociological interpretation that was a consensual product of their time and place. It was this interpretive consensus, not the original thought of Robert Park, that became the sociology of race relations. Though Park contributed significantly to its shaping, it was only partly his own construction; its major assumptions, in fact, were the antithesis of Park's own ideas about race relations.

When sociologists have sought to review the development of sociology, they seem not to have considered the place of the sociological group in sifting through and winnowing out from the cohesive body of thought offered them by a major thinker. Instead, they seem always to have assumed that the work of this more creative mind was incorporated in its totality into the mainstream of sociological thought. In Park's case, at least, that did not happen in developing the sociology of race relations. If the treatment of Park is a more generalizable case, then the reconstruction of the development of sociology requires something more comprehensive than a review of the work of its best minds. It requires the kind of reflexive analysis offered by the sociology of knowledge.

Sociological Continuity and Change

During the 1960s sociologists continued to do much of the same research they had been doing for decades: on prejudice, on the assessment of differentials in white and black income, education, and the like, and on persistent discrimination. But they had also to observe and report on powerful forces making for change: black rebellion, a powerful civil rights movement, the legal and judicial attack on discrimination, and widespread racial disorder. They did so in the face of criticisms of their theoretical perspective both within and without sociology and with a growing recognition that much of what had been previously assumed had now to be abandoned.

Before the 1960s were over, however, a few efforts were underway to give new shape and direction to the sociological study of race relations. One such effort came in books by Pierre van den Berghe and Richard Schermerhorn, who sought to convince sociologists that in order to escape an American parochialism they needed to undertake a comparative study of race and ethnic relations. But there were also several efforts to make up for the lack of a theory of race relations. The best-known effort was by Hubert Blalock, whose *Toward a Theory of Minority-Group Relations* produced a list of ninety-seven "theoretical propositions," which he acknowledged to be in the manner of Robin Williams twenty years before. Several years later, Graham Kinloch, in similar fashion, offered an "axiomatic deductive theory of race relations" that culminated in 253 propositions and theorems. Both books were directed toward the production of a quantitative and highly abstract theory of race relations. Between these two book-length efforts was a paper by Ernest A. T. Barth and Donald L. Noel that reviewed four conceptual frameworks as a step toward a general theory.[20]

Yet, in truth, neither the effort to make the American sociology of race relations a comparative study nor to formulate an abstract theory succeeded. There has, in fact, been no significant trend to alter the American sociological emphasis on more concretely empirical work oriented almost exclusively to the American system of race relations. In that particular sense, the sociology of race relations has remained the same over the last seventy years.

Throughout the 1960s and 1970s, sociologists continued to do research in race relations, much of which was a replication of work done in the past. A survey by Milton Barron found research on the demographics of race relations, on status dynamics, on prejudice and discrimination, on black and white stratification, on educational inequality and IQ differentials, and on assimilation and intermarriage. But there was also research on policies and programs of intervention: early childhood intervention, integration of schools and neighborhoods, busing, affirmative action and preferential quotas. By 1968 sociologists could not avoid observing the shift from integration to ethnic nationalism, as well as the emergence of a "New Pluralism," a movement of ethnic consciousness among a diverse set of racial and ethnic groups. Among blacks, it meant "developing a greater sense of unity and a positive black self-image." But it also meant that a "noticeable development of more hostile attitudes among black youth, a more critical attitude toward the institutions and values of white America, and a greater desire to associate only with blacks became evident."[21]

Nonetheless, there were developments in the broader literature on race relations to which at least some sociologists paid attention, particularly those engaged in teaching. There was, in the first instance, the discovery of a black protest literature that had existed for over a century, but which sociologists had largely ignored. But there was also an interest in the writings of black sociologists of the preceding generation or two, such as E. Franklin Frazier, Charles Johnson, and W. E. B. Du Bois, as well some less well known to a later generation.[22]

In addition, there was also the emergence of a radical social scientific literature on race relations, as well as a new literature by black social scientists often more critical than white sociologists of the prevailing reality and the pace of change. Between these two there was some overlap. The significance of this is that for at least a decade, from the mid-1960s to the mid-1970s, this more critical literature often provided the more widely read messages on race relations among undergraduate students in sociology classes.[23]

Optimists and Pessimists

In the 1960s, when sociolgists assessed the gains in race relations since World War II, many of them thought they could see the end of racial inequality in the near future. In 1962, in the twentieth anniversary edition of Gunnar Myrdal's *An American Dilemma*, Arnold Rose noted that the changes in race relations during the preceding twenty years "appeared as one of the most rapid in the history of human relations." Though there was still prejudice and discrimination in the land, Rose predicted that "change has been so rapid, and caste and racism so debilitated, that I venture to predict the end of all formal segregation and discrimination within a decade, and the decline of informal discrimination so that it would be a mere shadow in two decades." Though that would not mean equality between the races in that time, "the dynamic social forces creating inequality will, I predict, be practically eliminated in three decades."[24]

Three years later, another leading sociologist of race relations, J. Milton Yinger, was as optimistic as Arnold Rose about the future. Yinger thought it "highly probable that further extensive desegregation will take place" and that "within the United States race lines are fading." Though "racial disprivilege will outlive the twentieth century, though in less and less extensive ways," he predicted, "if the United States takes as many steps toward full integration in the next twenty-five years as she has in the preceding twenty-five—and this seems likely—the country will have accomplished a major transformation."[25]

Rose and Yinger were not unique in believing that the steady progress in race relations they had observed over the previous two decades would continue to a logical completion. Rather, these two distinguished students of race relations were here voicing the confidence of most sociologists in a steady trendline of racial progress into the future, a confidence that had begun after World War II and had been strongly reinforced by the developments of the decade of the 1950s. As the 1960s began, they possessed an assured sense that now the sociologist could predict the relatively early demise of significant racial inequality in the United States.

Yet, even then, there were sociologists with more pessimistic views of the future. Perhaps the first to offer a pessimistic forecast was Lewis Killian, one of American sociology's more astute observers of race relations, and Charles Grigg in 1964. In their *Racial Crisis in America,* they argued that what was underway was a significant and permanent racial change in the United States: "a new era of race relations" had come into being by the black challenge to segregation. But, they also noted, "this does not mean that in the new era race relations are going to be more harmonious, that the Negro's lot will soon become better, or even that segregation will disappear."[26]

Over the next decade, Killian followed closely the black struggle for equality, and the two editions of his study of the "impossible revolution" made gloomy forecasts. He could see no easy way out of the nation's racial dilemma and feared a backlash by white Americans unwilling to pay the price for racial equality. For Killian, the American dilemma was now one of increasing black demands for racial equality in the face of white refusal: "Neither politicians, social scientists, nor white voters beleaguered by their own growing problems have the answer as to what to do, and blacks indicated clearly that they will not accept any solution that they do not have a significant part in shaping."[27]

Throughout the 1960s and 1970s, sociologists and other social scientists presented evidence in support of both optimistic and pessimistic predictions of the future of race relations. Reports of increased gains for blacks in income and education throughout the 1960s led many social scientists and others to claim that considerable progress was being made in reducing the income disparity between whites and blacks. During the 1970s a number of studies by economists and sociologists continued to support that claim.[28]

But other sociologists offered a note of sober reassessment, arguing that, notwithstanding real gains, the differences between whites and blacks as measured by income, occupation, and education were not changing at a rate to ensure that racial equality would be attained in the near future. What may have been true for more educated blacks was not necessarily the case for the less educated. In 1969 Leonard Broom and Norval Glenn pointed out that the occupational gap between blacks and whites "obviously is still very wide and it is closing so slowly that it will not disappear within the next century unless the rate of Negro gains sharply accelerates."[29]

In another paper in the same book, Glenn undertook a careful assessment of the changes, pointing out that blacks made an "unprecedented improvement in their social and economic conditions" during the 1940s, for the first time closing "substantially and rapidly" the gap between blacks and whites in occupation and income. The 1950s saw continued but less dramatic gains. The gains of the 1960s, in turn, were "in many respects" greater than in the 1950s. But overall, he warned, these trends have not all been favorable to black Americans. In summary, he noted that there had been a "moderate acceleration" in reducing some dimensions of racial inequality, but a slowing down or cessation in others. While black Americans had improved substantially in an absolute sense, they had in several respects not improved relative to whites, who had also gained considerably in a period of economic expansion.[30]

In the 1970s there were similar sober assessments. For example, in a paper based on a critique of the methods used to assess black gains in income, Wayne Villemez and Alan Rowe made the case that most assessments had in fact exaggerated the gains blacks had made. They concluded that their findings "indicate that the magnitude of black economic gains in the decade of the 1960s has been slight. To be sure, gains have been made in some areas, but they are neither dramatic nor compelling."[31]

Perhaps the most severe criticism of the optimists was offered by Sidney Wilhelm, who argued that the claims of progress made by social scientists were a delusion. The black condition was worsening, not improving, Wilhelm argued, whether measured by housing, income, or education. His larger argument was that blacks were being rendered economically irrelevant in a technologically changing society, and this permitted whites to separate out the economically unneeded black labor and reduce the black urban ghetto to the equivalent of an Indian reservation.[32]

Even the otherwise optimistic Reynolds Farley, who saw a continuation of gains made in the prosperous 1960s sustained in the 1970s, particularly in education and occupation, nonetheless noted that the income gap had remained constant, due, he believed, to the increase of female-headed families among blacks. And black men, he acknowledged, suffered from a lack of employment opportunities, resulting in high rates of unemployment and nonparticipation in the labor force. His final assessment was that, while blacks had not, even during a recession, lost prior gains, "reductions in inequality are small when compared to the remaining racial differences on many indicators. A continuation of the trends of the 1960s and 1970s offers no hope that racial differences will be eliminated soon."[33]

Some of the differences in the arguments between those who optimistically saw considerable progress and those who saw much less can be attributed to their angle of vision. The optimists focused on a rapidly growing black middle class and the fact that the college-educated black found both job opportunities and relative salary equality to a degree never known before. The pessimists, in turn, offered data that made it clear that most of the black population did not share in these gains. Indeed, as far back as 1965 (in his controversial study on the black family for the U.S. Department of Labor), Daniel Moynihan noted "that the Negro community is, in fact, dividing between a stable middle class group that is steadily growing stronger and more successful and an increasingly disorganized and disadvantaged lower class group." The recognition of that difference grew during the 1970s and became expressed in the later disputed concept of the underclass. In noted and widely read books, both the sociologist William J. Wilson and the journalist Ken Auletta sketched out basic details about the conjunction of class and race, which was to become one significant way in which race was to be discussed in the United States.[34]

Such a sober reassessing of the prospects for racial equality took from even the more optimistic sociologists their once sure sense that progress since the 1940s in the reduction of discrimination made the attainment of racial equality a likely possibility in the near future. Race, it now seemed, was a far more intractable problem than the generation after World War II had realized. The loss of a confident optimism about the future of race relations was only further evidence that a once dominant perspective was in dissolution.

In 1901 W. E. B. Du Bois greeted a new century by proclaiming that "the problem of the Twentieth Century is the problem of the color-line." As the American nation readies itself for still another new century, indeed, a new millenium, it remains trapped within a still unresolved race problem. If the once secure color line has been often crossed in the last half century, and if it no longer clearly demarcates the proper and expected "place" of white and black, the fact remains that it has not yet been washed out of American life. Furthermore, a rising tide of public conflict over policies on civil rights challenges the legitimacy of the particular remedies put in place in the 1960s and also makes race relations a matter of severe public acrimony.

At such a time of public need, sociologists have little of value to offer a beleaguered public and a sorely beset civic leadership beyond the always useful measurement of attitudes and the assessment of the slow pace of racial progress. A sociology of race relations constructed decades earlier under far different circumstances can provide no adequate understanding of what possibilities there are for racial progress at present and in the foreseeable future. It is time to undertake the reconstruction of the sociology of race relations.

Notes

1. Robert Blauner, *Racial Oppression in America* (New York: Harper and Row, 1972); see especially his Introduction, 2–18.

2. Milton M. Gordon, *Assimilation in American Life: The Role of Race, Religion, and National Origins* (New York: Oxford University Press, 1964), 236.

3. Herbert Blumer, "Industrialization and Race Relations," in *Industrialization and Race Relations: A Symposium,* ed. Guy Hunter (London: Oxford University Press, 1965), 220, 246. Further references to this work will appear in the text.

4. Guy Hunter, "Conclusion: Some Historical and Political Factors," in *Industrialization and Race Relations: A Symposium,* ed. Guy Hunter (London: Oxford University Press, 1965), 255–56.

5. Edna Bonacich, "A Theory of Ethnic Antagonism: The Split Labor Market," *American Sociological Review* 37 (1972): 547–59; Edna Bonacich, "Advanced Capitalism and Black/White Race Relations in the United States: A Split Labor Market Interpretation," *American Sociological Review,* 41 (Feb. 1976): 34–51.

6. Gordon, *Assimilation,* 76 n. 26, 173.

7. Everett C. Hughes, "Race Relations and the Sociological Imagination," *American Sociological Review* 28 (Dec. 1963): 883.

8. L. Singer, "Ethnogenesis and Negro-Americans Today," *Social Research* 29 (Winter 1962): 419–32. Killian's citation from Singer's paper is in his *The Impossible Revolution? Black Power and the American Dream* (New York: Random House, 1968), 137–38.

9. Benett M. Berger, "Soul Searching." Review of *Urban Blues,* by Charles Keil, *Trans-action* 4, no. 7 (1967): 54–57.

10. Robert Blauner, "Black Culture: Myth or Reality?" in *Afro-American Anthropology: Contemporary Perspectives,* ed. Norman E. Whitten, Jr., and John F. Szwed (New York: Free Press, 1970), 351–59.

11. Historians went through the same process of revising their history of slavery and subsequent black life, replacing an older, denigrating image of the black person with a new "slave community/culturalist paradigm," as the historian Clarence E. Walker labeled it. Now, however, there is underway an even newer revisionism that claims that this fully warranted rewriting possesses its own distortions: "Although no dominated population is ever completely socialized by its oppressors, the depiction found in slave community/culturalist studies of black life under bondage and afterward exaggerate the domestic autonomy and psychic health of the people being studied." Clarence E. Walker, *Deromanticizing Black History: Critical Essays and Reappraisals* (Knoxville: University of Tennessee Press, 1991), xiii–xiv.

12. Mary R. Jackman, "General and Applied Tolerance: Does Education Increase Commitment to Racial Integration?" *American Journal of Political Science* 22 (May 1978): 302–24; Mary R. Jackman, "Education and Policy Commitment to Racial Integration," *American Journal of Political Science* 25 (May 1981): 256–59; Mary R. Jackman and Michael J. Muha, "Education and Intergroup Attitudes: Moral Enlightenment, Superficial Democratic Commitment, or Ideological Refinement?" *American Sociological Review* 49 (Dec. 1984): 751–69.

Howard Schuman, Charlotte Steeh, and Lawrence Bobo, *Racial Attitudes in America: Trends and Interpretations* (Cambridge: Harvard University Press, 1985). For summary statements of issues about education treated in detail throughout the text, see pp. 137 and 199.

13. Leon Mayhew, *Law and Equal Opportunity: A Study of the Massachusetts Commission against Discrimination* (Cambridge: Harvard University Press, 1968); Gerald Benjamin, *Race Relations and the New York City Commission on Human Rights* (Ithaca: Cornell University Press, 1974), 256, 259.

14. Frances Reissman Cousens, *Public Civil Rights Agencies and Fair Employment: Promise versus Performance* (New York: Frederick A. Praeger, 1969), 113–14, 116.

15. Wilson Record, *The Negro and the Communist Party* (Chapel Hill: University of North Carolina Press, 1951); Wilson Record, *Race and Radicalism: The NAACP and the Communist Party in Conflict* (Ithaca: Cornell University Press, 1964).

16. Lewis M. Killian, " 'The Race Relations Industry' as a Sensitizing Concept," in *Research in Social Problems and Public Policy: A Research Annual,* vol. 1, ed. Michael Lewis (Greenwich, Conn.: JAI Press, 1979), 129.

17. Ibid.

18. Ibid., 135.

19. On the neglect of the politics of race by political scientists, see Donald R. Mathews, "Political Science Research on Race Relations," in *Race and the*

Social Sciences, ed. Irwin Katz and Patricia Gurin (New York: Basic Books, 1969), 113.

20. Pierre van den Berghe, *Race and Racism: A Comparative Perspective* (New York: Wiley, 1967); Richard A. Schermerhorn, *Comparative Ethnic Relations: A Framework for Theory and Research* (New York: Random House, 1970); Hubert M. Blalock, Jr., *Toward a Theory of Minority-group Relations* (New York: Wiley, 1967); Graham C. Kinloch, *The Dynamics of Race Relations: A Sociological Analysis* (New York: McGraw-Hill, 1974); Ernest A. T. Barth and Donald Noel, "Conceptual Frameworks for the Analysis of Race Relations: An Evaluation," *Social Forces* 50 (Mar. 1972): 333–48. See also William J. Wilson, *Power, Racism, and Privilege: Race Relations in Theoretical and Sociohistorical Perspectives* (New York: Free Press, 1973).

21. Milton L. Barron, "Recent Developments in Minority and Race Relations," Supplement, *Annals of the American Academy of Political and Social Science* 420 (July 1975): 128.

22. See, for example, Francis L. Broderick and August Meier, eds., *Negro Protest Thought in the Twentieth Century* (Indianapolis: Bobbs-Merrill, 1965); John H. Bracey, Jr., August Meier, and Elliott Rudwick, eds., *The Black Sociologists: The First Half Century* (Belmont, Calif.: Wadsworth Publishing, 1970); James Blackwell and Morris Janowitz, eds., *Black Sociologists: Historical and Contemporary Perspectives* (Chicago: University of Chicago Press, 1974); Elliott M. Rudwick, *W. E. B. Du Bois: Propagandist of the Negro Protest* (New York: Atheneum, 1969); W. E. B Du Bois, *On Sociology and the Black Community,* ed. Dan S. Green and Edwin D. Driver (Chicago: University of Chicago Press, 1978); E. Franklin Frazier, *On Race Relations: Selected Papers,* ed. G. Franklin Edwards (Chicago: University of Chicago Press, 1968).

23. See, for example, Robert L. Allen, *Black Awakening in Capitalist America: An Analytic History* (New York: Doubleday, 1969; Anchor Books, 1970); Louis L. Knowles and Kenneth Prewitt, eds., *Institutional Racism in America* (Prentice-Hall, 1969); Raymond S. Franklin and Solomon Resnik, *The Political Economy of Racism* (New York: Holt, Rinehart and Winston, 1973); Stokely Carmichael and Charles V. Hamilton, *Black Power: The Politics of Liberation in America* (New York: Vintage Books, 1967); Harold Cruse, *The Crisis of the Negro Intellectual: From its Origins to the Present* (New York: William Morrow, 1967); Joyce A. Ladner, ed., *The Death of White Sociology* (New York: Random House, 1973; Vintage Books, 1973); and Robert Staples, *Introduction to Black Sociology* (New York: McGraw-Hill, 1976).

24. Arnold Rose, Introduction to twentieth anniversary edition, Gunnar Myrdal, with the assistance of Richard Sterner and Arnold Rose, *An American Dilemma: The Negro Problem and Modern Democracy* (New York: Harper and Row, 1962), xliii–xliv.

25. J. Milton Yinger, *A Minority Group in American Society* (New York: McGraw-Hill, 1965), 72.

26. Lewis Killian and Charles Grigg, *Racial Crisis in America: Leadership in Conflict* (Englewood Cliffs, N.J.: Prentice-Hall, 1964), 8.

27. Killian, *Impossible Revolution;* Killian, *The Impossible Revolution, Phase 2: Black Power and the American Dream* (New York: Random House, 1975), 174.

28. See, for example: Daniel J. Moynihan, "The Schism in Black America," *Public Interest,* no. 27 (Spring 1972): 3–23; Leonard Weiss and Jeffrey Williamson, "Black Education, Earnings and Interregional Migration: Some New Evidence," *American Economic Review* 62 (June 1972): 372–83; Richard B. Freeman, "Decline of Labor Market Discrimination and Economic Analysis," *American Economic Review* 63 (May 1973): 280–86; Finis Welch, "Black-White Differences in Returns to Schooling," *American Economic Review* 63 (Dec. 1973): 893–907; Stanley H. Masters, *Black-White Income Differentials: Empirical Studies and Policy Implications* (New York: Academic Press, 1975); Reynolds Farley, "Trends in Racial Inequality: Have the Gains of the 1960s Disappeared in the 1970s?" *American Sociological Review* 42 (Apr. 1977): 189–208; James P. Smith and Finis Welch, "Black/White Male Earnings and Employment: 1960–1970," in *The Distribution of Economic Well-Being,* ed. F. Thomas Juster (Cambridge, Mass.: Ballenger, 1977); David L. Featherman and Robert M. Hauser, *Opportunity and Change* (New York: Academic Press, 1978).

29. Leonard Broom and Norvel D. Glenn, "The Occupation and Income of Black Americans," in *Blacks in the United States,* ed. Norvel D. Glenn and Charles Bonjean (San Francisco: Chandler Publishing, 1969), 27.

30. Norvel D. Glenn, "Changes in the Social and Economic Conditions of Black Americans in the 1960s," in *Blacks in the United States,* 43–44, 54.

31. Wayne J. Villamez and Alan R. Rowe, "Black Economic Gains in the Sixties: A Methodological Critique and Reassessment," *Social Forces* 54 (Sept. 1975): 192. The article has been reprinted in abridged form in *The Sociology of Race Relations: Reflection and Reform,* ed. Thomas F. Pettigrew (New York: Free Press, 1980): 363–75.

32. Sidney M. Wilhelm, *Who Needs the Negro?* (New York: Schenkman, 1970; Anchor Books, 1971). See particularly chapter 5, "Delusions of Progress."

33. Reynolds Farley, "Trends in Racial Inequalities," 208.

34. U.S. Department of Labor, *The Negro Family: The Case for National Action* (Washington, D.C.: Government Printing Office, 1965), 5–6; William J. Wilson, *The Declining Significance of Race* (Chicago: University of Chicago Press, 1978); Ken Auletta, *The Underclass* (New York: Random House, 1982).

Epilogue

The time has come to rethink the sociology of race relations and to undertake its reconstruction. Changes in the social definition and interpretation of race relations in the United States over the last two decades make that task imperative.

A change of vocabulary provides one mark of what has changed. Little is heard anymore of assimilation, and even integration is given little recognition. Instead, the talk (particularly within academia) is of diversity, pluralism, and multiculturalism, and some modes of separatism that once would be called segregation are now encouraged. Furthermore, the application of the concept of ethnicity to what once were defined merely as racial categories denies relevance, if not validity, to the once firm sociological distinction between race and ethnicity.

These significant changes are rooted in the Immigration Act of 1965, which increased almost fourfold the allowable number of immigrants in any year. Its new national quotas sharply reduced immigration from Europe and substantially increased it from Asia and Latin America. Since 1965, therefore, it has been a matter of national policy that there be a new ethnic and racial pluralism in the United States. It is a policy, furthermore, that will steadily increase the proportion of the population that is neither white nor of European descent.

The new ethnic pluralism, however, has been supported by more than a change in immigration law. Government, law, and the judiciary, aided principally by the institutions of education, have shared in the construction of this new order with its conception of group rights and affirmative action, reparations, race as a legal criterion, and the identification of victims of past discrimination.

Race and Ethnicity

In the new pluralism of ethnic groups, black Americans are increasingly identified as African-Americans, particularly within academia. Yet there is a paradox in this assigning of ethnic status to blacks in that the transition from a racial category to an ethnic one has neither decreased race consciousness among blacks nor reduced racial awareness among white people. The sense of race as a fundamental distinction between two categories of people remains a live and powerful force in American life, and thinking in racial terms is still a basic attribute of the national consciousness.

Such a development is a disappointment to those who thought that conferring ethnic status on peoples once designated solely in racial terms would lead to the discarding of the dubious concept of race. For over forty years some in the scientific community have argued that race should be abandoned as a term in the scientific vocabulary. But a nation still divided by a color line was not likely to abandon the concept of race, and what the nation did not do, biologists and social scientists did not do either.

The reminder that race may not be a scientifically viable concept has persisted, however, in both sociology and anthropology. Leonard Lieberman, for one, has pursued the issue since his first paper on the matter in 1968, wherein he reviewed within a historical and sociology of knowledge context the debate over race among physical anthropologists and found distinguished names on both sides of the issue. In other studies, he and collaborating colleagues have shown that anthropologists are no longer in agreement on the validity of what was once a core term for their discipline.[1]

Despite the steady if slow decline of the concept of race among anthropologists and other social scientists, it has shown no such decline in a larger public, even an educated one. If race is losing its status as a scientific concept, then it is as a cultural construction that it finds vitality and force and is no less real to black and white people, here and in the rest of the world. This commonsensical belief that race is real provides the restricted condition that gives legitimacy to the existence of a sociology of race relations. But sociologists need to constantly remind themselves, as well as everyone else, that race is a nineteenth-century construct that has been steadily losing scientific validity.

But while race still persists as a concept, it no longer stands opposed to the concept of ethnicity. And if ethnic pluralism is now taken to be an inescapable fact of American life, so is the value placed upon it. The old assumptions of a declining ethnicity and an increasingly homogeneous population were never simply facts, they were also values; the sociologists of race and ethnic studies spoke for a wider public when they proclaimed and approved the steady decline in ethnicity and, by virtue of assimilation, the increasingly homogeneous character of the American population. But no longer; now the message is that diversity and pluralism are to be valued and ethnicity is to be recognized, respected, and sustained.

At first glance it would seem that we are back to the 1920s and are hearing again the case for cultural pluralism that Horace Kallen and others so vigorously argued, but against which sociologists, among others, advanced the case for assimilation. From that came a grudging acceptance of the right of ethnic groups to maintain their identity but also an expectation of a value consensus within a national framework. But now, it seems to some contemporary observers, there is a new "corporate pluralism" in the making, with far different implications for national policy.[2]

Whatever the policy, it now seems that for some time into the future the American condition is to be one of heightened and institutionalized diversity of culture (and, to some extent, of language) among a pluralism of ethnic groups. Does that mean that the new pluralism will sustain itself indefinitely over the generations or will there again be assimilation? The sociological answer to the question has not been formulated. But it would seem useful to recall L. Paul Metzger's 1971 article and note his conclusions about assimilation, particularly his final point: "To abandon the notion that assimilation is a self-completing process will make it possible to study the forces (especially at the level of cultural and social structure) which facilitate or hinder assimilation or, conversely, the forces which generate the sense of ethnic and racial identity even within the homogenizing confines of modern society."[3]

But the existence of an ethnic pluralism and of social policies that give support and reward to ethnic status do not necessarily contradict the idea that there will also be an assimilative process, even if unintended. Sociologists cannot ignore the power of assimilating forces always at work: education (unless it is segregated or committed to inculcating pluralist identities); the marketplace with its meritocratic and achieved-status values (unless hiring and promotion operate on a quota basis); democratic politics (unless racial identity is institutionalized as the basis of political participation); the mass media (which can communicate across ethnic boundaries); and popular culture (the assimilative function of which remains largely unexamined).

Though sociologists can no longer accept the premise that assimilation is the inevitable endpoint of race relations, neither can they assume that the diversity and pluralism of the present will continue without change. Any number of possibilities fall between separate, self-preserving ethnic groups, on the one hand, and the steady assimilation of all of them into a single homogeneous culture. But in the present celebration of ethnic pluralism, little thought seems to have been given to the intermingling of racially pluralist groups in urban communities and large-scale organizations, or to the question of allegiances and identifications to the national society and the nation state. Instead, the struggle over instituting and legitimizing a new ethnic pluralism seems intent only on creating an atmosphere, buttressed by social policies and laws, that will protect and sustain the continuing identity and existence of each ethnic group.

But if assimilation is no longer to be the societal expectation, let alone the national policy, there remains a large and compelling issue of how to conduct public life. Given an established set of democratic institutions and values, how does a culturally diverse people interact in order to agree upon and accomplish the common good? If no one else will, sociologists need to talk about such matters.

A New Social Context

Whatever the contours of the new ethnic pluralism, it will occur in a new economic and political context. Since the early 1970s, the American economy has been unable to continue the postwar expansion that made possible a period of racial progress in which blacks and other minorities found new economic opportunities. And even as expansion has faltered, a new global economy has emerged. To this point, the ideological claims of its proponents point to the significance of new levels of education and skill for any nation hoping to do well in the competitive struggles of a new world market. Beyond the issue of what this means for the American working class as a whole, it clearly diminishes even further the chances of ghetto-dwelling blacks to escape a life of poverty. Their economic future cannot remain unaffected by the movement toward a new high-tech economy, a new world market, and a reduction in the less skilled forms of employment that have been the mainstay of the working class. If there now is or there becomes a body of largely unneeded labor in a technologically advanced economy, blacks, and especially black males, will make up a substantial portion of it.

If the concerns about a new world economy are yet a matter of peering speculatively into a still unformed future, recent changes in the status of black people are more clearly evident. One change of significance has been the expansion of the black middle class, assisted by affirmative action, college scholarships, and other targeted programs. But there has also come into being a strong white reaction against the programs that have served to advance blacks into the middle class. While there is an almost universal acceptance of the principle of equal opportunity, programs to achieve it, such as affirmative action and racial quotas, have produced what seems to most whites a contravention of the principle. Sociologists need to confront these most difficult and acrimonious issues of public policy, recognizing that these are not moral principles but social policies intended to be instruments of change. The opposition is both a significant part of the new racial tensions that beset the nation and a national political factor of enormous consequence.

Another significant change has been a worsening of the plight of the mass of poor blacks who inhabit the decaying inner cities. The central city more and more becomes synomymous with inner city and increases the separation of whites and blacks. Beset with such intractable problems as neighborhood decline, drugs, crime, and poverty, much of the central city seems to many middle-class whites to be a social wasteland from which they have withdrawn in fear and with decreasing sympathy and sense of obligation. Furthermore, no longer the target of ambitious government programs and suffering from a decline of even maintenance-level resources, the central city continues to deteriorate because the public sphere has undergone a severe contraction of resources. The massive riot in Los Angeles in the spring of 1992 indicates the explosive potential that lies just below the surface of daily life in such urban places, unchanged since the violent days of the 1960s. There is no reason to believe this will soon ameliorate.

But the significant changes affecting race relations are also political. Through legislation, judicial decisions, and executive action, government has become an active force in legitimating the existence of a plurality of ethnic groups identified as victims of past discrimination, and it has fostered and sustained the search for remedies. That, in turn, has made ethnic status a source of politically organized groups committed to advancing the interests of their members. The political process, in short, has become the social arena in which ethnic groups pursue racial equality. A reconstructed sociology of race relations will need to be more sophisticated about that political process than it has been in the past. It will need to recognize the key role of the national government in the making and executing of racial policy, both progressive and retrogressive, and in either case, subject to conflicting political actions. And it will also need to recognize the force and significance of what Lewis Killian has identified as the race relations industry.

Within this new context, there is going to be a difficult and complex process of struggle and adjustment among a plurality of ethnic groups in interaction with a white majority that will see its own numerical dominance in constant decline. That ensures there will be conflict, not only between majority and minority, but also among minorities. It will be the task of sociologists to provide a theoretical framework adequate to the task of making sense of that complex and conflict-ridden process and providing an understanding of what is happening, what might happen, and what it is possible to do.

In summary, then, a new sociology of race relations will be framed within a new sociological perspective, which will be grounded in a new social context. That context contains several basic factors: a new immigration policy that increases the racial and ethnic diversity of the American population while steadily eroding the proportionate dominance of those of European origin; the onset of an ethnic pluralism sustained by a new ideology that rejects assimilation and advocates a pluralism of ethnic cultures and identities; and the state and subordinate levels of public institutions as major actors in institutionalizing the new ethnic diversity.

It is within these new contexts that sociologists must build a new theoretical perspective on race relations. There are several contextual aspects that are not conducive to further racial progress, and taken as a whole, there is within them much that ensures that racial conflict will continue to be a significant if difficult dimension of American society for some time to come. The sociologists of race relations must now work out a sociological stance toward race relations that enlarges their and the public's understanding of what is going on and better assesses both the sources of racial conflict and the prospects for racial progress.

On a Sociological Stance toward Race Relations

From the beginning of their work in race relations, sociologists have described in detail the disadvantages that have been the fate of blacks in a white-controlled society, and they have measured the prejudices and discriminations of whites that have sustained those disadvantages. They have also measured any gains blacks have made in reducing those disadvantages; such reductions have defined progress in race relations. Though carrying out these basic tasks is still needed, it will no longer suffice. In a new era, when some key actors are intent on the celebration of a new ethnic pluralism, and when the political and judicial arenas are the center of the struggle for equal rights, sociologists need to learn new ways to examine race relations.

Sociologists lose when they take sides in the difficult struggle to attain racial equality. They need to be, and want to be, for racial equality (they are not value neutral), but they do not need to be, and should not want to be, partisans in the ongoing disputes about how to attain it. They need to continue to measure racial progress, but they also need to assess the efficacy of various programs, strategies, and policies (which always risks conflict with their proponents), to clarify existing disputes among partisan actors (which cannot be done by being aligned with one of them), and to provide an empathic assessment of the racial thinking of both black and white people. These are only accomplished by a stance that is independent of the committed partisanship so often entrenched in the politics of race relations. Indeed, for the sociologist, the actions of the partisan contestants in the political process should itself be material for sociological analysis.

Such a stance toward race relations remains intellectually free of whatever ideological interpretations are dominant at any given time. It is not the business of sociologists to be "politically correct" by advancing any required form of speech or behavior; neither, of course, should they be resolutely "politically incorrect." Instead, they should construct a sociological analysis that not only reports on what is going on in race relations, but seeks to make clear the depth and extent of the limits of and constraints on the possibilities for racial progress. The task of what might be called a critically disinterested sociology of race relations is always to examine the prevailing condition in order to assess the possibilities for moving toward racial equality.

This is easier stated than accomplished. It means, for one thing, to refuse to accept claims by contending actors, whether they be the state or any of its bureaucratic agencies, those who speak as racial liberals, or the representatives of organized racial groups, that their definition of the situation is the only correct one. There is always another ground on which to stand than the one the opposing partisan interests have stamped out as their own. It becomes the obligation of sociologists to mark out the contours of that ground, that is, to construct an intellectual position on race relations that informs and educates. In a time when sociologists seem to have become committed to the policymaking process, they need to revive an older democratic commitment to speak to a larger public that includes and cuts across the conflicting racial identities whose fates are inexorably bound together in the same historical struggles. Now, if ever, and here, if anyplace, is the need for the sociological imagination—and for a modicum of courage.

Notes

1. Leonard Lieberman, "The Debate over Race: A Study in the Sociology of Knowledge," *Phylon* (Summer 1968): 127–41. See also Leonard Lieberman, Blaine W. Stevenson, and Larry T. Reynolds, "Race and Anthropology: A Core Concept without Consensus," *Anthropology and Education Quarterly* 20 (June 1989); and Alice Littlefield, Leonard Lieberman, and Larry T. Reynolds, "Redefining Race: The Potential Demise of a Concept," *Current Anthropology* 23 (1982): 641–47.

2. Milton Gordon has drawn a distinction between an old "liberal pluralism" and a new "corporate pluralism." See his "Models of Pluralism," *Annals* 454 (Mar. 1981): 178–88.

3. L. Paul Metzger, "American Sociology and Black Assimilation: Conflicting Perspectives," *American Journal of Sociology* 76 (Jan. 1971): 644.

Index